Biblical Families in Music

Biblical Families
in Music

CONFLICT AND HETERODOXY
IN ORATORIOS, 1670–1770

Robert L. Kendrick

The University of Chicago Press
Chicago and London

The University of Chicago Press, Chicago 60637
The University of Chicago Press, Ltd., London
© 2025 by The University of Chicago
All rights reserved. No part of this book may be used or repro-
duced in any manner whatsoever without written permission, ex-
cept in the case of brief quotations in critical articles and reviews.
For more information, contact the University of Chicago Press,
1427 E. 60th St., Chicago, IL 60637.
Published 2025
Printed in the United States of America

This book has been supported by the General Fund and Donna
Cardamone Jackson Fund of the American Musicological Society.

34 33 32 31 30 29 28 27 26 25   1 2 3 4 5

ISBN-13: 978-0-226-83604-1 (cloth)
ISBN-13: 978-0-226-83814-4 (e-book)
DOI: https://doi.org/10.7208/chicago/9780226838144.001.0001

Library of Congress Cataloging-in-Publication Data

Names: Kendrick, Robert L., author.
Title: Biblical families in music : conflict and heterodoxy in
  oratorios, 1670–1770 / Robert L. Kendrick.
Description: Chicago : The University of Chicago Press, 2025. |
  Includes bibliographical references and index.
Identifiers: LCCN 2024024464 | ISBN 9780226836041 (cloth) |
  ISBN 9780226838144 (ebook)
Subjects: LCSH: Oratorio—Europe—17th century. | Oratorio—
  Europe—18th century. | Bible in music—History—17th
  century. | Bible in music—History—18th century. |
  Families—Biblical teaching.
Classification: LCC ML3220 .K45 2025 | DDC 782.23094—dc23/
  eng/20240603
LC record available at https://lccn.loc.gov/2024024464

♾ This paper meets the requirements of ANSI/NISO Z39.48-1992
(Permanence of Paper).

CONTENTS

List of Music Examples and Tables vii
Note on the Text ix

ONE Families and Representations 1

TWO Fratricide, Sin, and Despair 18

THREE Obedience and Division 39

FOUR Fathers, Sons, and Waiting Mothers 75

FIVE Sacrificing Daughters 105

SIX Fears, Returns, Blindness 138

SEVEN Grieving Spouses, Fierce Motherhood 170

EIGHT Connections 206

Acknowledgments 223
*Appendix: Metastasio/Caldara, Opening of
La morte d'Abel (Vienna, 1732)* 225
Notes 227
Bibliography 263
Index 275

MUSIC EXAMPLES
AND TABLES

Music Examples

2.1   Alessandro Melani, *Il sacrificio di Abele* [or: *Il fratricidio di Caino*], duet "Cara membra"; I-MOe, F. 731, fol. 89v   27

2.2   A. Scarlatti, *Cain, ovvero Il primo omicidio*, "Figli, miseri figli"; US-SFsc M2.1 M470, fol. 8r   35

2.3   A. Scarlatti, *Cain, ovvero Il primo omicidio*, "Piango il prole"; fol. 68r   37

3.1   G. A. Perti, *Abramo vincitor di se stesso*, "Per opra d'amore"; I-MOe, F. 925, fol. 14v   50

3.2   A. Scarlatti, *Agar ed Ismaele*, "Non posso, non lice?"; A-Wn Mus. Hs. 19164 (after Bianchi 1965: 40)   62

3.3   A. Scarlatti, *Agar ed Ismaele*, "Ingrato Abramo" (after Bianchi 196: 120)   64

4.1   P. Bencini, *Sacrifizio d'Abramo*, opening canonic aria; UK-Mp Ms.580bk51, fol. 8r   87

4.2   M. A. Ziani, *Il sacrificio d'Abramo*, "Se vanto, è di un gran pianto"; A-Wn, Mus. Hs. 19133, fol. 34v   93

4.3   C. de' Rossi, *Il sacrifizio d'Abramo*, Sara, Part II, opening ("Discostatevi omai"): A-Wn, Mus. Hs. 17306, fol.49r   96

5.1   A. Lotti, *Il voto crudele*, ending; A-Wn, Mus. Hs. 17695, fol. 88r   126

5.2   A. Sacchini, *Jephthes sacrificium*, ending, recitative "Omnia finita, solo remanet vita"; B-Bc, Ms. 1104, fol. 370r   136

6.1	J. Mysliveček, *Il Tobia*, "Qual tumulto"; I-Pca, D-V 1808, fol. 48r	158
6.2	Haydn, *Il ritorno di Tobia*, Sara, Part I, recitative (after Schmid/Oppermann 2009, pp. 57–58)	163
7.1	A. Ariosti, *La madre de' Maccabei*, Madre, ending; F-Pn, D.233, fol. 100r	186
7.2	J. J. Fux, *La donna forte nella Madre de' sette Maccabei*, farewell duet: A-Wn, Mus. Hs. 18186 (after Wessely/Kanduth 1976: 176–77)	192
7.3	P. Anfossi, *La madre de' Maccabei*, "Misera, che ragiono?"; I-Mc, M.S. ms. 8-1, fol. 112v	198
7.4	A. Sacchini, *Mater machabaeorum*, "Vos enarratis stellae"; I-Mc, M.S. ms. 233.2, fol. 42v	202
8.1	F. B. Conti, *L'osservanza della divina legge nel martirio de' Maccabei*, "Pria di tu"; A-Wn, Mus. Hs. 18167, fol. 37r	213
8.2	A. Caldara, *La morte d'Abel* (1732), Part I, opening recitative; A-Wn, Mus. Hs. 18146, fol. 7r	217
8.3	L. Leo, *La morte d'Abel* (ca. 1737), Part I, opening recitative; F-Pn, D-6867, fol. 11r	217

Tables

3.1	Differences between the ends of Bicilli's and Scarlatti's Ishmael oratorios	65
5.1	List of Jephthe pieces by venue in the later Settecento	110
5.2	List of Iphigenia pieces by venue in the later Settecento	110
A.1	Metastasio/Caldara, opening of *La morte d'Abel*	225
A.2	Aria (Abel), outline of structure	226

NOTE ON THE TEXT

RISM sigla are used for library abbreviations. For character names, I have used the Italian or Latin when referring to a personage in a given piece ("Agar") but the English form for the general character type or Biblical figure ("Hagar"). Works for which a score survives are marked by asterisks.

Chapter One

Families and Representations

Humans, being part of the family and of the state . . .

—Thomas Aquinas, *Summa Theologica*, Q. 47, art. 11

This book looks at Biblical families through the prism of those sacred musical-dramatic works known as "oratorios" in Italy and Catholic Austria/Germany, in the century after 1670. Many of the texts were based, often loosely, on stories from the Hebrew Bible/Old Testament, and in some the relationships among parents, children, spouses, and cousins played dramatic, didactic, and devotional roles. Here, the choice has been limited to the most striking narratives traced through a variety of audiences/publics, moments in piety, and musical changes. Family relations worked as both motivation in the stories as well as (anti-)models for contemporary Catholic life.[1] Although the genre began as hortatory drama in Lent, later in the Settecento it expanded out of penitential occasions and sacred spaces into theatrical seasons and venues, and it had social resonance with both the prescriptions and the reality of family life.

These stories are presented roughly in Biblical book order. Genesis furnishes the opening chapters: Cain/Abel; Hagar/Ishmael/Abraham; and Isaac/Abraham. Jephthe and the Sacrifice of his variously named daughter come from Judges 11; Tobit (chapter 6) comes from the eponymous book with a brief look at the story of Ruth/Noemi/Boaz; while the penultimate chapter (7) combines the Song of Songs in a Passiontide reworking with the Mother (and Seven Sons) of 2 Maccabees. Within any chapter/story, libretti and musical settings follow more or less chronologically (pieces whose music has survived are marked with an asterisk).[2]

Oratorios were made up of a combination of declamatory recitative, florid arias including ensemble numbers, and a few choruses. They were normally divided into two parts, separated by a sermon, and our stories present the case of at least one surviving sermon delivered between the two parts of a musical work. Audiences included court nobility, clergy, and the urban patriciate.

For these castes, the centrality of family to social position, devotional taste, and identity needs no underlining here. Later periods in Italian history might suggest the omnipresence of large nuclear or extended clans during our era. Yet the best demographic studies, including those on the underexamined South, have noted their relatively limited size, with perhaps two to four living children per family, even across social classes.[3]

The themes of murder, sacrifice and martyrdom run through the repertory. Thus mortal, as well as moral, resonances figure in the tales. For the Genesis stories, one marker can be found in early modern Bologna, where a reasonable estimate for the percentage of familial homicides in society as a whole seems to be slightly under 15 percent; a third of prosecuted crimes committed by women in the same time and place were violent, including infanticide, even if there is only imprecise evidence for the exact Italian level of the latter practice in the early modern period.[4] The sacrifice of children, of course, runs through the stories of Hagar, Isaac, Jephthe, and the Mother of the Maccabees. Obviously, infant mortality on all levels played into this, but for the well-off or patricians, the high clericalization rates for both sons and daughters also had long-term effects over generations. The example of two sons in the patrician Orsi family in Bologna, patrons of oratorio around 1670, highlights this phenomenon (with pieces discussed in chapters 3 and 5). Important recent work has underscored the idea of family experience of both oratorio and its cousin, opera, in several Italian cities.[5]

Further, new additions from post-Tridentine canon law began to change some aspects of Catholic marriage itself, along with the treatment of children and of in-laws.[6] One important question, then, is: How did oratorios affect both the reception of the Biblical stories and the actual family relations among their audiences?[7] In terms of this book's themes, several contemporary social realities had direct reflections in the pieces: the disinherited Ishmael, the aging Tobit, or the force of the Maccabees' Mother. Some cases—Jephthe and his daughter—were so extraordinary as to find no immediate social reflection, as the reactions of the exegetes and preachers (chapter 5) testified. As each of these stories is considered, I have attempted to include such conditions. Irene Fosi has magisterially traced how some of these family issues — not least polygamous fathers, like Abraham — wound up in the papal courts across central Italy.[8]

Overall, it is best to consider the details of oratorios' divergences from the Biblical accounts not as quaint curiosities or poetic license but rather as signs of the difficult effort to write musical versions of spiritual tragedy, thereby falling into the wider category of the post-1550 nonclassical trends in Italian literature.[9] Some of the stories end fully with death (Abel, Jephthe, Song of Songs, Mother of the Seven Maccabees), while others are near-misses (Isaac and Hagar).[10] Only Ruth and Tobit (chapter 6) have normative happy endings, while still raising issues of family relations. The search for appropriate spiritual tragedies occupied a notable place in early modern Italian literature. Although oratorio libretti, with the exceptions of those by Apostolo Zeno and Metastasio, did not possess the same generic weight as spoken tragedy, still the circumstances of their performance, and the musical expressiveness that went into them, rendered them an important part of the cultural landscape.

Indeed, viewing these works as spiritual tragedies with music brings us back to the music, in light of the historical insufficiencies of prose tragedy and the need for psychological expressiveness through music. The various shifts of the patriarch Abraham, in both the Hagar and Isaac stories, seem to have been best enacted by the combination of straight recitative, "arioso," and arias, evident in all the oratorios in which he was a character.

The other striking feature of these characters is their historical awareness of each other. Over and above their prefiguring of Christ's Passion, such characters as Abel, Ishmael, Isaac and Jonathan, Jephthe's daughter, and the youngest Maccabee recall or prophesy each other's fates at various moments of their own self-reflection. The most evident case of this is the final duet in Pietro Pariati/J. J. Fux's Viennese *La donna forte nella madre de' sette Maccabei** (1715/18), in which the Mother and her youngest son recall the Isaac/Abraham story, just before their own deaths for refusing to obey the pagan tyrant Antioco. The story of father and son, of course, comes from a favorite Habsburg Genesis account, one which had had its last previous version in the Imperial capital some seven years before.[11] But other such sacrificial flashbacks occur in other pieces as well, and thus there is a kind of internal genealogy to the stories across the Biblical books.

In a wider world, the parallels with classical myth are clear, and perhaps too obvious: Cain/Abel with the Antigone legend; the Binding as an incomplete Kronos tale; and Jephthe's daughter as a version of Iphigenia in Aulis. Of these, the last is the most revealing and is discussed in chapter 5 below.[12] On various fronts, my perspective on sacrifice cuts across the opera/oratorio divide.

Still, oratorio's audiences were normally in less extreme family situations than the dramatic Scriptural accounts. Thus, one question arises: How were listeners to bridge the gap between the seemingly distant—even if central to belief—Biblical stories and the texts plus music that comprised the performances? The genre was, at least nominally, educational; among this book's subjects, the most optimistic—that of Tobit's family—was mined by exegetes and orators for points on Christian family life, and some of the sacrificial pieces were redirected in the Settecento for female monastic professions. But the other themes used family as a vehicle for one or another conveying of the Passion, in or out of Lent. The Mother-Son relationship in the Passion would have implications for almost all the stories here, as well as being represented directly in oratorios.[13]

The shadow of Pietro Metastasio's libretti has hung heavily over this repertory, and indeed the seven sacred dramas written by him for Vienna had enormous cultural importance.[14] A recent study has traced the early nineteenth-century translations, published in Istanbul, of most of the oratorios into classical Ottoman Turkish written in Armenian script, meant not only for a mixed Christian/Muslim readership, but also probably as textual sources for court-style musical improvisation.[15] But overall, much of the discussion has been framed around the immediate impact of these texts and their pedagogical role. This study includes the two Genesis pieces by the Imperial poet, on Cain and on Isaac, seeking to place them in their immediate Viennese context, musical and devotional.[16]

At the same time, the debate over oratorio's lower rank as non-staged, or only rudimentarily produced, theater has diverted attention from the higher profile of its music compared to opera. Stage directions, occasionally in manuscript, occur in a number of these pieces, and the exit aria convention meant that singers somehow had to disappear from the actual performance space. Most importantly, the text and music took on greater importance, and the equivocal status of a few reworkings was evident in some missing imprimaturs, even in (or perhaps especially because of) the Roman repertory in Latin at the Oratorio del Crocifisso next to S. Marcello.[17] I have used both "on scene" and "on stage" to characterize the dramatic situation of these pieces.

Another Latin-texted corpus occupies a special place in this study, that of the four Venetian *ospedali*.[18] Their young female occupants were, as semi-orphans, cut off from most normative family relations, and their future as wives was always uncertain. Still, some of this book's themes—Jephthe, Tobit, Ruth, and the Maccabees—recurred in their repertory, especially after 1760 in a moment of increasing financial and social crisis for the institutions. These span the themes of children's deaths and of their more successful marriages (here, chapters 5, 6, and 7). The oratorio performances, especially at the institutions of the Derelitti (Ospedaletto) and the Mendicanti (the Pietà seems not to have hosted works on these stories), raise the tension between family ideals in the libretti, on one hand, and the social reality of the singers, on the other; they seem to have been sung (only) from behind the screens in the galleries where the women performed, without any hint of staging.

Most *ospedali* libretti, in their fulsome neo-Latin, do not display the complexity and dramatic interplay of the vernacular works, but they do often give the names of the women singing the characters, and hence make the works more performatively decipherable than was the case in most venues other than Vienna (where similar character lists are often present after 1690). I examine three works composed for the Derelitti by Antonio Sacchini, 1770–72, with libretti by Goldoni's great rival, Pietro Chiari (1712–81). The issues of family, because of the unusual demography of the Venetian patriciate, as well as for the young women themselves, suspended between their partial origin as foundlings, with futures limited or not to the four institutions, gave a special charge to the works considered here (as in the stories of Ishmael, Ruth, Tobit, and the Maccabees) as well as to the other *ospedali* oratorios that invoked family relations on some level.

The other disjunct between the music and its context that cannot be overlooked is the issue of Catholic domestic devotion. Some of the early Bolognese oratorios took place in patrician palaces, to be sure (as did a few others in Lucca and elsewhere, sometimes in the Marches), and of course all the Roman ones connected to cardinals' households were done for an invited audience including family members. But it is also true that most of these works were done in court chapels, urban shrines, or churches of religious orders. In their majority, these familial pieces were not done in domestic spaces, and their publics were varied and evidently large.

Hortatory Literature

Despite their location, the social reception of these works was conditioned by family realities and liturgical practice, and also by the words and literature available to oratorios' audiences.[19] The degree to which these libretti were influenced by Catholic family writings is clouded by the lack of studies on the latter. For the Seicento, Giovanni Leonardi's *Istitutione di una famiglia cristiana* (Rome, 1591) was reprinted until late in the century. His thought was continued by Costantino Roncaglia's *La famiglia cristiana istruita nelle sue obbligazioni* (Lucca, 1711; Roncaglia was a member of the order that Leonardi had founded, the "Leonardini"). The Jesuit Fulvio Fontana's pamphlet of 1705 was relatively brief, aimed at parents, and perhaps more a result of his missionary work than specifically urban.[20] The concern for bringing up daughters was evident in the thousand pages of Cesare Franciotti's *Della giovene christiana, ovvero Ammaestramento per una figliuola ben nata* (Venice, 1638), with its concern and anxiety about every possible aspect of a girl's life.[21]

But it was the French writer Jean Cordier (1599–1673), whose *La saincte famille* (1644, 2nd ed. of 1666) was translated into Italian in 1672, and which laid out the connection among family, political activity, and drama most tellingly: "We are in this world as if in a theater, and our life a play comprised of comedy and tragedy. . . ."[22]

In his preface, Cordier pointed out that sanctity was just as possible in family life as in monastic orders, and that three of the four divisions of Christendom found themselves involved in it. His Part I dealt with matrimony, its presuppositions, and its leading role for the bride's father, while comparing the perfect Christian marriage to the hypostasis of Christ (i.e., His two natures united perfectly in one being).[23] He then moved on to children in Part II, why they were generated and not created afresh, the reasons for rejoicing in many children, and, importantly for this work, why they were taken away in death at a young age.[24] In that sense, demographic reality had not markedly changed since the frequent deaths of Christian children in late Antiquity, and the positive spin given to such passings in Patristic writings.[25] Cordier went on to discuss their education in obedience, respect, and piety, and how to handle wills entailing the parents' property. Finally, Part III treated children's obligation to follow their parents' wishes, along with sibling relationships, and the relations with servants inside the family, which are also vital to this study.

For Cordier, filial obedience was the central point for the Isaac and Jephthe stories. His use of the Cain narrative was surprising: not only the inevitable effects of sin on marriage and reproduction ("the first reprobate"), but also as the first human condemned to Hell, and as an argument against forced monasticization ("il sacrificio di Caino," probably the mark on his forehead) of ugly or mentally deficient children. Tobit came up twice, once for the son's marrying only for "good cause" and once on the necessity of paying servants justly, while the Mother of the Maccabees was taken as the perfect idea of the maxims that parents were to impart to their offspring. The case of Hagar and Ishmael was harder, but Cordier repeated the Patristic opinion (see chapter 3 below) that Ishmael had been instructing his younger sibling to venerate idols and therefore had to be banned from the clan.

In Cordier, the emphasis was on strict family hierarchy cemented by domestic piety. The relative post-1648 population growth in Western Europe suggests that, despite the relatively small sizes indicated above, there was more social need for not only larger numbers, but also chronological extent (age differences) among child populations, as our period went on.

Beyond the family literature, both the surrounding culture of Lent—notably its sermons—and biblical exegesis take on importance for understanding the stories. Here, I have used several kinds of texts: (1) the performative form of sermons, especially those for Lent collected in print under the title of "Quaresimale"; (2) devotional and moral literature, ranging from individual spiritual guides to domestic manuals; and (3) Biblical exegeses after 1620, particularly those on the difficulties of Genesis or Judges. It is difficult to ascertain which sermons or literature a given oratorio audience might have known, and the task of localizing sermons in a given city is rendered more difficult by the itinerant careers of preachers. Still, the sermon of one Viennese oratorio of 1717 (Bernardino Perfetti's *Ismaelle*) does survive (chapter 3 below).

For all three kinds of devotional/exegetic literature, I have also concentrated on prints (1) held in multiple copies in Italy, or (2) with dedications to those princes, nobles, or prelates linked in some way to musical patronage. In all these materials, I have assumed a Seicento/Settecento divide, as the more variegated piety of the seventeenth century was replaced by Ludovico Muratori's "enlightened devotion" across Italy and Austria.

For the earlier century, Cornelius a Lapide's commentary is helpful also for its synthesis of Patristic and Scholastic authors on any given verse. However, Lapide was not the only exegete; I have included John Chrysostom, Ambrose, Augustine, and Jerome among Patristic writers. For the Settecento works in an exegetical present of 1730 — when Metastasio began his annual series for the Habsburg court — I have used among the "modern" commentators of the Hebrew Bible the following: the Jesuits Benito Pereira and Jacques Tiran (with the latter's complete commentary of 1632) and the French Benedictine Augustin Calmet (1672–1757), all of whom are cited in Metastasio's footnotes for one or another of his own oratorios. Still, commentaries on individual books are important, especially on such special cases as Tobit and 2 Maccabees, and these interpretations are cited below under the various stories. In terms of sermons, I have concentrated on the widely circulated works of G. P. Oliva (on Genesis), the Lenten series of Paolo Segneri, and other homiletic cycles that pay particular attention to the stories here while being reprinted in Seicento or Settecento Italy. After about 1740, there is a notable drop-off in both the commentaries and the sermon literature except for Tobit, this latter a central book for families and their devotion.

Up until roughly 1750, oratoric was a strongly marked penitential rite; even if it was used — as it was for some time after 1730 — for nuns' profession of vows or even on the feast of the patron saint of a community or a religious order (one example is given below), it still involved the interplay of sinful human behavior with the rules of family life, and as an expiatory ritual, it shared its approach to domestic relations with opera; both attempted to restore, or to learn from, shattered family norms.

But the oratorio repertory existed in no vacuum.[26] For Rome, Bologna, and Vienna in some years, I have considered the thematics of the immediately preceding Carnival opera season, for which we might regard the sacred works to be penitential continuations of the seemingly secular topics. This is particularly the case before 1730, as the oratorios functioned as anti-Carnival works, and therefore thematic intersections were quite likely.[27] In some places, the very same singers performed in both, sometimes as soon as the first full week of Lent, and hence some ten days after the last opera performance. In chapter 8, Farinelli's 1732 Viennese oratorio appearances — his only formal singing in the Imperial capital — help convey this overlap. Several other cases considered below underscore the relation.

For all that theatricality united the two genres, oratorio's production norms differed, especially in smaller centers. Its librettists tended to be non-professionals, and some of its composers younger, imparting the idea of its place as a stepping-stone to the secular form. In and out of sacral space, the hard-to-trace staging was more common than thought, a tradition continuing through Haydn's *Il ritorno di Tobia** (1775) and beyond.

Still, oratorio's onetime annual performances also removed it from clear public discussion in larger cities. Its slow move into theaters seems to have begun around 1750, and despite the slightly flexible seasonality just noted, until roughly that moment it remained linked to Lent and to the season's penitential messages.[28] Indeed, in some cases there were allusions to Lenten readings for Mass or the Office. And the number of singers it required was normally fewer: for these stories, often four or five, as per Arcangelo Spagna's famed recommendations.

In some ways, then, the genre was a testing ground, on various levels, for opera. Still, those moments in which it was the only major dramatic means should not be forgotten, for times and places without secular music theater: in Vienna's unsettled 1684–85, the same court's 1693 mourning year, or Clement XI's post-1702 ban on opera in Rome. The sometimes exiguous martialing of artistic resources in oratorio shades against its ideological centrality. Still, in Emilian cities around 1700, Huub van der Linden's work has shown just how much social energy went into oratorio performances: libretto circulation, sets or set-like effects, patrician civic pride. This involved both performance venue and the family relations among the varied audiences. Some quite important composers were commissioned for pieces seemingly minor: for example, for nuns' professions celebrated by the Jephthe stories, David Perez in Palermo (1742?) and Niccolò Jommelli for the same city (1753, just as he was departing for Stuttgart). This tale generated a wide number of settings: about 120 different musical versions of about 80 different libretti, in 1650–1803.

Politics and Orders

The first systematic exploration of political allegory for Roman oratorios is found in a thorough and stimulating essay by Saverio Franchi for the patronage of Livio Odescalchi, and the not-so-hidden meanings of various Roman pieces associated with the latter around 1700.[29] In a different tradition, Handel scholars have suggested deep links between Biblical stories and immediate political conjunctions in the United Kingdom. For obvious reasons, the emphasis here is on the ideology and military/dynastic moments of the Habsburg court, the institution with the widest Lenten/Advent repertory in all Europe, from 1660 to 1740, along with the major events of the period: the European wars, and the use of some stories (e.g., the Mother of the Seven Maccabees) against the threat of the French Revolution in the 1790s.

Even here, though, distinctions should be made between those texts expressly produced for courts and those imported from other venues, with other possible agendas. For all that the Binding of Isaac might have been important in Vienna, the imported texts on such themes by Tommaso Stanzoni (as performed in an Abraham piece with music by Francesco Passarini*, 1692) or Girolamo Gigli (a setting by Attilio Ariosti of the Maccabees story*, 1704) had carried other original meanings. The nexus between Habsburg inability to produce surviving male heirs and the Isaac story implied that certain, quite subtle, touches in the local libretti would have personal implications for the royals: references to Isaac as "olocausto [sacrificial victim]" as a marker for dynastic loss, or the imagining of deceased male children as a future angelic cherub.

This latter allusion dated back to the dynasty's continual loss of male heirs from the 1650s to the 1680s, and again in 1715–40. But again, looking at the oratorios in conjunction with the themes of the Carnival and birthday operas in any given year helps provide a fuller picture of the Habsburg enactment of its values.[30] In the Imperial environment, stories that might not have had such familial resonance elsewhere took on a role in domestic education.

This development of Imperial ideology in oratorio is also notable in the Florentine repertory after 1740, at a time when the genre had ended at the Viennese court, making the newly Habsburg Tuscan capital a kind of alternative to the former repertory of the *Hofburgkapelle*. Of the roughly sixty oratorios done in Florence between 1737 and 1773, some twenty-five take up family-related themes noted in this study, including takeovers from mythology (e.g., Tommaso Traetta's setting of *Iphigenia in Aulis* redone as St. Iphigenia of Ethiopia; see chapter 5 below). This emphasis on the musical representation of family was accompanied by a massive importation of Metastasio's oratorio texts into the city, related to the early Habsburg efforts to reform family relations and legislation in Tuscany. As we shall see below, the mid-century works also manifested the new, "sensitive" devotion.

By contrast, and as Franchi showed, competing interests in Rome made for different, sometimes conflicting interpretations of that repertory; this could be extended to urban papal centers elsewhere (Ferrara, Bologna, Macerata).[31] As noted below, some thematic gaps in the corpus of these cities are not easily explainable. Still, the urban nature of the genre in central Italy leads to the overlapping family programs of city patriciates and the local Oratorians, the order most responsible for its cultivation across the peninsula (although two other sermon-oriented congregations, the Conventual Franciscans and the Discalced Carmelites, also played a role).

Morelli's now-classic studies have shown how Oratorian practice and literary traditions influenced the entire genre into the early Settecento, really until the tidal wave of Metastasianism spilled into northern and central Italy around 1740. Still, their specific social placement elsewhere needs further work, especially in Florence, Venice, Perugia, and the Marches. Some of the Oratorian foundations—for example, L'Aquila—had active musical and devotional lives without hosting oratorios.[32] The role of their major intellectual figure, Pier Matteo Petrucci (1636–1701), famed as a preacher and devotional writer—less so as a fairly prolific oratorio librettist—has suffered from the long debates over Italian Quietism and his role therein. Although none of his oratorio texts deal specifically with this book's stories, his influence in and out of his order should not be underestimated.

As in other cultural forms, the level of Jesuit interactions with oratorios was dependent on any given city's sacred economy. Although they were renowned preachers—indeed, Segneri produced a popular Lenten collection—the order's engagement with the genre was quite specifically local and sometimes non-existent. For instance, there is almost no trace of music at the Jesuit church of S. Lucia in Bologna, as compared to the many pieces done at the Oratorian foundation of S. Maria in Galliera (and other confraternity churches in the city), and this kind of difference needs to be incorporated into any local study.

In those places (Rome, Florence, Bologna, Modena, Venice, Vienna to 1740) in which multiple oratorios were produced during Lent, I have looked at an entire annual corpus as a kind of musical *quaresimale*, a penitential and familial program expressed musically.[33] To the degree that such programs were organized, certain themes emerged among the various oratorios independent of any given librettist or composer. In those cases where oratorio was the only local production in any given year, I have attempted to examine the politics, ascertainable sermons, and the Catholic exegesis that might have been known in such places.

Many of these stories have no happy ending, no matter how reworked in the oratorio libretti: Cain, Jephthe (until 1743), the Passion meditation of the Song of Songs, or the multiple martyrdom of the Maccabees. The seemingly inexplicable stories of Cain and of Hagar, with the Divine refusal of the former's sacrifice and the Banishment of the latter for no blatant crime—and to some degree the Binding of Isaac as well—also counseled obedience and patience with Divine will. By contrast, the versions of Tobit normally ended in universal happiness, consisting of the successful marriage of Tobit the Younger and Sarah; the restoration of the family fortune, due to the retrieval of loaned money; the similar reknitting of the older Tobit's marriage; and not least the restoration of his sight. The possible relationship of these last themes to Lenten devotion will be discussed below.

As a genre, oratorio fitted into problematic categories from the start. Compared to opera, its generally more limited character sets (except for special works in Vienna and at the Venetian *ospedali*), along with its more direct narrative trajectory, marked it as a site for less experienced librettists and composers throughout the period, with some important exceptions among our works. Handling a more limited and more affectively predictable cast made it easier to write the text and music of arias.

In that sense, then, oratorio might have had its apprentice aspects as a locus for young composers to try out their music-dramatic skills, but it could also work at the level of *opera seria*. The musical overlap between our somber pieces, especially in the eighteenth century, and the operatic repertory is suggested by some of the comparisons here. Outside court situations, it also had some of the flexibility of comic opera, and from its beginnings into the Settecento, our family stories were also marked by the tradition of sacred dramatic plays, performed largely in the oral tradition even if the occasional early Seicento print embodied one text/scenario; the latter is the case for the Cain, Isaac, and Tobit stories discussed here.

Another historiographic verity is that of oratorio's non-staging. Although the genre seemed less expensive to produce than opera, still the costume and some set expenses are evident from the pieces considered here. The 1666/67 copy in I-Bc of a Bolognese piece (twelve scenes, no interval; chapter 2) on the story of Cain and Abel has manuscript marginal notes for sets and gesture that do not appear in the printed text (for the purposes of studying or following the libretto, they were not necessary); presumably other similar pieces from the Seicento also had practical stagings not reflected in the editions. Probably around 1705, two set designs were executed (one with indications for singers and instrumentalists) for oratorios in Pietro Ottoboni's new theater in the Palazzo della Cancelleria.[34]

Family relationships could have been indicated by costumes; the ways in which vocal writing was coded for generational differentiation will be explored below. Patrician palaces from Bologna to Palermo demonstrably hosted some seventy-odd oratorio performances from 1660 to 1770, for our current purposes those of Bologna around 1680 being most relevant. Moving the form outside of consecrated spaces also underscored its commonalities with opera, with direct ramifications for its "familial" meanings. The issue of how oratorios worked inside theaters—the first evident case being one in Perugia in 1715, followed by stagings in 1743–45 in Pistoia, Macerata, and Palermo—would take on special meaning in late Settecento Naples, as the theme of Jephthe moved onto public city stages (chapter 5).[35] The urban politics as well as the theatricality of the genre became evident.[36]

But as late as Haydn's *Il ritorno*, the staging (in the widest sense) of the pieces was important. Especially for the Seicento works, the tradition of semi-improvised sacred drama—the *sacra rappresentazione* in Tuscany and elsewhere—showed itself strongly in our stories: Cain, Hagar, Isaac, Tobit. Much of the Settecento repertory even before Metastasio suggests attempts, as early as that of the Sienese poetic improviser Bernardino Perfetti and his work on Ishmael for Vienna in 1717, to overcome the long shadow of this drama, a project pushed further by Apostolo Zeno's works for the same court in the following decade. Popular sacred drama featured, among other things, characters who speak in a low register, along with allegorical figures, stage noise (or other sonic effects), and a clearly didactic purpose (and its deictic elements are clear, e.g., one character asking "Chi sei tu?"/"Who are you?"). The vernacular tradition continued into the seventeenth century before being overtaken by such forms as the oratorio.

The least traceable aspect in the performances is the sermons, although it should be remembered that they too were acts of improvisation. However, homiletics' close performative relation to oratorios underscores the reason for the incorporation of Lenten sermons in the present work. One has to presume that all of the two-part works framed a homily of up to an hour; the sermons might have started and continued on a different heuristic track than that of the oratorio libretti.

There is a special place in this study for the Latin-texted oratorios at the Crocifisso in Rome, 1680–1710, besides the later ones in the classical language for the Venetian *ospedali*.[37] The evident Imperial ties of the former institution, along with its regular, almost weekly schedule of works around 1700, encourage its consideration as a place at which unusual Biblical stories, including some of the family histories, were presented in some kind of organized fashion. Even if its public is not entirely clear, here the Crocifisso pieces figure as part of the Roman scene at the moment. The libretti's language was usually simple enough, and close enough to that of serious opera, that their message was probably understandable by more than just the literati present in the audience.

The four Venetian *ospedali* offer more direct issues of family linkage, for their musicians were in an oddly liminal state: somewhat dissociated from the families which had born them, some young women would marry, others pursue professional careers (notably Adriana Ferrarese del Bene), and others remain as lifetime residents. In a sense, their own links to each other substituted for family and kinship support. Still, the repertory here presented stories of daughterly piety, sacrifice, and heroism (Tobit, Ruth, Jephthe, Maccabees) in ways that might or might not have been paralleled among the real social relationships inside the houses. More scores survive for the Venetian repertory than for the Crocifisso, and I have concentrated on several works by Sacchini. In both institutions, I have tried to take the Latin libretti as seriously as vernacular texts.

Settings in the Fields

Although the genre seems both urban and Lenten, in small-town and rural situations these conditions did not always obtain. In Puglia after 1660, as a recent study has shown, many occasions were festive, for saints' or Marian feasts along with nuns' clothing ceremonies, and almost none can be traced to Lent.[38] Similarly, the three Rogation Days/Lesser Litanies (just before Ascension) in the agricultural center of Castel S. Pietro (Terme) near Bologna witnessed more than thirty oratorio performances between 1722 and 1769. Given the "rural" nature of the stories of Abel, Ishmael, Isaac, and Jephthe, these must have felt appropriate for these festivities; one of the earliest Cain/Abel oratorios, Maurizio Cazzati's *Il Caino condannato* (Bologna, 1664; chapter 2), makes reference to the characters' agricultural and pastoral labor, putting the Killing onstage.

A particularly "agricultural" setting was that of the Book of Ruth, based around female relationships, marriage, and harvesting labor. The farming work in the Ruth story set up a pastoral context for these tales of womanly fidelity and hard-won Christian marriage, perhaps a reason for their emergence in the Settecento and not before. Although these stories had relatively few reflections in oratorios, one such piece is discussed below. The rurality of the story was evident in the short oratorios performed in Castel S. Pietro around 1740.[39] Many of these were sponsored by the local Eucharistic confraternity, and the link between the Abel story and the Sacrament was evident. The Rogation processions, with their litanies and Psalms, called down blessings on the upcoming crops and farm animals in rural Catholic Europe.

The anonymous 1733 oratorio on Cain and Abel in Castel S. Pietro fit into this kind of current echo, and, strikingly, it eliminated God's Voice in favor of the parents'. This *L'innocenza oppressa dal perfido Caino* begins with the parents' extreme self-mortification (hence a link to the penance of the Rogations; the 1733 Adamo goes as far as calling himself a "parricide," as his disobedience to God the Father has ruined the human race), and God's different reception of the two brothers' sacrifices is postponed until Part II, in which the murder actually happens on "stage," in front of the parents. In that sense, the opening parallels that of Alessandro Scarlatti's piece discussed below (chapter 2), although its lexical tone is much stronger.

Still, Abel had already earned his brother's enmity in Part I of the 1733 piece, as his encomia of Divine Creation contrasted strongly with Cain's obsession with sin. Abel's Christian optimism also resonated with the other part of the Rogations, the hopes for good summer weather and harvest, and so the story becomes one of sacred pastoral gone horribly wrong. Cain's fury only increases in Part II, leading to the killing; it is amazing that this libretto, with its total exclusion of the Divine, could receive an imprimatur from the curia of the hardline local archbishop Prospero Lambertini, a figure soon to attempt a belated reform of all Catholicism as Pope Benedict XIV. With its lack of a chorus—solo singers must have been imported from Bologna—this is in many ways the most "natural" treatment of the story, one which emphasizes parental guilt and fraternal degeneration.

The town would continue its tradition up to 1769. In 1752–54, the stories were linked by the successive performances of pieces on the Binding of Isaac, Jonathan's condemnation by his father Saul for an eating infraction, the Mother of the Maccabees, and then further iterations of the Binding (in this book, chapters 7 and 4). Overall, the Castel S. Pietro repertory included works on Adam/Eve, Cain/Abel, Abraham/Isaac, Jephthe, and the Maccabees; Tobit was heard in nearby Imola in 1727.

In 1769, the town witnessed a Sunday piece on the Transit of St. Joseph, one of the most important Catholic family tales, followed by a Monday work on St. Philip Neri, and then a short and unusual version of the Cain-Abel story, which involves only God and Cain, omitting Abel (!) plus the parents, this almost two generations after Metastasio's seemingly canonic *La morte d'Abel* (1732; chapter 8). Most of this one-part item is devoted to God's reasoning with Caino against his jealousy for his brother. Without a break, he kills his brother offstage and vaunts his revenge, evidently in the Divine presence, until realizing what he has done, self-interrupting, and hearing God's punishment of his future life hated and shunned by all. This was followed on Wednesday by another short oratorio on the Annunciation, after which—perhaps due to excessive spending—the tradition stopped.

Another striking example was the anonymous (both musically and textually) piece on the Hagar and Ishmael story, put on in 1727 by the male Discalced Carmelites at their important and large basilica of San Valentino in Terni (Umbria), amid the festivities celebrating the canonization of their very own St. John of the Cross by Pope Benedict XIII that year. Why this story of discipline, exile, and despair would have seemed appropriate on such an occasion seems inexplicable—unless we consider one passage from John's spiritual works. In Book III (chapter 42, section 4, and chapter 44, section 2) of the *Ascent to Mount Carmel*, the mystic discussed the personal sanctification of interior spaces of contact with the Divine, using Hagar's story of Genesis 16:7–14 (her contact with the Angel during her first attempt at flight, not the later Banishment account; it should be remembered that hers is the first Biblical case of humans talking with angels) as an example for individuals' sanctifying such places in their own psyches.[40]

This piece does not quote her words from Genesis 16:13 directly ("Profecto hic vidi posteriora videntis me" [Truly I have seen only from behind here (or: "the future works of") Him who sees me (which would put this verse into St. John's voice)]). Still, John's own use of the story had come in a discussion of sanctifying place, after his account of Jacob's Dream: "And Hagar put a name on the place where she had seen the Angel, esteeming it highly, and saying: 'Truly I have seen . . .'" The closing part of the oratorio goes out of its way to underscore the Angel's promise to Agar of her son's future progeny, taken from the later part of the story after her Banishment (Genesis 21:18). In that sense, Ishmael's "risky" life and future glorification paralleled the history of the newly minted saint. In this apotheosis, the

Discalced Carmelite Congregation itself was the child of the spiritual parents Teresa and John, and the piece was appropriate for sanctifying, not a place but rather a person. Indeed, the miracle of Ishmael's rescue resonates with the Carmelite narrative of John himself, considered as a personal marvel, not to mention the various wondrous acts attributed to him during the recent canonization process.

A final case from Lucca upends preconceptions about oratorios in general. On Tuesday, 10 September 1697, a "cantata" (but in two parts, thus an oratorio) was sung in the meeting hall of the local literary society, the *Accademia degli Oscuri*. This piece, the anonymous *Ritratto dello sposo celeste inviato dal Cielo alla sposa de' Cantici*, took up another narrative thread elicited later in this book (chapter 7), that of the grieving Sponsa of the Song of Songs as an embodiment of the individual Christian soul mourning Christ's Passion. Here, however, the male Sponsus (Christ) has sent an image—Lucca's famed statue of the Volto Santo supposedly crafted by Nicodemus—as a portrait token of love, and the Sponsa is the city herself. The libretto text used the Song of Songs sparingly, but reiterated the identification of city/Sponsa, and adumbrated Christ's Passion at length; the performance might have been connected to an unveiling of the statue (which lived, as it does today, in the cathedral). The grieving Sponsa is consoled by Fede and Amor Divino, and Nicodemo recounts his part in the Deposition, Burial, and the creation of the statue. Earlier oratorios the previous Lent in S. Maria Cortelandi had included works on Cain/Abel, Abraham, and various saints, but no operas had been heard that year.

The evening ended, however, with dancing by the local elites in attendance, a feature of communality which attracted its condemnation by the local curia for its "unsuitability" to the sacred, just two weeks later.[41] The piece was one of three annual works in honor of the Volto Santo, 1696–98, and one has to presume that the following ball had historically simply been a normal part of the performance event up until the curial intervention. Oratorios, then, were a part of the entire worldview of Lucca's patriciate, and not some kind of marginal genre. The ways in which they enacted Biblical family drama are the subject of what follows.

Chapter Two

Fratricide, Sin, and Despair

Corre sopra le sabbie favolose
E il suo piede è leggero.
O pastore di lupi,
hai i denti della luce breve
Che punge i nostri giorni.

—Giuseppe Ungaretti, "Caino"

CHARACTERS: Cain and Abel

BIBLICAL SOURCE: Genesis 4:1–16

NARRATIVE: Cain, the firstborn of Adam and Eve, brings agricultural products as a sacrifice to God, only to have the Deity reject them. Then his younger brother Abel brings a lamb for sacrifice, and God's acceptance of this is marked by a flash of lightning on the altar. Cain complains to God to no avail, then takes his brother into the fields and kills him. He lies to God about the murder, while his parents discover their second son's body. Cain is marked eternally as an outcast to human society.

WORKS DISCUSSED AT LENGTH IN THIS CHAPTER: Cazzati, *Il Caino condannato*; Anon., *Abele* (1666); A. Melani, *Il fratricidio di Caino*; Anon., *Agnus occisus*; Pusterla, *L'innocenza svenata in Abele*; A. Scarlatti, *Cain, ovvero Il primo omicidio*

PLACES: Bologna, Rome, Castel S. Pietro, Vienna

Family conflict began early. Cain's murder of Abel was the first sinful result of the Fall, and the first death recorded in human history, according to Genesis 4. It was also the first violent crime. For early modern Catholics, it gave a host of lessons and differentiations on murder, jealousy, and individual sacrifice to God. In its social distinction between farmers and herders, and the chapter's further detailing of the divisions of occupational labor, the story also provided a foundation story for inequality. For the present purposes, any minimal character set—two parents, two sons—would have been coterminous with the entire human population at this moment, and this was not lost on early modern listeners, as was evident in the commentaries and sermons. The tale's effect, then, was to prioritize sibling relations (and their failure), and the destructive universality of sin.

In the Settecento, that universality came to be questioned by Cain characters in oratorios, who demanded to know why the parents' sin should fall on him and his farming labor. Although some of the earliest oratorios did feature a demon or demonic voice, this "Pelagian" motivation for his discontent and crime would have a surprisingly long life, until being banished definitively by Metastasio's *La morte d'Abel* (1732; see chapter 8), in which pure, non-demonic jealousy and resentment slowly seize hold of the character, leading to an offstage killing of his brother.

Beyond the family group, many of the pieces feature parts for God (or His Voice), sometimes Lucifer (occasionally an angel), and often Abel's Blood, the last anthropomorphized also as his Voice. The musical ventriloquization of voices was known, of course, in opera, but this is one of the few plot lines to allow for multiple such hidden parts. How these were to be made dramatically effective, apart from placing the singers somewhere in the wings of whatever space, is not present in the libretti or scores.

The stark nature of the crime, Cain's semi-remorse alternating with the desire for escape, and the lasting consequences for humanity were evident already in the Divine warning of sin's omnipresence in Genesis 4:7 ("[if you do] ill, shall not sin be present at the door?"). Most centrally, the allegorical meaning of Abel as Christ focused attention on the two brothers plus the laments of their parents, normally the closing section of the libretti. Other features take on priority: the parents' relationship to their offspring, and the roles of Adam and Eve, not present in Genesis, in which the only dialogue is between Yahweh and Cain.[1] The addition of the parents leads to parental responsibility, communication, and lamenting.

Strikingly, there is only one other Lenten piece on another major fraternal battle in Genesis, that of Jacob and Esau (Genesis 25).[2] The antithesis story to fratricide—that is, the happy ending of Joseph and his brothers in Genesis 39—would emerge around 1685. Metastasio's *Giuseppe riconosciuto* would later become the classic formulation of this positive view.

Explaining Fratricide

Another problem with the story as it emerged from the *sacra rappresenta-zione* tradition was Cain's motivation for his unimaginable sin. Beyond the possible demonic character, the supernatural tracing of Cain's hatred for his brother would continue into the eighteenth century. The previous popular versions (as was typical for the vernacular play genre) had emphasized the low literary register of the characters, highly simple dialogues, and possibly the use of instruments to symbolize Heaven or Hell, or to provide atmo-sphere for the affect of a given moment. The parents' different behaviors were also part of the libretti's thematics from the very beginning and are central here.[3] The degree to which Adam also, besides Eve, took on the role of lamenter varied from libretto to libretto in the early repertory, but the story necessarily required mourning.

For all that parental reaction was evident in the earliest libretti con-sidered here, later on Metastasio switched back, at least in terms of the number and consistency of *versi sciolti* recitative lines, to Cain's inability to overcome the sin of jealousy and anger, thus reaffirming the centrality of Genesis 4:6–7 (God's advice to the older brother on how to emend his life before the actual murder).[4] Indeed, the latter verses and their warning against sin made the story useful for all moments in Lent.

The Cain story also played a devotional/political role due to its emblem-atic place in Augustine's *City of God* for its division of the two cities sym-bolized by the brothers. Given the Doctor's centrality to Seicento thought, and the use of the story in his own teacher Ambrose's *De Cain et Abel*, this tale underscored the most devastating consequences of sin on a fraternal level, uniquely suited to oratorio's penitential tasks. Still, the actual number of oratorios was limited.

In its division of brothers, one of whose sacrifices was pleasing and one not, it also set up anti-Judaism, with "marks of Cain" explicit or implicit in the libretti. The story's meaning (older brother Cain = older popula-tion of Jews), going back to Augustine, would continue as late as the final chorus of a 1763 Milanese cantata, with music by G. B. Sammartini, for a confraternity in the local Jesuit church of S. Fedele, *L'invidia giudaica . . . in quella di Caino adombrata* ("Jewish Envy . . . as Displayed in that of Cain"): "Vendica eterno Dio / Invidia, e crudeltà; / L'empio Giudeo ravvisa / nel traditor Caino, / e in Abele divisa / il divino redentor" [God eternal takes His revenge on jealousy and cruelty; see the evil Jew in Cain the traitor, and the Divine Redeemer in Abel].[5] A Neapolitan Oratorian also warned parents of the story's implications, should they not allow their firstborn to take monastic vows in the interest of preserving patrimony or of strategic (female) marriage alliances.[6] In this unlikely way, sacrifice and virginity were linked.

In his *Frutti del Carmelo* (Rome, 1667), the Discalced Carmelite Emanuele di Gesù Maria connected the different sacrifices of the brothers to the willingness and promptness in the fulfillment of vows.[7] Since Abel's were spontaneous, his sacrifice was accepted, while the grudging nature of his brother's caused Divine rejection. Although the tome was nominally occasioned as reflections on the congregation's Rule, Emanuele held the lesson valid for all Christians.

If some of the stories in this study had less social resonance, such was not the case with sibling murder. On a social level, in and around Bologna in the Seicento actual cases of fratricide came before the Tribunale del Torrone, anywhere between 2 and 5 percent of all homicides.[8] Allegorically, however, the overwhelming meaning of the Cain story was Eucharistic, due to both the sacrifice theme and Abel as a shepherd, prefiguring Christ.[9]

Early Cains

The local Emilian tradition of the story had a prehistory well before Castel S. Pietro's Settecento performances. Maurizio Cazzati's 1664 *Il Caino condannato* for Bologna, with a text by the *letterato* Giovanni Francesco Savaro (di Mileto; ca. 1610–ca. 1682), is one of the only three-part oratorios on any subject in the entire repertory, and this is due to its switches among different dialogues without ever bringing together a tutti except for the final choruses; the effect is that of a *rappresentazione*, still used today among Emilian confraternities. These groupings proceed in the order Caino and Dio; the parents; the brothers; and Caino and allegorical Vices. Each part's montage-style succession of scenes was introduced by instrumental music, signifying the profound affects of the Biblical story; this semiotic use of local instrumental style would recur a few years later in the Bolognese pieces on Hagar (chapter 3).

The original performance of Cazzati's piece was sponsored by the Confraternity of the Trinity in the Blessed Virgin on the organization's patronal day, Trinity Sunday (8 June) 1664; the 1669 reprise was done in the city's basilica of S. Petronio, this time by the more informal devotees of a sacred image of the Madonna near the city's butcher yards ("Beccarie"). The Trinity Confraternity, on the city's walls near Porta Lame, ran a hospital for the convalescent poor; the latter organization seems to have been one (or both) of the two "congregazioni delle anime" attached to the painting, which was located on a wall over the Avesa (Aposa) creek near the Torre della Garisenda.[10] However, the Marian character of both sponsors should be remembered; evidently part of Savaro's text was meant for Eve's lament over Abel to have its New Testament parallel in the mourning for Christ. The church of the Trinity Confraternity had been expanded to some 120 square meters in the early Seicento, suggesting a capacity of up to 200; S. Petronio's space was, obviously, much larger.

The 1664 edition was inscribed to Curzio Maria Guidotti, a canon of the Cathedral, the clerical director of the confraternity, and a dedicatee of literary editions, as well as a figure in the marriage efforts for the singer Margarita Salicola two decades later. Savaro began his opening at Genesis 4:5, the rejection of Caino's offering, with an angry solo aria for the farmer, followed by a dialogue with God. The narrator who had opened the work returns to introduce the allegorical figure of Jealousy (Invidia) appearing to Caino in a dream. It is Invidia (not Lucifer, who is not a character) who suggests the idea of killing his brother, and then convinces Caino to do so. Part II opens with the narrator and Abele, the latter singing the praise of a devout heart. God appears for a dialogue in which He warns Abele of jealousy's power, but the innocent shepherd seems unable to understand the veiled prophecy. Caino then appears to suggest going into the fields; the parallel slot given to the dialogue with Invidia in Part I is occupied by a passage between Adamo and Eva here in Part II. Ironically, this colloquy features the couple expressing joy for their children as a palliative against their Original Sin.

Cazzati's Part III returns to Genesis 4:5b, with Caino beating Abele to death onstage with pieces of wood (a prefiguration of the Crucifixion). The theatrical proximity to the *rappresentazione* tradition is perhaps most clear here, in that the killing is enacted in front of the audience. Adamo and Eva come back to find Abele's dead body onstage, and wonder what could have happened; meanwhile, Caino has been stricken by remorse and (with the parents offstage) sings two arias until God returns and prophesies his bleak future as in Genesis 4:9–15. The final chorus sings of the inevitable punishment for anyone guilty of homicide. Here it is simply allegorical Envy that seizes hold of Cain.

Several features of this early work are striking: the lack of a separate lament for Eva; the presence of no more than two characters onstage at any given moment; and its seemingly separate purpose as a warning against blood feuds and killing in general. The Torrone tribunal records give enough local evidence for the last of these. The reality of the allegorical Invidia not only recalls the *rappresentazione* but also, as a secular figure, points to a new kind of psychology. Liturgically, the 1664 performance would have resounded with the final reading of Mass earlier in the day on that Trinity Sunday, and the substitution of Luke 6:36–42 (appropriately enough, on forgiveness and on overlooking the mote in a brother's eye) instead of the normal reading of the Last Gospel.

Another approach to the vernacular tradition was evident in a 1666 Bolognese work, the anonymous musical *rappresentazione* noted above for its indications of staging and set entered by hand into the printed libretto. This *Abele* was written as an introduction to the ritual posing of the catechism questions ("dottrina cristiana") in the parish of S. Benedetto, sponsored by its instructors, and set out in some eight tableaux (a total of twelve scenes).[11] Here, Adamo and Eva begin by snarling at each other in the wake of lost Paradise; Lucifero and Invidia decide to take advantage of the situation and of Caino's rejected sacrifice; and the brothers talk twice, separated by Invidia's plans for the killing. Abele also links proper sacrifice to honoring one's parents: "Il primer honor giocondo / ha Dio; i genitori hanno il secondo" [God has the primary joyous honor; parents, the second]; and the link to the domestic dialogue of the catechism seems no accident. All this is followed by a quartet for the whole family, then the parents' worry and discovery of Abele's body. At this point the demonic forces come back to rejoice over the successful offstage killing of Abele, and the parents lament the latter.

Although its popular style (S. Benedetto was a downtown parish near the cathedral of S. Pietro, with evidently a large and varied population) might suggest something closer to recitative, there are eleven arias and five ensembles, perhaps close to an hour in performance (the music is lost). Its mixture of Biblical and allegorical characters is also typical of the vernacular tradition, and it was followed by the parish children's responses to the catechism questions and then a *licenza* by the character of Felsina (the ancient name of Bologna), in honor of Cardinal Giacomo Buoncompagni, the archbishop. Here an oratorio on good and bad children came socially very close to the actual religious education of youth, suggesting that these popularizing pieces formed a bridge between education and oratorio.

In scene 8, the parents and children sing to each other: "Delitie del seno, / mia prole gradita" [Delights of our heart, my beloved offspring] and "L'affetto / ch'è in petto / ai Genitori sta" [The affection in our heart belongs to our parents]. The irony is that this moment precedes the sons' departure to the scene of Abel's murder. In scene 9, Eva has intuited Caino's jealousy, although her fears are dismissed by her consort. The libretto follows the traditional sense of deeper maternal than paternal perception of children's wrongs. The plaints over Abele are interrupted five times (according to the added ms. stage directions in the I-Bc libretto) by the parents' breaking down into tears, in which it is Eva who picks up the language of Marian lament over Christ ("Ah, troppo infausto legno / se con opra sì fiera / fosti strumento a un fratricida indegno" [Oh, all too unhappy wood, if you were, with such an overweening action, the instrument of an unworthy fratricide]).

Laments in the Family

If these Bolognese pieces show the links to popular tradition, not long thereafter—but at a very different social level—Alessandro Melani's *Il sacrificio d'Abele** (also known as *Il fratricidio di Caino*) is cast in a more literary mode. It is preserved in both a source in Modena from 1677 and a Viennese score for its 1678 Lenten performance there; it might first have been created for the 1675 Jubilee Year in Rome. The 1678 libretto and score attribute the text to the young Benedetto Pamphili. It was also produced (anonymously) in Bologna in 1682 and in Mantua for 1687 and seems to have been the most popular piece on the theme until Alessandro Scarlatti's. This work starts with a dual self-lament for Adamo and Eva (again, this is a work in which there are only four singers, with no Testo, Dio, nor Demonio).[12] It is a purely human/family piece, anticipating the 1733 Castel S. Pietro text by several generations.

It also differs strikingly from Savaro's 1664 work in its setup and premises. Eva begins her first long recitative with a cutting recollection of her own (Original) Sin as ruining her sons (recitative: "Figli, traditi figli," followed by the aria "Mite il ciel per voi splendea / io l'armai di crudeltà" [Heaven shone benignly for you; I armed it with cruelty]). This would serve as a model for Antonio Ottoboni and Scarlatti's opening of their *Cain, ovvero Il primo omicidio**, "Figli, miseri figli," a generation later and discussed here. The sons are onstage to hear this, and the subsequent dialogue reveals how all the characters react to this first guilt in different ways: the parents and Caino pessimistically, but Abele optimistically in praising Divine Creation, even if fallen. His aria, addressing his brother and probably his parents, invokes hope: "Agli inviti di dolce Speranza / la Costanza / festeggi nel sen; / e rieda il seren / in quel ciglio, che mesto si duole; / dopo nube di duol si speri il sole" [Celebrate constancy in response to the invitation of sweet hope; let serenity return to that eye which is sadly pained; after the cloud of pain, then hope for the sun].

Both parents then encourage the sons' sacrifices, but a thunderstroke and smoke from above destroy Caino's offering, and in response he rejects Heaven. Abele's own offering is delayed until Part II, as the shepherd ends Part I by singing of the beauty of his lamb/Lamb, a Eucharistic reference. The parts are bridged by his solos, ending one and opening the next, as he also praises the devout heart with which he presents his offering, a clear contrast to Caino's pessimism and fixation on his parents' sin. In a Lenten context, this is an invitation to joyful penance.

However, this is too much for Caino, and the brothers quarrel. As the parents come out onstage, Caino strikes Abele down, despite the pleas for mercy from Adamo and Eva. Again we have a murder enacted on scene, and this time even with the parents present. Abel has time for a martyrdom aria ("L'ignoto martire"), followed by Eva's lament over him that recalls Marian plaints for the Dead Christ, as she finishes with an aria ("Crudo figlio, spietato germano") that reproaches Caino directly. In contrast, Adamo is given a recitative that gruesomely describes the physical process of this first death in human history, due ultimately to his own sin, without the long reproach of his son.

In this extended mortality scene, Abele has a final recitative consecrating his blood to God, and here again the Eucharistic connotations would have been quite evident. Without a Divine (or Voice of God) character, it is left to the parents to castigate their child, and Caino closes the entire piece with a recondite aria on the thorns of agricultural labor which will become pricklier because of his evil heart, "e saran chiuse punture / pene tacite d'un empio" [the silent pains of an evildoer will be scabbed puncture wounds]. Oddly, this defeated ending resonates with the pessimism that had occupied much of Part I except for Abel's optimism, as it equates the pain pricks of sin with the stabs of everyday work.

To examine the piece from the perspective of family relations, Pamphili's text had emphasized the role of Eva as opposed to Adamo, and indeed the latter does not have his own aria until after six other numbers (including two duets). Her role is clear from her first aria, "Mite il ciel," with a drone bass on C♮, as its long and difficult melismas function to reflect on the lost splendors of Eden and her own role therein. Similarly, her second solo, "Del piacer," was set by Melani with a large string ensemble, employing a D tonality, and is fixated on sin. Her description of the thunder showing Divine anger at Caino's unsatisfactory sacrifice, "Con voci di tuono," at the end of Part I returns to C-type tonalities, and to the stormy affect of her first aria. Finally, she opens Part I's concluding trio and receives the lion's share of the music.

Her next aria is her angry reproach of Caino for killing his brother, and moves in a different tonal world, that of B♭ (1♭). This long ABA number (B section: "L'innocenza oppressa langue") precedes the dialogue lament aria over their son for her and Adamo, "Care membra." Indeed, this "Largo" duet (ex. 2.1) is the first moment since the beginning spat that brings the two together. It is cast on C (1♭), with some twenty statements of two related ostinato gestures in 6/4 time. Adamo describes his son's pallid body, while Eva compares his outpoured blood to her own tears. This is the most extended lament in the piece. Strikingly, neither here nor in their short closing recitatives do the two ever come together again, and this suggests that the disaffection staged between the two at the piece's outset has not been—and will not be, despite the future birth of Seth—overcome. It is no surprise that Melani's score has been praised for its laments.[13]

Clearly, the other major character in Melani's work is Abele, and for the present purposes his relationship with his parents is important. His range of affect and technical difficulty in Part I was already quite wide, but his martyrdom evoked two different moments in the score: a first ostinato aria over some eighteen different statements of two related ostinati; and then a recitative, "Io moro, o madre, o genitore," with a vocal high point on "a cui l'alma donai."

Finally, Caino's aria "Questo suol di spino" also recalls the opening in its C♮ tonality (used for the opening and "Con voci di tuono") and especially the drone bass on C, which recalls the aria "Mite il ciel." There were good reasons for the popularity of Melani's piece around 1680, traveling as it seems to have done from Rome to Eleonora II Gonzaga's chapel in Vienna, Modena, and Mantua. This work is one which shows the ties among the Roman scene, the Habsburgs, and northern Italy.

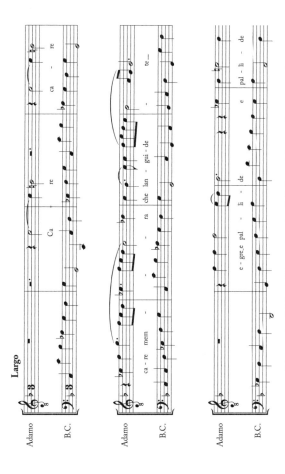

EX. 2.1 Alessandro Melani, *Il sacrificio di Abele* [or: *Il fratricidio di Caino*], duet "Cara membra"; I-MOe, F. 731, fol. 89v.

28 • CHAPTER TWO

Roman Connections

Just how far some of these libretti stray from normal interpretation is evidenced by a comparison with two sermons, one on each of the story's two brothers, by the Jesuit Giovanni Rho (who had a more famous missionary sibling in China, Giacomo), in his *Orazioni sagre sopra la Divina Scrittura*, part 2 ("The Patriarchs"; [Milan, 1671]).[14] In his sermons 5 and 6, Giovanni first praised Abel's innocence, virginity, and trust, while his following oration blamed Cain's downfall on his early melancholy and lack of faith in Divine Providence, as opposed to any allegorical temptation. These interpretations take the relatively simple story in specific ways: sacred vows and Christian optimism. Around the same time, as Morelli has shown, Bernardo Pasquini's *Caino e Abele* gave special prominence to its demonic Satano and the non-familial aspects of the text.[15] Again, the topic was not touched for some time after the Jubilee Year of 1675, and—since the homiletic literature continued to mention it in the late Seicento—it is not entirely clear why it was absent.[16]

A generation later, the background to Alessandro Scarlatti's *Cain, ovvero Il primo omicidio** is formed by a series of Roman pieces just before and after the work's putative origin around 1705.[17] From a devotional perspective, the first of these works was the 1699 Latin-language piece *Agnus occisus . . . in Abele* for Friday after the Fourth Sunday in Lent at the Crocifisso, which presented an unusual approach (it had only an indirect relationship to the day's Mass and Office readings, the resurrection of Lazarus; no librettist is named).[18] Although Francesco Scarlatti's music does not survive (it had evidently been sent up from Palermo, where the composer was active), the opening text gives us a Pelagian Cainus, who argues with his guilty parents against the ongoing effects of "their" Original Sin as affecting him, and it is from this disagreement that the piece's conflicts stem. Abel reproaches him for inhuman cruelty, but Cainus's anger liberates a Chorus of Vices from Hell, who appear with some eight members.[19]

After the chorus announces the arrival of Death in the world at the end of Part I (another gesture from the *rappresentazione* tradition), the action is postponed until Part II, opening with Abel's Sacrifice, just as in Melani's oratorio. Without any parallel offering on Cainus's part, the latter tells the former of his plans to kill him, to which Abel responds by begging for a kiss. This gesture of fraternal affection recalls, of course, Judas on the Mount of Olives.

This scene of the Killing is extended, with some four pleas from Abel to the increasingly irate Cainus. Urged on by the chorus, the latter ignores his own doubts, and the murder of the pitiful Abel takes place onstage. In terms of brotherly relations, the most pathetic feature is the latter's pleas: "My brother, can you wound me? Kill me if you can, but even dead I will love you. . . . Spare me, cruel Cain, with their tears, their cries, their laments, Nature and Love want you to relent, and spare Abel's love." This kind of pathos seems entirely new in the story at this point.

Suddenly both concerned for his own life and remorseful, the fratricide flees from the piece with no dialogue with God, as the chorus celebrates the Victory of Death. The rest is left to the Vices and then to the parents, who seek their son, then discover Abel's body, lament him, and prophesy the Second Abel (Christ). As with much of the Crocifisso's repertory, this piece mixes some recondite theology with features coming directly from popular culture. If its text was indeed by the Jesuit Alessandro Pollioni, it would also have resonated as an anti-Quietist gesture against those who would deny Original Sin.

Several other works on the theme came out in Rome around 1700, and another Pelagian Cain was heard in Francesco Pusterla/Mattia Laurelli's 1703 L'innocenza svenata in Abele. The piece was dedicated to the Venetian ambassador (1701–6) to the Vatican, Giovanni Francesco Morosini, and performed at the Chiesa Nuova/Vallicella's Oratory.[20] Here the four-voice casting, and even the opening distribution of affect, are taken over from Melani's piece, although there is a different resonance in Eva's opening: "Adamo, piangi pur, / che piango anch'io" [Cry away, Adam, as I cry too]. This is a direct reference to the beginning of Girolamo Gigli's 1688 oratorio on the Mother of the Maccabees (chapter 7), known in Rome because of Gigli's campaign to have his own texts published there.

In Pusterla's 1703 work, Caino then comes onstage to blame his parents: "Ma poi che deggio anch'io / per i vostri delitti / pianger l'error non mio? [Aria:] Molle è colui, che questa vita chiede" [But now am I to lament an error which is not mine, because of your sins? (Aria:) Anyone who asks for a life like this is weak . . .]. Ironically, Adamo defends the propagation of his sin to all future generations, and Abele appears to accuse his brother of arrogance in turning against Divine decree. Also, as in Melani's piece, Abele sings an aria ("Quanto è cara, e quanto è grata / a quel Dio dell'alma amante" [How dear and thankful to God is the sacrifice of a loving heart]) in praise of the human soul, with Caino's response being one of proud fury. The part is closed by four arias, one for each character: Abele on not all sacrifices being pleasing to God (and so anticipating Part II); Caino, as the firstborn, on not being a servant; Eva, a pessimistic piece on all Nature as allied against her and her family because of her guilt; and Adamo's own wish to die immediately because of his sin.

At the beginning of Pusterla's Part II, Abele's successful sacrifice provokes his brother's immediate fury, an affect that had been building all throughout Part I, as Caino threatens to cut his brother's throat just as the shepherd had done with his own sacrifice (a gruesome irony). The placement of the sacrifice is as in the earlier works on the topic. Before the parents can arrive, Caino moves into action, and Abele dies with another (but only one) martyrdom aria stressing his innocence. Caino repents immediately, with no moment of revenge or victory, as had been the case in Savaro and in Melani, but rather calling on the Furies to kill him. Here the affects of the parents diverge, as Adamo continues to repeat that it was his first sin that really killed his child, while Eva simply laments her lost son in a Marian vein. But, as in Melani's work, Caino ends this piece, looking vainly for someone to put him out of his misery: "Son tanto infelice / che per mio contento / non posso morir" [I am so unhappy that I cannot even die in order to make myself content].

In some ways, *L'innocenza svenata* enacts the complete breakdown of the original family. Its ending is all the more unusual in that by the close, Eva does not consider herself to be the primary sinner, handing off that guilt to Adamo, and in that sense the retrospection on Original Sin follows an inverted approach compared to traditional exegesis.[21] These two works, *Agnus* and *L'innocenza*, go out of their way to provide dialogue and conflict even at unlikely junctures in the story. Both Roman pieces show notable degrees of intertextuality and of cross-reference in their specific vocabulary as well as in their character dynamics. Only Part II of Pusterla's text begins to differentiate between Adamo and Eva in terms of their reaction to Abele's death.

A generation of Cain oratorios, in and out of Rome, seem to share a cultural background of the *rappresentazioni*, as well as bleak denouements of a bleak story. In the hardening devotional atmosphere of century's end, it is also possible to view all of them as justifications for the doctrine of Original Sin, aimed indirectly at any hint of Miguel de Molinos's ideas on human perfectibility that might have been circulating among oratorio audiences.

Happy Endings?

How all this would change became evident in just a few years. There is some chance that Alessandro Scarlatti's treatment of the topic had Roman origins, for all that its first recorded performance seems to be datable to Lent 1707 in Venice, based on the Venetian printed libretto dated 1707 but with "L'anno 1706 M[ore] V[eneto]" on its title page. In addition, the copyist's score (US-SFsc) gives 7 January 1707 as the completion date for his *Cain, ovvero Il primo omicidio* (probably of the copying, given the excision of some lines from the printed libretto and the duplicate aria mentioned presently).[22] The reason for suspecting a Roman origin is a long recitative in God's Voice present in this libretto but not in the score, which refers to the historical Temple of Jerusalem being transferred to the Eternal City. This number also contains a synopsis of salvational history from Adam through Christ and Mary, all the way to the Last Judgment. In response, the entire work ends with a duet for the parents on the theme of "O felix culpa," here Eva's "Contenti, / presenti, / brillateci in sen," labeled "allegrissimo" in the score. This moment, with its joyous tone and God's promise to end future vendettas, is unusual, especially given the somber Roman pieces that form the immediate background.

In that sense, one might posit a 1707 Venetian performance of Scarlatti's piece literally on the last day of "more veneto," that is, the Vigil of the Annunciation (24 March 1706, Venetian style; = Friday after the Second Sunday in Lent), in honor of Mary and the happiness of the Incarnation. This would then connect to the "O felix culpa" idea that closes the oratorio, and even to Eva's prophecy of the Cross in her second aria, "Sommo Dio, nel mio peccato." That no institution is given on the libretto's title page marks this as a private performance, without even a palazzo indicated.

In order to sort out issues of tone and characterization, it is necessary to differentiate among the printed Venice libretto (this was repeated in Rome at an unspecified location during Lent 1710), the score, and the rewriting of the literary text performed as *L'Abele* in Rome's Palazzo della Cancelleria the following year with presumably new music by Filippo Amadei and Cardinal Ottoboni himself, who is the likely candidate for having recast his brother Antonio's original libretto.[23] This Lent and this venue were also the same for P. P. Bencini's *Il sacrificio di Abramo*, discussed below (chapter 4), and, as noted, Ottoboni contributed music to this work as well. One other major difference in Amadei's work is the closing trio in Part II,

"O felice umanità!," another allusion to "O felix culpa" to be sure, but more penitential in its formulations.[24] In addition, Scarlatti's text was used in a female monastery in Palermo in 1713 for a Forty Hours' devotion, a clear Eucharistic inflection of the piece.[25]

This closing section is also the main site of the differences between the 1707 printed libretto for Venice and Scarlatti's score. The seven characters are the same, but the music features recitative cuts compared to the libretto. These score deletions include thirty-three "historical narration/prophecy" lines, referring to the Annunciation, Incarnation, and Passion in the Voce di Abele; six lines for Adamo replaced by five for Eva and two for him; the thirty-five lines cut to five in the Voce di Dio's recitative (this includes the references to the "Temple" moved to Rome and to the "winged Lion [of St. Mark]"); and seventeen in Adamo's closing recitative redone as seven new lines. Possibly these last were added in the Venice production to an earlier Roman piece to reinforce the Marian content.

The recitative and aria in Abel's Voice in Part II ("Non piangete il figlio ucciso") also have a second, crossed-out musical version in the manuscript score. Possibly Scarlatti (or someone else) chose this moment to rewrite the aria after the "historical narration" lines were deleted, perhaps for a different singer.[26] The score might incorporate an earlier stage in the accretion of the piece; notably, no arias are different between libretto and music. But the references to the "new Rome" in libretto lines suggest that the original text was crafted for the Eternal City.

Its unexpected end points to a wider feature: despite the seeming monotony of Antonio Ottoboni's *ottonario* meter, used for all the arias in Part I and a good deal of Part II's opening, the musical gestures are strongly contrasted between and among arias, rendering each memorable. The relatively low literary register, binary textual structures, and moments of instrumental representation all make Scarlatti's work more of a counter-Carnival sacred entertainment, a "trattenimento sacro" as both the 1707 and 1710 libretti are titled, rather than a Lenten penitential oratorio.

The contrast with the seriousness of the sin is striking. Although there was space for a sermon, the librettist must have deliberately intended a wider (if unspecified) audience and a greater linkage to the *rappresentazione* tradition than is the case for most of Scarlatti's oratorios. Against this patterned binary libretto, the aesthetics of discontinuity work well with more complex subjects and aria-based texts.

The 1707 libretto opens in symmetry, with two arias for Adamo, one each for Eva and the children, and two for the parents again, as Adamo invokes penance and Eva points to Marian intercession for her offspring. This sets up the sons' sacrifices, successful for Abele and failed for Caino. As Abele reacts with humility (including another Eucharistic allusion, "I am not worthy of Your glance," like "I am not worthy for You to enter my mouth"), Caino decides immediately to kill his brother.

The parents evidently do not hear this, as they turn to Divine praise, reinforced by La Voce di Dio, who enters to adumbrate obedience after a "grave and sweet" instrumental moment. However, the offstage Voce di Lucifero has indeed understood Caino; introduced by a dark and *concitato* instrumental section, he encourages not only the murder but also false warmth on Caino's part toward his brother. Lucifero recommends selfishness to Caino ("Poche lagrime dolenti / su l'estinta amata prole / spargeranno i genitori" [Your parents will shed few sorrowful tears over their dead and loved child]), which induces the deception. A feigned moment set as a duet ("La fraterna amica pace / grata è al mondo, e a Dio diletta" [Friendly fraternal peace pleases the world and is beloved by God]) is sung sincerely by Abele and mendaciously by Caino.

Scarlatti's Part II opens with competing arias on Nature between the brothers, and as Abele rests, his brother quickly kills him, to the accompaniment of instrumental music imitating blows and thunder, using wind instruments not present in the score. The Voce di Dio is immediately heard, with the famed "brother's keeper" quote (*Dio*: "Abel dov'è? [*Caino*:] Nol so Signor; forse del fratel mio / il custode son io?"). God prophesies Caino's future as a monster, and the killer asks for either protection or death; although tempted by Lucifero to suicide, Caino recognizes the infernal nature of the suggestion, and flees after long wavering, prefiguring Judas Iscariot and adding another Passion allusion. After God has demanded his repentance, however, he runs directly into the character of Lucifer's Voice, who advises him to fight Heaven. He rejects this, telling his parents they have lost one son to his action and one to sin.

After an implicit break, the troubled parents appear and hear Abele's Voice in the reworked section mentioned above, presumably from offstage, telling them of his death. As in some early Patristic interpretations of children's passing, Abele's Voice has an aria in which holy death is safer than life itself ("Non piangete il figlio ucciso"). Both parents thus have separate arias for lamenting both their living and their dead offspring, set up again as a binary double.

Adamo's next aria echoes Abele's Voice ("Piango la prole esangue") and begs God for another son, with the request that the Redeemer be born of this lineage. His prayer is heard, and the Voce di Dio sings an aria in *novenari*, promising a Savior even though His commands have been spurned. Adam, in another reworked section, prophesies the Incarnation as a way of atonement for his original sin. Thus, unlike any other work in this chapter, this one ends remarkably with the "duetto allegrissimo" between the parents because of the implicit promise of Christ's appearance on earth. It is this connection that underscores the appropriateness of the text for the Annunciation, the realization of that promise.

To examine the sections in more detail, the local breadth of arias' affect is evident in how family relationships are established at Scarlatti's opening: four *durus* items for each individual character, with Adamo's "storm of sin" piece in D; Eva's penance in A; Abele's pure sacrifice in a C as a *siciliana*; and Caino's laborious cultivation of the fields in E with a quasi-ostinato evidently symbolizing the repetitive nature of field work. Again unlike any other piece in the repertory, the work opens with Adamo's direct speech to his two sons: "Figli, miseri figli, / miseri perchè miei, / sol per mia colpa rei" [Miserable sons, miserable because you are mine, guilty only for my sin] (ex. 2.2). But Eva's reference to the serpent sets up a direct parallelism with her husband's recitative and aria, just as there follow the parallel statements of Abele and Caino. The symmetry—and unvarying *ottenari*—show the direct descendance from the vernacular tradition.

After the killing, Part II both continues the parallelisms and heightens the drama. Scarlatti's Caino bids farewell to his absent parents, quite aware of his guilt and loss ("due figli hoggi piangete, / l'uno per me perdete, / l'altro perchè peccò" [you lament two sons today, one whom you lost because of me, the other because he sinned]). Again Eva's maternal instincts foresee the tragedy, and the Voce d'Abele speaks, prophesying his brother's miserable fate. He also predicts his own time in Limbo until the Harrowing of Hell, with references to the Annunciation and Passion, all of which culminates in the salvation of the patriarchs (and hence another reference to the Incarnation).

He then disappears, and Eva launches into a *siciliana* in the flattest tonal region of the entire piece (C with 2♭) as she attempts to overcome her tears for both sons ("Madre tenera, e amante"). Adamo joins in with a parallel aria now on the sharpest region of the work (B with 2♯; "Padre misero,

EX. 2.2 A. Scarlatti, *Cain, ovvero Il primo omicidio*, "Figli, miseri figli"; US-SFsc M2.1 M470, fol. 8r.

e dolente"), again showing Scarlatti's local contrast between successive arias as noted above, as well as the dualistic structure of the speeches.

Another aria for Adamo ("Piango la prole esangue, / e chiedo prole ancor" [I mourn my bloodless son and ask for more children], on E with one sharp) is followed by a strikingly different one for the Voce di Dio, again in *novenari*, on the tonally removed F. It is also based on binary dichotomies ("L'innocenza peccando perdeste, / .o pietoso non perdo l'amor" [You two lost your innocence by sinning; I, merciful, do not lose My love]) (ex. 2.3).

Beyond pitch choice, Scarlatti's gestures for these last numbers in Part II match the libretto's variety. The parents' duet of worry before they learn of Abel's fate (Eva: "Mio sposo, al cor mi sento" [My spouse, I feel an unknown pain in my heart]) is set as another *siciliana*, with suspensions flowing into homophonic phrases. La Voce di Abele enters with *concitato* accompanied recitative, and direct representation for "io volo," followed by an *allegrissimo* aria for the idea of safety in death. This moment, in a sharp region around A, is answered by Eva's turn to flat regions in "Madre tenera ed amante."

The sense of tonal vertigo and affective surprise continues with Adamo's "Padre misero e dolente," at a new level of sharp pitches, an *andante lento*, and without any basso continuo in its opening ritornello, rather as if this father suddenly senses the lack of any foundation to his role, with no immediate possibility for children of any sort to continue his line. He explains the events as God's taking back his sons (an indirect reference to the Isaac story), Abel's death as telling him of his own mortality, and Cain's punishment as an example to others. La Voce di Dio responds in accompanied recitative, of course, and then His "L'innocenza peccando perdeste" aria is also a *siciliana*. This merciful response occasions Adamo's final joy, and the final duet of happiness is prepared, although only briefly. In the deleted recitative, God's Voice gives the salvational synopsis which includes the prophecy of long wars in the Holy Land and the reference to a "winged lion" (i.e., Venice) rising to help Rome.

This is certainly the most unusual ending to any extant Cain oratorio. To read only the libretto, the piece indirectly glorifies Mary without over-indulging in Eva's laments, considered as being parallel to the Virgin on Calvary. The lines that praise Venice as part of the defense of Christendom are also a strikingly direct political reference. The First Morean War (1684–99) had indeed united Venice, Vienna, and Rome, and had resulted in some Venetian gains among the Mediterranean islands and on the mainland; the Second War would not begin until 1714, and it would reverse the Venetian

EX. 2.3 A. Scarlatti, *Cain, ovvero Il primo omicidio*, "Piango il prole"; fol. 68r.

successes. The oratorio seems to reflect the interbellum situation, and to juggle various aspects: the original story, Marian praise, and current politics. In its gestures to Rome and to Venice, it seems to have ties with some Venetian family resident in Rome, although it is unclear which one.

Overall, the story had a surprisingly spotty performance history. The major changes among versions concerned the role of Eva as chief lamenter, the changing character of Cain, and Adam's guilt as the ultimate cause of the murder. Still, from Melani to Scarlatti, the theme generated some remarkable music. The issues of jealous kin would be transferred to two wives of a patriarch in the Hagar and Ishmael story.

Chapter Three

Obedience and Division

She [Sarah] sent us to the wilderness
like Ham stamped with sin . . .

—Honore F. Jeffers, "Hagar in the Wilderness,"
Outlandish Blues

Wer, wenn ich schriee, hörte mich denn aus der Engel
Ordnungen?

—Ranier Maria Rilke, "Die erste Elegie,"
Duisener Elegien

CHARACTERS: Hagar, Ishmael, Abraham, [Sarah]

BIBLICAL SOURCE: Genesis 16, 21, 23, *passim*

NARRATIVE: Sarah procures Hagar as a second wife for her husband Abraham so that he may have descendants, since she is infertile. Hagar is an Egyptian slave woman who tries to flee before giving birth, but is turned back by an angel. She gives birth to Ishmael, but later Sarah miraculously becomes pregnant with Isaac. While the two children are playing, there is some kind of dispute or mockery, and Sarah orders Hagar and Ishmael to be cast out. Abraham pauses, but is ordered by God to repudiate them. On their way into the desert, Ishmael almost dies of thirst, but is saved by an angel who brings water.

WORKS DISCUSSED AT LENGTH IN THIS CHAPTER: Ballati, *Il mistero ne' sogni*; Vitali, *Agare*; Perti, *Abramo vincitor di se stesso* (= *Sara*); Monari, *Agare*; Pasquini, *Agar*; Mesquita, *Ishmael*; A. Scarlatti, *Agar ed Ismaele esiliati*; Bicilli, ditto; Gini, *Agar et Ismaelis Exilium*; Gini, *Agar et Ismael in solitudine*; Caldaro, *Abramo*; Perfetti, *Ismaelle*

PLACES: Florence, Bologna, Rome

Then and now, the account in Genesis 16 and 21 posed a major devotional problem, not only for the story of Hagar, Ishmael, Abraham, and Sarah, but also in its presaging of Abraham and Isaac's Binding/Sacrifice. It made a relatively short but striking appearance in the world of oratorio, largely in the generation after 1675. Strikingly, none of the surviving libretti of this story are entitled after Sarah, although in Genesis hers is the main agency of the entire conflict (the one exception to this is the score, not the libretto, of Giacomo Antonio Perti's version for Seicento Bologna).[1] Early modern commentators also sometimes linked the three stories in sequential chapters: Sarah's being taken by Abimelek as the couple were in Gerar (Genesis 20; one of the "sister/wife" narratives); Ishmael; and Isaac. Although there is one oratorio on the first of these, no single piece combines all the chapters.[2]

The problems in Hagar's story are patent: a wife first giving her husband a slave/servant to bear his children (and thus a kind of female-sponsored concubinage); the latter fleeing, and an angel forcing/taking her back to her owners to bear the husband's child (all this in Genesis 16); then, in Genesis 21, the later rivalry between the two mothers and their children; and, finally, the patriarch condemning his own concubine and their son to exile and what seems like certain death in the desert.[3]

Paul and Augustine's interpretations of the Banishment had canonized the account's binary separation of the holy (Isaac) from the unholy (Ishmael), and so the New and the Old Laws. Paul cited the story (Galatians 4:21–31) as a prefiguring of the division between law (the "old covenant") and grace (the "new covenant"). This view dominated early modern exegesis, but it was far from univocal in the oratorio repertory. Beyond this level, though, the story took on personal and devotional resonance, much as it has in strains of twenty-first-century African American theology, via the role of Hagar.[4]

Patristic interpretation also raised various problems: bigamy; Abraham's quasi-sacrifice of his son; and Ishmael's putative place as the patriarch of many non-Judaic—and indeed, non-Christian—peoples. As oratorio began to spread in the seventeenth century, the tale's interpretation was similarly difficult in Catholic thought; Lapide had simply glossed it as Abraham's obedience to God's will, no matter how seemingly arbitrary, adding Paul's citation, and also using an interpretation (dating back to Jerome) of the verse (Genesis 21:9) on Ishmael's "playing with Isaac" ("Ismaelem ludentem") to claim that the slave's child had mocked his younger brother on the occasion of the latter's being weaned (and so deserved the Banishment). This latter detail played a role in some, but not all, oratorios. Most importantly, Paul's words were used in Lenten liturgy as the Epistle for the Fourth Sunday in Lent, and this was the only one of our stories to resonate immediately with the ritual of the penitential season.[5] Socially, then, it touched issues of both confessional identity as well as marriage and child starvation.

Early Modern Realities

The Jesuit superior, exegete, and homilist Giovanni Paolo Oliva (1600–1681) found even more difficulties in the passage, devoting some eight pages of "ethical commentary" to its various moments in his *In selecta Scripturae loca ethicae: commentationes in Genesim* (Rome, 1677).[6] He justified the Banishment by Hagar's status as a servant, and at the critical Vulgate phrase of Sarah's "seeing the son of the Egyptian Hagar playing with Isaac," his two-and-a-half-page explication of this sole verse blamed the slave exclusively, taking the children's play as a symbol of Ishmael's dynastic equality with—and not subjugation to—Isaac. Hence Oliva considered the Banishment not only necessary, but ethical.[7] He also faulted Hagar for her later despair in the wilderness and compared Ishmael's ultimate survival and growth unfavorably with that of another desert product, John the Baptist. The final point in Oliva's disquisition was a Pauline gloss on wives being subject to their husbands, linking Genesis and gender superiority in the tale.[8]

How far most of the oratorio repertory moves from these concerns will be seen presently. Most of the libretti begin with Genesis 21:9 (Sarah's demand for the Banishment) and continue through verse 20 (the rescued Ishmael). The narrative does, however, intersect with other stories considered here. For instance, its problem of sons at risk is shared with the Abel, Abraham/Isaac, and Maccabees narrations.

One passage in the homiletic literature tied the tale directly to lessons for early modern families. Lenten Sermon 22 of the north Italian Jesuit Giovanni Battista Manni (1606–82) concerned "the mutual obligations of parents and children," starting with the "effective male" parental love of fathers like Abraham. Manni again cited Jerome's explication of Genesis 21:9, which considered the "play" between the brothers mentioned above not as mockery but as Ishmael's instruction of his younger brother in idolatry, justifying Abraham's love via the Banishment. In his Sermon 26, "The palace of enigmas as the home of Divine Providence," Manni returned to the story to maintain the idea that God had heard the prayers, not of Hagar in the desert, but of her son; without explicit identification, he evoked Ishmael as a kind of penitent in the Lenten "wasteland" for his listeners, and underscored the power of enigma, presumably to guard against rationalist critiques of the tale.[9] The inexplicability of Divine decrees recurred in oratorios as late as Georg Reutter Jr.'s *La divina Providenza in Ismaele** (Vienna, 1732; chapter 8).

In a different and not totally coherent vein, Domenico Mayno used the story in his 1697 explication of the Ten Commandments: "Children's defects should be corrected with patience and charity.... The case of Sarah, Abraham's wife, is memorable, since when she saw her son Isaac playing with those idols of her slave's son Ishmael, ripped them away.... Now, o fathers and mothers, how many idols there are in your own homes? . . . With your own ears you hear the words of your daughter who likes that idol [i.e., suitor], and you do not close the windows nor banish the occasion; Jeremiah lamented, 'The daughter of my people has become like an ostrich in the desert' [Lamentations 4:3]." Mayno thus also supported parental control of marriage.

On the other hand, the Neapolitan Oratorian Antonio Glielmo considered the passage in a discourse on the "diffusion of God the Father's paternity" to imply that even slaves' children (i.e., Ishmael) could inherit the Kingdom of God.[10] In its social context, Glielmo's reference took on new meaning. The population of slaves in Naples, higher than almost anywhere else on the peninsula, would have given local relevance to the story; still, there were no oratorios on the topic in this major European city.

Quite apart from devotional issues, the contemporary social realities indexed by the story included: (1) illegitimacy and orphanhood; (2) bigamy (both known in Seicento Italy); (3) the perceived role of angels (also present in the Tobit pieces); and (4) the European genealogical imaginary of others. This last was related to ideas of Arabs and later Egyptians via speculations on Ishmael's descendants and—obviously—his mother's and his phenotype. Like Sarah, Ishmael is silent in Genesis's account. All the libretti invent dramatic personae for the two (a few three-character pieces omit Ishmael, concentrating on Abraham, Hagar, and Sarah). As in some of the other narratives considered in this study, the additions give a sense of Abraham's responsibilities.

The question mark hanging over the story and all the oratorios is how to interpret Abraham's ambivalence and Hagar's reactions, in addition to whether her final rescue is simply an instance of Divine Providence. Were her (and her son's) prayers and pleas equivalent to the Lenten penance meant to be encouraged by the performance of oratorios?

To start with the familiar social problems: legitimacy and disinheritance were quite present in seventeenth-century Italy, as men variously recognized (or not) their out-of-wedlock sons for purposes of family wealth. For those patricians or minor nobles who were patrons of oratorio, this was sometimes an issue. In addition, for all that bigamy might have seemed impossible in society, a number of cases did indeed make their way to the Roman Rota, as Kim Siebenhüner has carefully documented.[11] These situations ranged from honest mistakes of reported deaths which turned out not to be true, to Martin-Guerre-like impersonators pretending to return from war or pilgrimage, to spouses who simply left towns and remarried. However, the social class of those charged with this crime/sin was low, and there seem to have been no defendants' justifications heard in the trials which cited the examples of Abraham, Solomon, or other polygamous patriarchs. Both for oratorios' audiences and a wider urban public, however, illegitimacy was more common. In the Bologna where the Ishmael oratorios began, the *Tribunale del Torrone* considered these cases, along with those of abandonment and other crimes.

Although not as pronounced as in Netherlandish painting, the theme had visual resonance as well.[12] Given Guercino's two late-period canvases on the story—one for a private patron in Siena, and one (the 1658 Banishment now in Milan's Brera) a gift from his hometown Cento's patriciate to the Cardinal Legate in Ferrara—there seem to have been local/domestic echoes of the tale.[13] The 1658 painting—as Denis Mahon pointed out, the object of some financial/thematic negotiation between the painter and the Centesi—relates more clearly to the ideology of the urban patriciate as "proper" *patresfamiliae*, casting out the unholy.[14] It negotiated the space between this narrative and issues such as Catholic domesticity, order/obedience, and, in the case of the Angel, Divine Providence.

The other social reality was the presence of Mediterranean slaves in early modern Italy itself, and whether the references to Hagar's status ("schiava," "ancella," "serva"; "slave" [present once, only in Caldara's text], "handmaiden," "servant") inevitably racialized her.[15] Here again the visual evidence is ambiguous. Claude Lorraine's pair of scenes, painted for the same patron (Johann Friedrich von Waldstein) in 1668, suggests highly Europeanized features for Hagar. None of the various depictions of the Flight, the Banishment, or the Rescue by (in rough chronological order) Veronese, Giovanni Lanfranco, Rubens, Andrea Sacchi, P. F. Mola, Mattia Preti, or Pietro da Cortona represent her as being of color, for all the elaborate Orientalizing costumes in some images. Only in Francesco Ruschi's depiction (ca. 1645; Treviso, Museo Civico) does she even wear lower-class clothing.

Between Rome and Vienna, the possible references to real slaves seem more likely for the former, with its moderate-size population of baptized Muslims. On the other hand, only about four or five "Moorish" women are traceable in the Imperial capital in 1700, and these as servants for the nobility, with only one male African runner in Imperial service. Unlike the clearly racialized projections of Italo-African singers in Florentine comic opera, the evidence of cast lists and available singers suggests that the various Hagars seem not to have been inspired by real slaves.

To that degree, then, it is Hagar's status as upstart slave that plays a role in many libretti, and class is more evident than phenotype. Since some of the early pieces on the story come from Bologna, it helps to consider some detailed local demography from the Seicento. Although about two-thirds of the roughly 1,000 slaves recorded during the century in the Emilian capital were male, still (positing an adult lifespan of about thirty years) it seems possible that at any given moment anywhere between fifty and eighty slaves of color could have been present in the city.[16] It is unclear if any of the patriciate associated with the pieces discussed here actually owned any; the will of Count Astorre Orsi, discussed below, does not mention any such possession, although there must have been family servants of some kind.

An even more hidden issue is the degree to which any such female slaves were also the sexual property of their married masters, a situation which would parallel the Biblical story even more closely. At least for the Bolognese libretti, there seem to be no social or textual hints at an African identity for any of the Hagar characters, unless every "schiava" was presumed to be phenotypically African or Near Eastern. The number of slaves in Rome was higher, of course, although hard to estimate except from the documents on those who were freed.[17] Finally, both exegetical tradition and the context of the Ottoman wars could have suggested the child's role as a stand-in for Arabs and Ottomans (this is more evident with the visual clues in Dutch paintings of the tale); on the other hand, the sympathetic and pathetic depictions of the boy in a number of oratorios lead to rather different identifications.[18]

The other social reality, brought up by the story's denouement of Hagar's

Obedience and Division • 45

almost-abandonment of her child in the desert (or forest, according to the individual libretto), was that of parental desertion of their offspring. For lower social classes, this was almost something of a given, according to the Bolognese Tribunale records, and this coincided with Hagar's status as a servant. Given its troubled meanings, still the story did indeed make the jump from the *sacra rappresentazione* into oratorio in the first place. The fifteenth-century anonymous Florentine play on the subject was printed regularly up to 1610; it narrates the family's vicissitudes in third person, with an added prologue concerning a father (not Abraham) of two sons, one good, one bad. Indeed, this edition's title page noted that it was intended for an audience of "fathers and sons" (obviously marginalizing the women onstage and in the audience). It framed the story around "good" Isaac and "bad" Ishmael, justifying the latter's Banishment, and was meant as an example for males in families.

Strikingly, almost all the oratorios take a different tack, concentrating on Abraham's decision and waverings, along with the conflict between Sarah and Hagar and the pathos of the innocent Ishmael. Isaac usually does not appear, and the number of singing roles lies between three and five (one exception is a 1683 Latin piece for Rome by Salvador de Mesquita, noted below). In terms of fidelity to exegetical tradition, the roles for Sarah are telling; given Bernard of Clairvaux's comparison of her to the Virgin Mary, the oratorios' characterizations completely deviate from tradition. In a wider family context, her fierce defense of Isaac in this episode, as opposed to her complete absence in the next chapter of Genesis at the Sacrifice episode, also underscores the contradictions in her character. The number of characters normally is four, although many of the texts set up various dialogue scenes.

Given the mixed exegetical traditions, tracing a final, penitential moral in the oratorios is difficult. The Italian summary prefaced to Mesquita's oratorio text of 1683 explains Agar's two-stanza Latin aria "Nil desperet mens mortalia, / quam custodit coeli Numen: / inter umbras speret lumen / summis ope speret malis . . ." [Let the soul never despair of human (matters) as the Lord of the heavens guards them; let light hope among the shadows and through His strength hope even among the highest evils] as a reminder of the mutability of misfortune ("cavando la moralità, che il mutare un gran dolore in straordinario contento è opera solamente dell'onnipotente mano di Dio" [deducing the moral lesson that changing great pain into extraordinary happiness is the work only of God's omnipotent hand]).

For sheer dramatic intensity, it would be hard to match *Il mistero ne' sogni, ovvero Ismaele esiliato* (for the Florentine confraternity of the Purification and S. Zenobi, 1705), of Adriano Ballati and Antonio Giacobbi. Here, there are no supernatural figures whatsoever. As the title suggests, the piece opens with an evil dream for Abramo as he is sleeping with Sara. In his imagination, a monster (= Sara) has deprived him of Ismaele. He awakens to accuse his wife as responsible for the Banishment, to which Sara attempts a rationalist response. The entire part is devoted to their quarrel, and it goes as far as Sara's threat of truly becoming a monster, and of leaving if Ismaele and Agar are not exiled.

Part II puts all four characters onstage simultaneously, starting with Ismaele's pleas; the older brother has had his own dream, in which he was threatened by a giant and then lost a fight with his younger sibling. Agar tells him that a "great mystery" was present in the vision and attempts to pacify the situation by arguing for the benevolent nature of divinely inspired dreams. She insists on their power, and has her son tell his father of the story. Sara uses this occasion—and not the play between the two half brothers—to make Abramo expel Agar and Ismaele, both of whom have a lament. Based on the "evidence" of Abramo's dream, Sara insists on their departure. Then matters go downhill quickly, and the whole piece ends with the Banishment and a duet expressing general hope for Divine Providence, although nothing more: "Se si chiudon queste porte / s'apren almen quelle d'Iddio" [If these doors close (on us), at least God's will open].

Most striking is the omission of the Angel and of any explicit hope for salvation for the two. This renunciation of the most dramatic part of the tale, along with the intense interfamily arguments, pleas for pity, and exile arias, presumes a version of the story in which there are only human reactions to what is given as God's decree. There is no imprimatur, and Giacobbi's preface, addressed to the city's musicians, mentions only their reception of his work. Possibly it was performed on the titular day of the confraternity, Purification BVM (2 February 1705), although the linkage of its message to any possible devotional meaning of the feast is unclear at best, unless the "purification" of Mary had a symbolic reference to Hagar's own upcoming trials in the desert. Of all the versions of the story, this must be the furthest removed from the original.

In a less heterodox vein, the typical final scene of many oratorios, with Hagar and her son in the desert saved by the Angel, recalled Lent with reference to Christ's forty-day stay in the wilderness. A frequent conclusion from these happy endings in extremis was the unpredictability of Divine Providence for those who follow God's commandments, another theme in the century's devotion, and one which is a possible distant relation of Giacobbi's version.[19] This story also emphasized obedience, another leitmotif of Catholic family literature. But, as some marginalized exegetes had suggested, Ishmael's innocence also partially paralleled that of Christ.

Banishments in Bologna

The north Italian trajectory of the theme had evidently started with a Bolognese piece of 1671. Apart from the importations to Vienna, the story's spread was limited: essentially Emilia (Bologna and Modena), Rome, and Florence, and then fading after the 1727 work for Terni (chapter 1). *Agare*, with a libretto by the Bolognese canon Giovanni Battista Maurizio (the younger), was meant for February 1671 (before Lent started, i.e., as a sacred Carnivalesque entertainment) in the palazzo of Count Orsi in Via S. Vitale, part of a series of works sponsored by the family, often on unusual subjects; it had begun with an early Judith oratorio in 1668.[20] The 1671 piece featured music by the violinist Giovanni Battista Vitali, a feature evident in the number of arias marked in the libretto as being with ensemble accompaniment.[21] There are four roles plus a narrator, the Angel, and a chorus, perhaps five singers.

Clearly Astorre's wife Chiara Montecuccioli (1601–94) seems to have been as involved as her spouse in the oratorio productions, especially given the number of female protagonists in the pieces.[22] Although the couple had two sons, there seems to be no trace of family tension, and so the commissioning of this text may fit more into the tradition of depicting heroines than of the reconciliation of family problems. The postmortem inventory of Astorre's goods also lists no representations of any of the figures/narratives of the oratorios that the family sponsored, and no musical instruments, for that matter.[23]

The 1671 piece opens, unusually, with a two-stanza aria (not recitative) for the narrator, as if the story were already known to the audience and needed no introduction. The Testo first ruminates on the inscrutability of Providence, and then turns directly to Sara's residual resentment and jealousy due to her age and previous infertility. This early piece goes directly against Bernard's praise of Sarah, and its chorus begins unexpectedly and neutrally ("Of what is jealousy not capable?"), foregrounding her resentment. Abramo, entering, is incapable of placating her, and Sara's two-stanza aria turns into a catfight with the entering Agare, followed by another choral commentary.

The patriarch surrenders and orders Agare banished. In a pagan/sinful way, the slave calls on Fortune, is immediately reproached by the chorus, and then brings her son onstage for their painful departure. This is interrupted by a lament with strings, not for her but for Abramo, who resigns himself to the memory of his son. The following departure aria for Ismaele reiterates his own innocence, followed by another lament for Agare, bidding farewell to the city walls; she is consoled by her son, who repeats, echoed by the chorus, the unknowability of the Divine will, linking Part I's end to its beginning.

Already by this point, traditional exegesis and devotion could not have been turned more upside-down (it should be remembered that the librettist G. B. Maurizio was a cleric of a certain social standing). Sara is simply an aging jealous woman, there is no reference to Ismaele's interaction with Isaac (who is barely even mentioned), Abramo's indecision is unworthy of a patriarch, and the son has every reason to proclaim his innocence in the face of what seems to be certain death. Perhaps there was a reason for the missing imprimatur for the print, and its position essentially as a sacred opera.

Part II dispenses entirely with Abramo and Sara, concentrating on the despair of the banished mother and son (in this sense the character deployment is different from the 1705 work). The narrator again begins with a pitying aria, which leads to a lament with strings for Agare, which she addressed not to God but to the stars (another kind of "Fortuna" reference). Ismaele receives a sleep aria, after which, in a subtle reference to the opening of Part I, Agare asks the desert wildlife to eat her rather than her son. The whole section is a strikingly tender and long display of maternal affection, as in its duet Ismaele advises stoicism to his mother.

The Angel's subsequent arrival and his prophecy of the boy's descendants are framed by two one-stanza arias, the second with instruments; both refer to Fortune and to Hope more than to Divine intervention. After the messenger's departure, the joy of mother and son occupies no fewer than six arias (two of which are given to soloists from the chorus), and Part II has a balanced tripartite overall scheme. The final chorus then reiterates the inscrutability of Divine decrees and the transitoriness of life, its last lines the same as the opening of Part I.

The indications of instrumental parts suggest they were to be used in the three laments (and, strikingly, Sara does not get one of these). This text is so far from standard penitential fare that one might indeed consider it as a sacred Carnival piece. But there is one other familial topic: the maternal/filial affection between Agare and Ismaele, which occupies both sides of the break between the two parts as well as the ending. It would be hard to imagine which kind of sermon might have been heard here, except for one on Providence, and the whole end of the piece would have left its audience with the idea that sinners' fates were not merited.

A decade later in Bologna, the Sara of Giacomo Antonio Perti's popular *Abramo vincitor di se stesso** opened this new oratorio treatment via a semantic field of Petrarchan dichotomies of fire and ice to justify her own jealousy of Agar.[24] That this would be a different work was instantly clear from the immediate entrance of the Angel to console the matriarch. The 1683 premiere at the Bolognese oratory of SS. Sebastiano e Rocco took place on a Friday in Advent, the feast of the Translation of the Holy House of Loreto, suggesting Marian devotion; indeed, from early in the century, the oratory, halfway between the center and the city walls on Strà S. Vitale, had hosted sermons and music on all the *feste di precetto* for some time. Other oratorios, the first examples featuring its two patron saints, are recorded from 1666 to 1710.[25] The interior had recently been rebuilt; although there was no representation of Hagar among its artworks, still there was an altar with Mary Magdalen in the desert, an oblique reference to Hagar's exile.

Again, this is a piece from early in a composer's career. For Perti's listeners in 1683, it must have been a shock to hear Sara—as noted, for many commentators, the prefiguration of the Virgin Mary—begin the piece with an aria highlighting her jealousy and her own "exile" from sexual and emotional relations with the patriarch. This first scene gives two-stanza arias to Sara and to the Angel and their duet, followed by the Angel's flight to Heaven to obtain Divine wrath, leaving the rest of Part I to Abramo and Agar's highly sensuous love. This section is framed by an emblem-like aria on Amor's physical and emotion power, serving as a refrain and working around its own dichotomies: [*a 2:*] "Per opra d'amor, / [*Agar:*] Penoso contento m'afflige quest'anima; / [*Abramo:*] Soave tormento m'alletta il cor" [Through Love's power (*Agar:*) Painful happiness afflicts my soul; (*Abramo:*) Sweet torment delights my heart] (ex. 3.1). Here, "opra d'amor" still carries something of the early modern sense of Love's power/frenzy, again in a physical sense. There was also no imprimatur for this performance, although later versions would receive one.

EX. 3.1 G. A. Perti, *Abramo vincitor di se stesso*, "Per opra d'amore"; I-MOe, F. 925, fol. 14v.

In sharp contrast to Perti's Part I, the Angel begins the next part with an aria on Divine omnipotence, then frames his request for the patriarch to leave Agar with two arias (one da capo, one bi-stanzaic) surrounding the recitatives that demand the Banishment (which include a recall of previous Divine aid in the restoration of Sara from Pharaonic control while the couple had been in Egypt). The entire scene leaves Abramo incoherent and resistant, and so it undermines a directly "obedient" understanding of the story.

At this point, Agar bursts onto the scene, using her aria to call the Divine command "barbarous" and Abramo's heart "fragile." The ensuing trio recitative ("Cedi a me") ends in opposing demands on Abramo by the two women to give way, and his ambiguous "I will yield" is not clearly addressed to one or the other. The Angel and Agar wrap up their cases with different da capo arias, and the patriarch finally agrees to the Banishment in an aria, causing first anger and then lamenting tears in Agar's two subsequent arias. For all that Sara's surprise entrance at this moment, and the couple's ensuing professions of fidelity, did indeed lead to Abramo's aria on her "lieto e casto amor," the sense of an orthodox narrative is undermined by Agar's lyricism, rendering the Angel's concluding aria on the "bella vittoria" somewhat perfunctory.

The quick affectual changes in Part II, along with Agar's prominent role, render its derivation from any one exegesis or sermon difficult. Its contrast with the 1671 piece could not be greater. This work was done again in Modena (with a few revisions at court in 1685, as *Agar scacciata*), and in Bologna's Palazzo Caprara (1687); the most splendid revival was in Palazzo Pepoli (Via Castiglione) on 11 November 1689, for the traveling Ottoboni nephews (Marco and Antonio, but not Pietro) of the newly elected Pope Alexander VIII, complete with a new, family-specific introduction and *licenza*. As Francesco Lora has established, the surviving score in Modena is connected to the 1685 performance there. Overall, the emotional range of Perti's piece—with its double love duets (first Agar, then Sara) for Abramo, and Agar's move from fear to sensuous duetting to laments for her future—is wider than some of the Roman pieces to be addressed presently. The density of Bolognese palace venues is striking, and the popularity of Perti's work is also unusual.

Perhaps most remarkable was its 1726 revival, with imprimatur and again at the Estense court, by this point the center of Ludovico Muratori's rational piety. This late performance could be heard as a plea for reconciliation among Rinaldo I d'Este and his two sons in the early 1720s; sadly, the second one of the latter (Gianfederico) would die the next year in Vienna.[26] Certainly Perti's music, two generations old at that point but still attractive, must have been meant to underscore fraternal harmony as well.

The third Bolognese libretto on this story from these years was that set by the young Bartolomeo Monari, dedicated to the young noble Filippo Aldrovandi, and performed in the Oratorian church of the Galliera on All Saints' Day 1685, complete with imprimatur. This *Agare* begins with a Testo, leading us to expect a traditional approach based on Wisdom/Providence, but moves quickly to two laments for Agare (as opposed to Sara's opening jealousy in Perti's version of two years earlier). Sara's two following arias contrast with the opening, as she pauses her fury to remember Agare's own past sweetness to her. The balance of the part is evident, as all the characters open with two arias. The entering Abramo's indecision spills into both of his concerted pieces, and only Sara's raising the stakes by threatening to leave him moves him to the Banishment. Ismaele's arrival on the scene with two arias leads the lachrymose and guilt-ridden patriarch to exit, and Agare closes this part with another "Fortuna"-like, non-religious lament aria.

Evidently, this part had finished at night, as the Testo opens Monari's Part II with the dawn and with Abramo's anguish, answered but not resolved by Sara's two-stanza aria. Still at odds, the two depart, leaving the rest of the piece to a sequential narrative: Agare's two aria laments to Fortuna, justifying her "withdrawal" from her collapsing son (Genesis 21:16; in the Vulgate, this is not a complete departure, but rather Hagar's self-distancing "a great way off as far as a bow can carry," probably roughly 250 meters in classical antiquity); the Testo's description of the Angel's appearance (there is no sung role for the Divine messenger) with the saving water; Ismaele's jubilation at becoming a hunter in the woods of their refuge (a subtle reference to Genesis 21:20); and Agare's closing aria on Fortuna's favoring her.[27] It is hard to imagine which kind of sermon an Oratorian could have come up with between the parts on this 1 November, and the imprimatur probably had more to do with Aldrovandi family influence than with any devotional content in the text. Agare's Quietist acceptance of Fortuna was all the more striking in a Bologna still governed by Innocent XI.

This 1685 libretto is also noteworthy on one other count: all three of its adult characters reflect on the duties, honors, and disadvantages of being both a parent and a spouse. Far from Manni's admonitions, Abramo and Sara snap at each other in Part I: "[*Abramo:*] I am a father and a husband, and I feel love and fidelity take up equal parts of my agitated heart. [*Sara:*] I too am a wife and a mother, and Heaven wants it thus for Abraham and Isaac [only]; and so it pains me to witness that Abraham should share his affection and his riches with some other woman, some other son." She points to issues of patrimony and inheritance, another charged topic in early modern Italy. The duality runs throughout the libretto, and the most telling reflection is that of the saved Agare, whose final recitative, in a defense of unwed motherhood, answers the affect of her own opening aria, which had read: "A double care infests my breast, a double worry oppresses my heart: I am a mother, and a partner, and this double love destroys me through the rigor of a harsh fate." At the end of the piece, she finally reflects: "[*to Ismaele:*] Let us remain in this forest [miraculously no longer a desert]; I no longer care about the title of a wife, since I have kept that of a mother," a sentiment relevant even today.

In and Out of Rome

Far from the domestic scenes of Bologna, another set of spatial and textual convolutes, partially unified by the homiletic literature and by the patronage of the Oratorians, was found in Rome. Depending on the dating of the Biblioteca Vallicelliana collection (signature P. 2), the *Oratorio di Abramo quando scaccia Agar e Ismaele di Casa* seems indebted to the vernacular play tradition, here given a narrator instead of God's Voice, and with its entire second part given over to Agar and Ismaele's enactment of penance in the desert, another clear Lenten reference.[28] For all that its title recalls the past, its lexical field is actually rather elevated, and this seems to be a case of a piece from around 1660 which attempted to link popular tradition to newer developments in oratorios for a more restricted audience.

The convolute of pieces with imitations and effects began with the Jubilee Year performance of Bernardo Pasquini's *Agar* (on the Fourth Sunday of Lent, 17 March 1675, for the Florentine national community in Rome, with a text by Bartolomeo Nencini). At some point, possibly later, this version of the Hagar story was paralleled by a quite different libretto: Giovanni Bicilli's *Ismaele esiliato**. This second treatment of the theme was joined at some point by the best-known piece of this chapter: Alessandro Scarlatti's *Agar ed Ismaele esiliati**, which shares most but not all of its literary text with Bicilli's and was likewise exported to Vienna. Scarlatti's score in Vienna bears the copying date of 1683, while Bicilli's was performed at court in 1698, but both must have been composed earlier.[29] One version of the Scarlatti-Bicilli text was copied into a Roman collection of oratorio libretti as early as 1677, as Morelli has noted. But that text does not survive, and the earliest source for Scarlatti's libretto is a print from 1691 for a performance by a Marian confraternity in Palermo on Rosary Sunday that year.[30] Bicilli's literary text is preserved in a 1698 Viennese print (complete, as was normal, with a separate German translation). Unlike the Bolognese pieces, all three works traveled far.

The importance of the Hagar story around 1680 is quite clear. Nencini/ Pasquini's piece was meant for the 1575 Jubilee, and the appropriateness of the subject was evident in that the reading from Galatians was, as noted, the Epistle for the Fourth Sunday of Lent. Recent scholarship has placed the work in its Roman context, even if its libretto survives only in later and non-Roman sources.[31] One popular vernacular commentary on the Epistles of the church year referred specifically to the tale's penitential meaning that "chasing away the servant is the same as chasing away lasciviousness from the soul" and "chasing away her son is the same as chasing away the appetites and the works that are a result of this lasciviousness."[32]

The sermons for the Fourth Sunday in Lent of several Roman preachers do indeed mention the episode. There was a quadripartite background for this text: the two Biblical passages and their two uses in exegesis/ homiletics. Still, Agostino Paolacci's 1641 discourse had avoided stress on Paul's verses from Galatians that condemned Hagar and concentrated on Ishmael only as a case of Divine Providence.

For anyone in the original audience of 1675 who remembered Paul's words from earlier that Sunday, the opening of Pasquini's oratorio would have been both unusual and familiar. Abramo's hubris/*superbia* is set up by his rejoicing together with a chorus for being a father twice over, implying that Isacco was just born. Sara enters to voice her concern that her child will be disinherited, then raises the familiar topos of Ishmael's "scherzi" with his younger half brother, the offspring of a servant. This was the first, but not the last, mention of social class in the libretto. She demands their expulsion, and Abramo is divided.

The Angel enters to deliver the Divine command, noting that blood sacrifice would not be necessary yet (until Isaac or Christ; the reference is unclear), but tying the injunction, in a more generally penitential way, to human suffering in his exit aria: "Per sentiero di pene e martiri / alma forte al cielo se'n va" [The strong soul goes to Heaven via the path of pain and martyrdom]. Sara's joy—a two-stanza aria—leads into a duet with the patriarch, who immediately orders Agar (evidently coming onstage) to be banished. In that sense, Part I has already enacted Paul's points from Galatians.

But, as in the homiletic literature, matters are not so easy. Nencini's Agar accepts her fate obediently, but Ismaele brings the pathos of separation from his extended family onstage. For all that Part I had ended with the two setting off into exile under the star of Fortune, Abramo's ensuing unhappiness is eased only by Sara's exhortation to console himself with Isacco, demanding the patriarch's obedience, after which (as in Monari's 1685 Bolognese piece) the couple departs. Ismaele's own self-encouragement on this difficult path of exile makes him—not Abramo—into a Christian penitent who overcomes adversity by his own steadfastness, as in Manni's Sermon 26. After two sleep arias—one for the son, one for the mother— fail to ease the pain, and Ismaele has denounced Sara, thirst takes over, and Agar prepares to leave her somnolent and dehydrated son so as not to witness his death, until the Angel's intervention.

On a social level, then, another widespread issue comes into play here: the abandonment of sick or moribund children. The Angel immediately reappears to show the abundant water in the desert, seen as flowing from Ismaele's tears, a point made clear in a two-stanza aria. Ismaele is again refigured as a repentant sinner; Agar outlines her joy in a long two-stanza aria; and the penultimate lyrical moment is that of maternal/filial love. But his last words complete Ismaele's transformation into an example of a good Christian death: "Per divino volere / in grembo a morte a non morire imparo" [through Divine will, I, while in Death's lap, learn how not to die].

Again, it is a pity not to have Pasquini's score. This libretto manages to accomplish different tasks: to underscore Paul's interpretation, to leave Abramo and Sara happy (with the former's regrets), and to remake the young Ismaele as a penitent, along with giving a mixed picture of Agar's maternity. Its longevity seems justified.

Ramifications in Latin and Italian

In the following years, the story continued in Rome. In 1683 the Crocifisso witnessed another ambitious Lent, with the first Latin oratorio on the story paid for by one of the guardians of the confraternity, the sometime opera impresario Count Giovan Pietro Caffarelli, who commissioned a libretto

(*Ismael*) by the Brazilian-born Mesquita and music by the almost unknown Sienese figure Giacomo Fritelli, both in the service of Caffarelli and his brother Alessandro.[33] That year's Lent had featured other large-scale works on Joshua, Jonah, and the Abraham-related story of Abimelech (as noted above, from Genesis 20, another possible linkage among the three contiguous Biblical chapters), although — unlike in 1701 — there was no overriding trajectory to the topics. Possibly the four guardians of the institution had consulted among themselves.

Mesquita's libretto, however, recalls the *rappresentazione* tradition in its plethora of seven characters plus another *Vox Dei* (as in the 1701 Roman *Exilium* work discussed below), including a part for Isaac and a chorus of the younger child's friends. The text is remarkable on several fronts, not least the Italian summary of the story and its moral, both printed as prefaces to the libretto itself. It also evokes popular registers in its quick, montage-like movement among dialogue scenes. Still, Abraham's opening refers to double-choir music, which was just possible with the large cast hired for the occasion, while Ishmael immediately turns to his own jealousy as the persecuted firstborn (in a kind of scene 2). Sara jumps in with an aria quoting Genesis 21:10 ("Juste coniux, si parentis / nomen possides . . . eiice ancillam hanc et filium eius" [O just spouse, if you possess the name of a parent, send this slave and her son away]), and the patriarch wavers. In another moment taken from vernacular tradition, the Vox Dei intervenes, citing the chapter again, and Abraham obeys immediately.

Agar's response (scene 4) is a lament aria with Vergilian overtones, not addressed to the patriarch, and it is left to Ishmael to rescue her with a hopeful consolatory aria, followed by a duet for the two in which it is he who counsels obedience to the Banishment. For all that Mesquita rerouted details of the usual trajectory in this first part, the next one begins with a "symphonia laeta" of joy for Sara, followed by the expected (and unresolved) argument between the couple (Abraham mentions his "neglected children") and a duet of resignation.

Here the Banishment is into a forest, and Agar's first aria of this part notes their distance from the city. In a unique addition to the narrative, Isaac reappears (has he been spying on them?), with a reverse mocking aria of revenge against his half brother ("siccis Isaac si vos Genetrici / domo vidit exulantes"), and now Ishmael begins to faint from thirst. Most of this part deals with mother and son; Agar's aria expresses her desire to hydrate him with her tears (a gesture to the desert even though they are in a forest; "Si subsidiis aquarum / rupes carent duriores, / hoc vectigal lachrymarum / tuos leniat ardores" [If the hard rocks lack water, may this tribute of tears ease your suffering]). Just as she is shaken with horror ("horror quatior; nullus apparet latex"), the Angel appears, citing Genesis 21 again (like Abraham and Agar). This leads to two joyful arias for Agar, Ishmael's reviving, and the former's summary of the moral lesson quoted above, which concludes the work, without a chorus. As in the Bolognese pieces (which he probably did not know), Mesquita's text minimizes Abraham and Sarah, provides an extraneous and not terribly sympathetic part for Isaac, and apportions relatively large agency to Ishmael along with much lamenting for Agar.

One Libretto, Two Settings

It is against this Roman background that we might approach both Bicilli's* (*Ismaelle*) and Scarlatti's* (*Agar ed Ismaele esiliati*) settings of the story. The scores survive only in Vienna, due to their shipment northward. Given his years of association with the Chiesa Nuova, it seems more likely that the version mentioned in the 1677 Oratorian list was Bicilli's; the earliest date for Scarlatti's score is the inscription "Roma 1683" on the Viennese manuscript (the printed libretti are from later revivals). Strikingly, there is no evidence for a Viennese performance of the latter at any point. The two scores share what is essentially the same libretto, with minor but telling differences.

The Viennese choice of staging Bicilli's piece was no accident. As noted, in 1685 Eleonora Gonzaga had had his eight-voice allegorical *La vita humana* performed in her Lenten chapel, and his *Santa Cecilia* would be imported in 1700. His work* on the Maccabees (*Li Machabei*), which survives in Naples, also had a Viennese performance in 1686. The 1698 Vienna libretto for Bicilli's Ishmael piece mentions no author; the three for Scarlatti's claim variously Giuseppe Domenico De Totis (1644–1707), with the 1691 Palermo libretto and the Florence libretti of 1695 and 1697 assigned to Cardinal Benedetto Pamphili.[34]

The overall timing of this text's arrival north of the Alps in 1698 seems clear: this was a moment of transition in Viennese politics and culture, on the eve of the War of the Spanish Succession; as noted above, it came after Habsburg victories East and West.[35] As for Bicilli's oratorio, the importing might have had to do with the personnel situation: the long-standing court poet Nicolo Minato had died in January 1698, evidently in failing health from the previous summer, and so both the November 1697 opera and the 1698 *sepolcro* were repeats of previously composed works. New oratorios for Lent were needed, which included Bicilli's joined by one with an anonymous text (?Donato Cupeda/C. A. Badia), on the unique subject of Jehosaphat's alliances and victories (2 Chronicles 17–21). This latter was a highly political piece about good and bad counsel to sovereigns in a shifting military landscape. At least in Vienna, Bicilli's work must have carried some kind of external meaning, anti-Ottoman or not; possibly its shipment from Rome was facilitated by the controversial Imperial ambassador, Georg Adam von Martinitz.[36]

Placing Scarlatti's score in Vienna is harder. If the "Roma 1683" is a copying date, then this would have referred either to the very first weeks of January, in time to get the score to Vienna by Lent, or perhaps in autumn for the following year. But Lent 1683 in Vienna was already filled with some six other oratorios, and of course the court then fled in summer ahead of the Ottomans, spending a limited and divisive Lent 1684 in Linz. Possibly the piece was copied in 1683 and somehow squeezed in during Lent of the following year. There would have been good reasons for not performing the piece in either year, although given the 1693 importation of Scarlatti's *Il trionfo della Grazia/La Maddalena* and then the 1695 production of the composer's *La Giuditta* (with Pietro Ottoboni's text), its seeming neglect seems unusual.

The 1691 Palermo revival of Scarlatti's work was in the *Oratorio del Rosario* attached to the Dominican church of S. Cita (Zita), as the printed libretto makes clear. This small but spectacular space (probably capable of about 150 audience members) had received its stuccos focused on the Rosary Mysteries by Giacomo Serpotta in the 1680s, and the performance of the Scarlatti—outside Lent on Rosary Sunday—seems to invoke the ambiguous Marian interpretation of the story (there seem to be no other performances of any piece at the oratory).

Evidently it was done without a sermon (its title page calls it "Cantata," and there is no break between the parts, as in all the other sources). Possibly it was meant for a celebration, not a penitential moment, on the first Rosary Sunday after the completion of Serpotta's stuccos. Strikingly for Ismaele as a character, the chapel was also next to Palermo's *Conservatorio dei Fanciulli Dispersi*, the city's foundling school used for musical training.[37] Similarly, the 1695 Florence performance was sponsored by the famous youth con-

Obedience and Division · 59

fraternity, the *Compagnia dell'Arcangelo Raffaello*, with a long tradition of oratorio performance.[38] The issue of the almost-lost Ishmael might well have played a role here. As will be seen in chapter 6, this institution had a special affinity for the Tobit story in its patronage. Two years later, the other major musical confraternity in Florence, that of the Purificazione, picked it up again (anonymously but with an unchanged text).

The differences among the libretti (Bicilli/Vienna 1698, vs. Scarlatti/Palermo 1691, then Florence 1695 and 1697, plus the one derivable from Scarlatti's score in Vienna) are most audible at the end of both parts. Ismaele proclaims his innocence and filial attachment almost all the way through Part I before finally abandoning hope of remaining with his father, in a move reminiscent of Cazzati's 1671 *Agare*. The final aria of Part I, "Chi non sa, che sia dolore" (with a reference to Guarini's *Il pastor fido*), is given to Ismaele in Bicilli's libretto and its local German translation, after a recitative for the child trusting in God, not in his father.[39] The aria emphasizes hidden pain along with Stoic resistance thereto. However, in Bicilli's score, and all of Scarlatti's sources, it is sung by Abramo, and the change affects the meaning of Part I entirely: either Ismaele ends with a focus on disinheritance, or Abramo rounds off the part with his "unseen" paternal anguish. The latter feature resonates with some of the Bolognese works.

But matters are more complex, and more difficult, at the end of Part II. In Bicilli's version, Agar sings her penultimate aria ("L'innocenza oppressa langue") as Ismaele seems moribund, and she castigates Abramo's cruelty. Passing to a recitative on her departure (because of not bearing to watch her son die), she is interrupted by the Angel, whose long recitative on Divine help ends with the title of Giulio Rospigliosi's opera, "Chi soffre, speri." In her last and long (three-section) aria, Agar then calls on her son to revive ("Torna, torna, anima bella / quelle membra a risvegliar" [Beautiful soul, revive your limbs]), briefly mentioning his glorious future, and then recalls Divine pity on those who suffer, with a veiled jab at Sara ("A chi soffre ardor crudele / dona il Ciel ampia mercede / e ad un'alma, a Dio Fedele, / spesso il riso al duol succeed" [Heaven gives great mercy to whoever endures cruel force; and laughter succeeds pain in a soul faithful to God]), and the piece ends.[40]

However, Scarlatti's Palermo libretto moves directly from "Chi soffre, speri" to a chorus on a commonplace text "È folle, chi paventa / eterno il suo dolor; / se il ciel saette avventa / stilla rugiade ancor" [Anyone who fears eternal pain is mad; if Heaven shoots arrows, it also drops down dew] (a subtle reference to the water for Ismaele). If this ending—also present in Scarlatti's Vienna score but as a solo aria for the Angel—seems an unusual close for a passionate oratorio, it is; found as an aria for the shepherdess Dorisbe, closing the 1688 Roman production of De Totis's secular opera *L'Aldimiro*, it was a new addition to this reprise of his 1682 libretto. This neutral and worldly moment ends an already complicated text. Perhaps, rather than being borrowed from the opera's revival, the lines were already in what must have been De Totis's original oratorio text, then reused for his 1688 opera reprise. At some point Rome or Vienna replaced it with the more orthodox passage of "Torna, torna anima bella . . . dona il Ciel ampia mercede."[41]

There are more passages of other origin. Scarlatti's Agar has a two-stanza aria (in all sources) in Part I, condemning Sara's greed, "Non ha limiti, nè mete/il desio d'avaro cor" [The desire of a greedy heart has neither limits nor fears]. This text was set (different music) by Giuseppe Celani in a cantata manuscript now in I-Vnm.[42] All told, the lexical similarities point up the shared worlds of cantata, opera, and oratorio.

Beyond the meaningful differences of the versions, their overall trajectory moves symmetrically, as both parts in Bicilli and Scarlatti begin with disputes between Abramo and Sara, and both continue with both the former's internal conflicts and Sara's rejoicing. These end with extended scenes for Agar and Ismaele (and in that sense the libretti are like Pasquini's and Monari's pieces). The texts begin *in media disputationis* with a kind of oral deixis by Sara ("Udisti, Abramo, udisti i miei desiri?" [Did you hear, Abraham, did you hear my desires?]).

The entire opening, through the appearance of Agar and Ismaele, works around three binary statements: *Sara* (at the opening): "amor di madre, e gelosia di figlio" [a mother's love, and jealousy for her son]; *Abramo* (in response and defense of Ismaele): "Zelo di Genitor, pietà di figlio" [a father's zeal, and pity for his son]; and *Agar* (in her opening plea, referring to Sara's lying accusations as destroying "amor di padre, e fedeltà d'amante" [a father's love, and a lover's fidelity]). As Abramo then vacillates, another binary juxtaposition leads to Agar's full fury: *Abramo*: "non voglio, non deggio . . . non posso, non lice" [I do not want to (revoke the Banishment), I should not . . . I cannot, it is not allowed]; *Agar*: "'Non posso? Non lice?' o cruda favella!" [You say "I cannot, it is not allowed"; what cruel words!]. The two moments are telling (ex. 3.2).

An equally striking moment in recitative comes just before Agar's penultimate aria, as she watches her son languish: "Già di rigida Parca acerbo strale / discioglie a danni tuoi rapido il volo, / e rende un colpo solo / semiviva la madre, il figlio estino. / Hai vinto, Sara. Ingrato Abramo, hai vinto" [(O Ishmael,) the sharp dart of fierce Fate quickly launches its flight to harm you, making your mother half-alive and her son dead in a single blow. Sarah, you have won; ungrateful Abraham, you have won]. Although this whole passage is in the 1691 Palermo libretto, it does not appear in Bicilli's 1698 libretto/score; in addition, "Ingrato Abramo"—perhaps simply too much for more orthodox audiences to stomach—was omitted from the Florentine libretti (although Scarlatti set it musically as an extrovert *stile concitato* moment with repeated pitches and fifths in the continuo line)[43] (ex. 3.3).

If Bicilli's version was chronologically first, this phrase must have been added later. Table 3.1 summarizes the differences in the two settings. The most theologically unorthodox section of the libretto is Agar's accusation that Sara is motivated only by greediness for her son, an inversion of Sara's suspicions in other libretti of Hagar's designs on the patrimony; the aria with a text set elsewhere by Celani is one example. Just before, Abramo seems to admit his wife's desire for riches, as he refers to the Banishment: "a l'alito nocente, / che sparge de la colpa il rio veleno, / cade estina la fede, Amor vien meno" [Fidelity falls dead, and Love perishes in reaction to the harmful breath (of Sara's demands) which the evil poison of guilt spreads]. Ismaele's resignation to his fate in Part I reiterates this: "In van, s'affligge, in vano, / l'avida genitrice. Al mio minor germane / cedo quella ragion, che a me più lice" [(Isaac's) greedy mother worries for no reason; I yield that right, due more to me, to my younger brother].

In Part II, the patriarch's final words enact his own kind of Quietest subjugation: "Gran Moto de le sfere, / son padre; adoro i tuoi decreti, e taccio" [Great Mover of the spheres, I am a father; I venerate your decrees, and am silent]. Abramo's belated paternal feelings come in response to Sara's extended—and musically florid—jubilation after his moment of regret opening Part II. But to the degree that Agar defends the innocence of Ismaele, the slave woman has already won the moral high ground in the libretto, whatever traditional exegesis might have said.

The Angel appears only at the very end as a kind of deus ex machina. Contemporary listeners would have had to have known the Biblical story and to infer from hints in Sara's recitatives that she was acting as an agent of God's orders to secure Abramo's salvational paternity through Isacco alone.

EX. 3.2 A. Scarlatti, *Agar ed Ismaele*, "Non posso, non lice?"; A-Wn Mus. Hs. 19164 (after Bianchi 1965: 40).

EX. 3.2 (continued)

EX. 3.3 A. Scarlatti, *Agar ed Ismaele*, "Ingrato Abramo" (after Bianchi 1963:120).

Obedience and Division • 65

TABLE 3.1. Differences between the ends of Bicilli's and Scarlatti's Ishmael oratorios

Passage	Bicilli 1698 score + libretto	Scarlatti 1691 libretto	Scarlatti, A-Wn score
Con frode gradita	Dialogue	Duet	
Abramo, pietà	Duet	Trio	
Part II indication		Deest	
Intrepido sprezzato	Deest		
Final section	Agar: Torna, torna anima bella	Chorus: È folle, chi paventa	Angel: È folle, chi paventa

Musically, the two versions should be taken together, whatever their origins. If they both date to Rome in 1675–80, there is some chance of influence one way or another.[44] Bicilli's overall pitch structures move from G to C, whereas Scarlatti's piece begins and ends on the far more unusual B♮ (= "church-key 3 transposed up a major second," in Seicento terminology). Scarlatti used the arrival of the Angel at the end of Part II to bring back this tonal area from the oratorio's beginning.

A good deal of Agar and Ismaele's music in Scarlatti (e.g., the lengthy duet in the second part, "Quando, o Dio, quando sarà?") is set with accompanying strings and based on the pitch center E, a tonal choice evident in some of Agar's other solos (= "church-key 4/quarto tono"). Bicilli used flat (mollis) sonorities much more frequently, especially for Ismaele's pathetic restatements of his innocence and for his willingness to leave, both toward the end of his Part I. The turn to these sonorities starts with his entrance ("Padre?") and continues through his later resignation to the Banishment about two-thirds of the way through the part (the passage of "In van s'affligge" noted above is firmly around E♭).

Despite her departures halfway through both parts, Sara receives quite flashy music in both versions, notably in her first long aria in the unusual decasyllable meter ("Chi lo sguardo sublime e constante" [Whoever (does not fix) their high and constant gaze on Heaven]). In both, her character is also capable of local affective inflections.[45] The difficult melodic writing for Sara tends to mitigate her textual harshness; that is, in both works she essentially out-sings her husband, despite the libretti's characterization of her persona.

For the two composers, Abramo's most musically impressive moment is his remorse in Sara's presence that opens Part II; this is also the moment of his greatest explicitness around parental emotion ("Affetti paterni, / che l'anima amante, / con stimuli eterni, / ogn'hora affliggete, / tacete, tacete. / Decreto costante / de l'alto Motore / m'astringe al rigore / de l'essiglio, che impose il labbro mio" [Be silent, you fatherly feelings that continually torment my loving soul. A firm decree from the Great Mover constrains me to the rigor of exile that my lips imposed]).

Still, the slave and her son have balancing music. The most striking moment in the long series of their laments and prayers that close Bicilli's Part II is the beginning of an adagio aria for Ismaele preceding the arrival of the Angel ("Tu, morte clemente / col freddo tuo gelo, / del foco, ch'io celo, / estingui l'ardore" [O kind death, with your cold ice, put out the burning of the fire (= his thirst) inside me]; f. 71v ff.). Bicilli set this as a long chromatic descent in the voice, touching every possible pitch from G5 down to G4, extending the last line before returning to the motto of his previous aria ("Speranze, ch'il core"). In that sense, the innocent child has the most pathos-laden passage in his entire piece. Scarlatti, by contrast, kept this section linked to the opening "Speranze," using string echoes and a chromatic neighbor-note gesture (e.g., D4−Eb4−C♯4−D4) to convey the affect.

Since the libretto gives a good deal of onstage duration, as well as verbal intensity, to Agar, the musical differences for her two musical representations are also noteworthy. Strikingly, two recitative sections can be compared between Bicilli and Scarlatti: first, her plea to Abramo for her son ("Questo figlio innocente . . . son colpe d'Ismaele i tuoi tesori") after she has turned the patriarch's words ("non posso? Non lice?") back on him and Ismaele has condemned Sara. In Bicilli, this is quite simple, as she recites largely on F3 and C4 inside a clear pitch center of F. Set on G/*durus*, Scarlatti's passage is not quite as recitational, with a turn to flat inflections for the ending, "quell' / invida face, / che le [Sara] desta nell'alma odii, e furori: son colpe d'Ismaele i tuoi tesori" [that envious flame, which sparks hate and furor in her (Sara's) soul; your treasures are nothing but Ishmael's faults].

Similarly, Agar's two-stanza aria in *ottenari* takes stock of the desperate situation, as she believes her son dying ("L'innocenza oppressa langue; / gode, e regna l'empietà: / madre afflitta, e figlio essangue, / son trofie di crudeltà" [Oppressed innocence languishes, (while) impiety rejoices and rules; both the afflicted mother and the bloodless son are trophies of cruelty]). This linkage of parent with child, and the parallels with Mary's

Obedience and Division • 67

laments over Christ ("figulio essangue"), evoked different responses. Bicilli's motto aria (f. 74 ff.), again firmly on F, is marked "fiero [proudly]," with a varied repeat for the second stanza ("Cieca invidia"). Scarlatti set his version on D, without the varied second stanza, but marked "grave" and with a long sustained A5 for "empietà." The slight differences in the mother's characterization are telling.

Overall, the two pieces give three different kinds of parental attitudes, none coinciding with the sermon or exegetical literature: Sara's fierce determination for the (absent) Isaac; Abramo's vacillating resignation; and Agar's denunciation of injustice followed by her concern for her child. All seem far from the Roman homiletic literature of the late Seicento, and there are some intersections with Pasquini's text. Still, the rejoicing at angelic salvation is minimized and the actual moral to be drawn from the oratorio perhaps even less clear.

Pursuing Ishmael

Rome continued to be a site for the story. The only case of two sequential pieces on the Hagar theme comes from the Latin repertory of the Crocifisso in 1701, a site under the patronage of Prince Livio Odescalchi and hence close to the Habsburgs. This was something of an "off" year in the city, just after the Jubilee and under the shadow of the hardline turn of the newly elected Clement XI; it had featured only one new opera at Carnival along with other sanctoral oratorios, these likewise under Odescalchi's influence, and also academic performances of tragedies with incidental music (including a series of Pierre Corneille's plays). For the Fridays before the Second through Sixth Sundays of Lent, whoever planned the Crocifisso's topics picked only prominent Old Testament women, good or bad: Jael, Abigail, the two Hagar pieces, and Jezebel (i.e., Jehu), distributing the duties among four different librettists. Possibly this reflected some kind of hidden female patronage for the series, like that of Chiara Orsi in Bologna a generation earlier. In any case, the Fourth Sunday's Epistle reading was anticipated by the first Hagar oratorio and followed by the second.

Both texts (*Agar et Ismaelis Exilium* and *Agar et Ismael in solitudine*) were crafted by the occasional sacred librettist Paolo Gini (the lost music was by Gregorio Cola and G. B. Pioselli, respectively). The division of the story neatly demarcated the Banishment from the Exile/Rescue. Set for four adult characters (Ishmael is disenvoiced), the first piece features God's

Voice as a role, replacing the Angel. Gini's habit of mixing the theologically orthodox with the looser formulations of vernacular oratorios is on display in the first piece, opening with the Voice addressing first the audience, then Sara, who demands the Exile of her slave from her husband. The patriarch wavers, and is moved only by the Voice, ending with Agar's own consideration of flight (a subtle nod back to Genesis 16). Part II begins with Sara's joy, continuing with the Voice's demands, a fight between the two women, with the Voice finally intervening to force Abraham to send Agar away with bread and water, and an obedient Agar (and Ishmael) resolving to set off hopefully.

The second libretto begins with another spat between Sara and Agar (as in Bicilli/Scarlatti) just before the latter's definitive departure, followed by Abraham's quasi-remorse, stilled only by the Angel's command (here substituting for God's Voice). *In solitudine*'s Part II is less obviously coherent; it reintroduces Sara with a lullaby for Isaac. There follow the Angel's entrance; Sara's singing to her son (a clearly Marian touch) interwoven with both Abraham's dream vision of his dying boy along with Agar's mourning; and the final angelic consolation to Agar, along with her ensuing joy and the Angel's moralizing recommendation of Divine Providence. In his layering of Sara's *ninna nanna* on top of the patriarch's anxious vision and Agar's frantic despair, Gini deployed various affects simultaneously. In order to express all these, *In solitudine* features some twenty arias, and it is no surprise that Vivaldi's future musical collaborator Nicola Romaldo would reset it—but not *Exilium*—nine years later for the same venue. The interest of the Crocefisso's audience, however, is beyond doubt.

For one final local version of the story, Antonio Caldara's *Abramo* (no named author, for reasons to become evident presently, no score, and like Giacobbi's without an Angel) must have been written for Rome, although the only libretto comes from a possible performance at Bologna's Oratorians of S. Maria in Galliera, perhaps around 1715.[46] Its version of the tale serves as a kind of link between Rome and Vienna. At first reading, its praise of—and leading role for—Sara (a prefiguration of Mary) would seem to emerge from a more orthodox exegetical tradition.

Still, Caldara's text suggests otherwise, not least in the scoring omitting the Angel. It opens with an aria for the suspicious Sara ("Un sospetto nel cor mio"), who immediately moves to the accusation of Agar's greediness, as the latter and Ismael come on scene. Sara does not mention the boys' play

Obedience and Division • 69

as heretical or socially inappropriate. She exits, and mother/son remain to worry about her intentions. Abramo enters to reassure them, and they depart with a duet, leaving the patriarch alone to wonder about the discord between his wives. Sara's re-entrance emphasizes her own status against that of the slave woman, and a possible disinheritance of Isaac: that is, without any reference to Divine command. Abramo considers both sons worthy of different kinds of paternal love.

This moment is underscored by Ismaele's solo and pathetic entrance. Although the patriarch reproaches him for his anger at Sara, Abramo wavers to the point of pledging to depart himself if Agar were to be banished. But the slave woman's closing aria for Part I prophesies — and accepts — the upcoming Banishment, even though the patriarch opens the next part with his vow to leave together with Ismaele, scornfully dismissed by Sara ("Ragion lo vieta").

Sara then invokes the Divine command in her first aria of this part ("Chi s'oppone al ciel ch'è giusto / tema sempre dell'offeso / la vendetta, e il rigor" [Whoever opposes just Heaven, may they always fear its revenge and harshness for their offense]). Abramo finally addresses God, just in time for Agar's entrance, as the latter's plea for her future is rebuffed, although the patriarch refuses to articulate his plans ("Chiedilo [il destino] al cielo, ei te lo dica" [Ask Heaven (for your fate), let it tell you]). Caldara's Agar resigns herself to the Divine command, despite her deepest fears ([*Aria*:] "Agitata dal dolore / ho in orrore / la speranza di goder" [Agitated by pain, I think horribly of enjoying hope]).

In Caldara's version, Ismaele then appears ([*Aria*:] "Madre, se vuoi ch'io mora / dimmi almeno il perchè" [Mother, if you want me to die, at least tell me why]), and the high pathos of this moment is theatrically interrupted by the furious Sara, a character lineup not found in other oratorios ([*Sara*:] "In me riconoscete la crudele, / che a penar mi condusse / la gelosia d'un parziale affetto" [Recognize the cruel woman in me, whom the jealousy of a partial love (i.e., from Abramo) led to suffer], another avoidance of Divine command). The departure of Agar and Ismaele is then followed, again uniquely in the repertory, by a long closing scene for Sara and Abramo, as the slaves disappear. This thirty-four-line ending opens with Abramo's aria of self-doubt ("Un fiero tormento / il cor m'inonda" [A fierce torment floods my heart]), in response to which Sara claims heavenly inspiration for her actions. Without further reference to Divine design, Abramo reiterates his continuing affection for Ismaele, while Sara's closing aria ("Mi sento nel core / un ben gradito" [My heart feels a pleasant good]) balances out her opening "Un sospetto nel cor mio" in Part I.

A univocal interpretation of Caldara's text seems hard. On one hand, the straightforward Banishment, along with the triumphant (and prominent) Sara, could point to a commonplace Pauline/Marian understanding of the latter's character and of the story, one at least acceptable for the Bolognese Oratorians' devotion to the Virgin at their S. Maria di Galliera. Other features, though, militate against this: Agar having to take Abramo's word for the Divine command, the lack of much reference to heavenly decrees, and the wrangling over the patrimony all suggest that this was originally written for a private performance, perhaps in a family in which issues of sons' inheritance and illegitimacy were extremely acute. The lack of any printed libretto would underscore how it was never meant to be heard publicly.

Habsburg Recalls

This text's oddness may explain why Vienna hosted a new version in 1717 after Caldara's arrival there. That the Habsburgs were interested in the story is shown by a sermon done between the oratorio's parts on Thursday after the Fourth Sunday in Lent. This was one of the three weekly Italian-language homilies that the court preacher that year, Giacinto Tonti (1666–1726), devoted to Genesis 21 and the Ishmael story, and which does survive.[47]

Here, Charles VI seems to have commissioned a libretto from the famed poetic improviser Bernardino Perfetti (1681–1747) from Siena, with a setting by the veteran composer C. A. Badia, whose score survives also in Meiningen (this work's title is Ismaelle*).[48] Perfetti's style, as might be expected, is syntactically clear; he was considered by his contemporaries, however, as more mediocre in his prewritten than in his extemporized production, which again complicates the reasons for the import.

The work was premiered on 4 March 1717, which might have been the reason for its placement after works earlier in Lent respectively on Yael/ Sisera and Saint Ferma (both these latter with possible anti-Ottoman overtones). The Carnival opera that year had been Pariati/Conti's Sesostri, and the Holy Week work would be Pariati/Fux's Cristo condannato (there is a possible hint at this latter topic in the final prophetic aria of Perfetti's

Angel character, telling Ismaelle that he was only a "shadow" of Christ: "Non il servo, ma il Signore / benchè giusto, ed innocente / assetato un dì morrà" [Not a servant, but our Lord—though just and innocent—will die one day of thirst]).[49] The gesture, of course, was a standard move in Habsburg libretti from Minato to Metastasio. However, the opera, with its Egyptian setting and standard plot of a disguised son winning his rightful reign and spouse, seems further from the oratorio's themes.

What would have been most immediate was the continuation of the Ottoman wars, with the Habsburg victory at Peterwardein in autumn 1716 and new Turkish attacks in spring 1717.[50] The question of Providence and of unexpectedly good resolutions therefore might be more immediately related to the choice of subject. Perfetti's text has the standard five characters and the printed Biblical summary in its libretto. The libretto starts completely in medias res, as Agar tells Ismaelle to stop mocking/playing ("scherzando") with Isaac, as noted above the nominal reason for Sara's rage and demand for the Banishment. For all of its prominence in Perfetti's version, this translation is problematic; as Trible has observed, the original Hebrew verb has no direct object ("Ishmael [was] playing") and thus no reference to Isaac.[51] For all that some preachers, like Manni, cited the Vulgate incorrectly ("iocantem," with more derogatory overtones), Jerome's final version actually used "ludentem," a more neutral term, at least in classical Latin. Still, the Latin commentaries, and the universal translation of this as "scherzando," forced Perfetti's highlighting of this phrase into a pejorative meaning.

Here, the distribution and sequence of arias also points to a different approach: Sara has four of these, as many as Ismaelle and one more than Agar, and most of these in Part I. One might expect that Perfetti's work, like Caldara's, represents a rebalancing of the story in favor of her; after the opening arias for Ismaelle and Agar, Sara has two (plus a shared *risposta* with her husband). However, at this point—early in the piece—the Angel intervenes with one of the most remarkable justifications of the punishment to be found in the repertory, in an aria of *ottenari* referring to Ismaelle: "A cert'anime più elette / qualche calice di fiele / spesso Dio porgenedo va" [Often God offers a chalice of gall to certain, most select, souls]. This praise of suffering seems crafted for the dynastic patrons of the piece.

The closing chorus of Perfetti's Part I prophesies indirectly the upcoming Binding of Isaac in its choice of "earthly loves as sacrifice," and Part II opens, unusually, with an aria for Ismaelle directed to his father (the Banishment having happened in the meantime). Abramo claims piety as his motive, only to be disputed immediately by Agar (who turns the "teneri amori" of the preceding chorus against the patriarch) and Ismaelle, and this farewell scene occupies three arias. Still, as in Perti's treatment, Sara's victory is short, and the scene of thirst in the desert is ended by a loquacious Angel, whose first aria recalls Divine Providence (the second moment, prophetic of the Passion as is universally the case in the Viennese repertory of any kind, is mentioned above). The final chorus calls for hope in the face of seeming affliction, again perhaps a political reference.

To read Tonti's sermon, delivered in some form between the oratorio's two parts, in light of the libretto also shows emphases. The homilist had also referred to Hagar as Abraham's "consorte" and not his "schiava." Like the librettist, the preacher stressed Abramo's great love for Agar and Ismaelle, and, in a reference to Part I's closing chorus, he related the two stories of Genesis 21 and 22 by taking the Banishment as an indivisible part of the patriarch's overall sacrifices; the expulsion was linked to the Binding, the former as division, the latter as privation. But Tonti reversed the stories, claiming that losing Ishmael was worse than Isaac because no official sacrifice was involved. The homilist's point of comparison for the patriarch was, unsurprisingly, the dynastically favored figure of Job, for whom the preacher claimed lesser value because of his passive acceptance of suffering. This sermon seems to have been generated by the libretto, leading to an interpretation against most traditions of Biblical exegesis, a single product giving a clear sense of the priority of media at the Viennese court.

After this moment for Perfetti's text, though, the story would lose some ground. Apart from the 1727 work in Terni noted above, the theme almost disappeared in the oratorio repertory, as "rational piety" seemed to have its difficulties with this story as a learning or penitential experience. A 1731 four-voice version (*Agar, oratorio per musica a quattro voci*) for the court of Joseph von Lamberg, Prince-Bishop of Passau, was not Perti's, but rather an attempt to balance the discrepancy between Agar and Sara: it starts with the Banishment already decided, and with Abraham and his slave wife wrangling. The Angel comes onstage early to demand obedience, and the tangle between the two women is expressed largely in class terms (Agar as "ancella").

Part I of this 1731 piece ends with the definitive Banishment, but Part II is careful to involve all three human characters (the children are devoiced), with two solos of Agar pleading for salvation, two duets for Abramo and

Sara, a final word from the Angel promising a lineage to Ishmael, and a final tranquil duet for Abramo and Sara. More than the Seicento pieces, this one keeps Sara in play until the very end. Perhaps in accord with the not overly zealous Lamberg's taste, it provides an orthodox take on the story while allowing Agar some very bitter pleas. The composer of the music is unknown.

The topic found its last expression quite late, and in a changed devotional and social context, a Florentine reworking of Nencini/Pasquini's 1675 text for 21 December 1747 (i.e., in Advent before Christmas, more than for St. Thomas), set by the Duomo's vice chapel master G. N. Ranieri Redi and dedicated to Archbishop Francesco Incontri, who had been placed in his see by the new Habsburg rulers of Tuscany, a figure of increasingly anti-Jesuit sentiment.[52] This *Ismaele in esilio* was meant for the Oratorian church of S. Firenze, and its emphasis on family relations should be seen in light of the order's concern with domestic piety, starting around this time (chapter 7 below).

This final version's preface claimed that "this story contains profound mysteries, explained by the Apostle Paul (Gal. 4) and by Scriptural exegetes. Equally, it provides teaching and resignation for us all, when God is pleased to deprive us of something dear, and [teaches us] faith in Divine Providence, if someone finds themselves in any kind of anguish or need." In that sense it took over the lessons from the 1717 Viennese piece, using a different text to repeat Habsburg trust in Divine benevolence. Here, Abramo rejoices, Sara predicts an "unhappy ending" from the two boys' playing together, and Abramo expresses his ambivalence in an aria, "Combattuta [his "costanza"] dall'affetto" [my constancy is embattled by my affection]. The Angel again repeats that blood sacrifice is not yet necessary; Agar surrenders immediately to the demand of Banishment; and mother and son end Part I by predicting their own complaints to the other. Sara, in what seems to be a prediction of the Binding, notes that the only difference between her husband and his second son is their age; Abramo promises to remember Ismaele forever; and the two exiles find themselves in a forest, with a recitative lament for the son; a duet of imploring God; and finally a lament for Agar.

Nencini's original symmetrical structure was preserved intact. The Angel arrives with the indication of water and, as in Nencini, the scene switches back briefly to Abramo and Sara, as the former voices his concern for his older son. Still, the piece ends with a trio for the Angel, Ismaele, and Agar, whose B section, given to the Angel, points to the same kind of penance that would have been appropriate for Advent: "A sincere penance, Heaven's gift, makes the ungrateful human heart worthy of pardon."

Overall, a review of all these Hagar settings highlights some remarkable variants from the didactic literature: Perti's emphasis on the physical love between Abraham and Hagar (spousal sexual relations elsewhere being claimed by Sarah); the widespread wavering of the patriarch, even after the Banishment (one wonders how audiences would consider his obedience to the Sacrifice of Isaac in the next chapter of Genesis); and the centrality of Hagar's maternal feelings in the wilderness, even after her withdrawal from her son. The emphasis on Ishmael also obtains in the Roman pieces (Pasquini, Bicilli, Scarlatti). For all the many musically florid moments apportioned to his mother, the texts (and some of the arias' musical procedures) figure him as the penitent and provide even a disinherited child a way back into God's family, if not that of his birth. In that sense, they hint at Ishmael's further inclusion in a kind of extended sacred family, as intimated by Genesis 21:21 and 25:9.

Of all these stories, Ishmael's has some of the most heterodox expressions and disappears the earliest from the stage. In terms of tragedy, it is closest to the Isaac and Jephthe plots in its nonclassical motivation for the Banishment, while in some oratorios, the omission of the "play" between the two children makes the tale even more irrational. In a negative way, this points to the tale's unsuitability for an age of family sensitivity. But the contradictions and the role of the innocent Hagar made it useful in the Seicento, with the range of composers' choices being on display in Bicilli's and Scarlatti's two settings. Strikingly, almost no Hagar works are linked to the master narrative of the Binding of Isaac, to which we now turn.

Chapter Four

Fathers, Sons, and Waiting Mothers

Cold steel, cold steel in the father's hand
Tears falling from the sky
The angels, the angels did not understand
Why the righteous, the righteous boy should die.

—Joan Baez, "Isaac and Abraham"

CHARACTERS: Abraham, Isaac, Angel, [Sarah]

BIBLICAL SOURCE: Genesis 22

NARRATIVE: After he has grown into boyhood, God orders Abraham to take Isaac to an altar on Mount Moriah and sacrifice him. Just as he is about to do so, an angel appears and stops the patriarch from the act, praising Abraham's faith and obedience, and a ram is provided for sacrifice to replace Isaac.

WORKS DISCUSSED AT LENGTH IN THIS CHAPTER: *L'Abramo* (Palermo, 1650); Pichi, *Il sacrificio d'Abramo*; Bencini, ditto; Leopold I, ditto; Passerini, ditto; M. A. Ziani, *Il sacrificio d'Isacco*; de' Rossi, *Il sacrificio d'Abramo*; F. Manzoni, ditto; Metastasio, *Isacco, figura del Redentore*

PLACES: Palermo, Rome, Vienna

Thematically, the Binding (Sacrifice) of Isaac (Genesis 22) links with, and is parallel to, the Banishment of Ishmael in the preceding chapter.[1] Still, the former became the model for all sacrificial prefigurations of the Passion; it was a kind of metastory of equating Isaac on Mount Moriah with Christ on Calvary. Its long Patristic tradition dated back even before medieval and early modern commentators, and its paraphrase dramatization (with added voices for Sarah and Isaac) had begun already with the famed passage from the Church Father Gregory of Nyssa's oration, in which the characters (including Sarah) were given reactions at various points in the narrative.[2]

Gregory's central text would be cited by late librettists (e.g., Francesca Manzoni in 1738 and Metastasio the next year), and its dramatization stood at the beginning of the tradition for early modern exegetes.[3] There were numerous earlier *sacre rappresentazioni* of the story, and its Seicento musical appearances started with some of the earliest small-scale dialogues, as well as cropping up in France (Charpentier) and even Protestant Germany.[4] Needless to say, it was also frequent in the devotional literature; one popular text identified the descendants of Isaac as "an allegory of the New Testament" while the "Jews, Hagarines, Ishmaelites, the Saracens, and the Isaacicides" were equated with the progeny of Ishmael.[5]

The great Jesuit preacher Daniello Bartoli considered that "the whole world, all humans, would be worthy to be the spectators and admirers of this action. . . . Was the father more ready to kill his only-born son [Ishmael tends to disappear in such accounts], or was the son more ready to receive death at the hand of his own father?"[6] The answer to Bartoli's semi-rhetorical question can be found in the different treatments among the oratorios discussed here. Certainly the thought of prepared, but not completed, filicide moved even Metastasio's Abramo to exalt supernatural grace over Nature's instincts.[7]

The story prefigured not only the Passion. Abraham's faith and obedience were to be models for any believer, but—for the present purposes— the filial virtues of Isaac were also to be displayed in oratorios, as well as his glorification as the second prefiguration of Christ (after Abel) to be found in Genesis. In the Bible, of course, his speech was limited to two verses plus monosyllabic responses to God and the Angel. Any expansion of his character—along with the envoicing of Sarah—was due to librettists' and composers' approaches. In terms of family, then, this is only triangular: Abraham, Sarah, and their son, except for one case noted below.

Indeed, Genesis 22 is so oblique and objective in its narration that, although the symbolism of Isaac as Christ seems obvious, the various depictions allow some rough charting of devotional and dramatic changes over the period from 1690 to 1739/40 (the date of Metastasio's *Isacco, figura del Redentore*). It will be noted that the span of performances is actually shorter than the cases of Hagar and, as will be seen, Jephthe.[8] For whatever reason, the appearance of the story in oratorio was rather late. Another striking contradiction is that there seems to have been no single canonic text before

Fathers, Sons, and Waiting Mothers • 77

Metastasio's—most versions not even repeated (unlike, e.g., Perti's Ishmael piece), with one exception—and no widely diffused score of Metastasio's libretto until Niccolò Jommelli's from 1742.

One Story, Many Nuances

Since some of the following examples will be from around 1700, one place for explicit discussion of the interconnections of God and of Abraham as Fathers is in an Advent sermon printed in 1706 by the Jesuit homilist Carlo Tommaso Morone, "On God, converted from Judge to Father." Here the parallels (Abraham sacrificing Isaac = God the Father offering Christ) are made quite explicit, with the addition of Mary—not made equivalent to Sarah—as the perfect Mother filling out the New Testament side of the equation:[9]

> Every tongue weaves the most flowery panegyrics to exalt it [the Binding], the pulpits resound with admiration for it, the plectra [stringed instruments] praise it with nobility, and the sacrificing Abraham and the sacrificed Isaac are the object of the most learned speculations. . . . Help us, o holiest Mother of piety, to thank the Father of mercy, and teach us how, once we are remorseful for our past, we never again offend Him, but rather live in continuous thanks, and rendering thanks to you, through whom we obtain such good.

Still, this centrality of the Isaac story in the overall repertory of oratorios is not totally borne out by the numbers, especially compared to the parallel stories of Ishmael and of Jephthe, at least until Metastasio (whose *Isacco* banished most other libretti just as his *Morte di Abel* had done with the Cain story). For all its earlier presence in seventeenth-century dialogues, the story's rarity in the oratorio literature, at least up until Metastasio's text, is something of a surprise. The ritual place for this passage from Genesis was among the "hopeful" Prophecies read during the Easter Vigil, and so its linkage of Christ's Sacrifice to Christian obedience and penance was not entirely evident.

Because of a relatively well-known piece in Mantua in 1622 (*Il sacrificio d'Isac*), the chronological ties between the late *rappresentazioni* and the earliest oratorios are closer than is the case for some other stories in this study.[10]

Carissimi's short piece on the topic, hewing fairly close to Genesis 22, is different in its highly virtuosic and extroverted narrator ("Historicus") part. Although scored for five voices, it omits Sarah entirely, and gives only short moments to God and a longer speech to the Angel at the end, speaking in Divine voice for the promise of Abraham's descendants. The "Historicus" is also allotted the description of Abraham's anguished state, and the text adds Nyssa-like dialogue between father and son, with another case of a father unable to tell the truth when asked directly. However, its use of the narrator to depict Abraham's extreme emotions upon internalizing the reality of the Divine command is also a kind of Patristic gloss on the Genesis passage.[11]

As oratorio as a genre was beginning to take shape at mid-century, it would not have been easy for the Palermo Jesuits in 1650 to come up with a counter-Carnival sung entertainment (*L'Abramo*) which narrates the Isaac story, to be sure, but includes an anxious Ismaele and "Acan" (?the latter's servant) who see father and son head off for Mount Moriah and who believe their dream of the Binding. Sarah is omitted from the cast. All of the young characters sing *canzonette* at various points, and although a traveler who had seen the father and son ascend the Mount adds to their fears, Isacco's cohort finally performs a song with the safely returning child before the piece ends in general rejoicing.[12] Along with one other Roman piece from the same time (Lelio Palumbo's *Sacrifizio d'Abramo* of 1648, a tragicomedy in music with a long preface justifying the art's usefulness), this represents one of the closest convergences between the *rappresentazioni* and oratorio, and it is no accident that it occurred in a frequently used story. The number of added youthful characters also raises the question of the audience for the popular tradition.

What is most striking in this 1650 Sicilian *L'Abramo* is its conception of family (the music is lost). It imagines an Ismaele who is not only present but quite concerned with his younger brother even after the Banishment to share his worry and eventual joy at the final result of the Binding. This signaled a remarkable Jesuit willingness to compromise Scripture in the interest of creating a holy kinship among the sons which was to counter the individualistic and sinful behavior of Carnival in the city (including the possibility of fraternal violence). The order was responsible for the piece's "compilation" ("azione . . . accresciuta'), implying also the use of popular song in its *canzonette*, or perhaps even the Jesuits' reworking of a pre-existent vernacular play. It served simultaneously to preview the Passion and to reinforce the bonds of family, especially among brothers. The Roman composer Giovanni Conticini must have been commissioned to come up with some thirty minutes largely in *stile recitativo*, blended with the more oral-tradition items, in order both to convey the fraternal tone of the characters as well as to compete with the other festal songs in the streets. The Palermo piece is perhaps only the most extreme case of such mixture.

Still, given the story's prehistory as musical dialogue, it took some time to circulate as oratorio. Some versions (e.g., Florence 1701 or Rome 1736) were done on the First Sunday of Lent, as a kind of motto for the penitential season as a whole; only the first and last Viennese ones (1660 and 1740) seem to have been performed in Holy Week. All told, there seem to be about twelve different printed libretti in Italy before Metastasio, compared to the roughly fifty for the Jephthe story in the same period. Oratorio's reversal of theological priorities could not be clearer.

Here, of course, composers' choices for tempi, musical gestures, and textual repetitions in the arias could also override the setup of any librettist, no matter how famous. The questions for the father, then, are: (1) when and how does he hesitate; (2) which kind of emotional proximity to his son, as opposed to pure obedience, does he express; and (3) how is the actual moment before the almost-Sacrifice figured? Overall, though, any relation to a social reality of filiocide was less present than the fratricide of chapter 2 or the abandonment/cohabitation issues of chapter 3. The Binding was simply unthinkable in early modern social terms.

In comparison to the use of oratorios in (forced or not) monasticization for daughters, it is striking that the story seems not to have been used as an allegory for the male taking of religious vows or for the departures of missionaries overseas.[13] But Abraham's willingness to execute the orders, and his apparent lying to the boy ("My son, God will provide a victim for the sacrifice"), presented librettists both problems and opportunities.

Including Mothers

However, where this left Sarah's dramatic position in the pieces where she did first appear was another issue. Her first appearance in a specific oratorio text came in a collection dedicated to Pietro Ottoboni; this was Giovanni Battista Pichi's *Sacrifizio d'Abramo*, printed in his *L'arpa celeste* of 1702, and likely dating from a few years before.

Pichi's seven-character work might have had a certain circulation, although there is no clue as to the music's composer or the original performance.[14] Like the 1650 Palermo piece, this one is close to the vernacular dramatic tradition in its relatively low-register vocabulary, its parallel stories (and brief side appearances by Sara and Ismaele [!] temporarily postponing the drama of the Binding), and most strikingly its uniting of the Ishmael and Isaac tales. A tender scene of harmony begins the work, with Sara teaching Isacco the Creed, only to be interrupted by Agar's entrance, together with the slave woman's preference for Ismaele and designs on Abramo's inheritance. The brothers' play and Abramo's affection for both are interrupted by Sara (and so far Genesis 21 is still followed fairly closely), and she demands the Banishment, backed up by God Himself. Part I ends with its enforcement.

Pichi's Part II then finishes Genesis 21 and moves to the next chapter, with Isacco missing his brother, Agar's plea to God causing the arrival of the Angel, and then including a good deal of resistance on Abramo's part to God's order for the Binding. The irony of the journey to Mount Moriah is evident, as the young child goes off happily singing and praising God's Nature, interrupted by Sara's worry about her son's and spouse's fates and by Ismaele's own longing for his sibling. When Isacco naively asks why he is being bound with ropes, his father replies that it is "to free his soul," and this Angel's descent to stop the proceedings happens almost at the very end. The only moral in the final chorus is that of sinners' "hearts which should desire God." Pichi's piece is almost ironic in its flouting of traditional modes for recounting the story. It is also almost the only one to collapse Genesis 21 and 22 into one work.

But, influenced by Pichi or not, the 1707–8 biennium had four cases with Sarah present: M. A. Ziani's sepolcro for Good Friday 1707 for Vienna; Camilla de' Rossi's oratorio the following year for Habsburg Lent; and, in the Roman Lent of 1708, a Latin-texted piece for the Crocifisso (Fourth Friday of Lent) titled *Isach immolatus*, with music by Francesco de' Messi, along with another Italian work dedicated to Ottoboni and presumably performed in the Palazzo della Cancelleria: *Il sacrifizio d'Abramo*, with a libretto by Girolamo Buonaccorsi and music by P. P. Bencini (and possibly the prelate himself).[15] The question of whether Sarah knew of the Binding was first addressed by Augustine in his *Sermo 73 de tempore*, who replied in the affirmative, but it was still novel enough in 1739 that Metastasio also had to cite this authority in his preface to *Isacco* (as had Francesca Manzoni, the librettist of an identically themed oratorio in 1738). The examination below of the four Viennese and Roman pieces from 1707–8 gives a sense of Sarah's role compared to that of her immediate family.

Why this new presence of Sarah should have come up in the same years in two major centers is not as clear, especially given her variable appearances noted below. There were few oratorios on the topic in Rome, but her next appearance was in Antonio Bencini's 1736 *Sacrifizio d'Abramo*. As for other added characters after 1700, Gamari—the companion in the 1740 Viennese libretto who fills in for John the Evangelist on Calvary—seems to be original with Metastasio's text, and his presence explains the highly Johannine theology underpinning the libretto noted below.

Rome beyond the Rappresentazione

The Roman pieces of the years around 1705–10 took on different characteristics. Francesco Clementi's Latin libretto for the Crocifisso of 1708, *Isach immolatus*, contains the usual vernacular *argomento*, although one would hardly think it necessary (de Messi's music is lost).[16] Again the four characters are simply the parents, son, and angel. The summary remarked how the story was known to all, without mentioning specific exegetical or devotional literature. But, uniquely in the repertory, this text's opening invokes an absent family, namely Isach's longing for his lost brother Ishmael; as a de facto only child, he wishes even for death before exiting ("Sed si fratri dolenti / ire non datur suos comes Amori / saltem, quod minus est, liceat mori").

This opening soliloquy is followed by a parallel one for the ruminative Abram, who also misses his elder son. Given the narrative conventions that had accumulated around this text, the combination is striking; Sara is excluded at the opening, and the part (Genesis 21) of the larger story that is supposed to be over is the first thing mentioned. The patriarch ponders the inscrutability of Divine decrees as he prepares for the journey to the mountain, and we find ourselves in a moment of deep separation between father and son.

In an unexpected turn in *Isach immolatus*, Sara then appears with Isach to reassure her son that his brother will live (recitative: "Vivit Ismahel, vivit / ergo quid tuum dolorem / adhuc ages dolendo!"). However, she takes the occasion to disparage the absent Hagar as a servant, full of *voluptas*. The references to the previous Hagar repertory (chapter 3) of the Crocifisso would have been clear. Sara then turns to the rejection of earthly love in an opera-like aria ("Amor est suavissima flamma"), as if this piece for the Friday after the Fourth Sunday of Lent were meant to reprise the theatrical season that had ended a month before.

In Clementi's text, the entering Angel wakes the patriarch from his reveries, and the latter's reaction is to question the Divine command of which the messenger has reminded him ("Isach manu est immolandus?"). At this end of Part I, he attempts to dominate his own unwilling natural emotions, without any interaction with his son (aria: "Rerum omnium faecunda creatrix [= Nature]"), falling asleep again, and Clementi placed a narrative question mark over the whole story.[17]

Part II of Clementi's work begins with the Angel waking the patriarch once more to undertake the journey. Sara erupts into the scene to tell her husband of her evil dream that he is going to sacrifice their child, but her aria ends, she exits, and there is no response from Abram. There is a switch to father and son on the journey, as Isach praises the beauty of Nature, evidently moved by the pastoral journey; Clementi might have included this passage as a moment of irony before the Binding. Finally the two engage in dialogue, as the son perceives his father's unspoken sadness. At last, Abram gives in to tenderness (the name of "son" being sweet and sad simultaneously) and marks himself as both father and (sacrificing) priest, carrying the fire of love and the sword of constancy to the mountain.

In a long (three-aria) soliloquy, Sara then takes over most of Part II. She recognizes that her dream was true (the orthodoxy of this gesture was at best equivocal; again, the libretto had no imprimatur); her second aria calls her missing husband "barbarous" ("Ah vade, barbare") and she works herself into an unanswered frenzy of invective against Abram; while her final solo blames "ungrateful fate, by which I would never have had such pain had I not been given over to your favor; you cruel man, you made me a mother and gave a child to this infertile woman, so that I might be fecund only with pain." She then disappears from the piece, leaving space for a finally tender dialogue between father and son. Isach accepts his fate, never doubting his father's love, and Abram turns to God, asking Him to guide the sacrificial blow. It is at this moment that the Angel appears to bring matters to a happy end.

The piece must have been so successful that it was repeated at the Crocifisso the next year (the note on the I-Rv copy of the 1708 text was "buono"), and this might have been due to the unexpected twists in the libretto. In

Fathers, Sons, and Waiting Mothers ◆ 83

accord with Gregory of Nyssa's treatise, the two parents never talk to each other directly, nor does Abram achieve any kind of intimacy with his son until almost the end of Part II (it will be noted how this contrasts with the opening of Metastasio's *Isacco*, in which father and son are already quite close). Besides his innocence, this Isach seems to be a model child in his longing for his missing brother, and then his quick acceptance of his fate. De' Messi's music would have mixed single-stanza and da capo arias, and perhaps some of the success was due to the setting.

But this final Isaac piece for the Crocifisso—the last one of any kind, Latin or Italian, in the city until 1736—gives a varied portrait of Sara, somewhat in a traditional vein, but far more loquaciously than was the case before 1700. The reticent father is clearly taken from tradition, but the prominent role for Isach is notably new by Roman standards. Why the piece has no reconciliation for Sara is not immediately clear.

The second Roman work of these years was Giacomo Buonaccorsi/P. P. Bencini's *Il sacrifizio d'Abramo**, done for Ottoboni at some point in Lent 1708.[18] As with some other works secular and sacred, the cardinal must have contributed some arias (the title page of the libretto says "posto in Musica dal Signore Pietro Paolo Bencini, e dall'Eminentissimo, e Reverendissimo Signor Cardinale Pietro Otthoboni"). This text is of a higher and clearer literary level than Clementi's; it begins with a long—but almost satirical—dialogue for the Angel and Abramo, in which the former tells the patriarch of a new test, while the latter's opening aria ("Del mio Dio un cenno solo") shows him utterly willing to comply with anything asked. At first the skeptical Angel tells Abramo to kill, not his son, but his tenderest affects, before turning to the actual victim. The patriarch's second aria is perhaps the closest to overstatement ("Parricida fortunato / io sarò della mia prole"), and the Angel recognizes the patriarch's all-too-eager disposition in a fast recitative dialogue which culminates in the point that Abramo will kill two victims: his son and his emotions.

Even with respect to the Patristic and exegetical traditions, the inversions of this opening are striking. The patriarch, unrealistically eager to obey but with no sense of the real emotional stakes, represents not a sinner, but rather a completely unconscious subject whose difficult enlightenment will be the piece's real theme. In a parallel duet scene, Sara and Isacco then appear, with the mother in a new role: that of preceptress. Buonaccorsi chose to emphasize the intimacy between mother and son, and in light of Abramo's preceding eagerness to complete the sacrifice, their relationship seems entirely different from that between father and son. She lists Creation's beauties in an aria ("Tu pur mɪri i fior del prato"), and her son replies with another ("Ingrato, e perchè") reproaching ungrateful humanity.[19]

This, however, is interrupted by his father's brusque entrance telling of God's command for the journey. Abramo, in an equally insensitive way, tells Sara that this is her last farewell, without saying why. His shocked wife replies in an aria ("L'ultimo addio?") echoing his words, and it is the parting dialogue between mother and son that finally makes the patriarch waver (aria: "Tacete, affetti miei"). He refuses to tell her the specifics, while rejecting her request to select a sheep to take up to Moriah as the sacrifice (a clear maternal substitution effect, but also a Eucharistic reference).[20] Although one might expect the part to end with the departure of Abramo, there is instead a farewell duet between mother and son.

Buonaccorsi's structure is clear (Angel/Abramo; Sara/Isacco; then *a 3*), with the uncertainty of the journey functioning as the close of the part. The opening of Part II makes it clear that Abramo has learned nothing, as he soliloquizes his ambivalence while grouchily enjoining silence on the boy, and his son notes his father's anguish. Against tradition, Sara has set out for the mountain herself, noting the falling streams as being like her heart (aria: "Quel rio mormorante"). Buonaccorsi then scene-switched to a long passage for father and son, as the former finally reveals the Binding. Echoing his parent, Isacco is quite ready, with an aria insisting on being bound tightly ("Stringi con forti nodi/questa mia fragil salma"), with his spirit and his heart being strong at his fate. This is the only example of such a masochistic tone in the entire repertory, and it represents an exaggerated parallel to the all-too-willing Abramo of the piece's beginning.

After this striking aria, Buonaccorsi turned back to Sara, this time underway looking for her son (and husband). From some distance (i.e., "offstage" in the Palazzo della Cancelleria's newly constructed theater), she hears her son's voice, but is close enough to see the preparations for sacrifice that are being made. Abramo tells his son to be silent, finally revealing that Isacco's words are testing his resolve to go through with the execution (aria: "Taci più, non parlar"), before he self-interrupts and tells God that he is ready, as the Angel had predicted in Part I, that he must first sacrifice his affection ("ecco ch'io sveno / pria gl'affetti del seno. . . . / parracida mi rendo, e in te mi scolpo" [behold, I, above my heart's affections, am about to devein him. . . . I make myself a parricide, and in you (Isaaco) I see myself]). For all that this might seem to resonate with his self-description of Part I

Fathers, Sons, and Waiting Mothers • 85

("parricida felice"), this is a very different father indeed, finally tormented in Part II if not before. Again, the distance between Abramo and Sara is noteworthy.

In an aria ("Altro non brama / Iddio da te"), the Angel appears (possibly on a machine), and, with his two arias and long recitatives, turns out to be one of the most loquacious examples of his character type in the repertory. Sara, still watching from offstage, has a single aria on her hope and her trust in God (emotions not exactly borne out by her earlier arias and recitatives; aria "Non m'ingannasti, no, / cara Speranza"), after which she disappears.

This allows the talkative Angel to make the promise of descendants (aria: "Non son tante in ciel le stelle"). He explains the Binding as an example of infinite Divine love (recitative: "E sì infocati nell'eterna mente / diffuse i raggi la pietade ardente, / che in questo Sacrifitio / di due bell'alme a lui dilette, e care / pretese Iddio di palesare al mondo / il suo amore infinito"; [Thus, His ardent pity diffused the rays of his burning pity into His eternal mind so that, in this sacrifice, God took it upon Himself to show His infinite love to the world]). Isacco ends with a happy aria, calling on humanity to rejoice at infinite Divine mercy while avoiding sin that provokes His wrath.

This text is probably best understood in the context of the other new approaches to traditional topics (e.g., the Passion in Scarlatti's *Per la Passione* of 1706) that Ottoboni sponsored, sometimes with his own texts, in the first decade of the new century. On one hand, the vocabulary and even the seeming tone of the piece are high culture. On the other, the implicit mocking of the unaware patriarch, and the sympathetic portrait of Sara (whose conflict with her husband is limited to the merely necessary), make this into another kind of Binding piece. In the context of Ottoboni's personal oratorio repertory (including the sequels to the Passion work), Bencini's piece represented a different way of telling the Isaac story.

Devotion also intersected with politics. One might consider Buonaccorsi's piece for the Francophile Ottoboni as representing a different kind of dynastic sanctity, in its lengthy promise of Abramic descent for rulers. On the other hand, the patronage of the Crocifisso seems to have placed the confraternity in the world of "Imperial" Roman circles, and de Messi's libretto could be considered with those of Ziani and Rossi as Habsburg works, concerned with the immediate relation of father and son in the middle of the War of the Spanish Succession and amid the concern over Joseph I's lack of an heir.[21] If Morone's "flowery panegyrics" referred to a cultural rebirth of the theme around 1700, then different political entities had hurried to put their own stamps on it, using oratorios as a means. These different emphases, however, also had implications for the family relationships inside the works.

Bencini's music seems aimed at connoisseurship as well as modernity. Abramo's first aria on his absolute obedience to God's will is a strict two-voice canon (with string ritornelli), musically enacting his following Divine commands, at least at first (ex. 4.1).[22] If the opening scene between the Angel and Abramo is otherwise not musically striking, matters change with Sara and Isacco's appearance, with a long opening aria ("Sorge l'alba") for the boy, and a descending ostinato in the *bassetto* aria for his mother, "Tu pur miri." Her diagnosis of Abramo's real intention in her aria "L'ultimo addio / dal figlio mio / prender io deggio?" fluctuates among affects and time signatures, while her "Luci de gl'occhi miei" features soli for cello and archlute. Similarly, Isacco's attempt to reassure his father of his sacrificial readiness, "Sol ti chieggio, e sol desio," is quite extended. Within the limits of Buonaccorsi's libretto, Bencini's score seems to have emphasized mother and son, and not the father.

Viennese Sacrificial Anxieties

The frequency of this story in the Habsburg repertory, with different versions sometimes premiering in successive years — as if the Binding had to be reenacted obsessively — seems at first glance linked to moments of dynastic succession and their crises at just the same moment as the Roman works. A generation earlier in Vienna, Leopold I (the younger brother who had succeeded to the throne after the unexpected death of the heir apparent Ferdinand IV) had first set it in 1660*, showing the Binding's importance among dynastic stories. At the end of the period, the complex process of getting Metastasio's *Isacco* produced and finally staged at the very end of Charles VI's life seems to round off the cycle, given that Manzoni's text on the same subject had premiered with L. A. Predieri's music* just before. In between this beginning and end of Habsburg court oratorios, there came other treatments: Francesco Passerini's imported (1693) *Sacrifizio d'Abramo**; the pieces of 1707–8, plus another short anonymous version* whose length seems to point to the seventeenth century, seven works in about eighty years. In the Imperial context, then, the issue was not so much the Binding as it was the promise of offspring, always an issue in Vienna.

EX. 4.1 P. P. Bencini, *Sacrifizio d'Abramo*, opening canonic aria; UK-Mp Ms.580bk51, fol. 8r.

The various pieces associated with the court approach this in different ways, and one point of demarcation might be the promulgation of the Pragmatic Sanction, allowing for female Empresses, in 1713, something not to become Imperial law until 1732 (chapter 8).

To begin, Nicolo Caldana's 1660 text *Il sacrifizio d'Abramo* with Leopold I's own music seems related to the latter's situation: with four of his full siblings, and two half siblings already dead by the time he turned twenty, his expectation of his own future children's deaths could have combined with his lifelong concern with contrition to render this exercise in dramatic composition a sort of musical self-preparation for both future loss and current penance. This piece — evidently the second Viennese *sepolcro* — couples a Roman-like dialogue on the Binding (Part I) with an enactment of contrition (Part II), but the text is hardly a model in this light. This one begins with no Divine command, but simply Abramo and Isacco en route to Moriah, with the former beset simultaneously by Umanità and Ubbedienza in a *sacra rappresentazione* style. Two servants prepare the penultimate part of the journey, but Abramo is so occupied with his continuing doubts that he has little time for paternal affection during the final ascent, instead singing a *sdrucciolo* aria on the horror of the Binding ("Con faccia impavida").

Isacco reproaches his father for his impassiveness, and on the mountain, Humanità reappears to dissuade the patriarch while comparing both Isacco's and Sara's moral characters favorably to Abramo's. Isacco and Ubbedienza split Christ's prayer on the Mount of Olives ("Father, if it is possible, let this chalice pass from Me"), giving a clear sense of Passion identification, until the Angel intervenes. It is here that the dynastic succession appears, as the Angel ventriloquizes God in recitative: "Io ti benedirò, / e moltiplicarò / il seme tuo, come del cielo fulgido / le stelle serene" [I will bless you, and multiply your seed like the constant stars of the bright sky]. Part II is largely composed of a virtuoso solo part for Penitenza plus the cries of some four sinners. It is possible that these latter were meant to represent the deceased Ferdinand III, along with his son Ferdinand IV, and the former's two children with Eleonora Gonzaga. This idea would link all the Viennese Abraham pieces to the dynasty's succession and to its mourning for the many males who had passed away. The piece yokes together two different kinds of texts, both related to Latin or Italian dialogues.

The next Viennese staging of a work on the topic was a generation later: Passerini's large-scale piece, imported from Bologna during a Lent of 1693 marked politically by the anti-Ottoman wars in Transylvania. But the entire winter had been ruined by the December 1692 death of Maria Antonia of Bavaria, Leopold's only surviving child from his first marriage to Margherita Teresa, in whose early education various oratorios, *sepolcri*, and operas had played a vital part. For all her problems, her father had been close to her throughout her troubled life. She had died from complications after the birth of her only surviving son (and third child), and the mourning period for her bled into the twentieth anniversary of her mother's death back in 1673. The two sets of grief were marked by exequies and urban bell-ringing in Lent 1693. Like two decades earlier, there were no Carnival operas or serenatas during the period, and both sons and mothers were being mourned at court as Passerini's oratorio was being produced.

The Lent 1693 lineup consisted largely of reprises: Leopold's own oratorios on St. Anthony of Padua* and on Mary's Seven Sorrows*; Passerini's imported piece; Scarlatti's *Il trionfo della grazia/La Maddalena pentita** (a gesture to the living Empress); and a short piece by C. F. Pollarolo on St. Philip Neri excavated from a Brescian performance in 1680. The Friday *sepolcro*, the only freshly composed work, was another collaboration by Nicolo Minato and Antonio Draghi, this on the Blood and Water (*Il sangue e l'acqua*) flowing from Christ's side on the Cross. Three pieces mourned Maria Antonia directly or indirectly, and the motto — God's post-Sacrifice promise to Abraham (Genesis 22:17) — affixed to the elegantly produced score of Passerini's work seems almost ironic: "I will bless you and multiply your seed like the stars of Heaven . . ." — were it not for the Emperor's indefatigable optimism, according to which the deceased family members were in Heaven, and his own two surviving sons were a proof of Divine promise. Indeed, this quote comes up in the Angel's final recitative of Passerini's oratorio, after his praise of father and son's constancy: "il real sangue / in propagarsi al mondo andrà al pari / alle stelle del cielo, / all'arene del mare" [this royal blood will reproduce itself on earth equal to the heavenly stars and the sea's sands]. Here again, as in 1660, Imperial self-reassurance seems to have been accomplished through the oratorio's performance.

Passerini's score has a libretto by the Bolognese Tommaso Stanzani (ca. 1647–1717), aimed at roughly the same audience as the Ishmael works from the city; it had premiered at the Oratorio of SS. Sebastiano e Rocco back in Bologna, and was intertextual with the preceding Genesis chapter.[23] As in the Biblical model, Sarah is not a character here; her role at this point would have needed interpretation for its dynastic tasks in Vienna. But one unusual aspect, not in the father-son relationship, would have made it appealing for the court: toward Part I's end, the Angel appears first as a living spokesperson of the Beatitudes, and in this guise announces the centrality of strength, hope, constancy, and faith to the boy, well before the latter intuits the upcoming Binding. Stanzani's Beatitude-Angel follows this up with two arias sung to Isacco and ending the part ("Quel cor è sol beato / che tutto a Dio si da" [Only that heart is blessed which gives itself entirely to God] and "O come lieta va / bell'innocenza / all'immortalità" [Oh how happily lovely innocence goes on to immortality]). Indeed, the entire piece ends with the Angel, Abramo, and Isacco claiming Charity, Hope, and Faith, respectively.

Whatever their original intent, these would have fit Leopold's sentiments well and served as lessons for the children present. Indeed, the situation of the 1689 Bolognese libretto's dedicatee of Passerini's original performance, the patrician Angelo Maria Angelelli, who seems to have died without a surviving direct male heir, suggests an immediate consolatory use for the original. Yet one further aspect would have increased the piece's attractiveness: this moment, perhaps implying only a costume change (into the Virtues) for the singers in Bologna, could also have been performed in the Hofburgkapelle, as any Imperial agent acquiring the work in Italy would have known.

Stanzani's libretto also hints at Christian optimism; arriving on Moriah at the beginning of Part II, Abramo sings an aria to his son praising Creation, despite his task ("Anco il sol"). He then contrasts his duties as father with those of sacrificial priest via another aria ("Come padre a te darò, / dolce figlio, amplessi e baci; / ma fra I nodi più tenaci / sacerdote io t'offrirò" [As a father, I will give you, dear son, embraces and kisses; but as a priest I will offer you up with the tightest knots]). This emphasis on the Binding and the knots is reiterated by Isacco's following aria ("Cari nodi, ah si, stringete / questa man, che voi darete / al mio cor la libertà" [Dear knots, yes, bind my hand, as you will give my heart its liberty]). That Abramo treats it again in yet another aria ("Io ti bendo, o cara fronte, / perchè sei fronte d'Amor" [I bind you, dear face, for you are the face of Love]), whatever the limited merits of Stanzani's text, links its meaning to the Binding of Christ in the Passion, far beyond any suggestion in Genesis. Indeed, there was a subtle implication of Habsburg devotion to Christ's wounded Face. Still, the mention of the knots picks up on the century's fascination with the instruments of martyrdom.

Types of Isaacs at Dynastic Junctures

As noted, another piece on the topic may have been performed around this time.[24] Still, a quick check of the Italian homiletic and devotional literature in North Italy and Vienna during the decade on either side of 1700 reveals no major shift in the treatments of the Binding story, despite the Roman activity discussed above.[25] The changes must have been internal to the Viennese situation. P. A. Bernardoni's 1707 *sepolcro* for Marc'Antonio Ziani—a genre at a higher level than oratorio per se—begins in medias res, with the command for the Binding having already been issued by God (who is not a character), and Abramo in dialogue with a wise servant (this latter sung by the important court tenor Silvio Gargetti). This *Il sacrifizio d'Isacco* took place in a far different political context than had its 1660 predecessor.

The Viennese winter of 1706–7 had been occupied by military problems in Hungary, Spain, and the Netherlands, while the upcoming wedding of the future Charles VI and Elisabeth Christine had been announced. Lent featured three oratorios on three different kinds of female sanctity (the Magdalene, St. Theresa, and St. Beatrice d'Este); a Tobit work (music by C. A. Badia); and probably one or two others. The Carnival opera, *L'Etearco*, had been on a royal daughter lost and found, and so there seems to have been a clear shift to topics for a female audience: the Dowager Eleonore Magdalene, the Empress Wilhelmine Amalie, and the adult daughters Maria Elisabeth, Maria Anna (soon to be married off in Portugal), and Maria Magdalena Josepha.

On one hand, Bernardoni seems to have been reacting to his audience in his Isaac work; on the other, several plot threads were left hanging in the *sepolcro*. This latter work followed the new post-Leopold norm of having narrative, and not allegorical, works for Good Friday. Here, Abramo orders the journey to Moriah and makes his servant hide that fact from Sara. He also prohibits her from coming along, should she discover the plan for the journey. Sara enters by reacting to the servant with twenty-two recitative lines on her concern, plus three successive arias, the last one lamenting her feared loss of her son, and it is here that the piece approaches its Good Friday thematics most closely, with the centrality of Marian grief for dynastic piety.

The *sepolcro* continues with the scene on Mount Moriah, with the ever-reticent Abramo unwilling to say at first which one of the two of them will be the sacrificial victim, until Isacco volunteers to take on this self-immolation; somewhat after the fact, his father tells him of the previous Divine command. Although the Angel appears at the correct moment, there is relatively little rejoicing after the Binding is blocked, and Sara never returns on scene, as the chorus finishes with the "O felix culpa" theme. This lack of any kind of happy ending was due, of course, to the Good Friday context of the performance. Most noticeable is the absence of anything about the Imperial succession. Since this was a *sepolcro*, not an oratorio, the only prophetic passages could be to the Passion, and this is what the Angel enunciates at the end.

As a whole, Sara is kept at a certain distance, for all of her Marian-like grief; this was only the second *sepolcro* whatsoever since Leopold I's death, and the first one using Abraham for Good Friday since the deceased Emperor's own 1660 piece. Possibly the norms of non-allegorical themes for Holy Week had simply not yet been established. Still, the mother's role here, especially in its lack of interaction with her son, seems puzzling.

As befitted a *sepolcro*, Ziani's music was, however, suitable to the gravity of the occasion. Abramo (a bass, in this case the experienced Rainaldo Borrini) begins his acceptance of the command (it should be remembered that *sepolcri* had only one part, without an intervening sermon) with a serious and long (thirteen oblong pages) aria on E, "Si che il Figlio ha da morir," in tempo giusto and with imitative strings, as he turns to address Isacco. The son has two arias before the first of Sara's (here sung by a woman, Anna Maria Badia) opening consideration of horror ("Un orror nel cor mi sento"), a shorter piece with a B section of sheer sadness ("Mesta son"), as she considers the Binding. This Sara is not only aware but also reactive. However, her second and third arias are relatively short, and the latter ("Se vanto, è d'un gran pianto" [If I take pride, it is only in my great sorrow]) marks the point at which she moves from family member to the Addolorata. This is marked musically by this aria's setting in F in flat regions, a sort of emblem for the sorrowing Virgin[26] (ex. 4.2).

The duet between father and son in which Isacco's fate is revealed to him is affectively less weighty (Abramo: "Della vittima il pensiero Dio si prese" [God has given thought to providing the victim]). To his credit, though, Isacco reacts with horror to the idea that the victim will be one of them, and here any sense of the perfect child disappears in the face of the sacrifice. But the son recovers quickly, in a "largo e spiccato" continuo-aria on E♭: "Io l'adoro e fiero in viso vado incontro al mio morir" [I adore Him, and with

EX. 4.2 M. A. Ziani, *Il sacrificio d'Abramo*,
"Se vanto, è di un gran pianto"; A-Wn, Mus. Hs. 19133, fol. 34v.

a proud countenance I go to die]. Ziani returned to the imitative string parts of the *sepolcro*'s opening aria for the Angel's (in performance, the well-paid alto castrato Gaetano Orsini) aria of reassurance ("Non è Dio crudel così"). The closing *madrigale* is relatively straightforward, and the question remains of where the specific weight of this piece lies. Although Sara is envoiced to some degree, she tends to sing in soliloquies, and not often to her son, let alone her husband. The need to gesture toward the Addolerata put further restrictions on her role.

One advantage to the genre was that of not having to interrupt the action for a sermon, something crucial for those who were used to the complex allegories of Minato's libretti in the previous century. This allowed Bernardoni and Ziani a more direct trajectory in portraying the events, rendering such moments as Isacco's wavering all the more surprising. The piece was the second of the librettist's directly Passion-oriented works for Good Friday 1706–9 (Calvary, Isaac, Christ on the Mount of Olives, and the Flagellation).

It was unusual that the theme would return as a normal Lenten oratorio the following year. Because of military problems in Hungary, Joseph I was gone from Vienna for some of March 1708; the Carnival opera had been *Il Mario fuggitivo*, the name-day piece in March was Fux's *Julio Ascanio*, and the two other recorded oratorios were *Il pentimento di David* and *La Costanza trionfante nell martirio di San Canuto re di Danimarca* (and then later the sepolcro *La Passione nell'orto*).[27] Although the audience was the same as the previous year, Joseph's presence was not assured. The 1708 *Il sacrifizio di Abramo* by the Venetian dilettante poet F. M. Dario and the Roman composer Camilla de' Rossi may have suffered from its text; the lack of named casting on the Viennese score might even raise doubts as to whether it was performed in the first place. That there was no part for a bass suggests that the envisioned ensemble of singers was different from that for Ziani's 1707 sepolcro.

In any case, this libretto for de' Rossi could not have opened more differently from Bernasconi's of the previous year. Dario foregrounded Sara and her praise of her son, starting the piece with direct address: "Di genitor cadente, / di già sterile madre / per un doppio argomento, / e di un seme, e di un seno / prodigio del mio Dio, figlio adorato . . . [*Aria:*] Chi non rimira in cielo, / opera eccelse e grandi / per se formar non può. / Se alla virtude aspiri, / al monte, al piano, al mar, / non cessa di adorar / quel Dio, che ti formò" [My adored son, (you have been born to) an aged father,

Fathers, Sons, and Waiting Mothers • 95

a previously sterile mother as double proof (of a miracle), of semen and of a breast both prodigies of my God . . . (*Aria:*) Anyone who does not look to Heaven cannot create great and noble works. If you aspire to virtue, then on the mountain (a covert reference to both Moriah and Calvary), on the plain, or at sea, never cease adoring the God who formed you].

Isacco replies in her praise and then sings his own aria lauding Creation, following his mother's instructions directly. This is followed by a long sleep scene in which the Angel (not God) appears to the drowsy Abramo to command the Binding, and Part I ends with a deeply troubled patriarch unable to tell his son the truth on their journey to Moriah.

Symmetrically, Sara opens Rossi's Part II with a soliloquy in which she asks for Divine punishment—which she intuits as aimed at father/son—instead to be directed against her, yet another substitution in grief which subtly recalls one Marian theme omnipresent in the Viennese repertory (ex. 4.3). But then again, she is silent for the rest of the piece, as on Moriah Abramo finally tells his son that he must die.

The patriarch holds off for a final recitative embrace of the boy, and then an aria ("Ti consacro la prole adorata" [I consecrate to You my adored child]), which together give the Angel enough time to intervene. But the final duet is for father and son, again without any return for Sara ([*Abramo:*] "Sin che io chiudo l'antiche mie luci / sin che spirto avrò nel seno / [*a 2:*] nume eterno, / di lodarti, di obbedirti / non cesserò" [Until I close my elderly eyes—(*Isacco:*) as long as I have breath in my chest, (*a 2:*) eternal Deity, I shall not cease to praise and obey you]).

But the most striking difference with Ziani's piece of the previous year is the Angel's emphasis on dynastic politics. After quickly stopping the sacrifice and pointing out the ram in the bushes, he rushes on to predict not only the personal continuation of the dynasty, but even the desired end of the War of the Spanish Succession, with Austria taking the Spanish realms: "la tua prole / quai l'arene del mar, le stelle in cielo, / cresca felice. E dove nasce il sole, / e dove al piè d'Atlante / precipita la luce e rompe il giorno, / nasca sembre, e tramonti, / suddito de tuoi figli" [let your offspring grow happily like the sands of the sea, the stars in the heavens. Both there where the sun is born, and where, at the foot of Mount Atlas, it starts daylight and makes the day break, may it (the sun) be born and set as a subject of your sons].

What exactly this might have meant in 1708 is unclear. There is one other clearly gratuitous reference to the Imperial eagle in Dario's text, as Isaac's seemingly final recitative, just before the patriarch's delay, invokes

EX. 4.3 C. de' Rossi, *Il sacrifizio d'Abramo*, Sara, Part II, opening ("Discostatevi omai"); A-Wn, Mus. Hs. 17306, fol. 49r.

the bird's mythology: "Che se l'aquila stessa tra gl'incendi del sol ai figli crede, / darà di me, tuo figlio / la fiamma dell'altar più degna fede" [Just as the eagle himself thinks to bring the sun's flames to his offspring, so too will the altar's flames give me, your son, a more worthy faith]. As time went by, Joseph I's infertility—and that of his wife—had become clearer, and although he was still young, the issue of the succession posed itself in terms of not only the Spanish throne but also the Empire itself. Perhaps both pieces of 1707–8 were either an attempt to hope for a miraculous pregnancy for the Empress, especially given the opening language, or rituals designed to exorcise the specter of missing heirs (and the future Charles VI was at the ready, although away on the war in Spain). If the operas of Carnival season were considered related to royal fertility, the following oratorios could also have functioned as penance and expiation for dynastic reproduction.

In any case, Rossi's piece allowed a wider expressive window for Sara, compared to the *sepolcro* of the year before. Although Dario disappeared from court life, Rossi was asked to do both text and music for the 1709 oratorio on the Prodigal Son, yet another family-related theme that had not been heard for some time in Vienna (Draghi's 1678 piece on the topic had been repeated in 1689), a real mark of confidence in her abilities.

Although often noted, her music has sometimes not been studied in depth.[28] The intimate nature of the libretto was reflected in the scoring for chalumeaux and archlute (the latter probably played by F. B. Conti). One immediately striking feature is the complexity of her bass lines, whether or not they feature the archlute obbligati; Sara's opening pedagogical "Chi non rimira in cielo" is built around two different motives in the continuo, against which she sings a complex but not flashy line; on the other hand, her Part II aria "Strali, fulmini," asking Nature to intervene against the Binding, features strings and a busy vocal line filled with *fioreture*. The first of these is addressed to Isacco, while the second is a soliloquy. Isacco's reply to her opening, on the other hand, "Dal sol ogn'astro apprende," is indeed extrovert, with a good number of melismas for "folgarar." This pairing of mother and son at the beginning, before a note is ever heard from the father, is one of the most novel features of Rossi's score.

That Abramo's first aria is a sleep piece ("Accostatevi a queste pupille") complete with chalumeaux enhances neither his authority nor his doubts. The Angel has to push him to accept the Binding ("Abramo, o forte Abramo"), and he needs a second aria ("Non entri il mio dolor/ad infestarmi il cor" [Let my pain not enter to infest my heart]) to regain his composure and proceed. This soliloquy does indeed bring him back to the musical level of the rest of his family, notably via the long melismas on "lo spirar." Despite the somnolent and distanced figure given her by Dario, Rossi set up the musical conflict in the patriarch by virtue of this aria, and the entire effect is to equalize the characters by the end of Part I.

Similarly striking is the aria with archlute obbligato: Isacco's "Già preparo seno al foco, cervice alla spada," his piece of determination to undergo the sacrifice, in a suitably "spirituosa" tempo and with arpeggios all over the instrument's range undergirding a largely syllabic and leaping vocal line. The virtuosity had been anticipated in the long, four-section sinfonia to Part II, with the archlute moving from arpeggio to tablature and a slow imitative passage for strings showing off Rossi's contrapuntal skills.[29] The score as a whole seems to have won her the commission for the text and music of *Il figliuol prodigo* of the next Lent.

The Binding a Generation Later

The Habsburgs would return to the theme in 1738 with Francesca Manzoni's libretto for the new court composer L. A. Predieri, in which the Milanese librettist claimed novelty for introducing Sara on Mount Moriah (even though Buonaccorsi had done so in 1708), stating the reason of prefiguring Mary on Calvary.[30] She cited the authority of Augustine and of Gregory of Nyssa (the latter via Lapide), which gives some idea of the Patristic source materials available to an educated laywoman. She emphasized Abramo's virtue and sacrifice of his own affections (hence the title) in an attempt to balance the Marian reference with the main theme of the text. To accommodate the large Viennese casting, she added Abramo's shepherd and servant to the four figures of parents, child, and angel.

As will also be evident in chapter 7, Manzoni's approach tended toward the expansive (although not at the very beginning of this text, with only thirty-eight recitative lines before the first aria). Like Metastasio's version intended for the following year, the 1738 *Il sagrifizio d'Abramo* began with a colloquy between Isacco and his father, in which the son first complains of the journey's length and then goes on to list the promises for his future (including those important ones made only after the Binding in Genesis 22). This sets up a soliloquy for Abramo, in which he wrestles with his own emotions, returning to Isacco plus his servants so as to prepare the ascent to the Binding, only to lie to the latter about his plans ("As soon as we have

Fathers, Sons, and Waiting Mothers • 99

complied with the Divine intention, Isaac and I will return to you here"). Still, the patriarch asks, at the end of Part I, why God had ever made him a father (Genesis 21 having been excised here again), and the shepherd notes the utter confusion of his emotions, before the chorus paraphrases a passage from John Chrysostom's *De fide Abraham et immolatione Isac* to close.

Part II begins with Abramo's ironic "our souls' emotions are burning even more than the pyre," as he explains to his son the identity of the victim. The patriarch gives a long explanation (in which Manzoni used both Flavius Josephus's and Chrysostom's accounts of the Binding) to his son, who is more than willing to obey. The Angel and Sara enter the scene simultaneously, probably from different sides of the Hofburgkapelle, but with the mother far enough away not to be perceived by her husband. After the halt to the killing, Sara gets close enough to talk with her family, much to their surprise, providing her own ekphrasis of the moments just before the planned execution, and emphasizing her horror at the idea, as she did not have her husband's and son's valor. She explains her pursuit of their not-so-secret journey, and her varied emotions, to which Abramo responds by citing his duty to hide the incomprehensible Divine command from her maternal love. There follows a familial trialogue during which the substitute ram is discovered, and a kind of reconciliation achieved with the Angel's repeat of the promise of Isacco's descendants, addressing the issue of the dynastic succession in a fairly clear way, and closing with an angelic chorus again singing the triumph over emotion. Manzoni added Sara not only for the purpose of the surprise encounter on Moriah, but also for the task of restaging the "victors over their own feelings" idea.

This was the setting, then, for Metastasio's text production of *Isacco, figura del Redentore* in early 1739, and it suggests that Manzoni's version was unsatisfactory in a way that mirrored the fate of Ziani's 1707 *sepolcro*. Predieri wound up setting two quite different libretti of the same story in successive years, while his music for both would disappear into the Viennese archives for the rest of the century; as noted, Jommelli's version of *Isacco figura del Redentore* (perhaps originally for Venice) became the first widely diffused score.[31]

Still, Metastasio's verses, demanded personally by Charles VI, differed from anything else that the court might have experienced, and their addition of "Gamiel" (Isacco's companion, and a stand-in ultimately for both St. John and the individual "rationally devout" soul) affected—and to some degree distanced—family relations in the 1739–40 libretto.[32] The Imperial poet's version would take off in the decades after its first performance.[33] After Charles VI's (as it would turn out, temporary) recovery from his illness of 1739 (which prevented the text's performance that year, substituted by *La Maria lebbrosa*), *Isacco figura del Redentore* would be the last *azione sacra* that he would hear in spring of the following year. But the work would be almost as popular as *La Passione* or *Giuseppe riconosciuto* in Metastasio's output, with something like ninety settings throughout the rest of the century.

Despite Metastasio's title, which emphasizes the Christological role of the son, the clear primacy of Abramo—whether or not he seriously doubts the command for the Binding—is evident even from counting recitative lines plus arias for the 1740 characters (Abramo: 202 + 2 arias; Isacco 87 + 2; Sara 90 + 2; these numbers could change in revivals). In this text, Metastasio narrowed his normally wide citational field (outside Genesis itself) to some notable, and not obvious, examples. On the other hand, the sense of the Binding necessitating the later Passion seems to have been behind his use of Lamentations as a text envoicing the individual believer's grief.[34]

The most obvious characterization is that of the loquacious and gentle patriarch. *Isacco* opens with a moment of filial intimacy, as father and son conclude an all-night session of history-telling covering the highlights of Genesis 12–18—but with no mention of Ishmael or Hagar. Abramo finally tells Isacco to leave—which he does not, waiting for the (here anticipated, as in Manzoni's libretto) promise of future descendants and possessions. Metastasio gave Predieri his usual long recitative introduction of some eighty-eight lines, evoking Isacco's "holy fear" at the thought of glory, before the first aria, sung by the boy on his "pure heart."

At this point, with the arrival of the Angel (substituting for God's Voice), Metastasio picked up the story of Genesis 22, notably with no mention of Sara to this point (she does not appear until the middle of l. 158). Thus, in contrast to most earlier pieces, the centrality of the father-son relationship has been restored here. The Angel's aria underscores both the "rare gift" of Isacco's birth and gruesomely predicts the sacrifice in its B section ("[Dio] Vuol che rimanga esangue / sotto il paterno ciglio" [(God) wants him bloodless under his father's eyes]; ll. 124–25).

Following this, in the parents' first, long colloquy (ll. 158–229), Abramo is about to send Sara away without an explanation, but realizes immediately that she needs full explanation and justification ("oda l'arcan").[35] Compared to the other patriarchal roles in this chapter, this is a remarkably rational approach. To this point, the temporal durations of recitative and arias have been roughly equal. In a passage seemingly meant for *accompagnato*, Abramo doubts the command, but in a break from all previous treatments he changes his mind and decides to tell the truth about the Binding at this point to Sara, in a "dialogue" during which she has only three complete poetic lines out of fifty-one. She breaks into tears, and his only response is an exit aria whose B section finally evokes the "triumph over one's own emotions" trope ("Chi una vittima gli svena . . . / a lui fa dono / della propria volontà"; ll. 221–29).[36]

It is at this point, after a final quote from a Passion sermon of Bernardino of Siena, that the references turn to John and Jeremiah. In seeming contrast, although Abramo had referred to his paternal feelings, Sara's maternity takes over, along with her mutual affect for her son. Metastasio then brought her together with Isacco and Gamari, thereby prefiguring the scene on Calvary, as she decides also to conceal the truth from her son, while equating her own pain to that of Abramo's affections.

Isacco sings his second aria of trust in his father to her and to Gamiel (thereby musically cementing his position as the second protagonist of the piece; "Madre, amico! Ah non piangete," ll. 269–75), expressed in Johannine terms of Christ's departure and return (i.e., Resurrection).[37] He leaves to join the patriarch, while, alone with Gamari, Sara finally gets her aria, adoring God even in her pain and wishing to suffer even more than her son. This provides both a Habsburg Marian flavor and a reminiscence of the Mother of the Maccabees (chapter 7). By the end of Part I, she has been transformed from a non-entity to a grieving mother, and finally into a superhuman heroine who seems to have vanquished her affections entirely. Despite the post-Arcadian gentility of the language, the underlying emotions move quickly and can be quite grim. In that sense, this part seems to be the victory over family, and Sara's aria, compared to her relatively short recitatives, underscores this transformation musically.[38]

Part II has the task not only of providing the happy denouement, but also of restoring conjugal and parental relations. This is evidenced by the opening: after a brief—and fully traditional—delirium "Deh parlate, che forse tacendo," in which Sara again imagines her dead son and the actual blow of the sword. Gamari returns to tell of Isacco's carrying the sacrificial wood (i.e., the Cross), and then, relatively early in Part II, father and son return safe and sound. This is the first time that the whole family is on scene together, but there is no difference in the proportion of communicative roles from Part I; Sara simply offers brief interjections to her husband's retrospective account of the Binding and the angelic intervention. Indeed, Abramo and Isacco have the first two arias in this passage, and the retrospective telling allows the listener the same sort of meditative distance that Sara and Gamari, as the on-scene "audience," would have had.

It is Sara's Part II aria, after her praise of her spouse, "Sian are i nostri petti" [Let our hearts be altars] (ll. 523–31), that performs the duty of overcoming emotion in a highly charged way ("vittime sian i nostri affetti / figli del nostro cor, / svenate a Dio" [let our emotions be the victims, and sacrifice to God the children of our heart]). The filial metaphor for emotions, in the voice of the mother, is striking, and explains the lack of conjugal affection between husband and wife in this passage. Even though there were quiet hopes at court that Elizabeth Christine would die, and Charles live long enough to father a son after her death, in the actual performance of the text, this invocation of progeny—by now a constant in the oratorio repertory—was only a dream, one which had to be repeated in the Lenten and Holy Week repertory as a kind of prayer that it, too, would miraculously come to pass.

Metastasio also was theologically circumspect about the succession. The descendants "numerous as the sands of the sea" promise is rushed through in one recitative line (ll. 539–40), and the Angel then passes to direct Passion prophecy, which leads the patriarch to ecstasy as he foresees the salvational presence of Christ in some twenty-three recitative lines (ll. 554–77); that is, general human salvation outweighed dynastic continuity, notably changed from the works of 1707–8.

The presence of the Passion from the beginning of the poet's text onward, highlighted by different citational and poetic usage, inflects the entire libretto with a sense of tragedy even if all audiences were aware of the happy end of the Binding story. Only in Part II do Sara and Gamari take on their role as a devotional public, suggesting that the process of meditation took some dramatic time. But in this sense the purification of the emotions made the classical vision of tragedy re-emerge, for all the work's happy ending.

Other settings of Metastasio's text started with a first non-Viennese version, for Habsburg Florence (by F. N. Rainieri Redi in 1741). Perhaps the most interesting detail of the 1740s is that of the added arias—the opening ones for both characters—of Abramo and Sara, present in the Venetian copy of Jommelli's score (I-Vsmf, no. 5) and (always in *virgolette*) in most but not all libretti, even those not for Jommelli's setting.[39] The two inserts follow each other as non-exit arias, and Abramo's plea of "Col tuo braccio ah reggi il freno" [Ah, guide the binding gag with Your arm] interrupts his own call to the servants and Gamari to wake Isacco so that he can unwittingly be taken to the Binding. It emphasizes the uncertain state of the patriarch's affect in its description of his doubts about the Angel's order.

Even more interesting is the added interruption, in this Venice score, of an extra moment for Sara, as she hears her husband's doubts about the Binding. She has observed his torment and humbly articulates that her own sufferings will gain her merit (this may be another Marian touch): "Sollecito, dubbitoso, / taci, mi guardi, e pensi . . . / merito nel soffrire / acquisterò per te" [Worried and doubting, you are silent, look at me, and think . . . / [but] through you I will gain merit in my own suffering]. While far from Metastasian in both placement and vocabulary, the addition has the effect of using conjugal communication for the sake of intimacy.

In Jommelli's setting, the patriarch's (tenor) plea for Divine aid is a florid piece, ranging up to high B4, simultaneously stopping the action and under-scoring his articulateness. Sara's (soprano) line consists more of syllabic interjections (its tonal distance of E♭ from the preceding G major is also noteworthy) with a quick and virtuosic first violin part. She is significantly envoiced much earlier than in the 1740 original, and perhaps it is no acci-dent that this double insertion would remain in some productions into the 1770s. This kind of addition means that, in the vocal partbooks of the Venetian source, her total number of pages rose to forty, twice that of the Angel and more than Isacco's *parte cavata*.

Sara's Part II opening in the 1742 version is a *scena* with the longest accompanied recitative in the whole work (starting in D minor/major, and extending the duration of her vocal presence), "Chi per pietà mi dice," one of the composer's famed accompagnati, followed by another aria with no opening ritornello, "Deh, parlate," as she addresses the shepherds who have been on Moriah. This F-major piece, reflecting her distraught state in its string tremolo, then moves to a closing passage in which, having decided already that her son is dead, her line is reduced to a series of F4s for "tacete." Her delirium of the actual sacrifice constitutes the B section ("So che spira quell'ostia sì cara" [I know that the (sacrificial) Host, so dear, is dying (with a Eucharistic reference)]), set largely as octave D4/5s over descending bass lines as symbols of lament. Jommelli's Sara is a vocally more prominent, and varied, figure than the libretto would suggest, and one whose emotional distance from her husband is partially compensated and partially transcended in the 1742 Venice score.

After 1740 and then the quick success of Jommelli's version, there were also other non-Metastasian texts for music still circulating. Besides the Castel S. Pietro piece, these included works in Genoa, an *ospedale* work in Latin by Galuppi (1764), and Cimarosa's 1786 Naples *Sacrificio d'Abramo*, a sacred opera with the same character names as in Metastasio but a completely different text. For all that audiences could not get enough of the Binding and its very different father/mother-son relationships, there developed some sort of cultural need for a version in which the filial sacrifice was clearly wrong (just as the Isaac story was theologically—if not emotionally—clearly right).[40] However, even more striking is the case of achieved child sacrifice, Jephthe's Vow and its disastrous consequences, the subject of the next chapter.

Chapter Five

Sacrificing Daughters

Siate fedeli, e a ciò far non bieci,
come Ieptè a la sua prima mancia
cui più convenia dicer "Mal feci"
che, servando, far peggio . . .

—Dante, *Paradiso*, V:65–68

CHARACTERS: Jephthe, his Daughter, [his wife and counselors]

BIBLICAL SOURCE: Judges 11

NARRATIVE: In Mafta, the Jewish Galaadites are hard-pressed militarily against the Ammonites. The Jewish leader Jephthe decides to wage the battle and takes a vow that he will sacrifice the first living thing that he sees on his return should he triumph. He has the victory, but the first sentient creature he sees is his daughter, who has come out to greet him. At first, he cannot speak, but eventually he resolves for the sacrifice and tells her. She asks for two months before the sacrifice to bewail her fate and childlessness, which she does on the hills outside the town. Although it is not explicit in Judges, we presume that he carried out his vow after the two months.

WORKS DISCUSSED AT LENGTH IN THIS CHAPTER: Molarchio, *Il Gefte*; Carissimi, *Jephthe*; Mesquita, ditto; Giubilei, *Iephthe*; Acciarelli, ditto; Balbi, *Il Gefte*; San Carlo, *Il riso e il pianto in contesa*; Frigimelica, *Jefte*; Pariati, *Il voto crudele*; Salio, *Il sacrificio di Gefte*; Caldara, *Jefte*; Perez, *Giefte*; Sacchini, *Jephthes sacrificium*

PLACES: Rome, Vienna, Venice

"And he [Jephthe] did as he had vowed. The difficulty is most serious. Come now, let us resolve it, by discovering new aspects of the sacred act in which

we are participating." In a sermon for a nun's profession of vows in 1673, a Spanish preacher summarized thus the enormous problems around the exegesis and understanding of Judges 11 and its story of daughter sacrifice.[1] The less allegorically inclined Augustin Calmet commented on the Vow in his 1730 *Dictionnaire* that "there is something so extraordinary in the vow by this head of Israel that, even though Scripture speaks of it in precise, quite clear terms, one continually finds difficulties in it that embarrass the commentators."

Then and now, the chapter has generated a good deal of exegesis. Questions for early modern Catholics included: Why did Jephthe take a vow for battle victory which included sacrificing the first living thing that he would see (as opposed to restricting it to animals)? Why was his daughter anonymous? What about other family members? And centrally, was the chapter to be taken literally in that he actually did go through with the Vow and sacrifice his daughter on the Israelites' altar? These ambiguities in the story's core might have generated the high numbers of oratorios based on it, especially in the second half of the Settecento.[2]

There are several moments in the entire story present in some musical versions. These begin with the dubious origins of Jephthe as general and his previous disagreements with both the Ammonites and the Hebrews' leaders; his choice as leader of the Galaadites by acclamation; his triumph, with all its martial expression; the encounter with his daughter; the agonized working out of the Vow; the Daughter's two months of lamentation in the hills; and the final Sacrifice (which had been silently omitted in Carissimi's famed oratorio).

For present purposes, the possibility of adding characters to the oratorio libretti — including the mother, and/or one of his lieutenants betrothed to (or in love with) the Daughter — involved further family complexity.[3] The protagonist's return, the moment of father-Daughter meeting, and their mutual perplexity are normative in almost all pieces, except those few that start after the pre-mourning in the wilderness. With four characters, there was enough for a modest oratorio already, and some are even smaller at two and three characters, in which there is no escaping the centrality of the parental relationship.[4] Still, the major issue here is that of the relationship between parent and Daughter, clearly running throughout the whole set of oratorios from beginning to end.[5] How the Daughter comes to her resignation, and how she asks for the lamentation period, also vary among pieces. She is sometimes simply "La Figlia di Jefte"; one favorite name, taken from pseudo-Philo's *Biblical Antiquities* (chapter 40), is "Seila," while other works give various names ("Noema").[6]

This problem is not limited to the final Sacrifice. In a very few pieces, Jephthe takes his Vow onstage (as opposed to informing those present, including the Daughter, of a pledge previously taken), and there is normally some martial music for his victorious return. Even while he is in battle, and before she knows of the Vow, the Daughter often worries in general terms about both her own and his fates, and the issue of whether he informs her of the Vow immediately upon seeing her—the case in Carissimi—is not universal, sometimes leaving the end of Part I open.

In a certain sense, the number of libretti, as opposed to the few pictorial representations, meant that the story was most widely conveyed via oratorio. The difficulties of the tale, however, also excluded it from the Italian sacred cantata repertory. Examining both a somewhat wide range of cultural moments as well as some libretti/scores in depth is probably the deepest way to get at its cultural meanings.

Of all the tales in this study, it obviously bears the closest relationship to classicizing tragedy, evident also in the parallels with the Iphigenia legend. Some of the early plays with incidental music are mentioned below; these seem not to have been Lenten works, however, and thus the question remains of how the oratorios are meant to be penitential.

The story's implications for filial relationships found any number of musical versions for expression. Some of the early linkages to music, even before Carissimi's oratorio, came from the religious orders. In Rome, a 1624 Latin tragedy by the Belgian Benedictine Jacques de Lummene de Marcke (1570–1629), without specific indications for music, was dedicated to Cardinal Francesco Barberini. In the presence of the Bavarian Wittelsbach, a 1632 *Jephthe ductor Hebraeorum* was performed as a five-act tragedy in Salzburg's Benedictine theater, with seven musicians, probably singers from St. Peter's Abbey or from the cathedral. This latter version provided the entire story, not just the vow and sacrifice, of the Israelites' predicament in Judges 11, hewing strictly to the Biblical account, including the completed Sacrifice, which occupies most of act 5. But it starts with the leader's birth from a prostitute and his difficult relationship with Israel. In the piece, presumably the musicians were imported to sing choruses at the end of each of the five acts.

Why Filial Sacrifice?

An overview of early modern meanings for the story would be almost as extensive as a list of its roughly 120 different stagings of about eighty different libretti from 1670 to 1800. In the absence of a single authoritative commentary on Judges around 1700 beyond Lapide, the story's reception history needs to be pieced together, especially in the later Settecento. The sacrificial denouement of the story remained in some libretti until the arrival of the French Revolution in Italy. For all that there had been non-martyrial interpretations of the denouement of Judges 11 since at least Nicholas of Lyra in the fourteenth century and continuing through Juan de Mariana's (1536–1624) *Scholia* (Madrid, 1619), such endings did not seem to arrive in the Italian-Austrian Catholic musical repertory until after 1740. Indeed, despite Lyra, Mariana, and a few other dissenters, the overwhelming majority of the exegetes, preachers, and librettists seem to have sincerely believed that the Vow trumped a daughter's life.[7]

The social history of filicide is also unclear. Demographers have disagreed about whether the cases were ever reported, in which case they would not appear in such records as that of the Bologna Torrone files. One categorization leads us to consider that a third of violent crimes were committed by women, but these are not broken down by homicide, fighting, infanticide, and so on, although there seems to be agreement on a generalized rise in crime in 1655–75 in the Emilian capital. The first exception to the tragic ending appeared in a Florentine piece of 1743 for a nun's profession; however, France was a different story (literally).

The most basic issue then is: Why the need for this massive representation of sacrificing daughters? Besides the pieces for nuns' vestings considered below, on some level there might have been an attempt to steer young noblewomen into unwanted marriages (by comparison with the Daughter, who laments not her death, but her virginity and her lack of contribution to the genetic reproduction of the family, an Old Testament value noted even by Settecento observers).[8]

Frequency and Familiarity

After Carissimi's famed Roman version of the story, a series of new works started in Florence and moved to Emilia, Vienna, Rome, and finally Naples (roughly similar to the diffusion of the Hagar stories). Up to about 1730, there was an average of almost one per year across Italy and Vienna, with a slowdown until about 1740, when the story again took off without ceasing all the way to century's end. The continual recourse to the story is all the more striking in terms of the changes in Italian piety in the second half of the Settecento, in which these kinds of "rough" Scriptural episodes were either sorted out or neglected.

Indeed, some of the libretti were taken to Germany as the new century progressed. David Perez's *Giefte* made it to Würzburg, perhaps around 1770, as part of episcopal patronage by Prince-Bishop Adolf Friedrich von Seinsheim, some twenty (or perhaps thirty; see below) years after its premiere. Besides the 1754 Dresden reworking of Galuppi's original 1749 *Il Giefte* discussed presently, there was also Matteo Verazi and P. P. Sales's long oratorio of the same name, done at the Catholic court of Mannheim in 1762, while Girolamo Torniello/Pietro Avondano's *Il voto di Jefte* was the second Italian oratorio done at the Portuguese court in 1771 (after a *Betulia liberata* in 1768). A German version, *Jephthes Tochter*, was given under Bishop J. M. Baader in Eichstätt's Hofgarten theater, like the case of oratorios in the Munich court theater. All this spread was part of the sacralization of opera, a much wider phenomenon whose slightly later manifestations across Italy have already been well discussed in the literature.

Another parallel with Gregory of Nyssa's dramatic exegesis of the Isaac story was the two-page envoicement of the Daughter's lament found in the Jesuit Saverio Vanalesti's 1743 sermon for Passion Monday. This homily consists of a reimagining of all her thoughts during this time, and her self-resolve at the thought of the Sacrifice, all used as a model for preparing oneself for a Christian death.[9] To the degree that the libretti highlight this moment—the lamentation was not universally present—this meaning, combining Lent and penitence, may be relevant to the Settecento pieces.

Methodologically, the sheer quantity of this story's representation forces this study into more selective patterns of works discussed. Some of the sites are familiar from other chapters: Emilia around 1680; works in Rome from Carissimi to Caldara (1715); and the Habsburg fascination with the tale. Some of the earliest come from the world of religious orders, academies, and universities, and these are discussed first. But the numbers also raise questions which have not yet been answered in the literature, evident in the comparative table below for the number of musical settings of Jephthe stories and those focused on Iphigenia in Aulis.

Whatever modern perspectives might be, the question remains as to

TABLE 5.1. Jephthe oratorio stagings in Italy and Catholic Empire, Italian and Latin, by venue

	1671–90	1691–1710	1711–30	1741–60	1761–80	1781–1800
Venue: City > 50,000	7	8	10	10	7	18
Venue: City < 50,000	3	1	4	7	5	15
Venue: Court	3	3	3	2	2	1
Total	10	12	17	27	16	25

Source: For city size, Paolo Malanima, "Italian Cities 1300–1800: A Quantitative Approach," *Rivista di Storia Economica* 14 (1998): 91–126.

TABLE 5.2. "Iphigenia in Aulis" operas as above (only in Italian; includes "Ifigenia" and "Sacrificio in Aulide" pieces)

	1671–90	1691–1710	1711–30	1741–60	1761–80	1781–1800
Venue: City > 50,000	0	2	1	2	3	10
Venue: City < 50,000	0	0	0	3	0	3
Venue: Court	0	0	2	3	2	4
Total	0	2	3	8	5	17

whether the killing of daughters was as ultimately charged as that of sons (Theseus, Idomeneus), with all the political and dynastic implications of the latter.[10] It is out of the scope of this study to consider the British tradition from Buchanan through Handel, although there is a good deal of work on the 1751 London oratorio.

One moment when the story became specifically useful was that of the celibacy of non-marriageable daughters. This seems to be the case with the "happy ending" in Galuppi's original *L'Jepht* [*sic*] for the vesting of a nun (Maria Rosa Orlandini) in Florence's S. Maria Regina Caeli ("Chiarito") in 1749. Here the responsibility for the changed story was put, in Antonio Maria Vannucchi's (1724–92) preface to the libretto, on unnamed "holy fathers," probably in light of Orlandini's clothing ceremonies:

What Scripture recounts about Jephthe's Sacrifice is so well-known that it would be superfluous to discuss it. Certainly the ancient fathers and exegetes agree that the Sacrifice really happened to the Daughter, but others are of contrary opinion. We have followed the opinion that seemed more suited to our plans. The characters' natures, which we have introduced into ancient tragedy, will sufficiently justify our choice, if they are compared to the natural movements of the human heart, which did not allow even the Hebrews, as human beings, always to breathe a venerable sanctity. We have also used some expressions only to serve poetic language, which is not always adaptable to rigid precision.

Vannucchi wrote on legal and scientific subjects but was also a Habsburg panegyrist, and this switch in the story, along with the 1743 *Il Gefte*, presaged a major turn in its conception. It is striking that the only recent version associated with nuns had been G. C. Canali's *La figlia di Gefte*, a prose *rappresentazione* used for the "virtuous entertainment" of female monasteries (and not for a vesting), and thus a play holding to the original story with its tragic ending, and not meant for music, dating from Bologna in 1714. The idea of reinforcing nuns' status by linking them to the vow that had been associated with Jephthe's military salvation of Israel represented a Christian "improvement" on the Old Testament, and the female solidarity evident in the Daughter's two-month lament with her companions also marked an ideal—not necessarily a reality—for monastic houses.

Use for vestings could also be implicit. The non-martyrial *Il sacrificio di Jefet* for Dresden's Good Friday (and hence a *sepolcro*) in 1754 (libretto in CS-Pnm) is, as noted above, a reworking of Galuppi's 1749 libretto, not related to Handel's piece. Oratorios and their ideology in the Saxon capital were closely related to Viennese models, even after the cessation of the form in the Austrian capital after 1740.[11] In this case, Frederick Augustus II and Maria Josepha of Saxony had no fewer than three teenage daughters, none of whom would ever be married, and two of whom would become Princess-Abbesses: Maria Christina and Maria Elisabeth.

In its relatively few arias and its long recitatives (before the indicated *virgolette* cuts, there are almost 100 lines of the latter before the first aria), the Dresden piece is a highly didactic work. Much of it is occupied by snarls between Jefet and Rebecca plus Gamiel (these latter two being respectively the daughter Sefa's [= Seila] mother and suitor). Sefa resigns herself early on (her last aria is in the middle of Part II), and with so few arias, she is in a certain sense devoiced compared to the other, more loquacious, daughters of mid-century versions. The non-martyrial conclusion is recounted by Gamiel, and linked to the Crucifixion, as Nature's signs at Christ's death (thunder, earthquake, etc.) are here anticipated at the moment at which Jefet is to sacrifice his Daughter on the altar, leading the local high priest to stop the act in a now-familiar trope taken from the Binding story. Here the sinful Jefet has become a kind of Abraham, and Sefa by extension a version of Isaac. Although other happy-ending works would pop up — for instance, a 1758 Roman libretto with an imprimatur, *Il voto di Gefte* (with no evident performance history), in which a chorus of rabbis intervenes at the end to spare the Daughter's life — still the tragic Biblical ending continued in many works all the way to 1800.[12]

Monastery, Court, City

Of the two non-sacrificial Florentine Jephthe stories from the 1740s, the first was associated with the young Maria Luisa Passignani's entrance into S. Girolamo in 1743. This brought her into a relatively large institution, not known for its cultural life (it belonged to the order of the Poor Gesuate). Whoever the librettist — nominally the Arcadian *letterato* "Peore Molorchio" — might have actually been, his preface is vague enough on the issue of non-martyrial endings that its close seems generated by both the vesting ceremonies and the new aversion to the representation of female sacrifice.[13] Molorchio's preface mentioned "Natale Alessandrino," that is, the French Dominican commentator Noël Alexandre, as a source for the "variety" of Patristic explanations of the Sacrifice. Volume 1 of Alexandre's *Historia ecclesiastica* (Paris, 1699) had discreetly left the door open to Lyra's view, without even mentioning names; the Italian edition of 1734 of Alexandre's work was published in the politically safe Republic of Lucca, and even had a local imprimatur. Perhaps this was why Molorchio thought that he could get away with doubting the story's ending and changing it to the fate of perpetual virginity, just as it was being enacted in the vesting ceremony for which the piece was written. Yet Alexandre's was hardly a revolutionary approach. He made it clear that he agreed with the traditional explanation, while referring only to "certain [commentators]" who, along with some of the rabbinical tradition, believed that virginity, and not death, had been the outcome.[14]

The author took advantage of this breach in exegesis. *Il Gefte* limits itself to three characters, father, daughter, and the sacrificing priest Abésan, who immediately begins with a recollection of Abraham's happiness in sacrificing Isaac; that is, Gefte's Vow has already been made known. Indeed, after Gefte reproaches the priest for the latter's lack of sympathy by singing an aria on his conflicted affect, Seila appears, having done her two months of mourning and hence ready for the Sacrifice (this may be a reflection of Passignani's having finished her novitiate). His daughter's constancy, paradoxically, causes Gefte to waver further, and the priest has an aria condemning him for his disobedience. After more arias of indecision, Gefte decides to wait further to hope in Divine mercy, and Part I ends with a duet for father and daughter plus interrogatives.

The following part begins with no sign from Heaven, and Gefte prepares himself, until the priest announces that a different sacrifice is necessary. The warrior believes this to be himself, until Abésan informs him that instead his daughter must remain as a temple virgin. Gefte tries to avoid this, but the priest is inflexible, and announces in recitative: "nel sacro tempio / ascosa agli occhi tuoi l'unica figlia / restar dovrà" [your only daughter will remain enclosed in the holy temple, hidden from your eyes].

Although Gefte resists further for a bit, he agrees to go to the temple, and Seila prophesies herself as the first presaging of Mary, even seeing Golgotha in her ecstatic view of the future. She gives a recitative reference, and then an aria, on nuns venturing as far afield as South Asia.[15] There is even mention of the Arno, along whose bank her new monastery was situated, and then a *licenza* addressed to Maria Luisa herself. The entire text becomes highly personalized, presuming a public for the profession of knowing patrician families. Indeed, the libretto was set by the Tuscan composer Beatrice Mattei, otherwise known only for keyboard works in manuscripts.[16] She is a hard figure to trace but might have come from a musical family (an "Orsola" and a "Cammilla" with the same last name sang occasional parts in local opera productions of the 1750s/60s).

The other Florentine case, that of Maria Rosa Orlandini's S. Maria Regina Caeli in via S. Gallo, was quite a different place, with both medieval and Renaissance altarpieces, and clearly its Augustinians enjoyed a rich cultural life. Not only was Galuppi commissioned for the Jephthe oratorio to be performed at the young woman's profession in 1749, but there are seven sonnets at the libretto's end for the event (not reprinted in the 1754 or 1756 reprises of the piece).[17] One striking moment in the libretto is the final chorus, referring to the vesting ceremonies and clearly meant for a convent audience: "O holy Religion [i.e., in 1749 this meant 'life according to Augustine's Rule'], you who light the pure flame in our heart, you who, in a white veil, descend to live among us; our heart awakens to its task through you; while you hide secrets in dark night, in vain the soul opposes itself to your victory, as you confound proud Reason; in your vast sphere the doubts of the intellect vanish." The anti-Enlightenment tone is evident.

That these non-martyrial pieces did not achieve immediate hegemony was evident in the striking difference with a 1753 Sicilian *Il sacrifizio di Gefte*. This piece was set for a nun's vesting in Palermo's S. Maria di Monte Vergine, and features a sacrificial ending, with its daughter Iftab who goes off to death over her mother's curses.[18] The composition was entrusted to Jommelli (no score survives), who must have found ample room in the short libretto for the conflicts and more extreme emotions that his writing was engaging in the 1750s; he could have done it just before leaving Rome for Stuttgart at the end of the year.

Yet the marked uptick in new versions (and restagings of older ones) started from this decade, suggesting a new definition of the relationship between fathers and daughters in society as reflected in this repertory.[19] The transfer of the story's use in various repeated performances had already been anticipated in the most canonical homiletic literature.[20] The other ideological explanation, that of a parallel to the Binding and the need to obey vows to God, was certainly present for early modern exegetes even at the beginning of the story's popularity. Whether this was intended to counter defections from the contemporary male clergy and their vows also remains to be seen. The performance on 22 November 1750 of Perez's *Giefte* by the Perugian Oratorians, who would likely have obtained the score from Rome, gives testimony for use on that day's feast (St. Cecilia, a martyred patroness with special meaning for the order's musical life).[21]

Early Daughters

Because of Jephthe's insistence on his own Vow, and the sheer amount of musical-dramatic space devoted to his agonizing in much of the repertory, there is a way in which the pieces are more about him than her. This is counteracted, as it was already in Carissimi's version, by the inclusion of multiple laments for the Daughter, not only her final months in the hills outside

Masfa, but also those sung to her father, mother, or beloved beforehand. Normally, both the added roles of mother and of beloved react strongly against the father's vow and against the Sacrifice. Several individual cases below show how this played out in given pieces.

Unavoidably, the Latin repertory leads to consideration of Carissimi's* *Jephthe*. Even before examining its "affective" additions to the Biblical text, it is still worth noting that there is nothing in the *rappresentazione* tradition on the story, and hence Lummene's piece seems to be the only Roman dramatic precedent, one which, given its Benedictine origin, was probably far from any audience either at the Collegio Germanico or at the Crocifisso, and so the story circulated among the religious orders.[22]

As is well known, Carissimi's text uses most of Judges 11:29–38, and certainly more of the Biblical verses than either the later Latin repertory or the earliest Italian pieces.[23] This passage, however, is interrupted by three tropes, the first two of which include verses:

Verses	Measures (Beat's source "A" = Charpentier 1)[24]
11:29–32	1–32
Trope 1	33–195, including 11:33–34 (martial)
11:35	196–216
Trope 2	217–69, including 11:36–37 (dramatic)
11:38	270–75
Trope 3	276–end (mournful)

For the present purposes, the dialogues between Jephthe and the Filia (Trope 2) are noteworthy for their immediate heightening of the chromatic pitch content, including every possible one between A4 and F4 in Jephthe's opening 11:35 ("Heu, heu mihi!"). Her first response is quite diatonic, and it is only his revelation of the Vow that moves her in a sharp/*durus* direction ("Pater mi, si vovisti"). However, unlike almost every one of the later versions of the character, she offers no resistance at all, but only acceptance in a long and tonally sharp descent to "antequam moriar." Her first venture into flat/*mollis* regions occurs with her final words to her father, "plangem virginitatem meam" (m. 267), although this inflection will take over her calls to the hills and caves around Masfa ("plorate colles," mm. 285ff). The end of this brutally sonic lament ("in sonitu horribili resonate") finally brings her line up to the high A5 (m. 336) along with a chromatic-sixth anabasis to an A♯ at "plorate virginitatem meam" (m. 343; the pitch is different from the many B♭s that have been heard up to this point).

The wording of the trope at this point ("Plorate, filii Israel, plorate virginitatem meam") raises several problems: first, this was supposed to be a lament of the daughter and her female companions (hence "filiae"), and second, according to 11:38, she alone was supposed to be the primary lamenter, assisted by other virgins of Jerusalem.[25] The female lamenters are repeated in 11:40, but the uni-gender "filii" of Carissimi's libretto seems to rework the passage for a mixed (even perhaps male-only) audience. In some way, the Jesuit origin of the libretto is cast into doubt by the clumsy reworking of 11:36 as the Daughter pulls herself out of the ropes that bind her for the execution (mm. 250–60: "My father, grant me—your only-born daughter—this before I die. *Jephthe*: But what can relieve your soul, precisely you who are about to die? *Filia*: Release me [for now], so that I can circle the mountains for two months . . .").[26] With a trope text as inelegant as this, essentially all the affect goes into the pitch relations (plus dissonances) discussed above. As popular as the work must have been—Marc-Antoine Charpentier made some three copies of it—it took almost two generations for the theme to return to public performance. Its audiences are not clear; if it was done as a Jesuit piece, which the presence of the chorus in Kircher's treatises suggests, it seems to have circulated in semi-private or internal circles.

Clearly, Jesuit exegesis is closest to the cultural world of Carissimi's original: Cornelius a Lapide listed all possible Patristic interpretations, and then concluded that, like the rest of the Old Testament, it was "flawed" in its unspecific nature of the sacrifice. Jacob Tirin made the comparison to the Iphigenia story in his brief commentary on the chapter, and overall it appeared that most exegetes took the episode seriously and literally, in terms of the Daughter's sacrifice.

The first complete linkage of drama to opera in this storyline is found in a kind of double presentation on 20 February 1686 at the Jesuit college of Louis-le-Grand in Paris.[27] This was formatted as a French *tragédie en musique*, five intermezzi for a different, unspecified Latin prose Jesuit drama in five acts on the same topic. We have essentially only the plot summary and one stage indication, for Jephthe's camp and the town of Masfa. It features a larger cast of characters, some five divided among seven student actors, and including Jairus, the captain betrothed to the daughter (here

"Seila," as she is often named, in line with pseudo-Philo's account of the story).

This was evidently the first piece which had a non-martyrial ending. Possibly the French music of each act preceded the Latin ones in a kind of foreshadowing. It has been suggested that Charpentier also provided the music, as he had for the similar double tragedy *David et Jonathas*.[28] Around the same time, Vincenzo Albrici prepared a Latin *sepolcro* for the Prague Jesuits: *Jephthe Dux triumphator* was done in 1684, in the context of his other work there after having left Dresden.

Roman Sacrifices

A generation later, four different Latin pieces for the Crocifisso from 1682 to 1703 also provide evidence for the diversity of family relations inside the story, and the heterodoxy that has already been seen in the institution's Ishmael works (chapter 3). For all of Salvador de Mesquita's Brazilian origins, the large cast of his characters for his 1682 oratorio (*Sacrificium Jephthe*, with lost music by Francesco Federici) on the topic (nine plus two choruses) and their paired setup recall the *rappresentazione* tradition strongly.[29] The opening resolve of Jephthe's friends to call on his aid explicitly cites Judges 11:3, 7–8, while also using 1 Maccabees 3:53. Mesquita's text embroiders the mission to Ammon (Judges 11:9–10) and Jephthe's final assumption of the Galaadites' leadership, encouraged by Seila (an early use of the name for the Daughter). The key verses 11:29–30 are skipped, and after a short aria the leader simply enunciates his Vow (11:31). The part ends with Jephthe putting the chorus of the Ammonites to flight amid warlike instrumental music.

The instrumental interlude before Part II is joyous for the general's return, but Seila's entrance is delayed until after the enumeration of the Ammonite cities captured (11:32–33). She has a long victory aria addressed to her two Companions ("Vos mecum sociae"). But Mesquita then, simply and shockingly, turns to the citation of Jephthe's "Heu mihi, decepisti me" (11:35), followed by an aria. Seila responds with her acceptance and request for the two months of lament (11:37), setting up a long scene in the mountains (and thus implying some kind of set at the Crocifisso, or perhaps staging things up to this point around the altar and then moving Seila up to the organ loft on the inner facade wall). There follow a duet for her friends; a lament aria for her; and then an echo passage which moves to some acceptance of her fate ("Jucunda moriar, si mori coelum iubet").

Jephthe then begins another scene with his return after the two months to accomplish the Sacrifice. But he falters, and Seila herself must encourage him to strike the blow, pointing out that she is no longer his property. Still, Jephthe gets an aria here, and ends the piece by consigning her corpse to the sacred flames. The setup does not allow for subtle explanation of father-daughter relations, or even much envoicing of the Daughter, although it gives a strongly classicizing touch to the whole execution scene.

This latter is also a feature of the second Crocifisso piece six years later, Pietro Giubilei's Latin text (*Iephthe, musicis concentibus*, as opposed to his Italian one of the same year, *Iefte*, for the Seminario Romano) for five characters, two of whom are soldiers. This was set by Giovanni Pietro Franchi and done on 26 March 1688. Here the Biblical quotes are entirely abandoned, but the piece once again opens in martial vein, with a soldiers' chorus. However, after some solo resolve for Jephthe, a parallel chorus of virgins ("Amazones Hebraeas"), together with the Filia, urge him on to the defeat of Ammon. Both in this text and his vernacular one, Giubilei's language has become classically pastoral ("Labris patulis rosa suspirat" in the second stanza of the Filia's aria at this point). The interplay of the two texts is noteworthy.

Part II of this 1688 work opens immediately with the post-victory encounter, in which Jephthe first concentrates on his own fate as his daughter's executioner and then almost loses the capacity for speech altogether in the following dialogue with the Filia ("Filia . . . filia . . . heu luctus . . . heheu . . . stultum . . . tace mea perdita spes . . . barbara . . . saeva . . . heu dolor," in which it is not clear whether the adjectives refer to the Filia or to his own fate ["sors"]). The preceding is all of the victor's contribution to about sixty lines of dialogue, including the two soldiers who sing more than he does.

After all this, Giubilei's Jephthe finally brings himself to explaining the Vow, which the Filia accepts, and he calls on the chorus of virgins to sing lamenting songs. She ends only with the plea for "time" (no two months) to mourn, with an aria ("Libens emior / victima numinis," already a sign of the classicizing distance from the original Book). Here, the daughter is allowed to end the piece with a lament aria ("Ad montes, / ad fontes") and finishes with a short echo recitative ("flete, flete") calling on her companions. Although this work is not much more specific in its father-daughter relations than Mesquita's, she still gets much more attention (and her father's inability to speak marks him as particularly lame).

The next two Crocifisso pieces on the topic move even further away from the original. The third one, Francesco Acciarelli's setting of a 1695 text, like Mesquita's 1682 Ishmael work, has a summarizing "argomento" in Italian, and opens, like Giubilei's, by paraphrasing the negotiations around Jephthe's return to the Israelites. Here, however, the other characters are composed of a Mother (one of the first occurrences of this character type in this story) and a fiancé ("Judas"). This piece opens with a Filia worried about the future but consoled by her mother; when Judas reports the Ammonites' belligerency, Jephthe prepares to leave. Oddly, the Vow worked into this moment is marked in the printed libretto by deletion quotes; presumably Acciarelli was told (or decided; there is no named librettist) not to set this here so as to heighten the dramatic tension in Part II.

This next part opens with a worried Filia again, conscious of the irony of her own weakness, but finally able to convince herself of an unproblematic victory. Judas thanks God for the triumph (perhaps one reason for the deletion of the Vow), and the very quick encounter of father and daughter takes as its motto the laughter-weeping dichotomy of "risus/fletus." Jephthe explains his Vow, finally, but first to his wife before finally telling his daughter. She obediently and quickly goes to her death without even the request for the two months' lamentation.

In some ways, Acciarelli's version marks an influx of sentiment into the topic, leaving space for the Filia, albeit primarily for her worries. On the other hand, Giovanni Antonio Magnani/Curzio Vinchioni's Latin work of eight years later (*Iephthe*) begins without an "argomento," using a summary of Judges 11 instead. Unlike the 1695 piece, its long opening solo is allotted to Jephthe, as he remembers his unhappy childhood and adolescence (11:1–3). Indeed, this is the most "musical" leader to date, as he addresses the nightingale to sing of his pain; meanwhile, two of the Israelite messengers try to convince him to lead them (there are only four characters and no chorus). Here too there is a deeply unhappy Filia, although she does not begin the piece. Indeed, she has recourse to the "risus/fletus" dichotomy before there is any mention of the vow.

Magnani—a friend and correspondent of the Arcadia's leader G. M. Crescimbeni—cast all this in a vocabulary so abstrusely classical that it is sometimes hard to decipher the narrative referents. Part II of the 1703 piece begins in the middle of the night outside the Ammonites' encampment, and it is only now that Jephthe takes the Vow. The following victory is celebrated by him and the Messengers until the Filia again irrupts into the scene, with her song and her "cymbalum." Again the leader is left speech-less, but in an even more lachrymose touch, he weeps at the sight of his daughter. Even though he begs God, using the example of Abraham and Isaac (another sign of the interconnection among these stories), there is no response; she calls on him to lament, but gives in fairly quickly, with her final aria predicting her two months of mourning, and her father is then left alone on stage to praise the "immortality" of her death, an abrupt close to a work that had compressed a good deal of action into its Part II.

The Crocifissso pieces, then, trace an uneven trajectory away from the Bible and from the *rappresentazione* tradition, in the general direction of character weakness in the face of events, and—especially in the case of Magnani/Vinchioni—a kind of aestheticization of emotional expression. The works popped up often enough that they suggest some wider trends in devotion and exegesis over the period, but they also point to a special appreciation of different versions of the same story over a generation of the site's audiences.

Roughly in the same generation, one Emilian work problematizes Jephthe as father. This was a collaboration between the experienced librettist Benedetto Balbi with G. B. Vitali as the composer. This *Il Gefte, overo il zelo imprudente*, also for Palazzo Orsi in 1672, moved the former to a lengthy explanation of his changes to the story. Balbi reduced the various Israelite princes and messengers to one each, and added "qualche verisimile fantasia, come il timore della Figlia" to the mix of affects.[30] Indeed, the cast of seven allows for a wide emotional range, starting with Gefte's desire for martial glory. The Figlia has every right to be worried, as her father declares "Amo la Figlia, ma più la Fama" [I love my daughter, but Fame more]. The Principe (who may be a proto-suitor) attempts to quiet her fears, and in a double scene switch, Gefte gives more space to his martial victory than to his offspring. At this point God and an Angel (another addition that Balbi mentioned) come onstage, the former foreseeing the Figlia's sacrifice and the latter pleading for mercy, a notable reworking of the story. Once again the oratorio repertory for the Orsi challenged many exegetical boundaries, and once again there was no imprimatur.

Austrian Jephthes

For all that the previous chapter has stressed the importance of the Binding story for the Habsburgs, still the numbers—if not necessarily the cultural weight of the pieces—favor Judges 11 in Vienna. From 1680 to 1730, there were six local productions of the latter tale, compared to four for Isaac. These include two for Antonio Draghi's 1680 piece on the topic (repeated in 1687), one imported from Siena around 1690, another from Padua (possibly 1692), a work from before 1702 (Girolamo Frigimelica and Carlo Francesco Pollarolo), and a final local one by Giuseppe Salio/Giuseppe Porsile in 1724. Just as the Isaac works were concentrated around 1700, these cluster around 1690, suggesting, however, an overall turn toward the former story, and perhaps a desire for happy endings.

For Lent 1680 in Prague, the court had obtained a copy of the libretto—but not Antonio Masini's music—for G. F. Apolloni's 1675 Roman oratorio on Jephthe's Vow.[31] Draghi* must have set the words quickly even if Lent was late that year, as his predecessor J. H. Schmelzer had died of the plague in January; he also composed two other texts for the penitential season. Since Apolloni's libretto is so martial, like some of the Crocifisso pieces, one clue to understanding its Viennese meaning is an open-air sermon by the famed preacher and writer Abraham a Sancta Clara. *Merck's wol, Soldat* (Vienna, 1680) was a call to the varied soldiers in Habsburg service—very much on the front lines against the still-victorious Ottomans—to follow proper Christian behavior. In his praise of the ultimate Christian warrior St. George, Sancta Clara came to mention Jephthe as an unwilling sacrificer, but in terms which praised his martial talent and which suggest a relatively sympathetic portrait—despite his manic outburst in Draghi's 1680 work.[32]

After the siege of Vienna, the reason for the 1687 repeat of the piece seems to have been a combination of mourning and organization. Eleonora Gonzaga, who had organized the oratorios since their beginning around 1660, had died on 6 December 1686, and so there was no Carnival opera. In addition, the responsibility would have fallen on Leopold, who had military problems with the Ottomans, and so the programming of the Lenten season was solved by repeating all three of his personally composed oratorios, and adding a "deathbed" piece from 1682 (*L'huomo infermo moribondo*), another tribute to Eleonora; a new work with music by Draghi, one which linked Lenten and Marian devotion (*L'entrata di Cristo nel deserto*, probably the first to be performed); and the 1680 Jephthe story, perhaps one that Eleonora herself had especially appreciated seven years earlier in Prague.

Three years later, it was all the more striking that the Discalced Carmelite preacher Girolamo di San Carlo (lay name: "Paolo Verospi")/Gaetano Rubini's *Il riso e il pianto in contesa** was brought in for Lent 1690; San

Carlo was himself present.[33] This work had first been done for Siena in 1688, with a surviving printed libretto; the Vienna score is not the work of a court copyist, but rather one of the outside hands involved in Passerini's work and other Italian imports to the court.[34] However, it seems no accident that the other Sienese oratorio by the same librettist and composer, *Il finto Smeraldo, o la vera Eufrosina* imported during the same Lent, also has to do with father-daughter relationships, and even perpetual virginal sacrifice, as it is the story of the fifth-century St. Euphrosyne of Alexandria, who fled marriage for a hermitage on Mt. Carmel. The local Italian newspaper noted Verospi/San Carlo's preaching at court in mid-Lent 1690, which was a moment for the two oratorios as well; only one other piece (Leopold's ever-favorite *L'amor della redentione*) was mentioned that spring. Both featured a kind of daughter sacrifice.

As the number of Eleonore Magdalene's surviving daughters grew, this overall concentration of works around 1690 is striking. The Carnival season of 1690 (which had been spent in Augsburg) had featured one large-scale opera, namely Minato's version of the Camilla story, *La regina de' Volsci*, also on issues of female agency. In his Jephthe work, the oratorio's librettist San Carlo, certainly a strongly orthodox figure (and Discalced Carmelite prior), centered the parent-child relationship by opening with a musically long duet for the two, this time concentrating on the father's fears. Gefte crowns his martial resolve with the Vow, evidently in his anonymous ("Anonima") daughter's presence. The "planctus/risus" motto of weeping and laughter returns in several dialogues, even in Part I and thus before the leader's return to Masfa. There are no other characters (perhaps a reflection of the originally scarce vocal resources for soloists in Siena), although members of the choirs of soldiers and of virgins have solos.

The festive spirit of Gefte's return is symbolized by the required trumpet parts, and the leader immediately reveals the Vow after his daughter's reproach aria. Gefte uses the "basilico/basilisk" reference (which San Carlo could have heard in Apolloni/Masini's 1675 approach to the story, since he had been preaching in Rome during that Jubilee Year), sings a two-stanza aria about his own pain ("Vedi, crudo dolor"), and then disappears, not unlike some of the contemporary Latin Crocifisso pieces. This allows the Daughter a long closing lament scena, comprising an opening chorus and then a long refrain aria with violins ("Cari monti amati"), saying goodbye to the hills.[35]

Overall, this work is quite close to the popular *rappresentazione* tradition, with its changing scenes and use of martial props. Given its ending for the Daughter and her companions, the complete disappearance of Gefte, and the amount of time at the opening spent on their relationship, it marks a different trajectory from the Euphrosyne legend; in this Jephthe oratorio, the father and his dialogues occupy a much larger portion of both arias and recitatives overall than is the case in the sanctoral work. In a certain sense, it also marks a full circle from Draghi's 1680 resetting of Apolloni's original Roman libretto.

In the next decade, Girolamo Frigimelica Roberti/Carlo Francesco Pollarolo's "tragedy in the form of an oratorio" *Jefte** was performed in Leopold's presence before the libretto's publication (1702), more likely at some point in the relatively tranquil 1690s, accentuating the presence of the story in this decade. It is part of a libretti group, all cast as five-act classicizing tragedies with scene divisions, which results in an enormous amount of recitative that Pollarolo dutifully set. This obeys the unities (hence there is no time for the two months of lament) while placing both the original Vow and the daughter's (Seila) greeting in the first two scenes, leaving a good deal of space for the actual revelation to her and for the reactions of her mother ("Bara"), who is the one to convey the Vow to her daughter (act 2, scene 3). Although Bara immediately starts planning to stop the Sacrifice, Seila gives in quickly to self-sacrifice, in a now standard move.

Frigimelica wove in the Ephraimites' rebellion from Judges 12 as a motive for urgency to the Sacrifice, while the central act 3, scene 3, excludes Seila, as it is the Mother's long denunciation of her spouse. The next scene highlights the daughter's emotional turmoil, not, however, extending to her disobedience. At the beginning of act 4, Seila begins to mourn her infertility, but still defends her father to her suitor ("Azaria"), while Bara holds firm in resistance.

Jefte proceeds with the sacrifice, and Seila enters the temple in which her stabbing occurs on stage in the middle of her final call ("Pa-[dre]"); this kind of *interruptio* would return as the end of Girolamo Gigli/Attilio Ariosti's *La madre de' Maccabei** (Vienna, 1704; chapter 7). For all the classicizing trappings of Frigimelica's text, this was simply shocking. Jefte claims that only his pain shows him to be a true father, while Bara follows by dwelling on her own suffering after the daughter's death, and the institution of the annual mourning period (11:40) closes the dialogue. Oddly, the final chorus returns to focus on Jefte ("O sfortunato eroe!"), leaving the real protagonist of this piece up in the air. As noted, Pollarolo had to compose extensive recitative for this libretto (which might not have bothered Leopold, a listener always open to long narrative passages). Obviously, the most striking is that of the actual moment of sacrifice, and the arias tend to be more static, in line with the aesthetics of classicizing tragedy.

The pace of Jephthe oratorios did not let up in the Imperial capital. Compared to some earlier versions (Draghi or Frigimelica), the next one—Pariati/Lotti's *Il voto crudele** of 1712—was smaller (four voices, one chorus), testifying to the difficult musical logistics in the court chapel around the transition after Joseph I's death in 1711. Still, some of the thematics were repeated, in the librettist's purified language: an opening martial Jefte, answered by a skeptical suitor ("Getro") who points to the *vanitas* theme in warning the general against overconfidence. The protagonist is bent on revenge against the Ammonites, although the Vow is held off until after the appearance of the other character pair, the Daughter ("Isi") and Mother ("Storge"), who have a recitative dialogue leading to a dialogue aria on their fears for the future. As Jefte is overtaken by the Spirit, and makes the Vow, Lotti shifts the tonal center from flat to sharp regions. This suggests some sacrality to the pledge, again out of line with Patristic tradition.

In a more sentimental way than before, Isi begins Part II by expressing her hopes for marital love; Pariati's sense of irony, which would return below (chapter 7) in his Mother of the Maccabees piece of 1715, is on full display.[36] Isi's aria in dialogue with Getro, "Del tuo ciglio, del tuo brando," was set by Lotti as a virtuosa piece for the daughter, and Gefte returns with a victorious aria, only to have the fatal encounter with Isi. There is a delay in his explanation of the Vow, postponed by two musically difficult arias for him ("Vanne, vanne o cara" and "Cor di Padre, e che farai?"). Once again this is a deeply musical but emotionally reticent father, and only Storge's aria ("Vi sento, sì") can elicit his recounting of the Vow.

Isi is silent at first during her mother's and Getro's subsequent resistance to the Sacrifice. Isi then breaks in by opening her breast with a dramatic call to her father to kill her immediately, followed by her aria ("Si convien") that shares its ritornello and affect with Getro's subsequent one ("Si vedrò"). As in his Maccabees piece for Fux a few years later, Pariati extended this scene of departure to the maximum within the work's limits: Gefte promises to follow his daughter in death; she has a long and moving siciliana ("Vivete pur"); and then there is her request for the two months of mourning. Storge reacts badly at being called by name (and not "madre"), but Isi seems intent on getting away to the hills. Her final accompanied recitative ("Padre, io ti perdono") was set by Lotti in a deeply flat F region, and the other three characters end—there is no closing moralizing chorus, as was normal in Viennese oratorios and *sepolcri*—with "O voto funesto, o voto crudel" (ex. 5.1). This version seems to condemn the Vow *tout court*.

Certainly Lotti's writing, especially in the longer arias, is worthy of his fame, not least in this piece produced at a difficult moment of re-establishing peace in the Empire before the Peace of Utrecht. The entire transition after Joseph I's death was marked by uncertainty and by the establishment of new ritual norms at court. The work, in a wider political sense, might have corresponded to its diplomatic conjuncture, and the staging might have been meant to reconcile the court to the necessary losses (e.g., renouncing Catalonia, and more broadly the entire Spanish Succession) which were beginning to be negotiated. Given the year of mourning for Joseph I, and the preoccupations of the court elsewhere, this oratorio—along with Caldara's St. Francesca Romana piece—were the only stagings of either opera or oratorio that spring, the latter having perhaps been selected to provide a model for the newly bereft Dowager Empress Wilhelmine Amalie.

Twelve years later, in 1724, although the same story opened the Lenten oratorio productions (Thursday of the First Week of Lent), it was farmed out to the young Paduan Giuseppe Salio and the middle-aged but already pensioned Giuseppe Porsile for the music. Here, there seemed no immediate political reason for the choice of the story, as the diplomatic situation had settled. Its premiere (probably 9 March, despite a misprint in the newspaper report) was called "Das Opfer der Jephthe"; it included an unspecified Italian sermon. Still, *Il sacrifizio di Gefte* was clearly based on Zeno's models for oratorio libretti, including the usual group of three counselors (here future leaders of Israel: Abdone, Elon, and Absane, given to some quite experienced singers).[37] Most striking in terms of father-daughter relationships was Salio's evident attempt at novelty by introducing a confidante ("Anna") for the Daughter ("Menulema"), a gesture taken directly from opera. The presence of the counselors serves—after the revelation of the Vow (toward the end of Part I)—as a long disquisition on its merits (the opening of Part II).

In terms of Menulema, this effectively confines her early appearance to the actual meeting with her father in Part I and then the long farewell scene and closing duet "Parto, tu resta—o Dio" with her father in Part II, as she departs for the mourning in the mountains. This may have been due to the 1724 casting, with the aging Regina Schoonjans singing Menulema and

EX. 5.1 A. Lotti, *Il voto crudele*, ending; A-Wn, Mus. Hs. 17695, fol. 88r.

the twenty-six-year-old Rosa Borosini as Anna.[38] The extended reaction to Gefte's confusion in Part I, and many of the reproaches in Part II of his decision to pursue the Sacrifice, were apportioned by Salio to the Daughter. In his long disputations among the counselors, and citations ranging over Judges 11 and 12, the young librettist followed Zeno all too faithfully. Again, it was left to Anna, not the daughter Menulema, to extract Gefte's defense of his Vow against her harsh criticisms of the leader. The libretto portrays the daughter as an almost superhuman figure of female martyrdom.

A better case can be made for Porsile's musical characterizations of the women. Menulema's Part I is restricted to her greeting aria, "Caro padre, amato padre," an extrovert number, while the long closing of Part II is filled with her humble pleas in recitative for forgiveness from everyone. But Anna's "ventriloquizing" aria, "Bella sorte," in which she recounts her daughter's reaction to the reality of the sacrifice, is not only a long adagio but one in which the penitential reference of the B section ("con le lagrime si purghi/questa vittima che è immonda" [let this pure victim be purified by her tears]) is set to tonal motion ranging from A to D♭ to B in the space of nine measures.

The lengthy farewell scene is interrupted by three choral interjections, and finally Menulema receives extended writing in the final "Parto, tu resta," a *siciliana* with dissonances and melismas. The final *madrigale* is purely on the theme of *vanitas*, "Ma tutto è vanità sotto del sole," an understated ending by Salio, rescued by Porsile's imitative counterpoint. In Lent 1724, the piece had been up against some strong competition: the Carnival opera was Conti's *Penelope*, and the penitential season would later witness a repeat of Conti's passionate *Il martirio di San Lorenzo*, along with the premieres of both his *David* and Caldara's *Morte e sepoltura di Cristo*. Still, Porsile's score was sent up to Brno for performance the next year at the local episcopal court.

Changes in the New Century

This would be the last Jephthe work at the Habsburg court; Zeno and Metastasio stayed away from the topic, perhaps because it was considered too gruesome and not immediately Passion-related. But Antonio Caldara's 1715/16 piece* for the Ruspoli household in Rome (*Jefte*), which never made it to Vienna, had marked another approach to the tale, one more balanced and economical even if consistent with the trope of the Daughter's (here "Zebea") heroic martyrdom. Its limited scoring for four voices means that most of the narrative is concentrated among Jefte, his spouse Orama, and Zebea. The libretto survives in manuscript in I-Bc and a score in D-MÜs, Santini Hs. 734.

Whoever wrote the libretto (perhaps even Ruspoli himself) did an efficient job in getting all four characters—Jefte, the soldier Andrìa, the daughter, and the mother—on scene quickly, as a short moment of martial resolve leads Jefte to the Vow. Most of Part I is occupied by dialogue between Zebea and Orama concerning their worries about the upcoming battle. Here, Orama has the longer arias ("Vorrei goder, ma non risponde un rio timor" [I would like to rejoice, but fearful terror stops me]) against Zebea's ("E dice mio cor"). Part I ends with a scene switch back to Jefte and Andrìa, as they rejoice in their victory and anticipate their return to Masfa.

Part II opens with Jefte's initial joy at returning, Zebea's arrival, and the leader's "Ohimè!" in reaction. Once again it is difficult to get Jefte to enunciate what has happened, even after repeated pleas from Onama and an accompanied recitative of indecision on the leader's part. Onama realizes the situation first (aria: "Chi di voi, terra od interno, me dolente"), and finally the father has to admit that "l'ostia tu [Zebea] sei." Still, Zebea is essentially obedient in response to her father's self-pitying aria "Si, mia cara sei, figlia sei," with her own aria "Padre, non più, consolati," and like a Habsburg heroine she takes the blame on herself.[39] Her B section addresses itself to her father and not her mother ("Caro, di me ricordati"), although Onama breaks in with an aria limning her own victimhood ("Promettisti una vittima sola"). Zebea runs off to the hills for her two months, and the final trio of the others reinforces this decision ("Tu te'n corri").

Caldara's version is noteworthy for the direct trajectory of its narrative, and, more subtly, the way in which the seeming closeness of mother and daughter in Part I is undermined in the tragic climax, with Zebea addressing herself to her father. Besides the now-familiar features of the initially reticent Jefte, and the all-forgiving daughter, the music features some difficult and effective vocal lines, perhaps more so in Part I than in Part II. The libretto gives more space to mother and daughter (seven arias each) than to Jefte (six), and for most of Part I, text and music combine to provide a sense of a close family, perhaps precisely because of such affective and "loving" arias as Onama's "Amo troppo, e troppo adoro" (f. 25 in the Santini score). Part I ends with a similarly gentle aria for Jefte, as he goes off to battle ("Cara prole, amata sposa," f. 46v).

Yet here still, the musical signs of grief precede the actual telling of the Vow. The encounter between Jefte and Zebea is marked by the former's F-minor aria, "Ti dirà il mio core afflitto" (f. 68v). Without knowing the details of the pledge, Onama responds with a no-exit *vanitas* aria ("Al par del vento vola," f. 73); and only after Jefte makes the Vow explicit does she turn to the lack of help from Nature ("Chi di voi, terra," in C minor; f. 78). Zebea's first aria is one of self-pity and doubt ("Infelice, e che farò?," f. 75v), but she is strong enough to stop her father's own self-absorption with her next aria ("Padre, non più," f. 85), although not able to halt her mother's unbearable grief (and here there is another Marian tinge to the story). The piece ends with a trio for the three ("Corro lieto al fato mio," f. 98), in which, unlike her mother, Zebea does not surrender to self-pity.

This is one of the gentlest and most family-cohesive pieces in the repertory. Jefte's return, Onama's grief, and Zebea's overcoming of her fate all happen quickly, but with arias that do justice to the conflicting affects. Given its rapid repeat the next year, the Ruspoli must have liked it a good deal, and for good reason.

Another connection of the story to Vienna via Caldara is that to the nascent set of operas on Iphigenia in Aulis. One case of this is the composer's name-day opera for Charles VI in 1718 on this mythological story, probably composed just a few years after his Sacrifice piece. This opera had a libretto by the newly hired Zeno, who declared himself inspired by both Euripides and Racine. Although the librettist claimed its ending to be "more realistic" than actual sacrificial operas, he chose the one that ended with the self-immolation of Iphigenia's *Doppelgängerin*, the princess known as Erifile, who was a secret daughter of Helena and who had also been given the name of the heroine at birth before changing it in the interest of disguise. Although Erifile is torn by her unrequited love for Achille, she self-sacrifices to allow the "real" Iphigenia to marry him.

Because of the genre's convention (double lover pairs, etc.), the trajectory of Agamemnon, and especially the changing role of Clitemnestra as heroic mother, do not easily map onto the normal Jephthe story, let alone Caldara's Roman version of it. Still, Agamemnon, involved in war and alliances (rather like Charles VI), plays less of a role as the sacrificial politics go on in acts 2 and 3. Clitemnestra's change from servile spouse to active agent is like that of Onama in the oratorio.

130 • CHAPTER FIVE

The Reality of Sacred Sacrifice

In order to get at these issues of the Daughter's agency and of parallels to the story of Iphigenia, less direct but no less telling is a reworked oratorio: Tommaso Traetta's *Sant'Ifigenia in Etiopia*, done in 1772 by the Florentine Oratorians as part of a series of innovative pieces and repeated by a local confraternity the following year. A semi-anonymous librettist ("M. O. R.") was drafted to make Marco Coltelllini/Traetta's *Ifigenia in Tauride* into a two-part oratorio recounting the tale of the martyred St. Ephigenia of Ethiopia (feast day: 21 September), possibly in her direct honor, and it was then reused by the Confraternity of Jesus, Mary, Joseph, and the Trinity ("the Melani," founded by a seventeenth-century castrato) for its titular feast of St. Joseph (19 March) the next spring, just before the organization was suppressed.

The model of Traetta's original 1763 Vienna piece was obvious. In the oratorio, however, Iphigenia is made into a Christian virgin who refuses marriage to a pagan and is martyred, thereby combining the Aulis and Tauris stories.[40] According to the *Gazzetta Toscana* of 20 March, the 1773 reprise had an "innumerable" audience, with doubled orchestra and chorus (i.e., two on a part) with particular mention of the recently retired castrato Giovanni Manzuoli and the bass Giovanni Gherardi, and a violin concerto by Pietro Nardini during the intermission, perhaps instead of a sermon. As the century went on, and the popularity of both stories grew, the numbers cited in the tables above show the continuing appeal of the Daughter's story.

For reasons of space, the comparison with Iphigenia is limited here to a few examples beyond Caldara. Then there is a case of both stories staged in the same Carnival/Lent season, that of Rome in 1751, with an opera by Jommelli and an oratorio by Perez.[41] In Jommelli's opera, Ifigenia accepts her fate already by act 2, scene 6, and it is only the stunning onstage entry of Erifile in the last scene, with her declaration of identity, her unfulfilled wish for a sacrificing priest, and then her own self-sacrifice by leaping into the sea, that satisfies the plot's demands—an enormous amount squeezed into the last ten minutes of a three-hour opera, with the sacrifice of a secondary, and not the title, figure. Here Agamemnone is rendered powerless, and it is Erifile's agency that drives the denouement.

The 1751 Rome performance of Sant'Angelo/Perez's *Giefte* must have been a repeat, as the libretto bears a "reimprimatur," perhaps from the previous year's performance in Perugia. Its original edition seems to date from

Palermo in 1742, written for the vesting of two women from the Notarbartolo family in S. Maria delle Vergini.[42] Perez's work consists of a long dialogue between Giefte and his daughter, with only a few interjections from the secondary roles of Caleb and Azielle (the latter the female guardian of Seila). Here the Vow is very much present from the beginning, in Giefte's first recitative and aria, and Seila arrives immediately at the triumph, to her father's silent rejection. But this is a model daughter; once the Sacrifice is explained, she capitulates more quickly than Ifigenia in the opera (this may point to its possible origin as a nun's veiling piece). Most odd here is the close of Part I, a long dialogue between father and daughter on her kissing his hand, the same one that will sacrifice her. Muratorian Catholicism in Enlightenment Rome might not be the only view that recognized the masochism of this idea.

This issue is paralleled by Part II's closing with Seila's attempt to kiss her father just before the Sacrifice. The daughter had been unsympathetic to her anguished parent earlier in Part II ("Or non è tempo / di tenerezza, o Giefte"), and for her dedication she is apportioned the standard moment of prophetic ecstasy at the end, as she mentions Abraham and presages the arrival of Christ in her last aria ("Sorga da eletta aurora"). Besides her vision, one striking feature of her character is the fruitless hunt for filial intimacy underscored by her quests for his kiss. In a particularly odd inversion, this is reminiscent of the opening of the Song of Songs ("Osculetur me osculo oris sui . . ."). Thus the two sacrifice stories are not all that close in their musical versions.

Beyond the tales of sacrifice audible in the Roman spring of 1751, the numbers also suggest the migration of the Jephthe story into smaller cities; these were typical of central Italy (in the 1740s, there were performances in Fermo, Ancona, Montepulciano, and Syracuse). Although there is a gap in the 1730s, the story from Judges seemed overall only to gain in popularity. This is most striking in the last two decades of the ancien régime.

Amid the sheer number and variety of Jephthe pieces in the last decades of the Settecento, and what would seem to be their progressive distancing from the original, a piece such as the Arcadian poet Angelo Scarpelli's *Jefte, azione sacra*, probably done around 1770 for the Roman Oratorians at S. Girolamo della Carità, is striking for its nods to tradition: not only the tragic ending, with Seila going to the hills for her laments, but also its five opening penitential citations from Baruch, its long debates among the Israelites as to the validity of the Vow, and its five closing Patristic quotes affirming its execution.[43] In a wider sense, it seems to comprise part of the Oratorians' feverish attempts in the century's final decades to reclaim Biblical family relations via local oratorios, a feature to be noted below (chapter 7) in the case of the Mother of the Maccabees.

Another example of this is the 1785 pasticcio sacred opera (three acts, seven characters, performance in the Teatro del Fondo di Separazione) *La figlia di Jefte* for Naples (the arias but not the recitatives are in US-CHu). At its end, Jefte feels "new strength" from Heaven, and Noema is sacrificed, blinded, on an onstage altar.[44] That this piece could go up and be repeated the next year (*La figlia di Gefte*) in conservative Bourbon Naples is testimony enough to the power of the orthodox interpretation.

Another piece with only a surviving libretto, this time Antonio Sacchini's *Jefte* staged posthumously in Vienna in 1788, might possibly have originated in Rome, as the composer produced other Italian oratorios there (two of which survive in Viennese copies) in the 1760s (this piece is not the same, even in translation, as Sacchini's Latin *Jephthes sacrificium** for the Venetian *Ospedale dei Derelitti* in 1771, a work discussed below). This vernacular oratorio takes much more emotional energy to get to its traditional sacrificial ending, as the Figlia is quite resistant at first to the idea of the Sacrifice. Jefte has long solos of anguished doubt just after announcing the Vow and again before executing it, while the Daughter provides a pathetic farewell aria for her Sposo. The Sacrifice just offstage is oddly vague, and the unsatisfactory ending is reinforced by a chorus of the Daughter's companions who finish with the un-Enlightenment moral of God giving and taking back all good. Perhaps there is a reason why no score survives from Joseph II's Vienna, despite textual cues for pathetic and despairing arias by the composer.

The enthusiasm for the story showed no sign of abating, starting with the 1776 happy-ending *Jefte in Masfa*, done in autumn (!) at Florence's Teatro del Cocomero (now Niccolini), with music by F. H. Barthélemon.[45] The original musical commission had been given by Grand-Duke Leopold, and this version ends with an actual happy marriage for the Daughter and her suitor, another sign of Habsburg emphasis on the family unit. Here Ifisa is allowed to marry her fiancé Siba, although Jefte starts the drama by revealing his vow to Siba alone and not to his daughter. Only in Part II, after suspecting Siba of infidelity, is she told of her fate by her father, with an explicit reference to Abraham and Isaac. But the Divine inspiration of the High Priest at the end of Part II annuls the sacrifice and opens the path to the wedding. Penitential filial sacrifice seems a long distance away from this work.

Among other popular works figures the 1785 pasticcio mentioned above, and there seems to have been an oratorio by Domenico Cimarosa on the topic. Barthélemon's piece fit in well with the massive reforms to piety and to theatrical life in Habsburg Tuscany, while the Neapolitan works are less easy to place in local devotion. Certainly the idea of avoiding the actual sacrifice fit in well with more "rational" devotion. The flood of Jephthe works from about 1780 onward is too wide to be examined here, and as noted above, the theme had a stage presence after 1800, including Meyerbeer's youthful *Jephthas Gelübde*; Pietro Generali's *Jefte* (Florence, 1827); Ruperto Chapi's *La hija de Jefte* (Madrid, 1875); and even as late as the first original Cuban opera, Laureano Fuentes Matons's *La hija de Jefté* (a preliminary version for Havana in 1878; later redone as *Seila*).[46]

Still, the move of such pieces out of sacred spaces into theaters was indicative of the loss of penitential and didactic content in treatments of the story. One late case of an "odd" resolution is the mention of the "ransom" of both the daughter's life and her nubility (i.e., she would be allowed to live and to be married) for thirty pieces of silver—a clear reference to Judas Iscariot—in Mayr's *Il sacrificio di Jefta* (probably early 1790s, possibly for Forlì).[47] This suggestion, about halfway through the piece's Part II and fiercely rejected for its mercantilism by the heroine, also seems a swipe at a Talmudic resolution of the story in this vein, but is not otherwise found in the oratorio literature.

Venetian Daughters

The one piece on the topic by Giovanni Paisiello, the undated *Jephthe sacrificium* for the Mendicanti in Venice, must be from 1779–81, as P. F. Gillio recognized.[48] Given that the composer was in St. Petersburg at this point, a distant spot for a commission, it is tempting to posit the "1774" date written in on the Rome copy of the libretto as being reflective of a now-lost, vernacular-language piece done by the composer for Rome or Naples in that year, then "Latinized" about five years later for the conservatory, as the institution finally began to use outside composers.[49]

Paisiello's setting is lost, all the more regrettably since the text is far simpler than Pietro Chiari's for a 1771 work on the same subject by Antonio

Sacchini.[50] This former piece is, however, more "familial," as it features both the mother (here "Rebeca") and the fiancé ("Gamar") along with a companion ("Saba") for the daughter ("Elcane"). The text also almost equalizes the loss on the fiancé's part, as it opens with him and Gamar returning for the Israelites' victory, during which their upcoming marriage is arranged. But this libretto works quickly: Elcane comes out immediately to greet her father, and although his reaction is less nasty than that of Judges 11, he leaves without even singing an aria or explaining his silence.

The consolations of Saba, Gamar, and the entering Rebeca do not work, and the Vow has to be elicited from the returning Jephthe. Saba is consolatory again and Rebeca excoriates her husband in what must have been accompanied recitative followed by an exit aria ("Carae gentes mala audite / genitricis desolatae"), while Saba and Gamar freeze in horror at the Vow. Without really addressing the others, Jephthe finally explains his torment, and Elcane obediently follows his decision. This is the only real dialogue between father and daughter, as Rebeca had disappeared after her denunciation of her spouse. Finally Gamar erupts in invective against Jephthe, and this sets up the final long trio section of the work, with father, daughter, and fiancé expressing their misery, obedience, and attempt at consolation, respectively. There is no happy end and no moral except for "oh inexorata mors!" It is indeed a shame not to have Paisiello's music for this extremely somber and unusual close. But the piece testifies to the ongoing power of the Biblical conclusion of the story.

Finally, the middle work* among Sacchini's three pieces for Venice's Derelitti in the 1770–72 triennium gives some sense of the composer's norms. This 1771 *Jephthes sacrificium* had to reconcile the "democratic" nature of multiple singers (seven here, as in his Mother of the Maccabees work discussed below in chapter 7) with the essentially two-character nature of the story. His librettist Chiari did so by holding his Jephthe off until a quarter of the way through Part II. Instead, the beginning is devoted to the Hebrews' concern about the battle with the Philistines; the Nuncius's report of the warfare; a Sponsus betrothed to the unnamed Filia; the dramatically male character Mara; and two of the Filia's companions (Saba and Noemi) urging her to celebrate her father's glory in the conflict. Again, the Filia's visions of the future prevent her from doing so, and the first long aria is given to the Nuncius, the famed Ippolita Santi (who will reappear in chapters 6 and 7 below). As was typical for this singer, the aria has to do with the Filia "flying" to her father to greet him ("Vola ad patrem"), and Sacchini, who knew the voice well, responded with a high-register aria typical of her style, with D6s and even an F6 as the last pitch of her line. The Filia decides to go alone to greet her father, telling the Sponsus to stay behind, and the part ends with a love duet for the two.

The Nuncius begins by calling for peace to enjoy the upcoming victory celebration, and again Santi has an "atmospheric" aria ("Quando in mare tacent venti"), this time relying not so much on the stratospheric runs as on the contrast between Nature's silence (sustained pitches) and human emotion. Chiari then breaks directly into the father-daughter meeting, paraphrasing the "decepisti me et ipsa decepta est" phrase of Judges 11:35 (*Jephthe*: "Ingrata! Siccine prima veniens, quo confides / genitorem occidis?" *Filia*: "Quare Pater?"). He calls on her to stop before her sorrow kills him (a kind of reversal between executioner and victim), and Sacchini set this entire dialogue/soliloquy as a remarkable thirty-four-page accompagnato, one of the longest ones in the Settecento, as Jephthe argues with himself and imagines the Sacrifice already. This culminates in a "Furies" aria for him (as sung by Domenica Pasquali; "Furiae abissi tenebrosi"), and Sacchini heightened the tension by linking this directly to the arrival of the Sponsus in a recitative dialogue which marks the beginning of the Daughter's self-lament, as she refers to "omnia finita / sola remanet vita" (ex. 5.2).

Alas, the only surviving copy of the score (B-Bc ms. 1104) ends in the middle of the A section of this last aria. But Chiari's plan is clear from the libretto: the aria begins her plaint, after which she goes off to mourn. Jephthe returns, and the piece ends textually with a series of duets and a quartet leading to the final sextet, with its curious recommendation of following vows as Nature gives glory to God ("Vota Deo, vota servanda / Dei voluntas veneranda: / caeli stellae rutilantes / maris undae fluctuantes / Deo volenti gloriam dant" [A vow to God is to be observed, and His will kept sacred; let the orbiting stars of Heaven, you flowing waves of the sea, give glory to God]).

Here the interchange between father and daughter has been reduced to the minimum, and there is no mother. What does come across—to some degree in contrast with the Ruth and Maccabees stories examined below—is the sense of solidarity among female Israelites with the Daughter, even beyond her fiancé's love, and the purely familial aspects of the tale recede in opposition to the social. But the brilliance of Sacchini's score

EX. 5.2 A. Sacchini, *Jephthes sacrificium*, ending, recitative "Omnia finita, solo remanet vita"; B-Bc, Ms. 1104, fol. 370r.

should not go unnoticed; in its long accompagnato, highly florid writing for both Santi and Laura Conti, and quick juxtapositions of affect, it is very much the equal of the other pieces discussed below, and worthy of Charles Burney's praise of the composer as inferior only to Baldassare Galuppi at this moment in Venice.

Chapter Six

Fears, Returns, Blindness

Wohin sind die Tage Tobiae
da der Strahlendsten einer stand an der einfachen Haustür
zur Reise ein wenig verkleidet und schon nicht mehr furchtbar?

—Ranier Maria Rilke, "Die zweite Elegie," *Duisener Elegien*

CHARACTERS: Tobit, Tobias, Anna, Azaria (Raphael)

BIBLICAL SOURCE: Tobit (esp. chapters 10–12)

NARRATIVE: In exile in the city of Tishbe, Tobit is old, poor, and blinded (by falling bird droppings) after having buried the Jewish dead. His wife Anna criticizes him for this. He remembers ten talents that he had loaned to his relatives in Ecbatana and decides to send his son Tobias to retrieve them. This family's daughter Sarah has become the object of desire by a demon, who kills each of her seven bridegrooms on their wedding nights.

The archangel Raphael is sent under the name of Azaria to accompany Tobias on his journey, during which the latter wrestles with a monstrous fish. Raphael advises Tobias to kill the fish and burn its heart and liver for later use. Tobias arrives in Ecbatana, marries Sarah, and on their wedding night banishes the demon by sprinkling it with the fish's remains. After three nights of chaste prayer, they are able to consummate the wedding and set off, Tobias ahead of his bride, back to Tishbe.

Upon arrival, despite his mother's earlier despair that he had met the fate of the other suitors, she rejoices to see him. Although Tobit resists at first, Tobias and the newly arrived Sarah are able to sprinkle the rest of the demonic liquid over his father's eyes, curing his blindness. Raphael/Azaria reveals his identity and takes his leave of the Jews. Tobit sings a canticle of praise, lives to a ripe old age, and dies, and his son and Sarah have numerous offspring.

Fears, Returns, Blindness · 139

WORKS DISCUSSED AT LENGTH IN THIS CHAPTER: Vacondio, *Jacob Fidelis Servitus*; Sacchini, *Nuptiae Ruth*; Galuppi, *Il ritorno di Tobia* (1782); Zeno, *Tobia*; G. Melani, *Il ritorno di Tobia*; García Fajer, *Tobia*; Casali, ditto; Anon., ditto (Florence, 1771); Mysliveček, *Tobia* (Padua, 1769); Haydn, *Il ritorno di Tobia* (1775/1784)
PLACES: Florence, Venice, Rome, Vienna

In some ways, weddings and marriages would seem to be at the center of any dramatic representation of Christian family—and, for early modern Lutheranism and Calvinism, that would be true.[1] But because of the penitential season of the original ritual, along with the necessarily unmarried status of cardinals, clerics, and other patrons, this was less the case for Catholicism and its musics. Still, with falling monasticization rates in the eighteenth century, marriages and the incorporation of new family members became more important.

In addition to the treatments of the Books of Ruth and Tobit noted presently, briefer oratorio libretti on Biblical weddings did indeed crop up on occasion, sometimes even as a trope for nuns' professions: Isaac and Rebecca, Jacob and Leah/Rachel, and one for David and Abigail (lost music by Sacchini in Naples, 1767). The first version of Isaac/Rebecca was found in a 1675 Lenten work for the Orsi family in Bologna, a piece which also displays the interconnections among our tales, as it begins with choral rejoicing after the Binding of Isaac. The choice reflects the domestic emphasis of the Orsi's commissions, as discussed above (chapter 3). Other works on these nuptials followed in the wave of the mid-Settecento: Monreale (1753), Ancona (1770), Spoleto (1775), and a twice-repeated Rebecca oratorio for Camerino (1776). How many of these were related to unmentioned local weddings is hard to determine. However, Jacob's sacred bigamy with Leah and then Rachel, recalling the Hagar narrative, was a harder nut to crack. Surprisingly, it appears in a work for the Oratorio del Crocifisso in 1702, *Jacob Fidelis Servitus* ("The Servitude/Slavery of the Faithful Jacob"), featuring the patriarch, his two wives, and his lying father-in-law Laban. This work had a text by G. B. Vacondio with music by the same Francesco Acciarelli who had done the Jephthe piece for the institution in 1695. Jacob's flight from Laban would be the subject of an oratorio by J. S. Mayr for the Mendicanti a century later, in 1791.

Like Mesquita's *Ismael*, Vacondio's 1702 oratorio has a long preface explaining the two Parts of the narrative, followed by a separate moral allegory for the otherwise unusable story. Here, Jacob's tricked first marriage to Leah was considered as symbolic of the active life, followed by that to Rachel as indicative of the contemplative one, the ultimate purpose being to combine the two into the perfect love of God. Again, as in the Jephthe stories, the Old Testament was taken as an imperfect foretelling of Christian doctrine.

Vacondio wrote some ten libretti for the Crocifisso, but perhaps none so hair-raisingly heterodox as this one. The piece begins with a dialogue in which Rachel spurns Jacob's courting; Laban then enters to practice his fraud of providing a bride to the prospective bridegroom, followed by Lia's (= Leah) appearance. Part II opens with Jacob's long lament about being deceived by his father-in-law, following by a snarling battle of jealousy between Lia and Rachel, once the latter has realized the deceit that has been deployed, and the fact that she is the object of Jacob's true affection.

As if this were not enough, Laban ends the oratorio by first promising to divorce Jacob from Lia after seven years so that he can marry Rachel, and then closing with a sermon-like aria on the dangers of *voluptas* (presumably Jacob's erotic attraction for Rachel) to the soul. This is decidedly not in the prefaced moral allegory, and there is a sense in which the latter was pasted in to get past any imprimatur difficulties — and indeed, there is no printed permission. Perhaps Vacondio wrote this as a challenge to show that any Biblical story could be reworked into an oratorio, although the additions to Laban's character seem gratuitous.

The complexities of this not insubstantial work — some twenty-three arias — suggest that, even in the absence of a score, its meaning functioned on various levels: the supposedly literal narration of Genesis 29 (deduced from the first part of the preface); the psychological reversals of the Latin text; the moral allegory given in the second part of the preface; and some kind of political or social meaning — not to mention the anti-sexuality Lenten *moralità* of Laban's closing aria. The Crocifisso's public on that 31 March 1702 could well be forgiven for their puzzlement at which of these — or perhaps all of them — was meant to hold the work together. Whatever it was, Vacondio continued his libretto production for the institution without evident objections from anyone.

Ruth and Tobit?

Two works considered here were based on another story from a minor Biblical book, a kind of female parallel to Tobit: Ruth and her relationship to her former mother-in-law Naomi (Noemi), all recounted in the epony-mous short book in Scriptures. Several of these works for female monastic vesting (Adria, ca. 1750, and a work by Nicola Conti for Naples, 1759) used the Ruth-Naomi-Boaz triangle as an allegory for the professing nun, Mary, and Christ. A more influential setting by Francesco Feo (text by the other-wise unrecorded Oratorian Giovanni Lupis, and not for nuns) follows the entire trajectory of the book. This *La Ruth* was dedicated to the powerful if not universally popular Silvio Valenti Gonzaga, Benedict XIV's Secre-tary of State (foreign minister), a figure with no other documented musical interests, for Palm Sunday 1743's evening at the Roman S. Girolamo della Carità. Again, it is centered on agricultural work and features a chorus of reapers; the flexibility of the genre, shown above in chapter 1's 1697 Lucca example, is also evident in this work. With a Roman repeat in 1757, it had already been picked up, with an unchanged text, for the Jesuits in Palermo in 1750 who were putting on a Forty Hours' piece during (not after) Car-nival in the city, and it fits also into the Oratorian project of creating new family models via oratorios.

For all that it may seem an innocuous story, this Book is not without its problems, starting with the various misunderstandings between Naomi and Ruth and the latter's departure to winnow in the fields, leaving her mother-in-law alone. In addition, it is Naomi's order that Ruth go to Boaz's tent after he has eaten and drunk, therefore setting up a kind of seduction scene (with more positive resonances of the Judith and Holofernes story).

The libretti do not totally iron out the issues. Cornelius a Lapide's com-mentary on 1:18–19 had taken Ruth as a type of the Church, coming to Christ (= Bethlehem) from among the Gentiles, while he viewed Naomi tropologically (individually) as a case of a woman whose joy had turned to lament. Although the exegete did not make the connection, this also underscored the suitability of the story to Lent, a kind of "joy of penance" piece of which this book treats other examples.[2]

Feo's 1743 version opens at Ruth 1:19, the return of the two widowed women to Bethlehem. Here, Ruth's opening aria focuses on her own strength compared to Noemi's dismay at the return to her native city: "Cara, consolati, / non tormentarmi, / tu mi vuoi debole / al par di te; / ma il core intrepido / non fa tremarmi / di nuovo in sen" [Console yourself, my dear, and do not torment yourself; you want me weak like yourself, but my intrepid heart in my breast does not make me tremble]. Ruth leaves for the fields, the servant Tigea encourages the reapers, and Booz has them leave extra grain for Ruth to harvest (a gesture to Ruth 2:16), although Lupis postpones the initial dialogue between the two future spouses to a later moment. Noemi continues to voice fear in an *accompagnato* and then, in her second aria, Ruth returns with grain and describes Booz without having met him, as Part I closes. This does not exactly mirror Lapide's guide to the story.

Tigea praises Ruth's beauty and character, and Noemi's advice to visit Booz's tent (Ruth 3:1–6; the seduction episode) is followed faithfully by her daughter-in-law. The denouement happens quickly, with Noemi onstage the whole time, along with directly self-identifying quotes from the Book ("Ruth Maobite io son tua umil serva" = 3:9) and a final duet for the new spouses. Noemi has as many arias as Booz, with only Ruth singing more; the use of this ultimately joyous and strongly female-oriented tale shows how the story had become unlocked from Eucharistic ritual meaning by mid-century.[3] Still, the Book provided what was essentially a positive view of marriage, in contrast to what has come up in the previous chapters, and its presence among oratorio topics also marks a shift away from penance and toward devotion.

The chronologically last Latin piece by Antonio Sacchini for the Venetian Derelitti on Assumption BVM in 1772 provides insight into how this story of female solidarity was reworked in a later generation, in this case markedly, for the *ospedali*.[4] His *Nuptiae Ruth** featured a particularly large number of added characters to accommodate nine singers; of these six additions, four are male in dramatic gender. Noemi was given to Marina Frari, with Ruth being Laura Conti and "Bohoz" (Boaz) the alto Francesca Gabrieli. The new personages fill out the casting for Bohoz's peasants, with the major star of the Biblical character trio being Gabrieli, who had not figured in the 1771 Jephthe piece.[5]

Here, the librettist Pietro Chiari set up a pastoral prelude which would have recalled the real agricultural labor for the day of its performance in mid-August in the fields of the Veneto, with the invented character Lamech's (= Elisabetta Pasquati) first aria in praise of Creation followed by a chorus and a second aria (on apian fertility, probably another Eucharistic reference). Ruth does not enter until after this aria, and it becomes clear that Chiari had started in medias res with Ruth already in the fields (Ruth 2:3 in a four-chapter Biblical book). She then has a sylvan duet with another invented character, the female reaper Zela (Lucia Tonello), and the entire effect is to distance her from Noemi as well as to suggest the multi-gendered nature of agrarian activity.

Chiari also kept Bohoz/Boaz away from all this agricultural action. Ruth's duet is rudely interrupted by another added role, the grouchy female overseer "Salemi," but the latter's reproach of Ruth gave the star singer Ippolita Santi, cast in this role, an occasion for a stratospheric rage aria, "Vade, superba." At this point Chiari brought matters back to Ruth 2, by introducing Bohoz's questions as to her identity, and then an accompanied recitative followed by an aria for Noemi (finally), "Ante thronum virgina-lem," again appropriate to the virginal women actually singing. Chiari col-lapsed Noemi's advice from Ruth 3 into a short recitative, and this part ends with one of his typical ensembles for the secondary characters, in this case a quartet. Once again, the possibilities for female solidarity, both in the story and in the reality of *ospedale* life, seemed outstaged by the importance of the marriage to Boaz and its place in the ultimate genealogy of Christ.

Unhappy Beginnings, Happy Endings

Still, among "marriage" oratorios, the journey and return of Tobias (= Tobit the Younger), together with his father Tobit's blindness, his mother's con-cerns, and the angelic (Raphael) guiding hand, were at the center of the imagery of Christian marriage and households.[6] For Italy, of course, this emphasis on domesticity and everyday Christian life had its roots in the *rappresentazione* tradition, and given the wide range of themes in the Bibli-cal book as perceived by early modern exegesis — inter alia the Seven Works of Mercy, duties to parents, financial responsibility, the morality of money-borrowing, Christian life in exile, and the growing cult of the Guardian Angel — its projection could have many meanings.[7] These other signifi-cations included devotion to the Trinity, Christ's Wounds, Mary, angels, St. Joseph, various other saints of "patience," and not least marital chastity, based on the three first nuptial nights that Tobias and Sarah spent chastely in prayer before consummating their union.

The story's opening, with an impoverished and blind Tobit, followed by the orders to his son to retrieve the ten talents from his relatives in Mede, could seem conventional. But the continuation, with the arrival of the angel (Raphael) to escort him, the journey to Mede and the encounter with a monstrous fish, followed by Tobias's wedding to Sarah, and the banishing of the demon who had killed the young woman's earlier bridegrooms, points to an uneasy mixture of ancient myth and early modern reality. In oratorios, the emphasis is often not so much on this "picturesque" part of the story, but rather on the return of the son and the miraculous healing of the father's blindness.

Given the use of the fish's bodily fluids in both banishing the demon and curing Tobit's blindness, the story was also suitable as a kind of protection of the job of apothecaries trained to use such materials. The issue of retrieving the money that had been loaned to their relative Gabael in Mede to alleviate the parents' poverty comes up in some libretti but not others, and the prosperity as a result of the angel's intervention gives some sense of the rewards following Divine instruction.

Time and again in the Settecento, the book was used as a touchstone for Christian family life. The Emilian Jesuit Carlo Tommaso Morone (noted above for his remarks on the Binding of Isaac) wrote an entire treatise on only the first chapter as an example of model *oeconomia*, the running of domestic and devotional duties.[8] The soon-to-be ex-Jesuit Giuseppe Luigi Pellegrini put it most clearly in Vienna in 1772:

> Others have believed that, since the world must continue with the succession of families, it should be the Lord's task to give us the true idea, both of the continuing dependency which [families] should have on Him, and of the sovereign protection that He would always have for them. This doubtless may well be, and if we consider the diverse perspectives of father, mother, son, and bridegroom observed diligently in Tobit [the Book], and the intersections of matrimony, family relationships, loans, and society precisely noted therein, then it seems truly that He wanted His views directed to this end . . . so may it be said, that in Tobit [the Book] the Lord has aimed to proffer an example to all of what a religious human being should be.[9]

A more hidden liturgical reference for the story is that to the Third Sunday of Lent. Because of Tobit's blindness, its Introit and Tract ("Oculi omnium"), both of which refer to "sight," provided a Lenten linkage for this seemingly joyful text. In addition, the father's physical—but also psychological—resistance to the hope of healing, clearly on sonic display in Part II of Haydn's *Ritorno di Tobia*, raises issues of physical disability.

This also includes the spiritual effects of infirmity, and a Christian response thereto. Haydn's work was premiered on Passion Sunday in 1775, while its 1783 Roman performance took place precisely on Lent's Third Sunday.[10]

The growing cult of the Guardian Angel, identified with Raphael, also generated interest in the theme. The most famous case is the Tobit repertory associated with the eponymous Florentine Compagnia dell'Arcangelo Raffaello, whose basic ideology, social practice, and oratorio repertory have been well studied. The issues of sons at risk, or boys in need of Divine social guidance, run through the repertory as well as through the activities of the Tuscan confraternity, and the number of oratorios generated by Raphael in Florence is noteworthy. Indeed, the presence of the story in the oratorio was very clear early in Giovanni Maria Casini's massive 1695 oratorio retelling of the whole journey, *Il viaggio di Tobia*, written for the Raffaello.

Especially around the idea of "ritorno," the Book could be used for other sacred motion in urban spaces as well. This is most evident in Catania's association of Tobias's journey linked to its 17 August festivities around the processional return of its patroness St. Agatha's relics. This mobile assembly of the city back to the church with her shrine featured various oratorios dealing with Biblical return journeys.[11] Even at the nineteenth-century Restoration, this was underscored by a cantata (in manuscript in I-Nc), *Il ritorno di Tobia*, written for the 1815 return of Ferdinand IV to a newly retaken Bourbon Naples, with a text by Giambatista Gifuni; the printed version of this was performed in a patrician household (Giuseppe Valuta's) with reference only to Raphael and not to an earthly sovereign. As in Lucca with its Volto Santo, oratorios enacted civic prestige and sanctity by taking a Biblical topos and turning it into urban ritual.[12]

Finally, in terms of ocular healing, the theme also resonated with the European spread of the Frenchman Jacques Duviel's new method (1748–53) for cataract surgery. Its use in Vienna is unclear, but Haydn's piece came at a time of changes to ophthalmology. This was most evident in the November 1773 appointment of the Maltese native Joseph Barth (1745–1818) to the first chair of ophthalmology at the University of Vienna, evidently the premiere such appointment in Europe, and one promoted by Gottfried van Swieten as well as the future Joseph II.[13] Barth pioneered a good deal of optical anatomy, although he seems not to have invented a new procedure for cataract surgery, but the issue of eyesight and its cure was quite present in the Vienna of 1775.

146 • CHAPTER SIX

Tobits and Tobiases

In terms of the Book's episodes, a few works concentrated only on the "early" parts of the story (Tobit 4–8): Tobias's experiences of his departure, his meeting Raguel's family, his future bride and engagement to her, the banishing of the demon who had devoured earlier bridegrooms, and the nocturnal prayers after the wedding—that is, the ideally chaste Christian marriage. This started with a Neapolitan work by Gaetano Veneziano around 1690 (*Tobia sposo*), with another contemporaneous one being a Raffaello confraternity piece for Florence by G. B. Viviani in 1692.[14] Highly specific in its destination was the work by Pietro Pignatta for the Clarissan nuns of the Königinkloster in Vienna the same year, while a generation later, *I due sposi felici Sara e Tobia* was done for the Pistoia Oratorians in 1718, and two years later in a different musical setting (Francesco Gasperini) again for the Raffaello in Florence, with a dedication to Violante Beatrice of Bavaria. The Tuscan works entirely omit Tobit and Anna, ending with Raguel's blessing of the new couple, and they deprive the story of its driving force, perhaps given the majority of orphans (hence without parental models) in the real audiences.[15] In this vein, a 1764 devotional guide to Catholic marriage preparation was named *Istoria di Tobia*.

As the cult of the Guardian Angel grew, Baldassare Galuppi's 1727 oratorio, sponsored by the devotees of St. Anthony of Padua at the Tempio Malatestiano run by the Franciscans in Ravenna, was entitled *Il giovine Tobia*. Since this piece also is set before the actual return to the parents, it seems a celebration of trust, miracles (with a hidden reference to Anthony and the sermon to the fishes), and Christian marriage, all meant to be performed at a typical annual moment for weddings after Ascension Day (Anthony's feast was 14 June). Penance and Lent were far afield. No author is given, but Franciscan involvement could well be suspected; the preface cites Tobit 6–8 only, the wedding story. The Ravenna work goes over the journey to Mede/Ecbatana and the wonders of Raphael's help to the young Tobit; the final chorus seems to praise Sara's constancy and hope: "Forte un alma in patir non cangia tempre: / chi ben ama il suo Dio, l'ama per sempre" [That soul is strong which does not change its nature in suffering; whoever loves God well, loves Him forever].

At the end of his life, Galuppi would return to the general theme with a five-voice piece*, but this time on the return of Tobias (no Sara among the characters, although the mirror figure of Nabat was borrowed from the

Book), a "cantata" without an institutional link, with a libretto published in 1782. Its text was by Gasparo Gozzi (1713–86; Carlo's older brother). This late *Ritorno di Tobia* begins with bitter reproaches from Anna to Tobit: *Anna* [ironically]: "Ecco gli eterni accenti // del provido Tobia. Quel che disperse, / tutti i tesori suoi / a pro d'ogni mendico; ora egli stesso / è in dura povertà.... [*Aria:*] A queste ossa eterno ghiaccio, / ombra eterna della morte, / date pace. Apri le porte, / fredda tomba, al mio morir" [Hear the never-ending words of the provident Tobit, him who dissipated all his treasure for every beggar, now *he* is in dire poverty.... (*Aria:*) Eternal ice and shadow of death, grant peace to my bones; cold tomb, open your doors to my death].[16] Azaria = Raphael then enters, and in a combination of the *rappresentazione* tradition with Tobit's blindness, the father asks him his identity, with no one else on stage. Part I closes with a chorus of hope.

In the following part, Tobias's return is marked by filial affection, and in this text, unusually, it is left to the Angel to tell of the journey. Anna is suitably penitent, and there is no space for the actual healing of the blindness. At the very end of our period, this version praises father-son affection, marking Anna by her anger and disdain and minimizing the miraculous aspects: the fish, the wedding, and even the cure of blindness. When considering how difficult Tobit's healing is in the contemporaneous work by G. G. Boccherini/Haydn, Galuppi's second approach to this story marks notably different emphases: the duties of a son, and the real role of angels. If it had been meant for informal or domestic usage, then its downplaying of marriage and its emphasis on sons' duties might come out of the demography of Venetian family reproduction.[17]

A similarly short piece (*Il ritorno di Tobia*) for the same second section of the story, the happy return of Tobias, was set by David Perez for a Forty Hours' celebration at the Jesuit college in Palermo (1753). Here, although there is some initial lamenting by Anna, Tobias quickly appears, and narrates the story of the struggle with the fish. The miraculous effect of the animal's organs and fluids is made equivalent to the power of the Eucharist as displayed, with little mention of the marriage (there is no role for Sara as bride), the chaste wedding vows, and the like. But this is another use of the story for Eucharistic glorification. Indeed, the *licenza* calls the Host "the antidote to all our evils," and so there is a non-familial take on the tale.

Another work without clear institutional connection that concentrates on the fragile and recovering Tobit was done around 1740 by Francesco Feo.[18] This Latin-texted *Tobias, sive justi consolatio* might have been written for the same Neapolitan institution that sponsored the composer's Latin oratorios for the deceased; in that sense, the context would push the piece in the direction of an *ars moriendi* as embodied in the passing of Tobit. In any case, its opening, with the self-laments of both Tobit (tenor) and Anna (alto), evokes a more popular register than many other oratorios on the theme, despite its Latin-language text.[19] It has relatively little music for the penitent Anna, who also points to the story as redemption from "voluptas," and the focus is on a fragile Tobit, who has more doubts than the normal such personage, and who uses his blindness to question his son's account of the trip and of the situation. This leads Tobias, not the Angel, to recount the whole story in Part II, and it is left to Azaria to refer to blindness as symbolic of "false mental images" in the sinner, these specters being swept away via the joy of penance and Divine praise.

The trajectory of these "return to family" works, as opposed to the purely nuptial ones, does not necessarily line up with the commentaries and sermons. In the Seicento, Casini's *Il viaggio di Tobia* had concentrated on the actual journey and the marriage, with relatively short emphasis on the healing of Tobit and the *lieto fine*. A few settings, among them Pignatta's (1692), set up the link to nuns' profession ceremonies in terms of "voyage"—here across the cloister wall—leading to marriage (to Christ), a stark contrast to the Jephthe-inspired works discussed in the previous chapter, and one in which gender is neatly reversed.

The continuing debt to medieval exegesis is evident in the preface by the author, Giambattista Antonio Visconti (1720–83), to a setting composed for the Roman Oratorians in 1752 by F. J. García Fajer.* Here, Visconti cited the fountainhead of the book's interpretation, the Venerable Bede; he added to this the thirteenth-century Dominican cardinal Hugh of Saint-Cher and—for the depiction of Sara as the ecclesiological incarnation of the Song of Songs, that is, the Sposa—he referred to Augustine. Visconti also cited Ambrose and the far more modern Calmet in his notes. The power of medieval thought is clear.[20]

Several comparisons give a sense of how all the possible themes of the complete story—ranging from Tobit's original impoverished misery in Ninevah, Anna's handiwork to provide income for the family (a gesture to proto-industrialism), the parents' fears, the mockery of the Ninevites, the Angel's power, and the curing of Tobit's blindness through to his happy old age and death—were variously selected for specific situations. Around 1720, settings of different texts by Giuseppe Porsile* and Antonio Lotti show the changes to the story; a generation later, the Roman Oratorians would stage both García Fajer's 1752 work and, three years later, G. B. Casali's *La pazienza ricompensata negli avvenimenti di Tobia**, and these works would be revived into the 1770s.[21] This latter would have a certain popularity, put on in Vienna in 1761 (and available in Haydn's world). Finally, Josef Mysli-veček's 1769 Padua oratorio* *Il Tobia* shows something of a homiletic men-dicant take on the story. In combination with Haydn's piece, these works were still equally attractive in the 1770s, and a comparison among these five pieces is illuminating for setting the situation of the decade.[22]

The Making of a Type

To begin with a piece reflecting the notable changes to the story as inher-ited from the Seicento, Zeno's *Tobia* with Porsile's music seems to have been premiered to Habsburg favor on 14 March 1720.[23] It formed part of a large-scale series of oratorios that year, without a Carnival opera: four other oratorios (by Badia, Caldara, Conti, plus Ignazio Balbi, whose work was sent up from Milan), and an *azione sacra* (Pariati/Fux) for the Tomb/ *sepolcro* services. The only other Old Testament subjects in the season were David/Absalom and the Deliverance of Moses, and so again here it is hard to pinpoint a single theme across Lent. Zeno's text enjoyed a relatively long life, being set in Habsburg Florence in 1749 by Giuseppe Orlandini, as well as forming part of the poet's canonical sacred output printed in the *Poesie sagre drammatiche*.

The libretto opened at an unexpected place: a long dialogic gloss of Tobit 2:15's references to Tobit's miseries — his blindness, which occurred in the wake of his burying the Jewish dead, and his poverty — with a lexical and citational field taken from the one extratextual reference that would have immediately resonated with the Habsburg imaginary: that of Job, a favor-ite trope for the Emperor since Leopold I's reign. Zeno took the names of Tobit's relatives Achor and Nabat from much later in the Book (11:20) to personify these reproaches before Anna even appears. In yet another case of this study's intertextual awareness, Tobit responds to their criticism by cit-ing Abraham/Isaac as models, but Zeno's hyper-citational practice shows as many references to Job as to Tobit, and none to Genesis. The father's mis-ery is taken up by the counselors, linking his personal misfortune with that of the entire Jewish nation. In this way, Zeno tapped into a long dynastic tradition dating at least to Leopold I's senectitude if not longer, that of the sovereign (here = Tobit) as beleaguered just man. The rest of the libretto would work out the reversal of this seeming ill fortune.

The entering Anna's complaint is taken from Tobit 2:19–23, but she is convinced relatively quickly of her mistakes. Still in Part I, Tobias's dog enters ("ecco il cane"; evidently an animal was let loose in the Hofburg-kapelle) to pre-announce the arrival of Azaria and Tobias, and the main family emphasis here is on the mother, with the blind Tobit evidently not able to grasp the magnitude of the moment. Zeno jammed in the healing of Tobit's blindness at the end of this part (in the book it does not occur until 11:14, after most of the other action).

Zeno's Part II has a retrospective narrative task, and it begins with the entering Sara, in book order (paraphrasing her wonder at her new city and family from 11:18, since she arrived a week after her groom), but then describes her bridegroom in vocabulary taken from both speakers of the Song of Songs (in this usage, G. G. Boccherini two generations later would follow Zeno as he crafted a libretto for Haydn). Anna enters somewhat suspicious of the newcomer—a situation that had repeated itself several times since 1666 among older Habsburg Empresses reacting to incoming brides—but their affection warms as Sara retells the story of her seven bridegrooms killed by the demon. The new daughter-in-law's personality also develops with references to unusual passages in Augustine on receiving good only if asking God for it, a theme that would take over the end of the text.[24]

Still, she reproaches Tobias for his heart being unaware of her arrival, and finally the discourse turns to the loan money retrieved and to the dowry which accompanies her.[25] Azaria/Raphael self-cites from Tobit 12:11–15 on his continuing aid to the faithful (a clear reference to Guardian Angel devotion); Achior and Nabat recognize the error of their initial criticism; and after a reference to Psalm 91 ("Justus ut palma florebit"), the piece ends with Tobit and the chorus paraphrasing his canticle from chapter 13. Like Minato, Zeno filled his footnotes with citations, not just to the book, but to other Biblical passages, and—in a sign of modernity—to current exegetes as well. Perhaps the most striking was his use of Lapide's citation of Augustine on the fish gall (Tobit 11:14) used to cure the father as being like Christ's Blood shed on the Cross; obviously, the "gall" also resonated with other moments in the Passion.

The issue of recovering lost money also resonated in an increasingly mercantile Habsburg economy. In some versions the issue is not even mentioned or is submerged amid the joy of Tobias's survival and marriage. Still, Joseph I's reign had marked a post-feudal turn in Habsburg fiscal responsibility, and Zeno's emphasis here, along with the underscoring of Tobit's poverty, marks either an overall sense of having debts returned or, in a less literal sense, the importance of paying dowries correctly.

In its professionalism and variety, Porsile's score is probably underestimated.[26] Its opening monologue for the Job-like Tobit is set as accompanied recitative, and he lavished particular care on the mother-son duet "Vieni agli amplessi" by tempo changes. The traceable singers in this performance included women as Anna (Maria Landin-Conti) and Sara (Regina Schoonians, at age forty-three; she lived ca. 1677–1759), and although the piece was never repeated, it seems to justify its initial reception.

Beyond Vienna

Elsewhere, a Tobit work with text by the Sienese Arcadian poet Girolamo Melani and music by Antonio Lotti was performed at the Bolognese Oratorians in 1723; the libretto is one of three done by Melani for S. Maria in Galliera that Lent (and was printed as such in an appendix to his *Poesie toscane* of that year). The imprimatur of 16 February suggests that this *Ritorno di Tobia* might have been intended for some point around the Third Sunday of Lent, making the liturgical connection to the Mass Proper items on vision.[27] It was part of a massive Lenten enterprise that included some seven oratorios—every week, including before the First Sunday of Lent—that year; it could have drawn from the fifteen-odd professional opera singers who had been in the city for Carnival. That spring, the order put on Old Testament (Adam, Esther) and sanctoral works; although the undertaking was large-scale, it is hard to draw a single devotional focus from the multiplicity of settings.

But Melani's emphases and tone are different from those of Zeno's piece; with only four singers, and a long text (some thirteen arias and lengthy recitatives; 480 lines), it indexes a far more colloquial register, without any citations of the Book, let alone Patristic or exegetical authority. Its opening is Anna's monologue, in which she variously blames herself ("madre omicida") and her husband for her son's absence, while also taking a swipe at lending or recovering money as she dismisses the ten talents that Tobias had been sent to retrieve. Tobit follows in further anguish, but in language that anticipates passages in the Maccabees works discussed below, he attempts to remind her of her Jewishness which trumps her womanhood: "sei donna, / ma figlia di Sionne al fin tu sei . . . perchè non hai speme? / Perchè fede non hai" [you are a woman, but after all you are a daughter of Zion . . . why do you have no hope? Because you have no faith]. The sharpness of this exchange is reflected, however, in Tobit's own self-references as a "vil peccator," which recurs in both parts and is notably absent from Zeno.

Still in Melani's Part I, Azaria and Tobias do appear, and the secular connotations of the Angel's discourse are evident in his comparison of the situation to the calm after a storm and the visibility of Castor and Pollux. Azaria miraculously "pre-arrives" to calm the couple before their son appears; Anna (who has left) then returns, and the part ends with a joyous family reunion. The healing of Tobit happens offstage during the sermon, but Anna continues to create problems at the opening of Part II, asking about Sara's whereabouts and (despite her earlier words) the money. Her character becomes degraded, and this slightly comic tone continues in Tobit's attempts to pay Azaria for his services. Without revealing his identity, Azaria depicts Tobias's ideal devotion to the Guardian Angel just as he departs, and another joyous trio between parents and son closes the piece.[28] Still, the tone of the piece could not be more different from Zeno's closely woven Biblical (and occasionally Augustinian) paraphrases and his concern for more subtle characterizations at the highest level of dramatic register. Melani's Tobit is at the center of dramatic attention, with some five arias (compared to Azaria's one), and despite Anna's continuing complaints, this libretto does share with Zeno's its emphasis on the suffering father as opposed to Anna (three arias).

Parts of Melani's 1723 text would have a long life. Casali's 1755 work takes over some of its recitatives, while changing all the arias; this was imported to Vienna in 1761 and could have figured in the memory of Haydn's original 1775 audience. Meanwhile, the Florentine Oratorians' libretto for a work in 1771 again kept much of the 1761 Bolognese recitatives, while changing the arias again. These versions, plus Fajer's, would survive into the 1770s, and so they were all in a certain sense contemporaneous with Haydn/Boccherini's piece. Casali's piece was later performed in Bologna for the feast of St. Cecilia (22 November), as Visconti's 1752 piece had been for the same festival in Rome; both these texts are quite long, with Visconti's at about 860 lines and Casali's about 700. Audiences would have been sitting in the Chiesa Nuova or the Galliera for well over two hours to hear these works.[29] Despite the references to various characters' sins and penance, for

Fears, Returns, Blindness • 153

the Oratorians this topic had clearly migrated to one of festivity, echoed by the 1754 setting for Rome of a work on the same topic by the Marquis of Santacroce, which they also sponsored.

Finally, a 1768 Roman cantata, *L'Angelo di Tobia** (in two parts, thus oratorio-like), following the canonization of José Calasanz, the founder of the pedagogical Piarist order, mixed the story (from Tobit 6, 11, and 12) with praise of the new saint, himself seen as a kind of Azaria leading Catholic youth in the path of virtue.[30] Meant for the Piarist Collegio Nazareno, its emphasis on the Angel's comings and goings (Tobit 12) also provided space for a new topos, that of Tobias's fears in the face of possible abandonment. Its music was commissioned from Rinaldo da Capua; this sanctoral occasion was paralleled by a 1773 repeat of Fajer's work in Pergola, this time for the sainted young Jesuit Luigi Gonzaga.

After a hiatus, from 1743 onward the Roman Oratorians put on a total of thirteen family-oriented libretti in the next seventeen years, not only García Fajer's and Casali's Tobit works, but also treatments of the stories of Jonathan, Adam/Eve, Ruth, and Jephthe. This density of domesticity must have something to do with these urban audiences, especially given the cleric-oriented demography of both cities: part of an attempt to establish new family models in a Rome that lacked them.[31] Similarly, the number of new commentaries until about 1760 explicitly on the Book was relatively small: Paolo Medici's (Florence, 1725), Alberto Maria Pontieri's (Palermo, 1730), and Orazio da Parma's (Venice, 1740). The story seems to have made its way into public consciousness via the oratorios as well as popular print, and it could be hijacked into other uses.

Here and in other chapters of this study, it is evident how the mid-century began to mark real changes in devotional expression, and this is also evident in newer settings with different possibilities in emphasis. García Fajer's piece was given in three successive years until presumably replaced by Casali's, but the Oratorians clearly wanted to project the story for their audience, and presumably the dedicatee of the premiere, the young and upcoming cardinal Gian Francesco Albani (1720–1803).[32]

Four Tobits at Mid-Century

To compare the texts set over twenty years by García Fajer, Casali, the anonymous Florentine reworker of 1771, and Mysliveček reveals more than just verbal dependency; the new texts for arias give a sense of changing devotional priorities, shifts that would recur in the treatment of the Mother of the Maccabees. Part I of each of the four reflects more differences than similarities, for all that Fajer's 1752 text splits its time between the quarreling parents and the dialogue of Tobias and the Angel. To begin, Visconti/Fajer's Mother recalls the Sacrifice of Isaac as she imagines the worst for her son, and the whole process takes some ninety-one lines of recitative before arriving at the first aria. In the next semi-scene, the Angel has to push Tobias on to the return voyage, as he has been distracted by the weeping of Sara, who is temporarily left behind. An *accompagnato* returns us to Anna, who believes a traveler's account of her son's wedding to Sara — and his presumable death like the latter's previous seven bridegrooms. Despite Visconti's exegetical citations, the amount of time spent on the inappropriate emotions of the older couple's snarling, and on Tobias's reluctance to come home, points up how Fajer had quite a different text to handle, compared to Zeno/Porsile.

Strikingly, the 1755/61 text for Casali repeats the entire opening recitative of Melani's 1723 libretto for Lotti (Anna: "Figlio, ahimè, dove sei?"). The first aria, however, was changed, while the second recitative (for Tobit in dialogue with Anna) was lightly rewritten, followed by another new aria ("Di tua giustizia") and the total excision of two arias from Lotti's version, so as to arrive more quickly at the next scene, the pre-return of Azaria and Tobias. Again the recitative was little touched, but Tobias's aria was replaced, and from here the new version of Casali's libretto took a different turn, having Azaria encourage the young man to filial piety, to be sure, but also to using the gall to cure his father's blindness in a longer and more expansive set of gestures. There is a moment of anticipatory joy for the parents, and the trio that ends Casali's Part I after the actual encounter expresses only family solidarity.

The 1771 Florentine libretto, *La pazienza ricompensata negli avvenimenti di Tobia*, opens again with essentially the original 1723 recitative, but rewrites and lengthens the second half of the passage substantially, with a self-interruption for Anna that moves from maternal to religious duties, rather like the language of the later Mother of the Maccabees works (chapter 7):"Ma come in preda al duolo / mi lascio trasportar? Evver son madre / tenera madre io son; ma pria di questi / dolci affetti or crudeli / alla pace del cor sarò costante. . . . [*Aria:*] Fra l'orror de' miei pensieri / splende un raggio di costanza" [But how do I permit myself to be swept away by sorrow? Yes, I am a tender mother, but before these sweet, now cruel, feelings,

I will be faithful to the peace of my heart. . . . (*Aria:*) Amid the horror of my thoughts there shines a ray of constancy]. In Habsburg Tuscany, this vocabulary could mean only obedience to the value of fidelity. As the score does not survive, it is unclear how much of Casali's original music was kept.

The entire dialogue between the couple is here notably expanded, with new arias compared to the 1755/61 version. The effect is a much longer discussion of parental duties and reaction to tribulation, another dynastic imposition of family values on the oratorio's Florentine public. Again, the dialogue between the arriving Azaria and Tobias reuses some earlier recitative by Melani, but also with new arias.[33] The finale of Part I in the 1771 work is also rewritten, with an actual physical touch between mother and son, and the entire effect in this later version is that of an expansion of familial affection, both in the absence of Tobias/Sara, and the tuttis provide a longer iteration of emotion.[34]

Mysliveček would have had his work cut out for him in approaching the anonymous libretto for his 1769 *Tobia** for Padua. Some sense of a public is given by the numeration of the eight surviving libretto copies in I-Pca, hand-numbered variously between 1 and 55. If one hundred copies were printed, probably an audience of twice that size could have been expected, although there is no indication of venue. The piece was repeated the next year in Prague (with recitative cuts), and later in Bologna and Rome, although it would not have the success of the composer's other works in the genre.

Although it is all placed in Nineveh, Mysliveček's version starts much earlier in the story, with Tobias's departure coming only after a long opening snarl between the parents on Tobit's poverty, blindness, and "excessive" good works, by now a typical opening to such libretti. Tobit reflects on sin and his punishment, and his son enters to ask mercy for his mother. The sentimentality of this scene is new, and Tobit responds with another new emphasis, that on paternal training of children using the Ten Commandments. At this point, Azaria enters, and the two finally set off after a final aria in Part I for Tobias. The didacticism of this libretto, and its ambitious scope, are evident.

The anonymous text is so long and pedagogical that its setting must have been on commission, probably from a religious order. Even the first libretto for the Padua premiere had massive *virgolette* recitative cuts in Part I, which recounts only the early section of the book before Azaria and

Tobias's departure on the journey. However, the non-autograph score gives uninterrupted music for all these, and Mysliveček seems simply to have set them all (there are eighty-six recitative lines until the first aria).

This verbosity does, however, provide Anna an occasion to express bitterness against her spouse. It is also necessary since Part II starts with a still-absent son and angel, and the return plus Sara takes up a good deal of space in this part. Strikingly, even in the beginning there is relatively little emphasis on Tobit's blindness, and later on there is also little time spent on its cure; that is, this text is one of family recomposition and enlargement, and not one of miraculous healing.

Still, this libretto casts Tobit as an almost superhumanly patient figure, who discards his wife's reproaches and insists on gratitude and faithfulness to God without wavering. The soprano (probably castrato) part for the patriarch becomes quite difficult, especially in the second part. The casting for Azaria and Sara (alto) is notably briefer, with the former (bass) evident in Part II with arias featuring triadic figures.

The cuts to the recitatives indicate the importance of the arias. Here at the beginning of Part I, before the voyage is even undertaken, there is a kind of trajectory, with Anna's first fiery reproach aria ("Veggio ben io") leading to a simpler but not insignificant one for her spouse ("Quando il vaso in colmo"); the parallels and differences with Haydn's piece are noted below. Again a simpler piece for Tobias ("Se folle io traviai") gives way to technically more difficult ones for the other three figures in the same order, Tobit's "Qual fumo in faccia" with cello obbligato and then the two others. The hardest aspect of this Part I is not Tobit's poverty, blindness, and discrimination, but rather the decision for Tobias and Azaria to undertake the journey. That said, despite Anna's reproaches, this is a relatively compact and loving family, a clear change from Zeno's 1720 libretto.

What is perhaps most memorable in the score, and a feature with the widest negative implications for family relations, is Anna's soliloquy at the beginning of Part II: a long accompanied recitative (the first in the piece: "Qual tumulto") on her troubles and hopes, which goes as far as asking to be killed herself rather than have anything happen to her still-absent son (more substitution in grief), with her criticism of Tobit now overcome (ex. 6.1). This culminates in her B-minor aria ("Ovunque m'aggiro"), which also becomes even harder toward the end of the passagework section. Here the mother has become something far more than simply a worried parent; rather, her own emotional state takes on importance. Perhaps it was this

EX. 6.1 J. Mysliveček, *Il Tobia*, "Qual tumulto"; I-Pca, D-V 1808, fol. 48r.

newly sympathetic portrayal, and a possibly growing female audience in the various reprises, that accounted for the work's relative popularity.[35]

In Part II of Mysliveček's libretto, the application of the fish gall to Tobit's eyes evokes a fiery anti-sinner aria from Azaria ("Empi, tremate"), who also advises Sara on marital fidelity, a point indicative of the moralizing ambitions of the libretto. Sara's long recitative recounting the story in Ecbatana (arrival, miraculous casting-out of the demon, and the wedding) was cut in performance, as was the paraphrase of Tobit 12:6–12, Raphael/Azaria's listing of the Works of Mercy and his own self-revelation as an angel. Possibly the length of Mysliveček's arias effectively blocked some of the extreme didacticism. Still, this was the most popular setting in the years just before Haydn's Lenten 1775 work.

The changes in these mid-century pieces also reflect the growing domestication of the story, as more emphasis was placed on the interfamily relations and less on the "fantastic" details of the tale. Even before Pellegrini's 1772 treatise came out, the oratorio repertory stressed the relationship among family members.

Aiming at New Model Families

All the various themes, domestic or miraculous, in the libretti found an extensive expression in the devotional tome of Pellegrini's *Tobia: ragionamenti* [sic; Venice, 1772], dedicated to none other than Maria Theresia. Pellegrini was also a court preacher in Vienna, hence the inscription. His fifty-five "chats" cover every possible aspect of the Biblical text. The dedication praised the Empress as a model of domestic virtue, an exemplary mother, and a sovereign.[36] With her multiple sons, Maria Theresia probably was not to be mapped onto any single female character in the Tobit story itself (except perhaps as the future Sara, the mother of multiple sons in the Old Testament); rather, she functioned as a kind of materfamilias. Still, if a Viennese (and not only; there are some twelve copies of the 1772 edition surviving in Italy, plus later reprints) reception of the story is needed for Boccherini/Haydn's work, Pellegrini's long tract would be an important point of departure, as it represents a recent view of the Book in Austria and north Italy.

As has been seen, many libretti begin with Anna's reproaches of her consort for his charity and Works of Mercy (e.g., burying the dead, at great risk to the family). In *Ragionamento* 14, Pellegrini had considered this criticism of her husband (Tobit 3) as equivalent to eighteenth-century libertines' denial of the soul. In terms of narrative order, though, Boccherini's 1775 libretto starts with Tobit 10 (with flashbacks), and here Pellegrini restricted the parents' feelings only to "sadness" at their son's absence and possible danger, with particular emphasis on Anna's fears; indeed, *Ragionamenti* 39–41 are devoted largely to the mother's grief at her son's unknown fate.[37]

However, pedagogy is never distant in Pellegrini's text. *Ragionamento* 42 turns to domestic devotion as transcending filial duty in the interest of obedience to God, although this point, central to Pellegrini's trajectory, is not as evident in the 1775 oratorio's text.[38] The next chapter then considers the Healing, and in it Anna transcends maternity in the interest of religion.[39] The cure happens unproblematically, and—unlike Boccherini's libretto—is done without Sara, who appears only in *Ragionamento* 44 (on Tobit 11:14), in the context of the difficulties for a daughter-in-law in joining a new family.[40] In that sense Pellegrini follows book order strictly, not exactly the case of the oratorio libretto.

In this light, any consideration of the 1775 Viennese *Il ritorno* should start with Boccherini's text, which has always been a subject of criticism, even in the early nineteenth century. The librettist had written some eight other works, including Salieri's *La fiera di Venezia* (1772) and his own *opera seria Turno, re de' Rutoli* (Vienna, 1767), the latter printed together with a recommendation from Calzabigi, and dedicated to the Viennese nobility. Boccherini tried to thread his way into both court and noble circles in the city.[41]

Still, the objections to the libretto, the first of which dates to a revival in 1808, are not without merit. Several questions come up here: (1) Where is the actual "return" of Tobias, and (2) How do family relations, especially between Tobias/Anna and later Sara/Tobit, play out in the libretto? At the same time, for all the problems of the plot, Boccherini's text does indeed show craft.[42] Two passages highlight this, first the very opening:

ANNA: Pietà d'un'infelice
Afflitta genitrice.
TOBIT: Pietà d'un padre misero
O Padre d'Israel!
TUTTI: Ritorni omai Tobia,
Salvo Tobia ritorni,
Cessin del pianto i giorni

O sommo Re del Ciel.

Calma, perdona i palpiti

D'un cor materno, e debole;

Premia la speme intrepida

D'un genitor fedel.

ANNA: (*osserva*) Nè comparisce oh Dio! . . .

(*tornando*) Oh Dio! Tobit, il lusingarsi è vano,

Il caro figlio, il nostro

Amabile Tobia,

Dolce sostegno

Di nostra etade, ed unico conforto

Di nostra schiavitù, è morto (*piange*).

G. G. Boccherini, *Il ritorno di Tobia*, ll. 1–19

Have pity on an unhappy afflicted mother; have pity on a miserable father, o Father of Israel! Come back already, Tobia, let him come back safe, and let the days of lamentation end, o highest King of Heaven. Forgive the shudderings of a weak maternal heart; reward the intrepid hope of a faithful father. Nor does he return, o God! O God, Tobit, deluding ourselves is in vain; our dear son, beloved Tobia, the sweet support of our old age and the sole comfort of our slavery, is dead [she weeps].

To be noted here are: (1) Boccherini's taste for chiasm and anaphora ("Ritorni Tobia . . . Tobia ritorni"); (2) the use of various line endings (*piano, sdrucciolo*, with particular emphasis on the latter) across an unvarying *settenario* meter; (3) the high literary register of the opening, something that will slip downward during the immediately following transition from marital unity into Anna's reproaches (ll. 41ff) of Tobit's optimistic dream (which, ironically, turns out to be the reality of Tobias's safety and marriage to Sara that have happened in the meantime, even if unknown to the parents); and (4) the Zeno-like linkage of the parents' misery with that of the entire nation, again underscoring Aquinas's connection of the familial and the political. A possible objection to usury and to mercantilism in general is marked only by Anna's reference to the return of the ten talents that had been the object of the journey, a kind of objection to reclaiming money at any human cost.[43]

It is evident that Boccherini's text deserves better than its critical reception. The libretto comes in at a Metastasio-like 640 lines, but Haydn's music chafes at the outmost length for such a piece, even in a theater context where there was no sermon (and this, along with the added choruses in the 1784 version, may account for the shortening of the arias, and even possibly for the disappearance of any 1775 score for Part I). Presumably Luigi Tomasini's violin concerto (or later a different cello concerto), played between the parts, would have added another twenty minutes to the evening. Fajer's and Casali's works had more text, even if some of their arias were shorter than Haydn's.

How Boccherini's opening degenerates quickly into Anna's reproaches is evident from the ensuing dialogue, in which she does not even allow her spouse to speak: "[*Anna*:] Folle, perdesti / per sovverchia pietà degl'insepolti / la luce de' tuoi lumi . . . [*Tobit*:] Ma . . . [*Anna*:] torna / col rischio della vita / a seppellir gli estinti, e a dargli tomba / in vede di cibarti. Un'altra volta / Ninive: anzi l'Assiria / ti pagherà di scherni. E dove sono / l'elemosine tue? Le tue bell'opre / quando mai ti fruttaro / se non un frutto acerbo, aspro, ed amaro? [*Aria*:] Sudò il guerriero / ma gloria ottenne" [Madman, you lost your sight because of your overarching pity for the unburied . . . But . . . risking your life, go ahead and bury the dead and give them tombs instead of feeding yourself (= Tobit 2:1−11); once again, Nineveh, indeed all Assyria will pay you with disdain. And where are your alms? Your wonderful good works, when will they ever flower in anything except hard and bitter fruit? (*Aria*:) The warrior sweated, but obtained glory . . .]. The Biblical text for this entire scene is simply Tobit 10:3−7, the book beginning the oratorio.[44] It parallels Mysliveček's libretto by having its first aria be a rage moment for Anna.

Haydn's setting follows the unexpectedly bitter irony: the opening recitative turns from C major to three brief establishments of B minor, ending on an F♯ chord which suddenly dissolves into the martial glory of the aria's first stanza in D major (ex. 6.2). These spouses speak different languages, as Anna storms off, and restoring this conjugal break would turn out to be one of the oratorio's tasks. Upon her son's return, Anna finally even takes on the "Nunc dimittis" of the New Testament's Simeon (ll. 233−26): "Ah venga, o figlio, / venga pur la mia morte. Io vissi assai / or che ti rimirai" [O let my son come; let my death come, too; I have lived enough now that I have seen you]. The emphasis, then, is on filial, not conjugal, relationships.

Another moment in the relation between Tobias and his mother occurs

EX. 6.2 Haydn, *Il ritorno di Tobia*, Sara, Part I, recitative (after Schmid/Oppermann 2009, pp. 57–58).

EX. 6.2 (*continued*)

as a duet in Part II, after Tobit rejects the cure of the fish gall for his blindness (ll. 522ff):

[*Duet*] TOBIAS: Dunque, oh Dio, quanto sperai
Di provar le gioie estreme:
È perduta ogni mia speme?
E schernita è la mia fe?
ANNA: Dunque oh Dio de' nostri guai
Gl'infedeli esulteranno?
E confuse rimarranno
Quanti oh Dio fidaro in Te?
TOBIAS: Oh che orror!
ANNA: Che duol!
TOBIAS: Che affanno!
DUET: Impossibile a soffrir.
TOBIAS: Piangi ah madre!
ANNA: Ah piangi, oh figlio!
TOBIAS: N'hai ragione,
ANNA: È giusto il pianto;
DUET: Io son pronto(a) a pianger tanto,
Che si plachi Iddio sdegnato,
O si versi dal mio ciglio
L'alma mia disciolta in pianto;
Ah sarà mia gran ventura,
Se di duolo avvien ch'io moia,
Quel momento che di gioia
Dubitai dover morir.
SARA [*entering in recitative*]: Qui di morir si parla, e tutto esulta
Il popol d'Israel.

G. G. Boccherini, *Il ritorno di Tobia*, ll. 522–48

Thus, oh God, how much I hoped to experience extreme joy; is all my hope lost, and my faith betrayed? So will the heretics exult over our misfortunes, and all who had faith in you will be confounded? O what horror, what pain, what misery, all impossible to suffer! O weep, mother; weep, my son; you are right, weeping is appropriate; I am ready to weep so much that angered God will be pacified. O let my soul dissolve itself in tears from my eyes; ah, it will be my great fortune if I doubted having to die from joy at that moment. Here you are talking about death, and the whole population of Israel is exulting.

Equalizing the mother's and son's emotions, this passage of breaking into tears recalls on one hand lachrymose drama and on the other the sense of penance. Some of Boccherini's same technical means seen at the beginning are at hand here (anaphora for "gioia" and "pianger," and the metrical basis of *ottonari*), while the syntactical displacements of the closing lines also lend a certain dignity to the passage, broken ironically (Boccherini also wrote *opera buffa* texts) by Sara's sudden and joyous entrance, after which she narrates her own agency in gradually loosening Tobit's blindfold and rendering him capable of bearing the burden of sight.

Haydn set this all up with two major-third catabases: an opening previous recitative ("Che fulmine improvviso!") in which Tobias tells of his father's resistance, which descends from an implicit B minor to G minor, and then the duet (noted for its scoring with English horns) in E♭ major. The moment is well known, but the absolute synchrony between mother and son is evident, not only in their parallel sixths, but also in the sudden turn to B♭ minor at the end of the opening modulation to the dominant (m. 94) for "impossibile a soffrir." Given the affect, it is striking that Tobias has the only strikingly florid moment in the duet (mm. 37–42), again suggesting that he feels this failure even more deeply than does his mother.[45]

Boccherini's text thus has its dark sides, and that raises the issue of the work's dramatic register. The first major problem in family relations is the miscommunication between father and son. Tobias first introduces Sara to his mother (ll. 222ff), not his father; Raffaello presents Sara to her future father-in-law; according to the stage directions in the 1775 Viennese libretto, Tobias only presses his father's hand (l. 246), and the moment of encounter features a full onstage tutti which undercuts specific father-son relationships. Without any precedent in the repertory, Tobit's refusal to let himself be healed at first (ll. 460ff), and his lengthy rejection of the advice of his wife, his son, and Raffaello, all combine to render this father a remarkably distant figure until the final *lieto fine*. This may have to do with the musical personality of the cast, discussed presently.

In that sense, the slightly ironic moments just mentioned, and the switches in dramatic tone, could suggest that this work functions on a plane one step closer to *opera semiseria* than oratorios were wont to do; the Return is accomplished by the end of Part I, but the other major issue is that of Tobit's resistance to the cure, and Sara's agency in having him take the blinds off slowly so as to get used to light, something not found in the Biblical account. The new moment is that of Sara's care with the blindfolds:

SARA: All'afflitto Tobil, che pria l'ardente
fuoco sofferto avria del dì lucente
per cenno d'Azaria
d'un nero vello ricomersi il volto
ed a miei prieghi
i lumi aprì. Sofferse
la tenebrosa luce
che traspirar potea del denso drappo
io le bende alternai più rade ognora,
e più copia di lume ognor sofferse . . .

At Azaria's bidding, I covered the face of the suffering Tobit with a black veil, he who had suffered the burning flames of daylight, and he opened his eyes at my pleas. He put up with the darkish light coming through the dense veil; I changed the blindfolds several times, and each time he tolerated more light . . .

This accompanied recitative traverses G, F, and even the E♭ of the preceding duet before bursting (m. 34) into a bright C major with trumpets and horns as Tobit recognizes Anna. Sara's work had been prepared by two arias, one in each part, praising her bridegroom's family and then Azaria, respectively, and one could argue that it is this kind of daughterhood that enabled her to be the conduit of Azaria's semi-miracle. Musically her place had already been cemented inside the family, and the restoral of sight sets up simply the final chorus of praise and Azaria/Raphael's return to Heaven without further family history.

Sight, Sound, and Pain

Overall, Boccherini's libretto shifts the story's emphasis to its post-return part, with another set of difficulties provided by Tobit in Part II, just as Anna had posed different problems in Part I. Although the text, with these

Tobit's initial rejection of the fish-gall cure (ll. 429ff) goes against Tobit 11:14, and is quite biting: "Più sopportar non posso / l'aspro dolor, che mi trapassa / penetrando pungente / dalle pupille al cor quell sugo amaro" [I can no longer stand the harsh pain that fills me as that bitter liquid penetrates from my eyes to my heart]. Oddly, this passage reverses the tears of penance that are supposed to flow from the heart to the eye glands. Raffaello supports Tobias in his three efforts, but the father continues to refuse the gall in an exit aria, turning constancy against the cure (ll. 480ff): "Invan lo chiedi, amico, / Invan lo speri, o figlio. / Io pria d'aprir il ciglio / costante morirò" [You ask in vain, o friend (= Azaria); in vain you hope, my son; before opening my eyelids I will die with constancy], and this leads into the scene of despair between Anna and Tobias quoted above. Continuing to use his slightly *semiseria* verbal register, Boccherini also parallels Anna's sin of Part I (despair at the lack of Divine help) with her consort's fault (obstinacy in refusing help).

There are other aspects to this *poco adagio* in A major, most notably an inserted phrase (mm. 102–6) addressing Tobias before returning to the main salutation of Azaria. This follows a long, muted section around F# and C# to express Tobit's visual shadows. Haydn's choice of repetitive address here suggests just the slightest added emphasis on his son as opposed to the (unknown) Angel, and the priority of family even in what seems to be equal address to the Divine and the human.

Sara's agency tends to balance the dramatic weight of the characters, finally taking on a decisive role beyond simply that of a grateful daughter-in-law, something unknown in the repertory up to this point. Starting with her ironic entrance cited above, and after her gentle persuasion of her new father-in-law to remove the blinds slowly, her account of the final Healing—and the story's crux, even more than the triumph over the demon and the marriage—is the most detailed description of the process in the repertory. Indeed, the happy marriage of Sara and Tobias represents a marked contrast to the conjugal squabbles of the older couple. As an outsider, the former is the only character to recognize that Anna, for all her problems, speaks in angelic parlance (Sara's Part II aria "Non parmi essere fra gl'uomini / della tribù di Neftali, / mi sembra esser fra gl'angeli / della magion del Ciel" [I do not feel that I am among the people of Nephthali's tribe, but rather among the angels of Heaven's habitation]).

Doctor Barth's discoveries meant new hope for the blind in Joseph II's Vienna. Anna even seems to allude to Barth's discoveries and appointment in ll. 160–64, reacting to the Angel's prophecy of her husband's eventually regaining his sight: "Il figlio mio del cieco padre / monderà le pupille! / L'opra tentata in van dale più dotte / mediche mani ei compirà?" [My son will cure the eyes of his blind father! Will he carry out that operation attempted in vain by the most skilled medical hands?].

The previous and future roles of the 1775 cast also give some sense of their musical presence in the oratorio.[46] Magdalene Spengler-Fribert, the Raphael, was of course the major singer in the Esterházy establishment at this moment, having done Vespina in *L'infedeltà delusa* (summer 1773) and moving onward to Rezia in *L'incontro improvviso* (August 1775). Tobit was the buffo bass Christian Specht, and some of the role's short-windedness may be due to this casting.[47] Tobias was Haydn's collaborator Carl Friberth, famed for his tenor roles, and Sara was sung by Barbara Teuber-Dichtler, a difficult part reflecting her roles in the operas of 1773 and 1775. The most mysterious career was that of Magdalene's sister Margarete Spengler, the Anna whose part was notoriously difficult in its leaps, runs, and trills, and she seems to have been brought in for the Vienna performance only, and not to have formed part of the regular ensemble. However, her famed first aria, "Sudò il guerriero," would have opened the piece with someone not a member of the Esterházy ensemble, and casts some doubt on the view of the piece as pure noble advertisement.

The immediate reception of Boccherini/Haydn's piece also testifies to the universality of its family models. In 1777, it was performed by a Berlin society of amateurs; in 1783 in Rome, and in 1784 both in the Lisbon royal palace for the name day of Dom José (1761–88), Prince of Portugal and heir to a throne that he would never inherit, as well as in the ducal Philharmonic Academy in Modena (a city with close Habsburg connections by this point). Still, the piece worked for Viennese patricians, Protestant concertgoers, the Roman oratorio audience, and the Portuguese royals, all of whom would have had different ideas of Christian family norms — a testimony to its cultural range.

Overall, the stories of Ruth and Tobit played a far larger role in the Settecento's imaginary than before. Like the other stories examined thus far, albeit in a happier mode, they proved themselves capable of small but important shifts in narrative emphasis and character development. Even these *lieto fine* plots show some kind of uneasy coexistence, and in the case of several Tobit stories, an audible level of spousal conflict between the older couple. The issues move from the miraculous (magic fish, supernatural healing) toward the familial. Boccherini left it to Sara, coming from outside, to heal the communicative gap between her in-laws. Past the oratorio's ending, Tobit 14:5 would note that she would eventually have seven sons with Tobias, and this returns us to issues of passionate maternity.

Chapter Seven

Grieving Spouses, Fierce Motherhood

Una volta mi chiedevi che cosa avevo e non ti rispondevo.
Ma è divenuto molto difficile
parlare delle ultime cose, madre mia.

—Franco Fortini, "In memoria I"

TOPIC: Passion dialogues based on the Song of Songs (Canticle of Canticles)
CHARACTERS: the female and male Spouses of the Canticle
BIBLICAL SOURCE: Song of Songs, *passim*, but esp. the opening of chapter 3
NARRATIVE: In these pieces, the female Spouse (*Sponsa*) of the Song of
Songs is taken as the individual soul, seeking the wounded (or dead)
CHRIST AT NIGHT IN THE CITY.
WORKS DISCUSSED AT LENGTH IN THIS CHAPTER: G. Gigli, *La sposa
de' cantici*; Furlanetto, *La sposa de' sacri cantici*
PLACES: Siena, Venice

TOPIC: the Mother of Seven Jewish Sons [Maccabees]
CHARACTERS: the Mother of Seven Sons, Antiochus, various Sons
BIBLICAL SOURCE: 2 Maccabees 7
NARRATIVE: Antiochus IV, Emperor of the region ca. 160 BCE, orders
all Jews to eat pork, which they are not allowed to do by Mosaic Law.
He attempts to force the seven sons of a mother to do so, but they each
resist, and each is put to death. The mother gives them encouraging
words for their struggle, and Antiochus cannot convince her even when
her youngest is threatened. Both she and the boy are martyred.
WORKS DISCUSSED AT LENGTH IN THIS CHAPTER: G. Gigli, *La madre
de' Maccabei*; Bicilli, *Li Maccabei*; Stampiglia, *Il martirio de' Machabei*;

Pariati, *La donna forte nella madre de' sette Maccabei*; G. Barbieri, *La madre dei Maccabei*; Sacchini, *Mater machabaeorum*

PLACES: Siena, Vienna, Rome, Venice

In contrast to the previous chapter, an entirely different trope of marriage between spouses as an enactment of individual Passion meditation brought one exegetical tradition of the Song of Songs into the oratorio repertory. Similarly, the state of widowhood—one of the most typical situations for early modern women of all social classes—seems largely absent from the corpus, except in a particular case of female heroism taken from the Old Testament. The first of these took a variant of the "tropological" (Sponsa = individual soul) threads in Song exegesis to meditate on the wounded Christ. The second one used a passage in a chapter from the Second Book of Maccabees on a mother and her seven sons who refused to eat pork as demanded by the ruler Antiochus in homage to the pagan gods, and who were thus martyred.

These two themes are unified epiphenomenally by both their original milieux and author: on one hand, the links between central Italy and the Viennese court, and on the other, Girolamo Gigli's role as dramatic innovator around 1700.[1] Although the two topics began in the late Seicento, their medium-term survival into the new century—albeit with notable changes—also sheds light on the devotional representation of these stories. Dramatically, both function at tragic levels even if they lack the trappings of classical tragedy.

Loss, Anxiety, and Canticles

The use of the Song of Songs in our texts was very much in an individual vein as articulated by the two Spouses. One other point of differentiation is helpful: the Canticle was sometimes used in a Marian—and not personal—sense for oratorios, in accordance with the most widely spread allegorical reading of the Seicento. For instance, Alessandro Scarlatti's *La sposa de' cantici** (for Naples; the score is now in US-STsu after previously being in the archive of the Cappella Reale) uses the "Veni, coronaberis" Biblical verse as a link to the feast of Assumption BVM.[2]

The text was also related to nuns' vesting ceremonies, in one case under the title of *La Sulamitide* ("The Sulamite," i.e., Solomon's actual spouse in the Canticle), found occasionally throughout the Settecento. The sensuousness inherent in this latter subject generated more than the usual number of imprimaturs in the works based on it, notably G. M. Ercolani's popular play (Rome, 1732). However, in 1755 Stefano Serrarrio (1722–90) turned the idea of the Canticle's Sulamite into an oratorio for the vesting of Cistercian nuns in Atri (music by Giuseppe Ventura), also with an imprimatur (and lengthy Biblical citations in the footnotes to avoid the suspicion of sensuality). Evidently the concupiscence of Solomon's love created serious problems for early modern clerics.

Obviously, the tropological interpretation of the Song had an ancient tradition. Still, the specific linking of the book's dialogic language specifically and exclusively to Passion meditation in oratorios seems to have been the work of two librettists in Vienna and Siena: Donato Cupeda and Gigli. The case of the 1697 Lucca oratorio mentioned in chapter 1 gives a sense of the civic use of the canticle as Christ's personal manifestation to the Sienese *polis*; its text might well have been known to both Cupeda and Gigli (the latter himself from the city).

As has been noted, there was a devotional background to this identification of the *Sponsa*, manifest in Cupeda's *Il fascietto di mirra*, a *sepolcro* for Holy Week 1701 in Vienna (M. A. Ziani's music is lost). Gigli's dedication to his 1702 Passiontide oratorio for Siena, *La sposa de' cantici*, immediately showed his differences with Cupeda's approach, while making gestures to tradition:

> The Sponsa of the Song of Songs is . . . the soul beloved by God and the lover of God . . . it finds its pleasure on the mountain of myrrh and makes its bed on the thorns of Calvary. . . . You know that all the anxieties of the Divine [female] Lover of the Canticles were only the living and explicit symbol of the loving worries of the soul for its ineffable union with Jesus Christ, the Divine Word made Human. It wished for this union, asking to be kissed with His Divine kiss.[3]

For all that Gigli's text might seem to be an enactment of any given soul's quest—and the libretto's dedication to the Medici magistrate and administrator ("auditore generale") for Siena, Aurelio Sozzafanti (or Sozzifanti; 1662–1721), highlights both the secular and the political implications of the allegory—the circumstances of its 1702 premiere point indirectly to more specific meanings. For the piece was first heard in the relatively small church of S. Caterina del Paradiso, the *chiesa esteriore* for a monastery of

Grieving Spouses, Fierce Motherhood • 173

not terribly musical Dominican nuns, which was an intimate space. Probably it was performed by outside musicians, possibly with a score (now lost) by Gigli's sometime musical collaborator Giuseppe Fabbrini, who also had written the music for *La madre de' Maccabei* some fourteen years earlier.[4]

The decoration of S. Caterina portrayed its patroness saint (i.e., Catherine of Siena) in two altarpieces, the main one by Francesco Rustici (1625) depicting a Pietà with the saint as intercessor for the faithful; and a slightly later (1649–51) canvas on her Mystic Marriage, done by Raffaello Vanni for a side chapel. Gigli was also active in promoting the saint's neglected writings and her cult in the city, as Jane Tylus has shown, and the text and its first performance might suggest Caterina, who often referred to herself as Christ's bride. A later revival of Gigli's piece in a Dominican church in Padua in 1706 made the reference to Caterina as the Sponsa explicit in its title.[5] The Esterházy establishment in Eisenstadt was impressed enough by the theme of myrrh/Canticle/Passion to commission the first German-language oratorio for their own Holy Week Tomb in the town's Bergkirche, G. J. Werner's 1729 *Fasciculus Myrrhae Dilectus oder das geliebte Myrrhen-Büschlein**.[6]

However, given the absence of the Song in the saint's own writings — a point first made by Bernard McGinn — and the relatively few references to the Biblical text in Gigli's own 1707 edition of her works, it seems clear that the poet was not using his oratorio libretto simply to ventriloquize her in the context of the Dominicans' public devotion.[7] For all that the context might have pointed to Caterina, this seems to place Gigli's Sposa as a clearly early modern figure, and the "familial" nature of her relationship is aimed only at her Sposo.

Gigli's Part I opens at night with the Sposa and her Compagna (the latter standing in for the canticle's chorus of young women), as both wait for the Sposo to arrive.[8] The Sposa's first aria alludes, without specific citation, to Canticle 2:10b (i.e., the Sponsus calling his beloved "my dove"), while the Compagna notes His nocturnal wanderings, a trope for the "absent Christ" in John of the Cross's terms of spiritual life. The Compagna's first aria has another implicit reference, this time to Matthew 25:1–13 (the Wise and Foolish Virgins, whose Gospel placement in Catholicism came just before Palm Sunday). Her following recitative lines explicitly invoke, for the first time, the Song: here the Sponsa's "Ego dormio et cor meum vigilat" (5:2a).

Gigli changed the speaker of Song verses early in the process, a trait found in the entire text. Moving in and out of wakefulness, the Sposa both recalls the beauty of the Sposo (implicitly referring to Canticle 5:10ff) and voices her worries at His absence, using Christ's words at His Capture ("the power of the shadows"; Lk 22:53). Again appropriating the Sposa's words of searching the city and then of seeking Him (3:2–4, followed by 1:6, the latter an aria here), the Compagna offers to find Him. Similarly, the Sposa takes over the questions originally spoken by the Biblical chorus (5:9), and the Compagna's next aria is generated by the Sponsus's praise of his Beloved (4:2).

In contrast, other outside quotes—this time from Ezekiel (22:27) and Lamentations (3:57) on voracious wolves hunting the Lamb—reignite the Sposa's worries, which not even her Compagna's recall of Canticle 2:1 (on the Sposa's beauty) can extinguish. Indeed, the Sposa's next aria is generated by two citations from Job, and the Compagna then uses Canticle 5:7 to predict her suffering during her nocturnal search for her Spouse. This continues with the Compagna's mixture of verses originally enunciated by the Sponsus ("Hortus conclusus"; 4:12; then "sicut turris David"; 4:4) and the Sponsa ("Veni, auster"; 4:16) to reassure the Sposa of her own worth, finishing with another use of the Sposa's phrase on her Beloved ("oculi eius sicut columbae"; 5:12). This ends the Biblical citations in Part I, and the Sposa concludes with two arias, the second a sleep piece, as the two characters finally drowse, ending with somnolent instrumental music.

That Part II opens with the first appearance of the Sposo and the use of Canticle 5:2b ("Aperi mihi, soror mea sposa" [Open up to me, my sister, my spouse]) suggests that Part I had been a long meditative interpolation between the two sub-verses of 5:2, as again the oratorio's ongoing trajectory changes its overall meaning. The Sposa hears His banging at the door (the Compagna remains asleep for the rest of the piece; i.e., this is a soul's personal encounter with the Sponsus), but she recognizes neither her Beloved nor even His words. This becomes a recitative *dialogo dei sordi*, in which the Sposo itemizes His Wounds, with even His voice changed by His experience on the Cross. The Canticle's 'dew in His hair" (5:2b, another reference to the opening of the entire libretto) has been frozen into the icicles of His Crown of Thorns, as the handsome Sponsus of the canticle becomes the Man of Sorrows.

Still unable to grasp the horror of the Passion, the Sposa returns to book order by citing 5:3 ("Expoliavi me tunica mea"), and only when the Sposo shows His Blood and Wounds does she realize what has happened and with Whom she is speaking. The Sposo's next two arias invite her to enter His Wounds (a recall of pseudo-Augustine) and to realize His love ("Mira il fianco, mira il petto" and "Amor fù quello, amor"), followed by new citations which turn away from the Song and to Job, Jeremiah, and Isaiah (53:2).[9]

Just when it seems that the libretto's lexical field has abandoned the Canticle, Gigli ends his text in recitative with a referential surprise: the joyous spousal "drunkenness" of 5:1b ("et inebriamini, carissimi")—that is, before the citation of 5:2 that had begun the piece's Part I—is taken as signifying the fluids of tears and of Christ's Blood, with a further note of Isaiah 16:9 ("inebriabo de lacrima mea" [I shall become drunk on my own tears]). The final couplet (*Sposo:* "Poi 'l tuo cuor la Tomba sia / del mio cuore [*Sposa:*] e'l tuo la mia" [Let your heart be the Tomb of Mine—and mine Yours]) is just detailed enough to suggest a deictic reference to a real Tomb of Christ constructed for Passiontide in the church of the *Paradiso*.[10]

Whoever the original composer, the piece had reprises in Siena and Perugia in 1704 and was set for Urbino, first by Giuseppe Aldrovandini for a local sanctoral feast in 1705, and then by Pietro Scarlatti in 1706 (with some textual cuts) for the "Oratorio della Grotta" underneath the cathedral, both with dedications to the local legate Cardinal Sebastiano Tanara. Alas, none of these scores survive. The lithic context of this last performance would have recalled the Canticle's "in foraminibus petrae" as symbolic of Christ's Wounds; together with the Mother of the Maccabees libretto discussed presently, it also projected Gigli's works in this temporarily important center under Tanara, a prelate with long and sympathetic experiences as *nunzio* at the Viennese court, including presumably its oratorio repertory. For all that Gigli's text circulated widely at first, it had longer-term effects, serving as a silent reference (but not a complete model) for a later libretto first done for the Venetian Oratorians in 1753 and then set to music by Bonaventura Furlanetto* for the same institution, probably in 1767.

This mid-Settecento reworking of a text in a marital vein deserves some explication.[11] Possibly to differentiate it from the earlier libretto, the 1753 Venetian piece adds a word to its title (*La sposa de' sacri cantici*). Although it was also meant for Passion meditation, its means differ from Gigli's. Like the earlier text, the 1753 oratorio begins at night, with a dialogue of the Sposa and her Compagna (here the Sposo is called the "Diletto," in a further differentiation from Gigli), and its debt to the 1702 piece is evident in the allusion to "Ego dormio, et cor meum vigilat" at its opening ("Che, sebbene dormo, ho sempre . . ."). Still, there are no explicit marginal citations to the

Song in the 1753 libretto, and the Diletto breaks in at an early stage of Part I with a self-referential aria to the Man of Sorrows ("Con le mie pene").

The 1753 text continues its shadowing of its silent 1702 model with a worried Sposa, deaf to the knocking, who resolves to seek her Beloved. Only her Diletto's use of the key Lamentations verse addressed to the world at large ("O vos omnes, qui transitis per viam"; Lamentations 1:12a) brings her to the recognition of His presence. He turns the Sposa's Song phrase ("Veni, dilecte mi") back to her ("Vieni, diletta mia"). The Diletto self-identifies as the Shepherd betrayed by His vassals, in response to the Compagna's silent reuse of another phrase from pseudo-Augustine's *Meditationes* ("Quid commisisti, dulcissime puer?" = "Che agistasti"), which rounds off Part I with a closing duet.

Since Gigli's Part II had opened with the banging Sposo and a long scene of incomprehension, the 1753 text's explicit iteration at this point of Christ's sufferings, led by the Diletto himself with reactions from the Sposa and the Compagna, stands in sharp contrast. As the piece is still nocturnal, the description of the Agony in the Garden is quite lengthy (and the frequent lexical use of "interno lume" both reinforces the text's omnipresent subjectivity and might even recall the emphasis on internal illumination that had gotten the Oratorian Cardinal Petrucci into such trouble three generations earlier). In a third-person, non-eyewitness narrative style, the Sposa and Compagna run quickly through the night's events: the Apostles' flight with the Trial and the Mocking, before the Diletto's longer description of the Via Crucis.

In the 1753 work, as the Diletto's aria manifests His desire for his Sposa to internalize the Cross ("No, mia Sposa, in te sol bramo / la mia Croce al vivo impressa" [No, my Spouse, I want only my Cross imprinted alive in you]), He is answered by her recitative "Se a Te sol basta / mirar la Croce Tua dentro il mio petto / nel sen piccol fascetto / di mirra mi sarai" [If it is enough for You to see Your Cross inside my heart, then You will be a small myrrh branch in my breast]. This finally reintroduces the Canticle, its myrrh bundle, and Cupeda and dell'Assunta's original devotional ideas.

Part II's third scene of visualization (after the Agony and the Via Crucis) then describes the Three Hours on the Cross, Mary on Calvary, and Christ's Seven Last Words, at the end of which the Sposa—not Mary, traditionally the fainting figure—swoons in tandem with the Eclipse and Earthquake at Christ's Death.[12] This highly specific meditative path suggests either a sermon fashioned around these three moments, or some image in the church of the Fava (S. Maria della Consolazione), or both. Its replacement of Mary's fainting by that of the individual soul points at a highly tropological understanding of Passion meditation. At the same time, in its lack of explicit Song citations (not to mention any underpinning by standard exegesis, traditional or eighteenth-century), its emphasis on the Christian self, and its arias generated by generic natural phenomena and not by any Scriptural reference, it seems less Metastasian than its technical debts to the Viennese repertory (line enjambments, third-person narration) might suggest. This text seems to be set at a lower cultural level and in a more sentimental register than the works from a generation before.

Overall, the character triangulation of (1) the model Christian wife, (2) the Sposa, and (3) the meditative, ungendered Christian soul works unevenly across these texts. Gigli's solution was to accentuate the Sposa's anxieties — not her desire for her Sposo — enough to dominate the entire libretto. Perhaps to avoid this, and to maintain greater equilibrium in Passion meditation, the 1753 piece took a more normative path. If its first version dates to Lent 1753, it would have sounded just after (perhaps even on) the dedication of the Oratorians' reconstructed Fava on 1 April, with its new organ and cantoria on the east wall behind the main altar, and the original *oratorio* from 1496 (taken over by the order in 1662) included inside the apse.

Furlanetto's musical setting exists in two copies (I-Bc and I-CHc), and probably was done originally for the 1767 Venetian revival. Later Oratorian performances of the 1753 text — Rome 1763, Bologna 1768, or Venice again in 1773 — did not mention a feast, but their Verona reprise in 1777 of Furlanetto's score noted Pentecost Monday, a day totally without Passion or Song resonances, while the 1781 non-Oratorian performance in Vercelli did indeed refer to Passiontide performance.

Given his more orthodox libretto, Furlanetto's musical choices were not entirely predictable. The opening aria sequence (Sposa, Compagna, Diletto) unfolds symmetrically around flat-pitch areas (E♭ – d – B♭), with a directly representational (high-tessitura) aria for the Diletto, as He notes how even the heights of Calvary had pity on His sufferings (noted above, "Con le mie pene in fronte . . . / mi vidde il colle il monte" [With My wounds on My face . . . the hill and mountain saw Me]). Furlanetto's writing for the Sposa is florid but not as high at first, leaving the latter range to the Diletto. Part I ends with a duet, and Part II begins with her aria, both focusing on her pain over that of her Beloved, as one performance (preserved in the Bologna copy of the score) stitched out the B section of the Diletto's showpiece aria "Non di fiume." The only minor-key aria in Part II is the final one, sung by the Sposa to her Diletto on the Cross, "Al grande affanno." By the time of the Sposa's aria prophesying the Last Judgment, "Tempo verrà," a markedly penitential moment, Furlanetto has brought her tessitura higher. In some ways, the tonal and textural choices show why the Oratorians would have wanted a newer, more modern and differentiated setting for their earlier text, pointing to the same kind of microshift in musical piety going into the last third of the Settecento that has been seen above.

However, the theme of the Song/Passion then moved to the Latin *ospedali* repertory, with a short version *a* 2 by Galuppi for the Incurabili (1770) and then Ferdinando Bertoni's thrice-repeated, longer piece *a* 4 for the Mendicanti on their major feast day of St. Mary Magdalene (1777, 1781, 1784, 1787). Both identified the Sposa and her companions with the young(ish) women singers in the institutions. Again here, their timbre literally enacted the voices of the Canticle. A final piece in Italian for the patronal feast of San Severino [Marche] on 8 January 1797, as the French Army was on the verge of entering, was held in the city's theater; it featured the Sulamite and her Companion in a pastoral setting along with Solomon.[13] Its recitatives draw freely from the Canticle, and, after separation/absence, it ends with the reunion of the two lovers. Again here, as in Lucca a century earlier, the Sposa must have symbolized the *civitas*, one which was about to be put out of business by the looming French Republic.

Mothering for Martyrdom

As noted above, Gigli's other successful libretto, this time on a historical book of the Old Testament, had both Viennese and Sienese antecedents. Even in early modern Catholicism, the story of the Mother of Seven Sons from 2 (and 4) Maccabees—technically not a member of the Maccabee family, although popularly identified as such—was rare in exegetical and devotional literature. Ironically, it had a wider projection via music, beginning in the 1660s but widening around 1700. Still, the Mother and children had their own *commemoratio* (1 August) in the post-Tridentine liturgical calendar, the only Old Testament figures represented therein, and their supposed relics were preserved in Cologne (the "discovery" of related objects in S. Pietro in Vincoli was an Ottocento development).[14] As noted above (chapter 1), the main Biblical source was 2 Maccabees, although the non-

Grieving Spouses, Fierce Motherhood • 179

canonical 4 Maccabees left its traces in more subtle ways in a few libretti.[15] In addition, several texts draw on Flavius Josephus's *Jewish Antiquities* and/ or the *Sepher Yosippon* (also thought at the time to be by Josephus, although in reality a much later compilation).[16]

Since, compared to other family situations addressed here, the Maccabees' story was somewhat marginal to Biblical exegesis, there was paradoxically a greater amount of freedom in treating the details.[17] The account starts (7:1–19) with the fate of the first six brothers who refuse Antiochus's demand for them to eat pork (and to follow pagan law), each of whom is given very short refusals which lead to execution. It then turns (7:20–21) to a third-person encomium of the Mother, which prepares her direct and retrospective address of fortitude to all the sons in 7:22–23. Next, Antiochus re-enters in 7:24–26, attempting to sway the only Hebrews left: first the last son, and then the Mother, who promises to "talk" to her child. Her second direct intervention (7:27–29; noted as being in Hebrew) urges her youngest to follow his brothers' example. The longest speech of the chapter (7:30–38) is that of this last son, and the account of Antiochus's final wrath by martyring the boy (7:38–41) mentions the Mother's execution only in passing at the end, a real problem for anyone writing a text named after her.[18]

The story could also be used as a model for religious orders. In a Jesuit vein, Oliva's in-house sermons for Jesuit foundations had compared the Mother's strictness with her children as analogous to the order's severity with its members.[19] Suitably enough, the Jesuits in Terni put on an oratorio using the story in order to celebrate the 1726–27 canonizations of their saints who had died young, Luigi Gonzaga and Stanislaus Kostka, in the same time and place that the Carmelites had employed the Ishmael story to commemorate John of the Cross (chapter 1).[20]

Although the individual speeches given to all seven Sons, plus the long reflections on the Mother's fortitude, found in the much longer version in 4 Maccabees might suggest this text's use in the libretti, still the latter's dubious status seems to have kept it out of formal footnoting procedures.[21] As the first librettist to tackle the whole story, Gigli had several issues for his Sienese *La madre de' Maccabei*, which premiered in 1688: (1) what to do with the first six brothers; (2) how to place the first encomium of obeying Jewish law; (3) how to envoice Antiochus; and (4) how to deal with the Mother's two relatively short Biblical statements, especially compared to the last son's peroration (as noted, this comes in 2 Maccabees after the Mother's final words).

Irony and Pedagogy

In a wider sense, librettists' problems consisted of balancing the last son's resistance with that of his mother, and the treatment of the mother-son relationship. Gigli produced his version to be performed at Siena's Jesuit-run Collegio Tolomei on Passion Saturday (like all other oratorios done there), a year without evident opera performances public or private in the Tuscan city. As noted, his text would enjoy relative popularity for a generation.[22]

Gigli's dedication to his contemporary, the little-known Count Augusto Chigi (1662–1744), largely resident in Rome, might have had its origin in their mutual ties to the Tolomei, and in the idea of the Collegio's students as model Christian "warriors." But it might also be a hidden tribute to Augusto's own mother, Maria Virginia Borghese, a feature suggested by its beginning, as its Madre disdains the offstage tyrant with an aria telling Antioco to mourn at the failure of his attempts to break the children, just as she mourns the upcoming deaths of her sons ("Piangi, barbaro rè, / che piango anch'io" [Weep, barbarous king, as I myself weep]; as noted above, this would be the model for the opening of Scarlatti's Cain/Abel oratorio later).

Gigli's Biblical reworkings in *La sposa* fourteen years later had been anticipated here. In the librettist's typically ironic way, the Maccabees libretto continues with her Figliuolo's two arias of semi-reproach, first for her weeping, then for his own physically smallest (as her youngest) heart, with less blood to be spilled than that of his siblings in his martyrdom. Her recitative response to him turns to musical metaphor, as she tells him of his future "conducting" the hymns "sung" by his older brothers' wounds, presumably in a heavenly choir, a clear if uncited reference to 4 Maccabees 14:3–8. Antioco bursts onstage into a trio with the two, set out typographically so as to make sense both vertically (i.e., for each character) and horizontally (as dialogic response). The Madre exits temporarily with a moralizing aria on how evil brings its own revenge, leaving a Consigliere who questions Antioco as to the wisdom of combating those armed only with *pietas* and beauty, and noting that their wounds would drip with *costanza*.

This section moves to a close-knit duet for the Madre and her Figliuolo on their desire for death, and its complete syntactical parallels highlight their union. An oddly self-doubting Antioco returns to close the part with the Consigliere, who suggests the idea of bribing the child to induce compliance (this is a paraphrase of 7:24 split between the parts). Possibly there was no sermon, as Antioco begins Part II with a direct flattering of the child, both for his beauty and for a possible golden future.[23] The youngest Son's refusal to recant generates a comment by the Consigliere on how moral character is formed by education, a clear reference to the Tolomei itself, with its hundred-odd pupils at this point. This is immediately followed by the Madre detailing how her laws were instilled via lactation (a hint at 7:27). She simply talks over Antioco's blandishments to her son, and the mention of gold leads to an ironic misunderstanding typical also of Gigli's opera libretti (e.g., *La fede ne' tradimenti*), during which she mistakes her Figliuolo's praise of the metal in the sword—soon to kill him—as being instead his apostate surrender to Antioco's offer of treasures and reproaches him accordingly.

Gigli then uses the last possible character combination in a dialogue between her and the Consigliere, and her son's following aria both expresses his wish to shed his blood and sets up Antioco's final rage. The Consigliere's advice to the tyrant for pardon falls unheard, and this sets up a Mother-Son duet indexing both his forthcoming blood and her milk; the echoes of the Double Intercession of Christ and Mary would have been audible. The child begins to die onstage as he calls on Antioco to drink his blood, and the tyrant, ordering the Madre's death, finds himself incapable of remaining to witness this, and flees the stage in a remarkable collapse. Finally the two martyrs die together, as the Madre closes with an aria marking her final repose on the bloody chest of her seventh Son.

For the present purposes, the most striking aspect of this libretto is Gigli's intertwining of Mother and Son, their communication also including some misunderstandings and irony, as noted above. Their combined resistance also causes, in complete contradiction to both 2 Maccabees and the Patristic literature, Antioco's antiheroic departure. Some of the vocabulary, along with the Passion Saturday performance context, points to Marian/Christological devotion, but other aspects index maternal piety. The text's longevity seems well deserved; despite its departures from the canonical sources, its 1719 performance in Jesi received the ultimate accolade to orthodoxy, as the local Dominicans chose it to be set (by the cellist Angelo Massarotti) for their feast of the medieval inquisitor St. Peter Martyr. Gigli's version was performed with Massarotti's music as late as 1728 for the seminary/college in Montefiascone, part of an oratorio tradition there dating back to 1701.[24]

Outside music, though, Gigli was not the first to highlight the Mother.

The long three-volume set of "moral lessons" on the Book of Jonah by the Tuscan Dominican Angelo Paciuchelli (Florence, 1646–50, with Italian reprints into the next century and even a Latin translation issued in Munich and Antwerp) came to the story in its "Lezione 42," dealing with Jonah 2:11 ("And the Lord spoke to the fish: and it vomited Jonah out on the dry land") as a trope for personal resurrection. Here, Paciuchelli (1594–1660) used the verse to explain how the hope for eternal life (like the prophet's salvation) had fortified martyrs and other Christians in the face of impending death, and then turned to the case of the Mother before even citing her sons. As a reproach of maternal tears in the face of death, he exhorted his readers: "That great, holy, and courageous Mother of the Maccabees did not do that [kind of weeping] . . . the memory of [Christ's] Resurrection arms and fortifies us for victories and triumphs. This consoled, strengthened, and gave an invincible spirit to those holy Maccabees."[25]

Paciuchelli also found contemporary parallels from far away, as he cited Francisco de Mendoza's account of a Japanese Christian mother ("Tecla") who had encouraged her several sons (presumably in the 1597 or 1626 waves of persecution) to martyrdom; the Dominican linked her example to that of the Mother. Even if the actual opportunities for Catholic women to become martyrs after 1650 were even more limited than those for men, still this exemplum brought the Old Testament story into intercontinental reality.[26] The story's interpretation had to do with Christian motherhood in the face of adversity, and in the character's willingness to stare down death.

Habsburg Maternity

For all that librettists praised the Mother's virtues, the question of whether, in such texts, women were a targeted part of oratorios' audiences seems most clear in the case of the Habsburgs, less so in Italian urban centers. Each of the cases here presents different kinds of possible female audiences for the story. As had been the case since early Christianity, there was also something of a Marian tinge.[27] Indeed, the 1688 Siena premiere of Gigli's Maccabees piece would have taken place the day after the Feast of the Seven Sorrows, although this would not be extended to the entire Western Church until 1727. This, in addition to the overall "strong woman" trope of some oratorios, rendered the treatments more widely usable.[28]

Like the "tropological Sponsa" just discussed, the representation of this topos seems to have begun in the Viennese *sepolcri* repertory, in this case as early as the 1660s. In scene 5 of a libretto written by Francesco Sbarra for the Dowager Empress Eleonora Gonzaga to be performed on Holy Thursday 1665, the "Madre de' Maccabei" appears along with Mary Magdalen, as the piece's plot—that of Christ's Harrowing of Hell—gives voice to the souls in Limbo, first St. John the Baptist, then Abel and Abraham, and then the two women.

Sbarra could have come up with this moment in *Il Limbo disserrato* ("Limbo Unlocked") as a tribute to Eleonora, possibly using the two female Biblical characters to represent both the "strong" and the "penitent" aspects of his employer's persona.[29] Sbarra's Mother addresses the Magdalen in an opening solo aria: "Bella afflitta, asciuga il ciglio, / Che il gran figlio / De l'eterno alto Monarca, / Da quell'arca, / Se ben morto, / Si vedra' presto risorto" [Beautiful, sorrowful woman, dry your tears, because the great Son of the eternal high King, even if He died, will soon rise from that Tomb (with a deictic gesture to an onstage constructed tomb)]. In a standard gesture taken from the tradition of sacred plays, the Magdalen asks her interlocutor's identity, and her response is: "Sono de' Machabei / La Madre celebrata, / . . . Hor Iddio si compiace, / Ch'io ritornando in vita / Possa ammirar' tra voi / L'Unigenito suo morto per noi" [I am the famed Mother of the Maccabees . . . now God has been pleased to let me, returning to life, admire His only-begotten Son who died for us]. After further reflections on the Harrowing of Hell, the Magdalen concludes the scene with a solo aria in the same meter (*ottonari e quadrisillabi*), cementing the identification of the two. Most strikingly, the Mother's sons do not appear, possibly due to the fact that two children of Eleonora had died as infants.

Of course, Sbarra had probably taken his idea from Augustine's *Sermon 301*, a Patristic text which began with praise of the Mother and went on to make links first to the Capture of Christ and then to personal penance. This Augustinian understanding of the passage seems to undergird the later Viennese versions, which went on until 1737; there may also be references to a sermon of Gregory of Nazianzus on her. After her cameo appearance in 1665, the Mother figured in a Lenten oratorio performed for Eleonora in 1686, *Li Maccabei*, which is the same as Giovanni Bicilli's *Oratorio de' Maccabei** with a score preserved in Naples (I-Nf).[30] The overall Lenten lineup that year was similar to previous years: repeats of Leopold I's own three oratorios, followed by a piece by Bicilli, suggesting that the singers were to put their energies into the newly imported Roman work. Later in Siena, Gigli could have gotten the idea from this repertory, given his own ties to the Imperial court, and the presence of a copy of Sbarra's piece in Lucca.

Bicilli's piece moves from narrative freedom to Biblical fidelity. After an opening chorus and solo on music, its Testo starts by praising the Mother and launching into a description of the vicious fight between her and the tyrant. There are also solo attacks on Antioco given to Sons #4 and #1 (the latter with an aria), and Part I ends with a citation of the dynastic "Fortezza e Costanza" Habsburg motto. But Part II begins with the first self-doubting Mother in the repertory, as she addresses herself to summon her own courage and dismiss her worries about her Sons' upcoming tortures. As matters return to the Biblical source, the Testo resumes the narration of the story, followed by more solos for the Mother (including her private advice to the youngest Son to resist, like 2 Maccabees 7:27–29, here in a two-stanza aria "Io ti prego, o figlio amato, / di mirar quest'ampia mole" [O beloved son, I beg you to examine this wide world]), overall adding substantially to the Biblical account of the Mother's rejection of Antiochus.[31] Even though the tyrant orders the youngest's tongue to be torn out, the child still manages to sing a two-stanza aria ("Questo mortale ardore"). As in 2 Maccabees, the Mother's own death is simply mentioned briefly before the closing chorus, which, in an uncited gesture to Bridget of Sweden's *Liber celestis / Revelations* (part I, chapter 31), referred to the Rose and Seven Lilies in the mystic's interpretation of a passage from the Apocalypse.

Attilio Ariosti's 1704 Viennese setting*, the only surviving score for Gigli's text, and also the first of three local versions of the tale inside a troubled decade, would have had some five adult female Habsburgs (plus two children, along with the present and two future Emperors) among its audience, and the subtle references, originally for Siena, to "education" and to "constancy" would also have made sense. The composer was fresh from composing the librettist's opera *La fede ne' tradimenti* for Berlin (1701) before transferring to Imperial service, and the oratorio's score (F-Pn) shows familiarity with the textual moves in the stage work. The abstract brilliance of Gigli's often epigrammatic text transcends purely emotive moments, while the verbal play and rapidly changing textual conceits lead one to wonder as to how Fabbrini's lost original music for Gigli must have worked. Leopold I himself, along with his consort Eleonore, would have remembered Bicilli's piece on the topic from 1686.

Ariosti's score, however, would have appealed to the musical aesthetics of the aging Leopold on several fronts: its florid vocal parts, especially for the bass role of Antioco; its contrapuntal string writing with virtuosic parts for celli and lute (the latter probably for his fellow Tuscan F. B. Conti); and, most attuned to Leopold's semi-professional connoisseurship, its striking movements among pitch centers. This is immediately evident at the beginning, as the Mother, an alto, starts off the piece around F♯ (for Ariosti, this would have been "Tuono 4" up two fifths; for us, a sort of proto-F♯ minor). Although she stays in sharp regions, Giacobbe enters with a tonal anabasis and change of system, to the flat sonorities of G (usually some kind of "Tuono 2" for Ariosti).

The composer's sense of variety further generated arias in a bewildering variety of tonalities; Antioco's numbers move at first in sharp regions. Another gesture to local practice is one aria for two solo celli, paired with one for lute, the latter probably a mark of Francesco Conti's improvisatory ability. Although there is no cast list (the Paris manuscript is clearly of Northern European provenance and bears no trace of the Vienna premiere), a castrato such as Gaetano Orsini (or Francesco Ballerini) must have sung the Mother, and Antioco's part could have been assigned to the virtuoso bass Rainero Borrini, the latter quite active in opera and oratorio from 1700 onward. It is unclear if Giacobbe was given to a castrato or to one of the women singing in opera and oratorio at court.[32]

The score is filled with striking moments—not least the bass arias for Antioco—but the close stands out, as the Mother attempts to plead with Heaven (or perhaps with the absent Antioco) for her last son's life, while he struggles to finish his dying words. Although set out as recitative in the Viennese libretto, the Mother repeats "Deh, lascia il rigor" as arioso. Giacobbe finally manages to utter—over his mother's cries—"Deh, lasciami dir: 'che dolce morir!'" as he expires.

The Mother's closing monologue begins with her reference to Creation ("Quando il mondo fabbricò quella man [i.e., of God]" [When God's hand created the world]), but ends mid-phrase with an *interruptio* just before the cadence: "tal anch'io mi ritrovo vo' sopra il petto sanguinoso del mio settimo figlio il mio riposo, il mio ripo- . . ." [so too I wish to find, on the bloody chest of my seventh son, my repose, my re- . . .] (ex. 7.1). Again, this is set on F with multiple flats, as the Mother ends on a seventh, and leaves the upper strings to finish the entire piece. Whether this is her death, or her Marian-like swooning, at the end is not as important as Ariosti's inspired close; it is also possible that the moment presages the traditional reference

EX. 7.1 A. Ariosti, *La madre de' Maccabei*, Madre, ending; F-Pn, D.233, fol. 100r.

Grieving Spouses, Fierce Motherhood · 187

to Mary's collapse on Calvary, a trope present in music since a 1616 motet by Alessandro Grandi. The sheer imagination present in this score gives some sense of how this very martial moment in court culture might have sounded in Lent.

Like those of Isaac and Jephthe, this story in different musical versions was repeated again and again at court, some five times between 1709 and 1737, and all in the presence of Wilhelmine Amalia. Silvio Stampiglia's 1709 libretto *Il martirio de' Machabei*, set by Badia* and done after the Imperial transition, is just as short, if not as epigrammatic, as Gigli's. Joseph I's busy schedule that Lent, as the Austrian attempts at the Spanish Succession were beginning to fail, may have been a cause of the brevity (as was noted above in the case of Binding pieces, 1707–8). It seems to have been listed as a "kleines Oratorium" on the Lenten Feast of the Seven Sorrows BVM that year, a day spent by the royals (the same complement in the audience as for the 1704 piece, minus the deceased Leopold I and the now-married Maria Anna of Portugal) first in the Hofburgkapelle, then in the Minoritenkirche, and finally back for the work in the court chapel.[33]

On first hearing, Stampiglia's relative brevity and four characters (here the Mother is "Salome") lead to some of the same abrupt shifts as Gigli's, starting with an aria for the Mother addressed to her son (instead of Gigli's "Piangi, barbaro rè"), followed immediately by Antioco's captain, who reports on the Jews' revolt in his own aria. Similarly to Gigli's 1688 text, the 1709 work passes to a trio standoff with Antioco, here retelling the latter's profanation of the Temple. Although first the tyrant pardons the son for the boy's reproach aria, still the Mother's continued resistance leads to imprisonment for Salome and all her offspring. Part I's ending emphasizes the tight communication of Mother and Son, but while the Figliuolo stresses his empathy with his mother's pain, she pushes on to the palm of martyrdom.

Dramatically, Stampiglia's 1709 Antioco opens Part II with the demand for all eight Jews to eat the forbidden food. Salome refuses, leading to the offstage execution of the first six brothers, and when the Capitano returns with their heads, the Figliuolo's wish to kiss them is turned down, a moment of further gruesomeness absent from Gigli. After a short bribe offer from the tyrant, the son follows Salome's instructions to reject this (without the irony and emphasis on gold found in the 1688 libretto). As martyrdom becomes certain, Salome sheds tears of joy, while her son echoes the end of Part I with an aria based on the idea that witnessing his mother's suffering is worse than death. Rather than fleeing as in Gigli, Antioco remains to watch, but the last aria is given to the Capitano, striking the mother's heart and the son's chest with knives/swords (another Marian "sword in the heart" reference for dynastic piety). The two die together, and the piece ends with a short chorus on "si nobil costanza," another Habsburg commonplace.

The symbiosis between Gigli's Mother and Son is also present here, although far more briefly. To examine the possible devotional political meanings for the two libretti in Vienna raises various issues: in a strict Sorrows of Mary sense, Stampiglia's is the more obvious, given Part I's ending and the Figliuolo's constant empathy for his Mother. Possibly the 1709 text downplayed the son's stage time since—unlike 1704—it was clear by this point that Wilhelmine Amalie, Joseph's consort, was not going to produce heirs of any kind. Reading the piece's Jewish constancy and martyrdom as a figure of Christian resistance to Islam is harder, given the temporary lull in the wars with the Ottomans until 1715. In terms of family relations, though, it would be hard for any text to match the constant proximity of Gigli's Mother and Son.

For all that the 1709 text might come off as a relatively short and highly martial piece, in line with other trends during Joseph's reign, the performance and singers suggest otherwise. Salome was sung by the operatic castrato Domenico Tollini, one of the most-employed figures in the chapel, and her Son by the stalwart Orsini, while the relatively important role of Antioco's Capitano was given to the prized tenor Silvio Garghetti. Perhaps the most emotional aria is the Figliuolo's "Seguir voglio io il desir della mia madre" [I want to follow my mother's desire], his final rejection of Antioco, a text which emphasizes the unity of Mother and Son (possibly an attempt in court circles to pave over the real differences between Joseph I and his pious mother, the Dowager Eleonore Magdalene).

At the same time, its martial aspects as encouragement against religious/political enemies were only partially hidden. Sbarra's use of the character had come in a difficult martial moment, after both the stalemate of the 1663–64 conflict with the Ottomans as well as the ongoing Low Countries war with Louis XIV. The 1686 Viennese piece, whatever its origin and date, fits into the general context of the ongoing battles against the Turks. Gigli's—whose Imperial sympathies were no secret—premiere followed the successful Battle of Mohács on Christian Europe's eastern front (1687). Similarly, the Viennese works were marked by the War of the Spanish Succession.

Distance and Detail

A few years later, Pietro Pariati's text for J. J. Fux's music*, *La donna forte nella madre de' sette Maccabei* ("The Strong Women [embodied] in the Mother of the Seven Maccabees"), was simultaneous with the outbreak of the Ottoman-Venetian War (1714/15), which would eventually involve Austria and lead to notable Habsburg victories. This performance continued the Habsburg trope of the "strong woman" and was another instantiation of Charles VI's famed emphasis on "costanza." A generation later, the last Viennese work* on the topic (Francesca Manzoni-Giusti/Giovanni Porsile; *La madre de' Macabei*) was perhaps meant as an object lesson for Maria Theresia in view of the uncertain succession to the heirless Emperor (and aimed at European enemies, not the Ottomans); her first daughter had just been born on 5 February 1737, six weeks before the premiere of Manzoni's libretto.

Certainly, after the peace of the Treaty of Utrecht which brought a certain calm to the court, Pariati/Fux's 1715 *La donna forte* picked up on Stampiglia's work at greater length (nineteen da capo arias as opposed to thirteen, along with "internal" choruses), and with emphasis on all seven martyred Sons, who sing as a chorus in Part I.[34] Its premiere seems to have been on 4 April 1715, the Thursday after the Fourth Sunday in Lent, while its later reprise possibly fell on 12 April 1718, the latter but not the former a Seven Sorrows feast; the numerical equation of Sorrows = Sons would have been reinforced.[35] With the addition of Elizabeth Christine, now Charles VI's reigning consort in 1715, the female audience for both performances returned to seven, and the hope for a male heir was still very much alive.

In both substance and style, Pariati's text marked a change from Gigli's, and even from Stampiglia's (although there are more lexical recalls of the latter). Most evident is the character build-up of Antioco's party, with two counselors/captains for the tyrant, and an opening scene for the three of these, meaning that the Mother's (here "La Maccabea") arrival is delayed for some nine numbers, even after the chorus of her seven Sons praising God. Still, the overall emphasis lies on the five different moments — three in Part I, two in Part II — of direct confrontation between the Mother and the tyrant.

Pariati's dramatic use of the chorus, and his varied arias for the non-Biblical counselors, meant that the actual paraphrase of 2 Maccabees 7 was held off at length, as late as Part II (#40, a dialogue recitative between the last son "Giacobbe" and Antioco). The narrative then returns to the Biblical account with Antioco's blandishments (7:25 = #50–#51) followed by the Mother/Giacobbe's colloquy (= 7:26–29; #52–#53) of resistance to the tyrant's final offer. Although the two have a duet (#53) as Giacobbe expires, the Maccabea stays onstage for a final aria on "Heaven's highest good," and then a simple concluding tutti *madrigale* in her praise, omitting any reference to her own martyrdom.[36]

On some levels, though, the libretto also blatantly flouts Arcadian decorum. This is most apparent in Antioco's closing order (#54) to rip open the Mother's chest and to stuff her son's corpse inside her body cavity, corresponding to his earlier threat (aria #30, "Mira che le tue viscere"). This detail seems not to be present even in the lengthier martyrdom account of 4 Maccabees, nor in *Yosippon*.[37] Similarly, the concern of Antioco's counselors Eliodoro and Nicanore with maintaining Roman religion appears to be another addition to the standard story. The real weight of this piece shifts, compared with Gigli and Stampiglia's, to the Mother's angry response to a plethora of opponents, perhaps a sign for the Ottomans, the still-powerful Bourbons in France and Spain, or both.

In this panoply of resistance and consistency across Pariati's text, two interactions between Mother and Son stand out: first, the moment of separation of the two, as Giacobbe is taken away following the third tangle between Antioco and the Maccabea (#31–#33); and then the son's request to the tyrant to have his mother brought back so as to instruct him what to do (this is the "filial" aria #43). The latter resonates with Habsburg ideas of maternal education. The first interaction between Mother and tyrant follows Antioco's brutal threat in an aria of *sdruccioli e tronchi*; the Maccabea continues to resist, and the tyrant orders Giacobbe separated from her (Pariati's recitative trialogue wittily splits the Imperial motto "Costanza e Fortezza" between the tyrant and the Mother), as the boy is dragged off. Her valedictory recitative turns immediately to flat-pitch regions ("Figlio, con te viene il mio core"). Giacobbe's temporary farewell is an exit aria, set as a pathetic *siciliana*, in the unusual hendecasyllables for an entire number ("Dammi, diletta madre, un bacio almeno"). The vocal line is accompanied only by solo *bassetto* strings, and the tonal structure works around G with contrast only as far afield as D. In the A section, Fux used two melodic gestures, along with some striking 6/4/2 sonorities. Since the Mother cannot

Grieving Spouses, Fierce Motherhood · 191

reply to him directly, she addresses God in accompanied recitative, that is, as an invocation.

The Maccabea steers matters tonally into sharp regions, from D to B, before falling back to G in a gavotte aria in *ottonari*, recognizing all her children as Divine donations to be returned to Him (and a special kind of Habsburg gift economy; "I miei parti, il viver mio, / sommo Iddio, sono dono tuoi" [My offspring, my life, highest God, are Your gifts]). Giacobbe's pathetic aria, on G in flat regions, is succeeded by his Mother's *durus* item on the same pitch, followed by the normal *madrigale* ending the part.

The next marked moment of filial sentiment is Giacobbe's profession of his obedience to her teachings, another *ottonario* sung to the tyrant who had called the Maccabea to gain her son's obedience ("Col suo latte e co' suoi baci," an expansion of 2 Maccabees 7:25). This continuo-only *passepied* is clearly on A, and Fux provided motivic connection between Giacobbe's learning via lactation and his childhood growth in Hebrew law (the A section's "m'ispirò" echoed by the B section's "Crebber gli anni più vivaci").[38] His exit does not overlap with the Maccabea's next entrance, which turns into another snarling battle with Antioco and his counselors, followed by a martial and prophetic aria for the Mother ("Si, vedrassi Giove e Marte / vili avanzi e tronchi indegni") on the future ruin of Roman gods.

Since this text, in some contrast to Gigli's, is more about faith-filled defiance than family relations, it follows that the Maccabea and Giacobbe get only a single farewell duet, in the unusual *senario* poetic meter (ex. 7.2). With no instruments to prolong the moment, the two sections are exactly the same length ("In faccio di morte"—their recollection of Isaac and Abraham mentioned in chapter 1 above—and "Io moro, ma forte" both span twenty-six measures), giving some sense of the slightly antiquated two-stanza aria. This moment is set up by a firm cadence on E♭ in the preceding trialogue recitative, and it is the first high-voice duet—another *siciliana*—in the whole oratorio. Pariati's rhyming of "cor" and "valor" moves the moment away from maternal/filial sentiment toward pure martyrdom.[39]

Fux's score follows Pariati's verses quite well, with a sense of restrained decorum not present in Ariosti. The first duet between Antioco and the Maccabea (#28; "Ecco il primo che già more") accompanies his execution of the first two brothers, while the Mother concentrates on their glory in Heaven. Fux set this up as a standard chamber duet with instrumental interjections. The tyrant's references to his tortures do not evoke any spe-

EX. 7.2 J. J. Fux, *La donna forte nella madre de' sette Maccabei*, farewell duet: A-Wn, Mus. Hs. 18186 (after Wessely/Kanduth 1976, 176–77).

cial musical gestures, a feature which holds for the martyrdom of the other Sons except for Giacobbe.

To understand this passage's meaning for the generation after Gigli and Pariati, Paolo Medici's 1724 explication is helpful, especially given his Jewish upbringing before conversion. Although the exegete began with the seven Sons in turn, in line with tradition, he soon inverted the Mother's gender: "She, not with a mother's feminine voice but with a father's masculine one, exhorted [her sons] to suffer patiently, and thus, filled with celestial wisdom (even though of the weaker sex), she courageously spoke to them thus: [there follows a paraphrase of her speech, 2 Maccabees 7:22ff]".[40] Still, after lengthy reworkings of the various sons' speeches of defiance, Medici followed the book in mentioning the Mother's death only incidentally, diverging from the many scenes of maternal martyrdom throughout the oratorio repertory.

Realistic Heroinism

Given Medici's fidelity to the Biblical model, the changes to the tale at mid-century are notable. The most popular version of the Mother story had a text by Giuseppe Barbieri (ca. 1724–69), an Oratorian from Vicenza working in Rome during the 1750s.[41] The 1785 Rome libretto for this *La madre de' Maccabei* mentions him by name, and his piece, probably for the Chiesa Nuova in Rome, was likely first set by Pietro Guglielmi on commission in the late 1750s. This now-lost score was taken to Würzburg for the enlightened Prince-Bishop Adam Friedrich von Seinsheim as soon as 1760.

His order was also anti-Jesuit, and his text shows strikingly different emphases from past versions, an example of Ludovico Muratori's turn to "rational" devotion. Barbieri's Italian text represents a major departure both in its depiction of its Mother (here "Anna") and in its new formulations of motherhood and childhood. The preface explicitly cited 2 Maccabees and "Flavius Josephus" (i.e., *Yosippon*), but not 4 Maccabees, and the piece begins after the martyrdom of the first six sons, with a dialogue between Antioco and his counselor Apollonio on their strategy to bribe Giacobbe and convince Anna. After their exit, Anna enters to reinforce both her unspeakable pain and her refusal to weep, encouraging the entering Giacobbe to resistance. Her son leaves, and her noncommittal answers to Apollonio reflect his mother's worries that he will give in. Giacobbe's return, and his second reassurance to her of his fidelity to Judaism, lead to Part I's closing duet of constancy.

Barbieri's differences with earlier libretti become audible at the beginning of Part II, with a long recitative for Anna, recounting her dreamed fears of Giacobbe's martyrdom and, even worse, his possible recantation. After a century of steadfast Mothers, this represents a shift toward subjectivity and doubt. On Giacobbe's third return, she tries to quell his "excessive" tenderness toward her, pointing out that "ha i suoi confini / anche il materno amor. / Se oltre si avanza, / colpa divien" [even maternal love has its limits; if it exceeds (them), it becomes sin], possibly an effort on Barbieri's part to quell proto-bourgeois family sentiment in favor of Christian duty. Giacobbe picks up on this, as the desire descending from Heaven for martyrdom ties him closer to her than does even filial love.

After Apollonio's return, Giacobbe refuses to go along with the tyrant's demands. As the tyrant reproaches her, Anna continues with the idea of transcending maternity ("Son donna, e madre, / ma son Ebrea" [I am a woman, and a mother, but (above all) I am a Jew]); as noted above, this is an inverse lexical reflection of Tobias's words to his wife (chapter 6). Apollonio reverses this opposition by using family *pietas* against her in an aria ("Se a mirar il tuo periglio / non ti scuoti e non paventi; / deh rivolgi al caro figlio di pietade un guardo almen" [If you do not tremble and fear from seeing your danger, at least grant your son a piteous glance]).

This first confrontation between the returning Antioco and Giacobbe brings the tyrant to try again with Anna, and her refusal to give in leads to her son being taken off to death; her interactions with the tyrant are more pronounced in this text than is the case in 2 or 4 Maccabees. Still, Giacobbe's final recitative and aria return to the issue of filial sentiment ("son pronto / la grand'opra a compir; ma sento insieme, / che son figlio, e sei madre.... [Aria:] A morir madre, m'invio, / ma tu resti intanto, e peni ..." [I am ready to accomplish the great work, but I still feel that I am your child, and you my mother.... (Aria:) I go to die, mother, but you remain and suffer]).

For all that this evokes images of Mary on Calvary, its continuation is quite different. Anna's two-page closing soliloquy moves first from grief to self-interruption, with an aria ("perchè non togliermi / l'alma dal seno?" [(You torturers,) why not take my soul from my breast?]) on her fantasy of stopping the tyrant before Giacobbe's martyrdom. Then, however, she transitions to a second self-reproach for excessive maternal affect via an epic self-interruption: "Misera! Che ragiono? Ah troppo io lascio / all'affetto materno / libero il fren! No, no si vada / di Giacobbe lo scempio / intrepida a mirar" [Miserable woman, what am I saying? I have kept the bonds on my maternal affection too loose! I will not go intrepidly to watch the slaughter of Giacobbe]. She remains far from the scene of her son's martyrdom.

It is precisely this disciplining of maternity that allows heavenly light to descend into her soul, making her a prophetess of the future Christ and Mary, as she imagines the Virgin watching the Passion, which is implicitly a greater suffering than her own. Anna's own martyrdom—necessary according to 2 Maccabees and the whole previous oratorio tradition—is here completely elided, as she waits for whatever the future may bring, and the piece ends thus.

The changes to the story are evident, and they seem present in neither Medici's view of the Mother nor that (1740) of Orazio da Parma.[42] They reflect a new kind of emotionality in the treatments of the story, as with the post-1730 versions of Cain/Abel and of Jephthe. Barbieri introduced Anna's doubts late in the text, postponing them to Part II, and then having her dominate the entire closing with her vacillations, ending in a Quietist vigil for what his audiences would have known to be her fate. If this was a new, Oratorian-sponsored idea of maternity for the Chiesa Nuova's public, the number of its musical settings testifies to its impact.

One widely circulated score was that of Pasquale Anfossi* for a 1765 Roman Lent. Its popularity is evident from the reprises of 1768, 1773, and 1785 in the Eternal City, and it traveled to Munich for Holy Week of 1770. A different setting by Luigi Gatti* seems to have premiered in Mantua's *Teatro Scientifico* in 1775, repeated with changes in 1793. In Anfossi's setting, Antioco's opening aria ("Vuol che spiri") already underscores the contrasts between Jewish and Greek laws around eating by musical interruptions (at "chi legge non ha," i.e., the Greeks had laws against self-martyrdom, while the Jews maintained their rules against eating pork) in a florid tenor line. In the libretto, Barbieri's apportioning of two arias to Antioco before we ever hear the Mother is a sign of his stature.

Anfossi has Anna react to Giacobbe's weeping at the danger and uncertainty with an opening aria of fortitude, "Chi spieghi col suono di flebili accenti" [whoever uses lamenting tones to show pain]. The end of the A section, at "palesa col pianto," goes up to high C6 twice in the context of a high register that recurs in none of her other arias. Whether or not Anfossi realized it, this vocal display for the Mother actually contradicts the text's meaning, that is, that weeping exposes only the "superficiality" of suffering, and that real pain is interior, treated in the D-minor B section (despite the printed libretto, this is a "dal segno" aria). Whoever the 1765 Anna was, this must have been a remarkable singer.

Anna continues in recitative, explaining to her son that Divine strength infused her with such constancy as almost to forget maternity. Giacobbe's answering aria is the slowest thus far, set with piccoli (appropriate for a child, instead of oboes; possibly a last-minute change in the Milan score), and at thirty-six pages of andante it is notably longer than his Mother's. After Apollonio's return, and the gesture to 2 Maccabees of Anna's promising to speak to her son, her last solo aria of the part is a soliloquy plea for eloquence in her encouragement of him ("Tu nel periglio estremo"), and her presence onstage continues through the duet and then into Anfossi's accompanied recitative that opens Part II with her doubts.

Indeed, the initial C major of this part collapses swiftly into her flattest regions so far (E♭, the key of her following aria), as she dreams of her youngest's martyrdom ("Veggio il sangue"). In turn, this breaks back into accompanied recitative as she questions his constancy ("sento, ma pur chi mi assicura della costanza sua?"), setting up an F-major aria of affective martial contrast inside her own heart ("Sento il cor di doppio affetto"), which heightens the *mollis* turn as far as B♭ minor. In other words, Anfossi's Anna opens Part II with a *scena* outdoing Antioco's dominance of Part I's beginning.

The abovementioned dialogue with the returning Giacobbe on natural filial affection versus divinely inspired piety, along with Anna's declaration of faith above motherhood ("son donna, ma son Ebrea") in the following trialogue with Apollonio, is all set to straightforward recitative (i.e., the novelty of the text works in different ways from the means of the music). Antioco returns to his final rejection with a revenge aria ("Giacchè crudel mi vuoi"), and another aria for Apollonio recalls the presence of the two of them at Part I's opening.

Anfossi's Giuseppe then initiates the climax with a return to E♭ major for his pathetic aria "A morte, madre, m'invio." Anna's reaction is in normal recitative until she imagines stopping the executioners ("Barbari, deh fermate"), at which point the accompagnato returns. Almost imperceptibly, this becomes an arioso as she substitutes herself in grief for her Son ("Non togliarmi l'alma dal petto"), and Anfossi sets her return to strength (the self-interruption at "Misera, che ragiono?") with a slow return to the tonal realm of C major, as at the beginning of her soliloquy (ex. 7.3). This pitch center undergirds her "prophetic" transformation predicting the Passion ("S'appressa ormai la pienezza de' tempi") while standing in marked contrast to the extrovert D major of the final chorus. Anna puts a good deal of vocal energy into her relationship with her son, to be sure, but her own pre-martyrdom blossoming into a prophet seems to have more to do with pitch relations than with vocal virtuosity.

Certainly one of the more surprising reworkings came from inside Barbieri's order itself. A somewhat different text with the same characters, the anonymous *La madre de' sette figli e martiri Maccabei*, was done in Habsburg Florence in 1773–74 for S. Firenze, the Oratorian church in the Tuscan capital. Its choral opening and parts for Anna and Giacobbe are new, compared to Barbieri's, but some of its Part II (including the Mother Anna's closing soliloquy) is the same.[43] This rewrote a good deal of the text, starting by adding chorus parts for Jews and Greeks along with an opening dialogue for Mother and Son, and a new preface, reusing only Antioco's opening aria and Giacobbe's penultimate one from Part II. Entirely absent were Anna's vacillations, doubts, and dreams (and a performance deletion included her prophesy of Calvary). The characters of the Greeks were also reinforced, along with the added choruses. The preface noted Giacobbe's offstage death (which had been the case in the Roman original of the late 1750s). There is no trace of Barbieri's name, and overall this seems like an attempt by the local order to adapt the ever more simplified piety of Habsburg Tuscany; it should be remembered that the Synod of Pistoia was only twelve years in the future.

For all that it premiered in Habsburg Lombardy, Luigi Gatti's 1775/93 setting* of Barbieri's full text placed its emphases slightly differently, most audibly in an expanded part for the Mother. The first performance was the first time an oratorio of any kind had been heard in Mantua since the 1750s. Here, Anna received an additional pleading (to Heaven) aria in Part I ("Per pietà deh vi placate, fieri numi"); some of Anfossi's simple recitatives were made into *accompagnati*. This was another piece to be performed in a theater, and some of the later additions might have been made for Katherine Lang, the 1793 Anna, who had come down from Munich for operatic performances in the Veneto (and might even have been recommended by Gatti himself, who was now in Salzburg succeeding Leopold Mozart).

EX. 7.3 P. Anfossi, *La madre de' Maccabei*, "Misera, che ragiono?"; I-Mc, M.S. ms. 8-1, fol. 112v.

Grieving Spouses, Fierce Motherhood · 199

If anything, Gatti's version emphasized the Mother even more than had Anfossi's, and—as in Catania—possibly this later revival carried not-so-hidden anti-French meaning as the revolutionary wars grew.

Martyrs in the Ospedali

In a different tradition but the same generation, Antonio Sacchini composed a Latin work, the *Mater machabaeorum** for the Ospedale dei Derelitti in Venice for Assumption BVM in 1770; this was followed by similar works for the Mendicanti by Bertoni (1781) and Lorenzo Baini (1784), and Domenico Fischietti again for the Derelitti (1793). Far from Barbieri's versions and its successors, the Venetian items in Latin for the *ospedali* were cast in a different mold. Besides its destination for the joyous feast of Assumption BVM at the Derelitti, the 1770 Latin text used other sources, with its Mother called "Jael" and four Sons (none of them "Jacob"). Its all-female vocal scoring thus puts even Antiochus into an alto register. The musical intertextuality in the score with Sacchini's operatic output (e.g., *L'eroe cinese*) of the same moment has already been remarked.[44]

Unlike Barbieri's treatment, the librettist (Pietro Chiari) divided the labor of resistance democratically among the four sons, with the youngest "Jonathan" given one solo aria and then a final duet with Jael. As in 2 Maccabees, Antiochus variously threatens, cajoles, bribes, and then condemns the sons all by himself; the first two are martyred between the two parts, and the piece ends with Antiochus's brush-off of the Jews (followed by the repeat of the chorus which had opened Part II). Jael's martyrdom is only implicit, and any political reference ("Antiochus = the Ottomans," who still ruled the Middle East in 1770) was similarly muted. For all this, the sense of the battle as a conflict of laws—present in Gigli, Pariati, and especially Barbieri—did have subtle resonances at the beginning and end of the Latin libretto.

Chiari began with a standard trope for the tyrant, answered in turn by Jael and four Sons who recall the martyrdom of Eleazar and the importance of Mosaic Law. That the discourse linked resistance and family was evident in the Mother's recitative reproach of Antiochus: "I beg you, stop tormenting this holy and hardened people [Jews] through this domestic matter." The tyrant attacks Mosaic Law by name; Barbieri's example of which law is to be obeyed is quite present. At this point, the star soprano Ippolita Santi (= "Jonathan") first gave a recitative synopsis of Jewish history, and then provided "Vos enarratis stellae," a contrasting virtuosa aria of high coloratura (perhaps inspiring Sacchini to highlight the "stars above" and "howling winds" in the text via tessitura) in praise of Creation and against the misery of human Fate (ex. 7.4). Possibly she had been chosen to represent the youngest Son because of her stratospheric range; among the other singers, the printed libretto lists Lucia Tonello as Onias; Laura Conti, Simeon; and Marina Frari, Melchi.

Still in Part I, the Sons' fierce resistance brings Antiochus to "call them to the table that they had resisted,' that is, to burn them alive and feed their flesh to the dogs of Idumaea (Edom). The Mother's scathing reproach of the tyrant ("Barbarian, will you not mitigate these things, will you not at least ease this inhuman judgment?") is set out typographically as two accompanied recitatives each framing an aria stanza ("Ite, felicia" and "Barbare, rex"), giving her a double number. After this textual and musical emphasis on her, the two brothers Onias and Melchi also resist, and the part ends with a trio for them and Antiochus, each singing the same text of resistance to each other.

By this point, it is obvious that any special relationship between Mother and youngest Son was to be held back in the interest of overall fraternal solidarity. Part II begins with a colloquy among the four brothers on the joys of martyrdom, and Melchi, who had not had an aria in Part I, sings a musically referential one ("Tibia, et citharae non tacent; / cara Sion, morior pro te" [Do not let the trumpets and lyres be silent; dear Zion, I die for you]). Antiochus re-enters to offer peace and mercy, but is rudely rejected by the brothers, leading him to launch into a long accompanied recitative detailing previous sufferings of the Jews, almost as if his offered peace were a favor, sparing the Hebrews yet another atrocity. In a subtle sense, this highlights a historically aware tyrant, one whose possible sympathy with his subjects remains ever so slightly hidden.

It was at this moment in the original performance that Charles Burney walked into the church, evidently not having been told by his local informants that some of the vocal fireworks would already have been over. However, as always, he was an attentive listener, remarking the musical if not literary aspects of the recitative as well as Francesca Gabrieli's (Antiochus) bravura in both recitative and aria ("Sinum monstro, et manum tendo" [I show my protection, and extend my hand]), the latter with a Jommelli-like B section ("Magis Iride serena / manus mea nubes colorat" [My hand colors the clouds with a serene rainbow]). Laura Conti's "Quasi per somnium," although semi-deprecated as too intimate by Burney, is an effective contrast dealing with the transience of earthly things.[45] This leads Antiochus to consign six brothers (implicitly) to the flames, and then in a final scene of duet recitative and aria between Jonathan and Jael, the aria ("Flammae carae") leads to their invocation of Faith, Hope, and Charity as they die together. In an unparalleled finish, Antiochus provides a short recitative summarizing and defending his deeds ("Whoever wants to die, let them die"), followed by a closing chorus.[46]

Chiari ran roughshod over 2 (and 4) Maccabees in his effort to emphasize combined fraternal resistance over Mother–youngest Son relations. Although his aria texts are neutral in a Metastasian way, he clearly had some idea of the general vocal personality of each of the women, tailoring the arias accordingly. Here the relationship between Jonathan and Jael, even if restricted to the final duet, is underscored by the music: set up in D minor, it is a triple-time Largo in a radiant A major. Still, the issue of youth solidarity was an implicit reference to ideal conditions inside the *ospedale* itself.

Sacchini provided effective, often inspired music for all the various moments (Burney's brief experience with this piece led him to rank the composer behind only Baldassare Galuppi among local figures). Again, the emphasis on "lex" in Antiochus's opening recitative suggests that the composer had understood the centrality of the Law in the libretto's ideology. Jonathan's "Vos ennarate stellae" is the second aria, and it put all of Salvi's talent on display: even in the first iteration of the A section, there are three C6s for "loquenti," and a D6 for the cadence. In this B♭ piece, the B section which contrasts "miserable earth" to Heaven turns to F minor, and then the repeat of the A section is reworked to be transposed up, not down, so that the vocal line reaches E♭6. Clearly the setting is meant to express the universality of Divine glory: "Vos ennarate stellae / Omnipotentis voces, / Et horridae procellae / Gloriam loquenti dant. [B section:] Misera terra ingrata, / Quid contra cælum vales? / Incerta hominum fata / In manu tua non stant" [You stars tell the words of the Almighty, and you rough storms witness to the glory of His speech. Miserable ungrateful world, what do you matter against Heaven? Uncertain human fate does not rest in your hand].

Jael's self-reference to her womb's products (i.e., her sons: "Ite, felicia et chara / viscera") includes a good deal of passagework in Gabrieli's alto register. The piece works, then, around different kinds of vocal virtuosity.

EX. 7.4 A. Sacchini, *Mater Machabaeorum*, "Vos enarratis stellae"; I-Mc, M.S. ms. 233-2, fol. 42v.

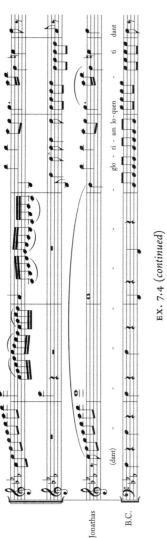

EX. 7.4 (continued)

The trio that ends Part I sets Onias and Melchi against Antiochus, all with different verbal affect for all that the musical material is shared. Tonally, Part II moves more clearly to flat regions (e.g., E♭ for Melchi's aria "Tristae umbrae," and even B♭ minor in Antiochus's recitative at his mention of Jael's tears: "Lachrymae amarae"). The latter's "Sinum monstruo" aria, expressing his fantasy of defeating the Jews, turns to D, and the final duet stands out for its imitations and passagework.

This piece was far from marking the end of the Maccabees tradition, as we have seen. But it did establish a renewed high level, textually and musically, in the Derelitti's oratorio offerings and, via Burney, contributed to the composer's Europe-wide reputation. In terms of its family relations, however, it also showed how a Mother figure could be central even in a work with several vocally virtuosic Sons, and in that sense it marked a different kind of change in the narrative tradition that went back as far as Gigli's 1688 text. Although tragically fated mothers have not figured prominently in the scholarship on late Settecento musical heroines, Sacchini's piece suggests that her model was an important one.

At the end of our period, the story would be mobilized against the spread of the French Revolution. A 1794 oratorio in Catania (Sicily) — nominally for the translation of its patroness St. Agatha's relics — seems to refer to the local populace as the Maccabees, fighting against the tyrant (= the French) threatening their religion/system; possibly the piece was repeated at the even more charged moment of the 1799 anti-Bourbon revolution, in Catania and in a clear pro-monarchist vein.[47] Even the 1793 Mantua revival of Gatti's setting, first heard in 1775, could have had something to do with anti-French fears in Austrian Lombardy, although the actual occupation would happen only three years later.[48]

One of the best examples of this anti-Republican use of the story is an anonymously printed pamphlet, without date or place (i.e., in a Republican-controlled Italian city after 1793), nominally against the introduction of the Revolutionary calendar, but including a 1791 prison letter from an anonymous Parisian pastor faithful to the monarchy. Here the faithful were encouraged to read 2 Maccabees and to use the example of the Mother and brothers as passive resistance against the tyrannical French who were abolishing Divine law, not least in decoupling Christ's birth from the calendar.[49]

The story of the Mother and brothers had many ideologically specific uses in the Settecento. Perhaps most interesting is the variety of inspired music that it generated: Ariosti's virtuosity, Anfossi's careful balance, and Sacchini's efforts to spread the musically significant moments across the whole cast. The topic certainly provided new accents in female heroism and agency. For various reasons, this obscure story played an outsize role in the century's imaginary.

Chapter Eight

Connections

A Familial Lent

Besides Charles VI's perpetual concern about his two daughters' devotional education, it is hard to find an immediate political reason for why the 1732 Lenten oratorio season in Vienna should have been focused on family stories.[1] The major diplomatic events in the moment had to do with winning British and Hanoverian support for the Pragmatic Sanction, a largely successful campaign. Still, three of the four pieces premiered that year came from among this book's themes: A. M. Luchini/Georg Reutter Jr.'s *La divina providenza in Ismael* (6 March); *L'osservanza della divina legge nella madre de' Maccabei* (Luchini/Conti, 13 March); and Metastasio/Caldara's *La morte d'Abel*, the Holy Week piece on Tuesday 8 April, in front of an already-erected simulacrum of Christ's Tomb. In addition, Zeno's Tobit piece back from 1720 was reimagined the following spring as *Il ritorno di Tobia* in a version by G. C. Pascuini/Reutter Jr.

The other major oratorio was Zeno/Caldara's *Sedecia* (27 March 1732), an Old Testament story but one not primarily on kinship.[2] This set of newly composed works allows us to examine the interaction of our stories in the Habsburg imagination at one moment early in the Settecento. Zeno's libretto has to do with Sedecia's bad kingship (i.e., his rebellion against Nebuchadnezzar II), a counterexample to Charles, although its events—set before the fall of the historical Jerusalem in 586 BCE—must have raised worries about the Pragmatic Sanction, the Imperial succession, and even the possible end of Habsburg domination of the Empire. As always with Zeno's texts, a prophetic character—here Jeremiah—plays a crucial role.

Still, for all the thematic connections, Lent 1732 was marked by another, perhaps overriding feature: the presence of Farinelli for the two last oratorios.[3] The castrato had come up from Turin after singing two operatic roles there during Carnival. After a trip of about two weeks, he would have arrived in early March, with about three weeks to learn his two title parts in *Sedecia* and *La morte d'Abel*, as the two performances would have happened within thirteen days.[4] He also sang privately for Charles, who, according to the castrato himself, told him, "Those gigantic strides [leaps], those never-ending notes and passages . . . only surprise, and it is now time for you to please . . . if you wish to reach the heart, you must take a more plain and simple road." This proto-Algarottian advice both gives us a sort of aesthetic for Viennese oratorios and may have played out in the repertory of 1732.

The Lenten oratorios proceeded in this order: Ishmael-Maccabees-[Sedecia]-Cain/Abel. If we consider these pieces as a kind of musical *quaresimale*, then a certain progression is evident: (1) obedience eventually resulting in salvation; (2) filial fidelity to the law and defiance of heathen oppressors; (3) disobedience resulting in disaster; and (4) the first human murder as a prefiguring of the Passion, with Eva's laments in a Marian tone and Abel as an obvious Christ figure. The highly Augustinian concept of "Divine Providence" set the tone for Lent as a whole. More subtle thematic connections emerge from the works themselves.

The Carnival opera that year had been Metastasio/Conti's *Issipile*, an aesthetically important piece (even if unknown today); in its own way, it was a complement to the others. This drama has to do with a father (Toante) and a daughter (Issipile), along with the issue of "correct" bride-grooms (Giasone) for princesses; this was ultimately an allegory for the much-desired future marriage between Franz Stephan of Lorraine and Maria Theresia. Having dealt with the obvious family situation for the opera, whoever (perhaps Charles VI himself) picked the oratorio season did so in order to depict other kinds of kin relationships. Still, there was a certain sense of cohesion around the idea of family to the entire Carnival-Lenten musical season; *Issipile* had featured the antihero Learco, an analog to Antioco in the Maccabees work and to Caino in *La morte d'Abel*. This is particularly true in the denial of free will common to Learco (act 2, scenes 6–8) and to Caino.

For the opening oratorio on the Hagar story, the casting gave a certain weight: Praun as Abramo, Barbara Pisani as Sara, Theresia Reutter as Agar, and Gaetano Orsini as Ismael (the last a clear indication of the non-coincidence between dramatic and real age). Luchini began his text with the infamous "playing" between Ismael and Isacco as benignly observed by Abramo, who is immediately reproached by Sara for Ismael's status as a slave's son. The patriarch cuttingly replies that giving Agar to him had been Sara's idea, because of the latter's infertility, and this battle becomes intense, as Abramo reproaches his wife for waiting almost fifteen years to banish his older child. Still, Sara gets the first aria, "Non creder," claiming that her efforts were born of her love for Isacco. The Angel arrives to back her up, and Agar, entering, hears Ismael's lament for his favorite lamb who has died, another clear presage of tragedy.

Luchini's symbolic reference in this passage both to Abel (as herder) and to the Eucharist is striking, undermining the standard figure of Isaac in the Binding story and replacing him with a slave's child. It also provided a link to Metastasio's upcoming work later in the season. Agar's technically difficult aria of response, "Pavido l uomo," is a presentment of Fortune's mutability, followed by the entering Abramo, who issues the Banishment in a long and not totally convincing recitative. This turns into a quartet *scena* of dispute, in which Abramo absolves Agar and Ismael of guilt while still exiling them. Ismael then gets a pathetic slow aria, "Padre, oh Dio," in which he repeats his love for his father, and this is paralleled by Agar's stoic "Andrò, / dove non so / in braccio a cieca sorte" [I will go, I know not where, into the arms of blind fate]. Part I ends with another set of arias for Abramo and Sara commenting on the departing exiles, with the former asking his servants for prayers invoking Divine benignity for them (with this performed by a closing chorus of servants). So far, the emphasis is on Agar.

Although far from the most heterodox text in the repertory, this Part I does have its Abramo go out of his way to emphasize the innocence of Agar and Ismael. In terms of the overall theme of "Providence," it underscored the idea that, for all the ills afflicting the innocent, still hope was an important virtue. Part II opens with Sara reproaching the miserable Abramo in an aria ("Cresce fiero in noi il tormento"), while the unhappy father wonders where Ismael and his unfortunate mother are at this moment, leading the patriarch to a flat-region aria of imploration, "Volgi, o Signor, pietoso lo sguardo Tuo," set out in the most serious texture possible, a *fuga a due soggetti*. To judge from L. A. Predieri's later correspondence (1738) with Padre Martini around writing sacred music for the Emperor, this kind of number was especially close to the monarch's sensibility, and it should be presumed as being directly reflective of his taste.

Luchini and Reutter's oratorio continued with a flashy aria for Ismael with *salterio*, of the kind that would also be heard in Caldara's *Sedecia* later that Lent, here "Fra deserti e vaste arene," sung by Orsini (as Caldara's would be).[5] Moving to *durus* sonorities, Agar's aria "D'una stella che risplende" portrays her as looking at the heavens for confirmation of her and her son's innocence, giving way to a prolonged thirst scene in which the mother goes away and then comes back (how this was staged in the narrow confines of the Hofburgkapelle is also not clear, except in the most symbolic way). Agar's aria in F♯, "Qui la fonte, o Dio, vorrei," again takes on pathos, especially as she remembers the site as the place of consolation by the Angel during her first flight back in Genesis 16; given the use of this passage by the newly canonized John of the Cross (chapter 1; Carmelite culture was highly prized at court), Luchini could have meant this as a metaphor for human communication with the Divine.

This scene of Ismael's slow death from thirst is lengthy, and moves entirely in *durus* tonal regions, including his aria "L'anima al gran tormento" and an accompagnato for his mother, "Di sterile deserto." Abramo and Sara have been left far behind in this Part II, as the Angel arrives pointing out a cave with water and adding an aria, "Fermo ognuno / lo squardo tenga / l'uomo al ciel" [Let everyone hold their eyes fixed on Heaven], in a totally different tonal region, a sudden shift to E♭. The messenger promises great descendants to Agar, a borrowing from the Isaac story, and the final chorus on Divine Providence is remarkably optimistic, given how serious the situation had been: "Humans are the object of Divine love, if they recognize the attributes of sublime Creation in themselves, and mortals contemplate their own image as if in crystal; [fugal *madrigale:*] thus God sees His gifts in you and is Himself honored."

This work, for all its seemingly lesser place toward the beginning of Lent, boasted a competent cast, a subtle libretto, and some clear tonal organization and affectual changes on Reutter's part. The emphasis on the basic benignity of human nature also shows the continuation of Christian optimism in the Habsburg worldview. And its overwhelmingly positive means and message also contrasted strongly with some treatments of the subject examined in chapter 3, although very few in the 1732 audience would have encountered these earlier works.

The librettist would have had a busy winter, as he also provided the text for Conti's Maccabees piece which followed. Faithful to 2 Maccabees, Luchini named only "The Mother" and "Sons 5, 6, and 7" of the Jewish family, and even the singers were largely different from Reutter's work which had been performed a week earlier (the only exception being the ever-faithful bass Praun; the Mother was the fairly experienced Anna Rogenhofer-Schnautz ["la Schnauts"]). Luchini did not use the individual statements of the Sons to be found in *Yosippon*. One question, then, is whether and how the poet might have been willing to overturn the family relations presented quite differently in an earlier generation by Gigli and Pariati (chapter 7; it should be remembered that Charles himself would have been present at the Viennese performances of both these earlier works).

L'osservanza della divina legge starts with a soliloquy for Antioco, with a cite to 2 Maccabees 7:1, and an aria on his majesty offended by the Jews' refusal to eat pork. The Mother enters to dispute him in a fifty-eight-line recitative dialogue via references to 1 and 2 Maccabees, joined eventually by Son #5 who, in response to Antioco's claims to divinity, sings an anti-tyrant aria ("Apri gli occhi, o cieco"), moving Antioco to his "eat pork or die" ultimatum. This opening is more like Gigli's confrontation than Pariati's delay, but the lexical field changes quickly as Antioco promises the most brutal martyrdom of the sons if the disobedience is continued.

After Sons #6 and #7 enter, the Mother demands to be the first to die, followed by Son #7, who reproaches her for dying before him and inflicting on him a pain worse than death: "Pria di me tu morir? . . . Ah, cara Madre, questo materno amor non è" [You die ahead of me? . . . Oh dear Mother, this is not maternal love]. Moving closer to Pariati, the first Son is then fried alive, and Sons #2–#4 dispatched (this is a paraphrase of 2 Maccabees 7:4–13, and therefore presumes that the Sons were watching and that this was somehow suggested on scene in the Hofburgkapelle). Sons #5–#7 and the Mother still refuse to change their minds, with one of Charles VI's key terms in an aria ("La Costanza è già si forte"), and leading even Antioco to question himself in an aside.

With four Sons dead, Part I's closing chorus of Maccabees paraphrases Lamentations (5:7) and prepares the Mother's first moment of self-questioning at the recitative beginning of Part II ("Ma pur son madre, e qual vorrei non posso / senza tumulti al core / spogliarmi il sen di ogni materno amore. . . . [*Aria:*] Tante morti una sol vita / sostener come può mai?" [Still, I am a mother, and as such I cannot banish all maternal love from my breast without tumult in my heart. . . . How can one single life stand so many deaths?]). The meanings for the dowager Wilhelmine Amalia and for the empress Elisabeth Christiane would have been clear. Still, the difference from the hitherto canonical Fux/Pariati version in its characterization of the Mother is notable.

Antioco enters to take advantage of this moment of weakness, sarcastically asking her how she has enjoyed the spectacle of the first four deaths. Luchini added hyperbole, as Son #5 asks for more poison in his wounds to make his suffering greater, then sings an aria ("Bramo più lunga pena" [I desire longer pain]), and dies, only to be succeeded by Son #6. The Mother has another moment of weakness as the next Son, paraphrasing 2 Maccabees 7:18–19, reproaches Antioco for challenging God, and then sings his own death aria ("Cede al rigor la vita / . . . mia dolce Madre, addio" [My life gives in to the harshness (of torture) . . . goodbye, my sweet Mother]).

Since the Mother is imagined as speaking to her Sons in Hebrew, in line with 2 Maccabees 7:20, Antioco does not understand her counsel. Luchini included her standard reference to faith being instilled in the Sons together with her own breast milk, and the tyrant turns to tempt the last Son directly (2 Maccabees 7:24), then the Mother. The Son believes that his mother will want him to recant, but she insists on his holding on to faith even at the cost of his life ([*Son #7:*] "Ah, madre, dunque? . . . [*Madre:*] Perder la vita a fronte di ricchezze . . . / come il Re a te promise, ella è follia" [So, mother, therefore? . . . To lose your life for riches . . . as the king promised you, that is madness]). For both the tyrant and for Son #7, there are arias with difficult string parts ("Sciocchi, andate" and Son #7's last aria, "Già atroce il dolore"). Antioco promises all tortures for Son #7, and Luchini worked the speech of this Son (2 Maccabees 7:30–37) into a single recitative, also giving him another dying recitative to his mother.

Since the Biblical text ends with only the brief mention of the Mother's execution, Luchini took advantage of the moment to insert her own desire for a martyr's death in a recitative ("Del sacrilege, mostro, sono paghi già gli sdegni," referring to Antioco) and aria ("Ah! Mio Dio! Ecco si avventa / il gran colpo a farmi esangue" [Oh, my God, now there arrives the great blow to drain me of blood]). In the B section of the latter, she addresses her children in Heaven and dies at the end of the A section's repeat (without Ariosti's *interruptio*). With a closing chorus of angels paraphrasing "Justorum animae in manu Dei sunt" (Wisdom 3:1, All Saints' liturgy), Luchini produced a text with some of Gigli's bite but without Pariati's gruesomeness. It did, however, manage to follow 2 Maccabees' verse order, at the cost of having the Mother address only Son #7 in her final advice.[6]

The martyrial concreteness of the text is reminiscent of an earlier, and equally original, oratorio by Conti, *Il martirio di San Lorenzo*. But this one is also inventive.[7] The composer certainly could give detail—in the Mother's first aria, "La costanza è già sì forte," the phrase "che la voce / non avrà mai per lamenti," the last word receives repeated surface chromaticism of D$\sharp$5– D–D$\flat$ to signal the "laments" (ex. 8.1). For the "burning grates" prepared for Son #1, Antioco winds up in the tonal region of C$\sharp$, but the immediately following recitatives of the Mother and Son #5 are in G and D, respectively, as distant as possible in the *durus* system.

Other aspects have to do with the overall affect of arias. Son #5's Part I aria on life as pilgrimage, "Nasce l'uom viator," is set again as a *fuga a due soggetti*, in line with many other arias in the overall repertory that invoke wisdom literature. Praun's skills at large leaps were used in Antioco's aria "L'arte più fiera e barbara / rinforzerò" to depict the varieties of torture at the tyrant's disposal.[8] The Mother's final *scena* also employs a combination of normal recitative, *accompagnato*, and then a last aria to give a sense of her peaceful resignation to death, with no further second thoughts. Conti's score was indeed varied and moving, and it is no surprise that a copy of the libretto, at least, made its way to the Stuttgart court at some point (now D-Slb).

The meaning for the Habsburg daughters was clear: to hold on to Catholicism at all costs, even in the case of some doubts. The work also prepared them for the loss of children (which did indeed happen to both women). To bracket it with *Issipile* gave a kind of marriage/motherhood slant to this particular Lent, with Maria Theresia about to turn fifteen and Maria Anna fourteen.

Shepherds and Castrati

Finally, in order to get a sense of the novelty of Metastasio's famed Abel libretto of 1732 against earlier local versions, and how the experience of Lent might have been for the court, it is worthwhile to remember some details from the most recent previous treatment of the story, Salio/Reutter's *Abele** (13 March 1727), which had been heard by the same complement of royals as in 1732. This earlier oratorio was the first Cain piece done in the Imperial capital since Melani's, two generations before, and it was staged on 13 March: the second oratoric in a very full Lent, after Giovanni Porsile's *L'esaltatione di Salomone* and before works on Isaiah, John the Baptist, and a repeat of Pietro Pariati/J. J Fux's *Il testamento di Nostro Signore*, the last for Holy Week). The thematic overlap with Genesis is not apparent. But Reutter's work of 1727 begins in a rather old-fashioned way, with two

EX. 8.1 F. B. Conti, *L'osservanza della divina legge nel martirio de' Maccabei*, "Pria di tu"; A-Wn, Mus. Hs. 18167, fol. 37r.

parental arias each for Adamo and Eva, plus one each for the sons, before Lucifero even appears to take advantage of Caino's simmering jealousy. The paired structures, and relatively low literary register, again reinforce this piece's relationship to vernacular drama.

This was reinforced by the casting: most of the singers had not appeared in the massive Carnival opera (G. C. Pasquini/Caldara), *Don Chisciotte nella corte della duchessa*, with its five acts and some eleven characters. The performers for oratorios, with the exception of the hardworking bass Christoph Praun, were separated from the operatic stagings. Abele was apportioned to the seasoned castrato Orsini, while Caino was the soprano castrato "Giovanni," with the parents given to the veteran alto castrato Pietro Casati and the experienced Maria Anna Lorenzani, and Dio the older tenor Gaetano Borghi. Four of these appeared in other oratorios that Lent. Even if the authors of text and music were somewhat marginal or young (Reutter Jr. was nineteen; this is a similar case to other oratorios discussed here), it was a relatively strong cast for the Cain piece.

The opening of this 1727 Viennese *Abele* thus paid homage largely to tradition, with its miserable parents, its concentration on parental duty (of which Eva's advice aria to mothers works on a popular lexical level, perhaps aimed at the very young royal daughters), and its emphasis on Lucifero. Given that it was the first piece on the theme locally since 1678, one might have expected a somewhat different solution. Caino is angry and unreasonable from the very beginning, as his complaints in Part I about his failures at hunting show, for all that he considers himself to be an "eagle." Clearly, he has not realized the condition of sinful humanity, as Adamo's opening recitative had already pointed out. He is pre-warned of the dangers of jealousy, not only by his father but also by Dio Himself, to no avail. Salio also directly juxtaposed the revenge-seeking Lucifero with Abele's pure-hearted sacrifice and Caino's furiously jealous response. Part I ends on the cusp of the murder.

As in some other libretti, the fratricidal act of this 1727 work takes place offstage between the parts (the sermon must have referred directly to this), but Caino opens Part II aware of his actions ("un fratello svenai . . . innocente" [I killed my innocent brother by bloodletting]). There follow four dialogues: the gleeful Lucifero and the impenitent Caino; Dio and Caino; a trio for the three, including the Mark of Cain imposed by Dio; and a final reckoning between Dio and Lucifero. This is strongly fortified by the long dialogues with Lucifero, and, for the present purposes, Eva's counsel to others: "Oh! Non aveste, o madri, / un core così tenero, / che meno penereste / per l'alme audaci e perfide / de' figli ingrati" [Oh, if only you mothers did not have such a tender heart, you would suffer less for the overweening and faithless spirits of ungrateful sons]. Despite the seemingly moralistic tone, Reutter chose two chalumeaux in the scoring to set the tender affect of suffering mothers.[9] Indeed, it is Eva who discovers Abele's body, followed by laments for her and for Adamo. The piece ends quickly and sadly, with only the briefest of prophecies about the future coming of Christ.

It is not surprising that the work was not repeated, nor that the theme would be addressed five years later in a totally different way. We might suspect that Charles VI wanted a better, more up-to-date, version of the story for Metastasio's third in the series of post-1730 oratorios. Stroppa has justly emphasized Abel's role in Metastasio's text as a moral beacon of innocence, evident already in his opening praise of Divine Creation, counterposed to Caino's refusal to recognize his own faults and his ultimate murder of his brother.[10] Abel's first discourse evokes the tradition of Christian optimism, here in a twofold pastoral setting: the fields of Nature in which the tragedy takes place, and Abel/Christ's place as the Good Shepherd, with Eucharistic references.

Besides Farinelli, Orsini, and the ever-faithful Praun (Adamo), Theresia Reutter sang both Amital in *Sedecia* and Eva in Metastasio's work; all four would have had to learn a good deal of music quickly. Her three arias in *La morte d'Abel* range from the prophetic ("Qual diverrà quel fiume") to the philosophical ("Dall'istante del fallo primiero") to the furious ("Non sa che sia pietà"), a testimony—besides her recitatives of concern and denunciation for Abel and Cain, respectively—to her dramatic range. Pisani, otherwise active in operatic performances, was the Angel in Metastasio's work.

Whether because of Metastasio's trust in—or perhaps disdain for—Caldara, the librettist posed a major problem at the opening for musical treatment: some fifty-two lines of recitative before the first aria (as opposed to the more common twenty lines, found in *La Passione* of 1730 or *Sant'Elena al Calvario* in 1731). Abel's joyous opening, and his description of the blinding Divine light greeting his sacrifice (a hidden reference to the Eucharist; one is reminded of the future Karlskirche's altar design), render the following tragedy all the more striking and are followed by a trialogue among Eva and her sons, setting the stage for Abel's first exit aria.

Daunted or not by this long stretch of *versi sciolti*, Caldara responded by setting Abel's opening praise as accompanied recitative, beginning with an extended sonority which a listener would have taken as preparatory to B♭ major (Appendix). Yet, prefiguring the tragedy in a way impossible in words, Caldara turned Abel's joy immediately to the flattest tonal area possible by inflecting a minor resolution to the opening chord, rather as if he were upstaging the newly arrived librettist via the setting.

At the most musical moment of praise in this *accompagnato* ("Sempre il suo nome / canterò" [I will always sing His Name]), a linear descent in the bass again moves to flat sonorities, and so one might have suspected that Abel's encomium would be brief indeed—until Abel/Farinelli sang his "Quel buon pastor son io/I am the Good Shepherd," a long (modern performances range from ten to thirteen minutes) moment also set in flat regions, with numerous opportunities for the castrato's *messe di voce*, pathetic phrases, and register switches, accompanied by the triple-time continuo and interlocking violin. This was a spectacular lament—not a moment of optimism (ex. 8.2). The differences with the 1727 work would have been quite audible.[11]

What do we learn from both the recitative and aria that would not be apparent in the text alone? The recitative is accompanied only for Abel; frequent shifts to flat regions, in all three voices (Abel, Cain, Eva), give a sense of the seriousness of the moment, and the ductus of Abel's vocal line leads up to a high F♯4 although Eva's overall range is higher, as befits a female character. The aria begins with Farinelli's patented held note (C4), followed by "sensitive" ornamented lines ranging up to a high A5 (at "e tanto il gregge apprezza"). The second vocal section works in a lower and flatter register, finishing with more sustained notes for the singer's *messe di voce*. As a vocal introduction to the character, Caldara provided both the trademark elements of Farinelli's style as well as an extreme prolongation of this first aria, its length in performance (eight poetic lines) being three times as extended as the preceding recitative.

Viennese tradition saved the F/3♭ tonality for moments of the greatest sadness or tenderness, so Caldara's was an aria designed to show off—perhaps in accordance with Charles's advice to the singer—the most emotion-laden, if not the most virtuoso, side of Farinelli's technique (there would be more difficult arias later).[12] In the aria's A section, the prolonged descent of the second vocal entry (mm. 56–59) provides closure to what might otherwise have come off as a sort of monotone affect at this opening moment for Farinelli, while the surface chromaticism (mm. 95–99) of the

EX. 8.2 A. Caldara, *La morte d'Abel* (1732), Part I, opening recitative; A-Wn, Mus. Hs. 18146, fol. 7r.

EX. 8.3 L. Leo, *La morte d'Abel* (ca. 1737), Part I, opening recitative; F-Pn, D-6867, fol. 11r.

B section's end underscores "il *tenero* pastor," the last word then reinterpreted at the return of the A section.

Some other details stand out. The tonal range is surprisingly wide, and the opening ambiguity of B♭ with flattened or natural third is also omnipresent. The overall move is from flat to sharp for the description of Abel's sacrifice, and back at Eva's entrance through the first aria. Most surprising is Caldara's decision not to emphasize Caino's first clearly negative words, his aside "cruel certainty" of being rejected, by any gesture. By way of comparison, Leonardo Leo's popular version of 1737 repeated the word "crudel," the first time with an augmented fourth (ex. 8.3).

Though this moment in Part I inhabits tonally flat territories, Eva's subsequent recitative dialogue with the increasingly frenzied Caino moves to equally sharp regions in order to express the latter's self-torment ([Caino:] "Ah, queste sono / la mia pena crudel, sian premio o dono" [Ah, these (Abel's glory), whether they be his reward or a (Divine) gift, are my torment] (with a literary citation to Cyprian, and a musical settling around E/*durus*).

For all that Farinelli/Abel might have stolen the musical show, Metastasio's libretto—as Stroppa noted—features Caino "on stage" far more than any other character; the royals would have heard more of the veteran Orsini singing recitative than they might have expected. Orsini had also figured in *Sedecia* as the prophet Geremia, again as a foil to Farinelli's title role. Evidently he must have made his impression largely over the course of the recitatives apportioned to him; other settings leave more room for virtuosity.

In Caldara's piece, Eva's first aria, "Qual diverrà quel fiume?" (on sin "poisoning" the river of life), is more extrovert than Farinelli's previous one, and Theresia Reutter would have had her work cut out for her. Caino's "Alimentando il mio proprio tormento" is a perpetual-motion piece on his feeding on his own torment, in direct contrast with Abel's opening about fifteen minutes earlier in the work. The latter's second aria, "L'ape e il serpe spesso" (on bees and serpents drinking the same fluids with markedly different results, an ironic presaging of the plot), works via larger leaps and more florid writing, more directly in Farinelli's accustomed style.

Other aspects of the libretto relate directly to Holy Week and the Tomb tradition. In Part II, as Eva sees the body of the dead Abel (ll. 583ff), her second moment of grief after she has heard of his offstage death, her deictic description of her son's body, dragged on "stage," implies that the simulacrum of the Dead Christ was moved out of the Hofburgkapelle's Tomb to reinforce visually the parallel between the two figures. Musically, in a stretch of twenty *versi sciolti*, the recognition generates a brief sharp shift from a framework on C to one on E, the opposite of her pitch trajectory at the beginning. As in *Sant'Elena al Calvario*, the single female role has an important part.

The final arias for the major characters give some sense of their progress. As the plot demands, Abel leaves early in Part II, having sung an aria, "Questi al cor," expressing his own amazement at the depth of his love for his mother, set as another pathetic piece, this time on B with two sharps. Just a bit later, Adam's final concerted piece is "Dunque si sfoga in pianto?," questioning the contradiction between Eva's spoken joy at seeing her sons depart together and the worry that afflicts her. Its setting as a *fuga a due soggetti* and its performance by Praun underline its status as a paradoxically authoritative question. Further on, Caino's "Del fallo mi avvedo" traces his too-tardy recognition of, and penance for, his crime. Orsini received another of his patented arias with solo obbligato instrument, in this case a trombone, perhaps signaling Divine judgment which he had heard from the mouth of the Angelo. Finally, Eva's "Non sa che sia pietà" brings us back to the flat regions of Marian piety (C with two flats). With Patristic citations, Metastasio used the B section to imagine a prophecy of the heavenly signs—the earthquake, the sun's darkening—that would recur at the Crucifixion. The leaps in the unison violins were Caldara's response to this cosmic upheaval, even if here present only in Eva's imagining.

Kinship on Stage

How might all three of these "family" oratorios have related to the Habsburgs' own situation in 1732, a dynasty for which the practice of family was second only to Christianity as its value system? The exclusion of Sarah from the Hagar piece suggests—as is obvious from the title—the role of Divine Providence in saving seemingly desperate family situations, not unlike that of the heirless Charles VI; it is the opposite of Caldara's work discussed above. The 1732 conjunction points at wider links between family and oratorio, a kind of musical *quaresimale* based largely around kinship (the exception, *Sedecia*, being a kind of penitential counterpart to *Issipile*).

Perhaps the 1733 work on Tobit, due to Giovanni Cesare Pasquali and Reutter Jr., best underscores the link between family and versions of oratorios. Certainly Zeno and his libretti had been de-emphasized after Metastasio's arrival, but the revival of this theme so soon after the older poet's 1720 work is striking. Although the performance of this *Il ritorno di Tobia* of 5 March 1733 was not noted in newspapers or court diaries, it was of a very different work from the earlier one. Pasquini crafted a Tobit story almost without conflict, and with Sara present from the beginning of the piece; he also omitted Zeno's interminable counselors and the question of the retrieval of the ten talents' debt. The parents quarrel over Tobit's choices and their poverty, but in a relatively subdued manner, compared to the snarling of the 1720 piece. Rather, again announced by the dog, Tobias and Azaria return calmly at the end of Part I, and the healing of the father's blindness is accomplished without problem. Sara has an early aria as she prepares to enter her new family, and some of the story is retold by her once she arrives. Although there are a series of quotes from Tobit 12:2ff, and the earliest citations are from Tobit 11, the number of Patristic references is high, and indeed Sara's lines are flooded by them.

As the sovereign was the same as for Zeno's 1720 work, the question is posed as to what had changed to occasion the switch. Given the pedagogical role of oratorios, possibly the now-adolescent Maria Theresia and Maria Anna were the intended audience of this piece, promising them a happy future domestic life, and instructing them about how to behave as new brides, with less emphasis on their parents; that is, the musical imaginary of family life came together with its reality.

Oratorio, Tragedy, and Family

As a whole, then, the corpus of works examined here continued to be an alternative to the shortcomings of spiritual prose tragedy. The latter was largely restricted to pedagogical work of the various orders, while oratorios — to judge by the social appeal of the Isaac, Jephthe, and Maccabees stories — took the problems of character, penance, and Divine judgment to a wider or more powerful audience.

In its own way, this oratorio repertory also held on to Aquinas's linkage (the epigraph of chapter 1). Culturally, the most striking feature is how the stories — all based on the same Scriptural verses — changed radically depending on audience, family members, and not least devotional/musical aesthetics, a feature best heard in the Jephthe, Song of Songs, and Maccabees works after 1750 (chapters 5 and 7). This even holds inside the seemingly happy Tobit pieces, as Haydn's oratorio makes clear. The social reality of family—illegitimacy, slaves, fratricide, widowhood—lurked at a deeper level, in terms of both the productions and their range of meanings.

Indeed, the ideological content of some of these venues—for instance, the mix of culture and sources in the Crocifisso pieces—is best reflected in their portrayals of family. The linkage of these stories with the patriciate in Emilia and Tuscany is also striking, in terms of both individual palazzo performances and more civic-oriented occasions such as Lucca's.

Kinship's inflections of these pieces—as noted, musically staged penance invitations—brought their moral meanings home to the most basic personal relationships of the early modern era. Still, the political implications of obedience, Providence, suffering, and even sacrifice came through in a surprising number of pieces. Some of the family situations (illegitimacy, new children-in-law, disinheritance) were quite familiar, others less so. But the deployment of the stories and their widely varying approaches, often to nominally sacred figures (Sarah), pointed up how both doctrine and family were being reworked for an age of new family realities as both devotional expression and demography took decisive turns in the mid-eighteenth century.

ACKNOWLEDGMENTS

My foremost thanks to Lucia Marchi for her support over several years. I am grateful to Arnaldo Morelli and Huub van der Linden for their unparalleled knowledge of Seicento oratorios, and to Martha Feldman for her thoughts on the Settecento works discussed here. I am also thankful to Marta Tonegutti and Kristin Rawlings from the University of Chicago Press for gently nudging me on to completion of the manuscript, and to Clay Mettens for music typesetting. I am grateful to the Press's outside readers for their comments. Several music libraries and librarians made access to sources easier: John Shepard at the University of California/Berkeley Music Library, and the staffs of Palermo's Biblioteca Comunale and Biblioteca Centrale della Regione Siciliana, Lucca's Biblioteca Statale e Governativa, and Ravenna's Biblioteca Classense.

Appendix

METASTASIO/CALDARA, OPENING OF *LA MORTE D'ABEL* (VIENNA, 1732)

TABLE A.1. Metastasio/Caldara, opening of *La morte d'Abel*

Speaker	Lines	Themes	Musical features
Abel	1–3	Creation	Accompanied recitative; resolution B♭/*mollis*
	4–6	Praise	High F4
	6–8	Sacrifice of lamb	C/*mollis*
	8–11	Humility	B♭
Caino	12–14	Lament/joy	Rec. semplice
Abel	15–17	Sharing	♯ tonalities
Caino	17–19	Vanity	–
Abel	20–30	Sacrificing affect	High F♯4
Abel	31–41	Light effects	C/*durus*
Caino	42–48	Doubts	Rising bass
Eva, Caino	49–52	Dialogue	Shift to *mollis*
Caino	53	(angry aside)	–
Eva	54–61	Good in Cain, return to work	C/*mollis*
Abel	62–66	Beloved sheep	B♭

TABLE A.2. Aria (Abel), outline of structure

Speaker	lines	Themes	Mm.	Musical features
A	1–4	A section:	1–19	Ritornello in F/*mollis*
	(*settenari*)	Vocal 1	20–44	Ascent to A5; move to E♭
		Vocal 2	44–79	Prolonged descent
	5–7	B section	80–99	C/*mollis*

Text: Quel buon pastor son io, / che tanto il gregge apprezza, / che per la sua salvezza / offre se stesso ancor. / [B section:] Conosco ad una ad una / le mie dilette agnelle; / e riconoscon quelle / il tenero pastor. [I am that good shepherd who prizes his flock so much that he offers himself up for their salvation. I know my lambs one by one; and they recognize their tender shepherd.]

NOTES

Chapter One

1. For issues on how "staged" the oratorios in the repertories considered here might have been, see below.

2. As is the norm in exegetical studies, I refer to the "Binding (and not Sacrifice) of Isaac."

3. On family demography, see Giovanna Da Molin, *Famiglia e matrimonia nell'Italia del Seicento* (Bari: Cucucci, 2000), esp. 125–58 on the size and breadth of families. One notable advantage of this study is its inclusion of southern Italy in the demographic data. Top-down efforts to remake family life in the era of absolutism were relatively few until the later Settecento.

4. Colin Rose, *A Renaissance of Violence: Homicide in Early Modern Italy* (Cambridge: Cambridge University Press, 2019), 28–29; and Sanne Muurling, *Everyday Crime, Criminal Justice, and Gender in Early Modern Bologna* (Leiden: Brill, 2021), 62–67.

5. Huub van der Linden, "A Family at the Opera: The Bolognetti as an Audience at the Theatres of Rome, (1694–1736)," *Recercare* 30 (2018): 145–200.

6. For the effects of legislation, legal theory, marriages inside Protestant territories, and especially the validity of marriage as "consecrated" not by a priest but by sexual relations or by physically transferring the bride, see Giuseppe Mazzanti, *Matrimoni post-tridentini: Un dibattito dottrinale fra continuità e cambiamento (secc. XVI–XVIII)* (Bologna: Bononia University Press, 2020), esp. 13–73 on "presumed marriages" without necessarily being present in church.

7. For the knowledge of the Biblical stories among a wide audience (as well as for women's writing well into the Seicento), see Erminia Ardissino, *Donne interpreti della Bibbia nell'Italia della prima età moderna: comunità ermeneutiche e riscritture* (Turnhout: Brepols, 2020). For instance, already in the Quattro-

cento Lucrezia Tornabuoni had rewritten the salient events from the Tobit story.

8. Irene Fosi, *Papal Justice: Subjects and Courts in the Papal State, 1500–1750* (Washington, DC: Catholic University Press, 2011), esp. 142–54 on polygamy, paternal authority, and same-sex relationships.

9. By taking this approach, I am following in the line of Virginia Cox (e.g., "Rethinking Counter-Reformation Literature," in *Innovation in the Italian Counter-Reformation*, ed. S. McHugh and A. Wainwright [Newark: University of Delaware Press, 2020], 15–55, and the "anti-classical" turn described by Marc Föcking and Daniel Fliege, "Implicit Anti-Classicism: Imitating and Exhausting Old and New Classicisms in Spiritual Tragedy and Spiritual Petrarchism," in *A Companion to Anticlassicisms in the Cinquecento*, ed. Föcking, Susanne A. Friede, Florian Mehltretter, and Angela Oster (Berlin: de Gruyter, 2023), 105–66.

10. Even if one were to consider the Isaac and Hagar stories as being examples of "tragedia con lieto fine" in Giambattista Giraldi Cinzio's mid-Cinquecento terms (cf. Föcking, *A Companion to Anticlassicisms in the Cinquecento*, 121–22), their distance from the Biblical models makes them into a different kind of genre.

11. On this duet, "In faccio di morte / d'Isaaco la gloria," see chapter 7 below. The previous Isaac piece had been Camilla de' Rossi's, performed in 1708 (on her setting and that of M. A. Ziani the previous year, see chapter 4).

12. For an incisive discussion of theatrical aesthetics and practice, see Enrico Mattioda, "Ifigenia e la figlia di Iefte: una polemica illuminista a teatro," in *Sacro e/o profano nel teatro fra Rinascimento ed Età dei Lumi*, ed. S. Castellaneta and F. Minervini (Bari: Cacucci, 2009), 213–29.

13. In 1709, the Milanese Theatines in S. Antonio Abate put on a performance of *Concerto di dolori tra il Figliuolo e la Madre* (libretto only: I-Mb; lost music by G. B. Brevi) sung in the chapel of S. Maria del Suffragio on Holy Thursday, followed by similar pieces concentrating on the same family relationship in 1714 and 1718. This sharing of maternal-filial grief was important for several stories here (Abel, Ishmael, Isaac, the Maccabees).

14. It should be remembered that the poet's texts, even the sacred ones, were subject to revision in performance. For instance, the 1739 Milanese *La Passione e morte di Nostro Signor Gesù Cristo* (I-Ma), performed by the Augustinian nuns of S. Maria della Stella (or della Consolazione), is a version of Metastasio's 1730 *azione sacra*, shorn of many arias. No responsibility for text or music is given in the print, although the piece is one of the last testimonies to the performance of complex music in Milanese female houses. For Viennese performances, see Alexander von Weilen, *Zur Wiener Theatergeschichte. Die vom Jahre 1629 bis zum Jahre 1740 am Wiener Hofe zur Aufführung gelangten Werke theatralischen Charakters und Oratorien* (Vienna: Alfred Hölder,

Notes to Pages 4–6 • 229

1901), and Herbert Seifert, *Die Oper am Wiener Kaiserhof im 17. Jahrhundert* (Tutzing: Schneider, 1985).

15. Vittorio Cattelan, "'Se desideri Allah / egli è in ogni creatura': Metastasio a Costantinopoli nelle traduzioni di Giovanni Eremian," in *Orizzonti della musica italiana a Costantinopoli nel primo Ottocento* (Lucca: LIM, 2021), 69–114.

16. Again, Sabrina Stroppa's notes to her edition (P. Metastasio, *Oratori sacri* [Venice: Marsilio, 1996]) and her *"Fra notturni sereni": Le azioni sacre del Metastasio* (Florence: Leo S. Olschki, 1993), esp. 81–116, continue to be essential reading, not least for the Patristic background of the texts.

17. This Roman repertory was first studied by Domenico Alaleona, *Studi su la storia dell'oratorio musicale in Italia* (Turin: Fratelli Bocca, 1908).

18. The standard work on the condition of oratorio at all four institutions is Pier Giuseppe Gillio, *L'attività musicale negli ospedali di Venezia nel Settecento* (Florence: Leo S. Olschki, 2006), 223–32, which also has a breakdown of arias and the like in pieces of the 1760s–1770s; other important studies include Helen Geyer, *Das venezianische Oratorium* (Laaber: Laaber-Verlag, 2005), and some remarks in Berthold Over, *"Per la gloria di Dio": soloistische Kirchenmusik an den venezianischen Ospedali* (Bonn: Orpheus-Verlag, 1998). For the practice of oratorios earlier in the century in the female foundations, see now Vanessa Tonelli, *"Le Figlie Di Coro*: Women's Musical Education and Performance at the Venetian Ospedali Maggiori, 1660–1740" (PhD diss., Northwestern University, 2022), for example 165–72.

19. All work is indebted to the studies of the massive set of volumes by Howard Smither, *A History of the Oratorio*, esp. vol. 1 (Chapel Hill: University of North Carolina Press, 1977); more detailed works include the standard studies of Arnaldo Morelli, "La musica a Roma nella seconda metà del Seicento attraverso l'archivio Cartari-Febei," in *La musica a Roma attraverso le fonti d'archivio*, ed. B. M. Antona, A. Morelli, and V. Vita Spagnuolo (Lucca: LIM, 1994), 107–36; Morelli, *Il tempio armonico: Musica nell'oratorio dei Filippini in Roma (1575–1705)* (Laaber: Laaber-Verlag, 1991); Morelli, "La circolazione dell'oratorio italiano nel Seicento," *Studi musicali* 26 (1997): 105–86; Morelli, "Un bell'oratorio all'uso di Roma: Patronage and Secular Context of the Oratorio in Baroque Rome," in *Music Observed: Studies in Memory of William C. Holmes*, ed. C. Reardon and S. Parisi (Warren: Harmonie Park Press, 2005), 333–51; and for Pasquini's works (the *Caino e Abele* and the *Ismaele* whose libretti's familial relations are mentioned below), Morelli's *La virtù in corte: Bernardo Pasquini (1637–1710)* (Lucca: LIM, 2016). Other essential work includes Saverio Franchi, *Drammaturgia romana*, vols. 1–2 (Rome: IBIMUS, 1988–97); Franchi (ed.), *Percorsi dell'oratorio romano da "Historia Sacra" a melodramma spirituale* (Rome; IBIMUS, 2002); Christian Speck, *Das italienische Oratorium 1625–1665: Musik und Dichtung* (Turnhout: Brepols, 2003);

Johann Herczog, *Il perfetto melodramma spirituale: l'oratorio italiano nel suo periodo classico* (Rome: IBIMUS, 2013); P. Besutti (ed.), *L'oratorio musicale italiano e i suoi contesti (secc. XVII–XVIII)* (Florence: L. S. Olschki, 2002); and Huub van der Linden, "The Unexplored Giant: Use Histories of Italian Oratorio around 1700" (PhD diss., European History Institute Florence, 2012). For Roman oratorios in Vienna, see Marko Deisinger, "Römische Oratorien am Hof der Habsburger in Wien in der zweiten Hälfte des 17. Jahrhunderts: Zur Einführung und Etablierung des Oratoriums in der kaiserlichen Residenz," *Musicologica austriaca* 29 (2010): 89–111. For general issues of rewriting Biblical texts, see Elisabetta Selmi, "Riscritture bibliche nel dramma sacro fra Seicento e Settecento," in *Gli italiani e la Bibbia nella prima età moderna: Leggere, riscrivere, interpretare*, ed. E. Ardissino and E. Boillet (Turnhout: Brepols, 2018).

20. The essential studies here are Daniela Frigo, *Il padre di famiglia: governo della casa e governo civile nella tradizione della "economia" fra Cinque e Seicento* (Rome: Bulzoni, 1985), and Giovanni Ciappelli, "Identità collettiva," in Ciappelli (ed.), *Famiglia e religione in Europa* (Rome: Edizioni di Storia e Letteratura, 2011).

21. It is striking that most of the stories in this book have to do with sons, with the exception of Jephthe and of Ruth.

22. Jean Cordier, *La famiglia santa*, bk. 2 (Macerata: G. F. Panelli, 1674); the I-Rn copy was owned by a Franciscan tertiary (and therefore possibly a husband and/or father), 170. In total, some twenty-three copies (most complete) of this three-volume work survive in Italy.

23. Cordier, *La famiglia santa*, bk. 2, pt. 1, 126–34, for the Hypostatic Union.

24. Cordier, *La famiglia santa*, bk. 2, pt. 1, 147–50.

25. See, for example, Maria Doerfler, *Jephthah's Daughter, Sarah's Son: The Death of Children in Late Antiquity* (Oakland: University of California Press, 2019).

26. This study thus takes some distance from the recent trend of discerning "Enlightenment Catholicism" in our period, not least because of the ongoing importance of Patristic and medieval thought in oratorio libretti as late as—and beyond—Metastasio (not to mention the eighteenth-century anti-Judaism also found in some of these texts). It is more accurate to conclude that Benedict XIV (1740–58) found an only partially reformed Church on his accession, and that many of the later Settecento's changes in devotion and model families, evident in the post-1750 libretti studied here, represented a catch-up attempt.

27. For the case of Pietro Ottoboni requesting an oratorio to be used as an opera with full staging, along with other examples, see Clotilde Fino, "Drammi e oratori nella corrispondenza di Francesco de Lemene con il cardinale Pietro Ottoboni," *Recercare* 30 (2018): 119–43. The best new work on the Settecento's

views of oratorio's aesthetics is Huub van der Linden, "Eighteenth-Century Oratorio Reform in Practice: Apostolo Zeno Revises a Florentine Libretto," *Eighteenth-Century Music* 26 (2019): 31–52.

28. As noted below (chapter 4), one of Metastasio's oratorios was done in 1749 in the Munich court theater.

29. Saverio Franchi, "Il principe Livio Odescalchi e l'oratorio 'politico,'" in *L'oratorio musicale italiano e i suoi contesti*, ed. Paola Besutti, 141–258.

30. It will be remembered that the Habsburgs controlled Naples and Lombardy from 1707 onward, the latter remaining Austrian until the arrival of French troops in 1796.

31. Juliane Riepe, *Die Arciconfraternita di S. Maria della Morte in Bologna* (Paderborn: F. Schöningh, 1998).

32. On the Oratorians outside Rome, see Stefano Boero, "Gli Oratoriani all'Aquila tra Seicento e Settecento: cultura e spiritualità," *Annali di Storia moderna e contemporanea* 16 (2010): 485–516; alas, there are no preserved oratorio libretti from this institution.

33. I have omitted Viennese oratorios after Charles VI's reign (i.e., 1740), but see Marko Motnik's very useful study, "Oratorien am Wiener *Theater nächst der Burg* in der Ära Durazzos," *Studien zur Musikwissenschaft* 60 (2018): 45–125.

34. First published by Smither, *A History of the Oratorio*, vol. 1, 270–71, they are now the subject of a detailed essay in conjunction with the documentary evidence from Ottoboni's accounts, Teresa Chirico, "'Balconi dorati per i musici': la prassi rappresentativa alla corte del cardinale Pietro Ottoboni fra il 1690 e il 1708," in *Spectacles et performances artistiques à Rome (1644–1740)*, ed. A.-M. Goulet, J. M. Dominguez, and É. Oriol (Rome: École Française de Rome, 2021), 151–65. For the 1666 Bolognese *Abelle*, see chapter 2 below.

35. On the move into theaters in Naples after 1780, see Franco Piperno, *La Bibbia all'opera: drammi sacri in Italia dal tardo Settecento al Nabucco* (Rome: NeoClassica, 2018); for the 1715 performance in Perugia's Teatro della Sapienza Vecchia, see the copy of the anonymous *Santa Maria Maddalena de' Pazzi* in I-PEc. On the interplay of an oratorio with the annual cycle of opera, ballet, dancing, and prose comedies in Pistoia, see Maria Fedi, *"Tuo lumine": L'accademia dei Risvegliati e lo spettacolo a Pistoia tra Sei e Settecento* (Florence: Florence University Press, 2011), 198–211, for performances in the Palazzo Comunale from 1716. There is also a record of Metastasio's *Gioas* in the Teatro dei Risvegliati in 1744 (Alberto Chiappelli, *Storia del teatro in Pistoia* [Pistoia: Officina tipografica cooperativa, 1913], 128). Later in the century, two important cases of sacred opera/oratorio performed in theaters are studied by Anthony R. Del Donna, *Opera, Theatrical Culture and Society in Late Eighteenth-Century Naples* (Farnham: Ashgate, 2012), 147–91; cf. also Piperno, *La Bibbia in musica*, passim.

36. I have used the verb "to stage" freely here; for oratorios that began to be staged in Italy as early as 1715, see below, and although it is hard to find payments for costumes and sets—suggesting that the "staging" was limited—there are printed deictic indications (and a few in manuscript) for basic sets.

37. I have deliberately omitted the fascinating works in the genre by J. S. Mayr, since there is an excellent monograph on them, and because they come at the very end of our period. For Sacchini's Latin oratorios, see the extensive overview in Geyer, *Das venezianische Oratorium*.

38. Antonio Dell'Olio, *Drammi sacri e oratori musicali in Puglia nei secoli XVII e XVIII* (Galatina: M. Congedo, 2013), esp. 83–106. This is evident in the pieces for the small town of Fasano around 1695, but other cities had witnessed performances prior to these.

39. These Rogation processions, often with a strong Marian component, continue in modern times in Castel S. Pietro, Bazzano, Imola, and other towns (e.g., https://www.ilnuovodiario.com/2023/05/15/dallentrata-alla -benedizione-in-piazza-il-racconto-per-immagini-delle-rogazioni/, accessed 21 December 2023).

40. This point was noted by Girolamo Clodenio, *Discorsi per la novena e solennità . . .* (Venice: G. G. Hertz, 1678), 572.

41. The anonymous account is given in Amachilde Pellegrini, "Spettacoli lucchesi: [anni] 1697–1700," *Memorie e documenti per servire alla storia di Lucca* 14, no. 1 (1914): 193–94.

Chapter Two

1. The further (and musical) ramifications of Adam's descendants—the birth of Seth, and the mention in 4:22–23 of Jubal and Tubalcain as instrumentalists and metalworkers—seem not to occur in the libretti discussed here.

2. This is the 1757 Palermo *L'Aurora foriera della pace fra Giacobbe, ed Esaù*. The passage from Genesis on Jacob and Esau was the Mass Old Testament reading for the Saturday after the Second Sunday of Lent.

3. The idea, still present in Metastasio, that Cain's real sin was not in killing his brother but in despairing of repentance for having done so, goes back to Ambrose and was reiterated by Angelo Paciuchelli, *Lezioni morali sopra Giona profeta*, vol. 3 (Venice: P. Baglioni, 1677), 343.

4. On this, see Stroppa's discussion in "*Fra notturni sereni.*"

5. *L'invidia giudaica contro N. Sig. Gesù Cristo*, (Milan: n.p., 1763; for the Friday after the Third Sunday; in I-Mb).

6. "Oh Padre, il primogenitor ha da far la casa. Si!, questa è la colpa di Caino, che *non de primis obtulit . . .*" (i.e., Cain did not bring his first fruits for sacrifice,

Notes to Pages 21–28 • 233

and he tarried in making it, earning God's wrath and non-acceptance); Carlo Lombardo, *Sermoni dominicali*, pts. 1–2 (Naples: Novello de Bonis, 1688), 413–14.

7. Emanuele di Gesù Maria, *Frutti del Carmelo, discorsi morali* (Rome: Filippo Maria Mancini, 1667), 343.

8. Rose, *A Renaissance of Violence*, 1–41.

9. This was evident in two Cain/Abel works sponsored by female monasteries in Palermo, the Stimmate and the Vergini (*L'Abele: Oratorio . . . per la solennità delle 40. Hore* [Palermo, 1713] and *Abele svenato per mano della vendetta* [Palermo, 1714]), both for Forty Hours' devotions.

10. Antonio Masini, *Bologna perlustrata* (Bologna: Vittorio Benacci, 1666), vol. 1, 148; and Antonella Ranaldi, "La chiesa di S. Maria del Soccorso e le chiese sulle mura. Domenico Tibaldi e il cardinale Gabriele Paleotti," in *Domenico e Pellegrino Tibaldi. Architettura e Arte a Bologna nel secondo Cinquecento*, ed. F. Ceccarelli and D. Lenzi (Venice: Marsilio, 2011), 221–22 and fig. 9.

11. All three copies of the libretto have manuscript changes from "1666" to "1667" on the title page; only the I-Bc copy has the stage action and set design indications. Now facing via dell'Indipendenza, S. Benedetto is large (~1,000 square meters, like the Madonna di Galliera), and there could have been a respectable turnout for the performance of this piece. Eva's lament would have evoked Alessandro Tiarin's side-chapel altarpiece of the *Lament of the Virgin* inside S. Benedetto's nave.

12. The incipit is: [Adamo:] "Folle Adamo!"; [Eva:] "Eva infelice." The *Il fratricidio* is found as the title for the 1678 score and libretto for Vienna.

13. Smither, introduction to Melani's *Il sacrificio di Abel* ("Italian Oratorio 1650–1800," 3; New York: Garland Press, 1986), [iii–iv].

14. *Orazioni sagre*, 46–78. The edition was dedicated to the Milanese civic leader Count Bartolomeo Arese; our Jesuit exegete (1590–1662), active around Milan, put out numerous Lenten sermons, hagiographies, and other exegetical works which were reprinted until century's end.

15. Morelli, *La virtù in corte*, 253–62; I refer the reader to Morelli's discussion.

16. For instance, Giovanni Battista Bigarolo's *Prediche quaresimali* (Milan: Francesco Vigone, 1686), dedicated to Leopold I, uses the story for the homily on the Thursday after Ash Wednesday, evidently considering it as the first act in the "history of sin." Various details of the tale are also mentioned in Carlo Antonio Menochio's popular "sermon-chats," the *Stuore* (Rome: Felice Cesaretti, 1689), vol. 1, 412–14.

17. For all that the printed Venetian libretto bears a date of 1707, the composer is not known to have had other commissions from the maritime city, and his piece is more likely to have originated in Rome a few years earlier.

18. The work seems to be a response to a poetic anthology of almost the

same name two years earlier, produced by the administrators and students of Siena's Collegio Tolomei (see chapter 7 below on this institution): *Agnus occisus ab origine mundi* (Florence, 1697), a literary collection (there is one three-voice "cantata" on Job) which lists various prefigurings of Christ as Slain Lamb but oddly enough omits Abel. The 1699 oratorio is listed, and the suggestion of its author Pollioni given, in Franchi, *Drammaturgia romana*, vol. 1, 744.

19. [*Abele*:] "Hear the words of Abel, your brother; whoever is cruel to parents is cruel to God; [*Aria*:] Cease wounding our mother with your ferocious words. . . . [*Cain*:] Shall I now say maledictions of Abel? For I am the older and the greater in strength. . . .

20. Morosini himself would that same year dedicate the reprise of Antonio Lotti's oratorio *S. Romoaldo* to Clement XI, giving a sense of his pro-Papal stance. On this piece, see Franchi, *Drammaturgia Romana*, vol. 2, 17.

21. For Arcangela Tarabotti's defense of Eve as a figure of free will, see most recently Erminia Ardissino, *Donne interpreti della Bibbia nell'Italia della prima età moderna: comunità ermeneutiche e riscritture* (Turnhout: Brepols, 2020), 244–51.

22. This is on the final f. 38; thus, the copying happened outside Venice, probably in Rome.

23. The piece is mentioned by Chirico, "Balconi Dorati," 154. No music is traceable.

24. "O felice umanità! / alla via da te smarrita, / se ritorni al fin pentita / il tuo duolo cesserà." There is a modern full score of the work at https://vmirror .imslp.org/files/imglnks/usimg/c/c7/IMSLP454385-PMLP621532-Scarlatti _Cain-full_score.pdf (accessed 23 December 2023).

25. *L'Abele. Oratorio da cantarsi nella Chiesa del venerabile monastero delle Stimate per la solennità delle 40. Hore* (Palermo: n.p., 1713).

26. This is on f. 31r. Although the score's title page says "Oratorio a sei voci," there are actually seven characters; presumably there was doubling for one of the "Voce" parts. The original score can be accessed at https://digital -collections.library.sfsu.edu/Documents/Detail/il-primo-omicidio-oratorio -a-6-voci-con-strom.-originale-cover-with-marbled-paper/3605?item=3680 (accessed 1 December 2023).

Chapter Three

1. The one traceable piece on Hagar's Flight (Genesis 16) is Bellardi and Salvolini's 1732 *La fuga di Agarre*, a work on the importance of humility (i.e., Hagar's obedience in returning to the family), done in Ravenna for the annual feast (not the feast days) of Sts. Gaetano Thiene and Philip Neri; presumably

Notes to Pages 40–42 · 235

it was meant to underscore the humility of the sixteenth-century saints. Perti's first, evidently 1683, version is, as Francesco Lora discovered, entitled "Sara" and preserved in I-Bsp, P. 54 (liner notes to the recording on Bongiovanni 2451–52; [Bologna, 2008]).

2. Flavio Lanciano's *Abimelech amor, et poena* was presented on the Saturday after the Second Sunday in Lent (22 February) 1704 at the Crocifisso.

3. The best discussion of the early modern interpretations is John Thompson, *Writing the Wrongs: Women of the Old Testament among Biblical Commentators from Philo through the Reformation* (New York: Oxford University Press, 2001), 17–99. A 1723 oratorio from Livorno—with a large Jewish community—considered that the Synagogue had been rejected in the Banishing of Hagar; *La sinagoga repudiata nella repudiazione d'Agar* (Livorno: n.p., 1723; in I-Pu).

4. For the history of African American theology appropriating Hagar as an emblem of Black womanhood, see Delores S. Williams, "Hagar in African-American Biblical Appropriation," in *Hagar, Sarah, and Their Children: Jewish, Christian, and Muslim Perspectives*, ed. P. Trible and L. M. Russell (Louisville: Westminster John Knox Press, 2006), 171–84. More recently, Andrew Prevot links her story, and its problems, to other theological trends (*Theology and Race: Black and Womenist Traditions in the United States* [Leiden: Brill, 2020], 1–79).

5. From at least the Pian Breviary and Missal of 1568/70 onward, none of the other stories here from Genesis, Judges, Song of Songs, or Maccabees appear verbatim in any weekday or Sunday Lenten reading in the Mass or Office.

6. Oliva's overall art patronage is discussed in Franco Mormando, "Gian Paolo Oliva: The Forgotten Celebrity of Baroque Rome," in *The Holy Name: Art of the Gesù, Bernini and His Age*, ed. L. Wolk-Simon (Philadelphia: St. Joseph's University Press, 2018), 225–51.

7. "The great crimes of children flow from their parents, and the sterility of branches can be traced to their roots. . . . For all that there may be two loves in Abraham's house, Wisdom should not level itself down to Charity. For the heavens know that, unless Hagar were to be banished with her child, Isaac's inheritance would not begin in his father's house"; Oliva, *In selecta Scripturae loca ethicae commentationes* (Lyons: Annison & Posuel, 1677), 90 (this edition was dedicated to Emperor Leopold I, which complicates the later reception of oratorios on this theme in Vienna).

8. Oliva, *In selecta Scripturae*, 94.

9. Giovanni Battista Manni, *Quaresimale prima* (Venice: Andrea Polletti, 1681; inscribed to the Dowager Empress Eleonora Gonzaga in Vienna), 358 and 422.

10. D. Mayno, *Il decalogo descritto e spiegato* (Naples: M. L. Nuzi, 1697), 253–54; Antonio Glielmo, *Le grandezze della Santissima Trinita* (Venice: li Baba, 1678), Discourse 15, "Paternity Diffused," 142–53. In a sermon for the Fifth Sunday after Pentecost (on Matthew 5), the Franciscan Giuseppe di Como managed to contrast Cain's anger and the slave-son evil of Ishmael with the beloved nature of Isaac, tying together Genesis 4, 21, and 22 (*Annuale* [Venice: P. Baglioni, 1670], 203–5). In a similar vein, the story was used as an example of why parents should check on their children's games by Menochio, *Le Stuore*, vol. 2, 203.

11. Kim Siebenhüner, *Bigamie und Inquisition in Italien 1600–1750* (Paderborn: F. Schöningh, 2006). I am grateful to Prof. Siebenhüner for her clarification of the social origin of these cases.

12. For the remarkable variety (perhaps some 140 surviving canvases) of both devotional understanding and visual representations of the story in Dutch painting, see Christina P. Sellin, *Fractured Families and Rebel Maidservants: The Biblical Hagar in Seventeenth-Century Dutch Art and Literature* (New York: Continuum, 2006), esp. 29–68 (devotional) and 69–150 (for the first Flight, Banishment, and Rescue episodes). Although there seems no possibility of cultural influence (most of the painters in this study were Netherlandish Protestants), the similarities with the character lability of Hagar, Sarah, and Abraham are still striking.

13. This palazzo still exists, but in private (Marconi family) hands and without housing any documentable image of the Biblical story. Hagar's story was normally painted for private collections, and the massive art holdings of Pietro Ottoboni included three paintings of her, two of the Sacrifice of Isaac, and one of the Tobit account (Edward J. Olszewski, *The Inventory of Paintings of Cardinal Pietro Ottoboni (1667–1740)* [New York: Peter Lang, 2004]), noteworthy in light of the Cardinal's contributions to P. P. Bencini's Binding of Isaac oratorio discussed below (chapter 4).

14. On the two paintings, see Denis Mahon's entries in *Guercino: Master Painter of the Baroque* (Washington, DC: National Gallery of Art, 1992), on the 1652 Angel and 1658 Cento works, 296 and 304. The recipient of the latter painting, Cardinal Lorenzo Mercuriali, seems not to have had musical connections.

15. The overall literature on Mediterranean slavery is too vast to mention here, apart from Salvatore Bono's lifelong works, summarized on a wide scale in his *Schiavi musulmani nell'Italia moderna* (Naples: Edizioni scientifiche italiane, 1999), esp. 21–45 for their origin (largely Turkey and the Middle East) and demography (largely in Livorno and Naples), along with his *Schiavi: una storia mediterranea (XVI–XIX secolo)* (Bologna: Il Mulino, 2016). Here I concentrate on Bologna as an important and understudied center, except

Notes to Pages 44–49 · 237

for Sarti's essay mentioned presently. It seems that there were few enough African/Eastern Mediterranean slaves in Vienna that few, if any, would physically be present in the Hofburgkapelle for performances.

16. On the Bolognese slave population and estimates for its size, see Raffaella Sarti, "Bolognesi schiavi dei 'Turchi' e schiavi 'turchi' a Bologna tra Cinque e Settecento: alterità etnico-religiosa e riduzione in schiavitù," *Quaderni storici* 2 (2001): 437–74. It should be remembered that Bologna was the second city of the Papal State, for all that its demography was different from Rome.

17. Bono, *Schiavi: una storia*, breaks these down by origin (e.g., 59–67 and esp. 71–75) on a Europe-wide scale.

18. On this idea inside Protestant understandings, see Thompson, *Writing the Wrongs*, 63, and Sellin, *Fractured Families*, 36–39; the latter's fascinating explication of Dutch visual exegesis of the story is not entirely paralleled by the Catholic literature and is omitted here. An argument for the interreligious nature of some of the libretti is given in Andrea Celli, "Figli di Agar e Ismaele: Riferimenti interreligiosi nei libretti per oratorio nel Seicento italiano?," in *Testi, tradizioni, attraversamenti: Prospettive comparatistiche sulla drammaturgia europea fra Sei e Settecento*, ed. A. Munari et al. (Padua: Padua University Press, 2019), 13–30. This essay concentrates on Scarlatti's setting and on a depiction of the Hagar story by the de Bry brothers which orientalizes her.

19. Filippo Setaioli's Christmas sermon imagined Divine mercy at Christ's manger, comparing her previous banishment from the world until the Nativity as being like the Banishment of Hagar; *Orationi e discorsi*, pt. 2 (Venice: Baglioni, 1678), 139.

20. The family's relationship to oratorio is well covered by Victor Crowther, *The Oratorio in Bologna (1650–1730)* (Oxford: Oxford University Press, 1999), 12–14.

21. Maurizio was the nephew of his namesake uncle, a literary figure in the local *Accademia dei Gelati*. No other writings by him seem to survive.

22. Information on the two is available at https://www.wandruszka -Genealogie.eu/Antonio.php. Astorre's son Antonio was the dedicatee of the 1670 Bologna reprint of Maurizio Cazzati's op. 3 motets (orig. ed. 1647).

23. Orsi post-mortem inventory, 26 January 1677, Archivio di Stato di Bologna, sez. VII/544, Famiglie, "Orsi": no slaves are listed, nor musical instruments. It is possible that Chiara possessed the latter.

24. Lora (liner notes to the Bongiovanni recording) carefully compared the Modena and S. Petronio scores as well as the various libretti, noting the following changes in the 1685 Modena performance: in Part I, an extra aria for the Angel ("Godi pur") plus minor changes elsewhere; in Part II, the expansion of the trio "Cedi a me," plus the replacement of Abramo/Sara's "Si mio

cor" with "Fra si dolci catene." He also listed the *licenza* in the 1687 libretto and the encomia of the Ottoboni for the 1689 revival, along with a different performance in Lucca that year.

25. Masini, *Bologna perlustrata*, vol. 1, 147: "le feste di precetto si fa l'oratione mentale, con sermone e musica, dal primo Novembre sino a Pasqua."

26. On Rinaldo's problems with his sons, see M. Al-Kalak's entry in the *DBI*, 87 (2016).

27. On "the distance of a bowshot" for the Romans, see Wallace McLeod, "The Range of the Ancient Bow," *Phoenix* 19 (1965): 1–14; in Bolognese terms, roughly from the front portal of S. Petronio to Palazzo Orsi.

28. This piece is given in Speck, *Das italienische Oratorium*.

29. On the 1675 commission, see Morelli, *La virtù in corte*, 38–39, and his previous work cited there; for the circulation of Bicilli/Scarlatti's text in 1677 via Oratorian circles, Morelli, "La circolazione," 132.

30. The literature has not advanced markedly since Lino Bianchi's 1968 edition of the work.

31. Morelli's magisterial *La virtù in corte*, 39. Here I concentrate only on the family relationships evident in the libretto.

32. Remigio Nannini, *Epistole e evangelii, che si leggano tutto l'anno alla Messa* (Venice: G. B. Gagliani, 1599), 108.

33. On Mesquita's oratorio production as a whole, see Rogério Budasz, *Opera in the Tropics: Music and Theater in Early Modern Brazil* (Oxford: Oxford University Press, 2019), 32–38; on Caffarelli as opera patron, see Valeria de Lucca, *The Politics of Princely Entertainment: Music and Spectacle in the Lives of Lorenzo Onofrio and Maria Mancini Colonna (1659–1689)* (New York: Oxford University Press, 2020), 223–25.

34. As De Totis worked under Pamphili's patronage in the 1670s, the ultimate authorship may be impossible to sort out.

35. In 1698 the Discalced Carmelites of Genoa hosted an allegorical oratorio by P. P. Mainero, *L'Europa in Asia*, dedicated to the Name of Mary (important in the anti-Ottoman wars) and featuring the victories of "Germania" over "Asia" (http://www.bibliotecamusica.it/cmBM/viewschedatwbca.asp?path=/cmBM/images/ripro/libretti/00/Lo00766/, accessed February 2022).

36. The 1698 Vienna printed libretto is the cleanest and most faithful to its musical score; perhaps it was checked by someone like the local court poet Donato Cupeda before being issued.

37. On both the Oratorio and the contiguous school, see Guido Palermo, *Guida istruttiva* (Palermo: Reale Stamperia, 1816), vol. 1, 306–12, and Vincenzo Mortillaro, *Guida per Palermo* (Palermo, 1836), 15–16. More recent studies of Serpotta (Vincenzo Abbate [ed.], *Serpotta e il suo tempo* [Milan: Silvana, 2017]) cover the Oratorio's decoration, without mention of music (except for the stucco *Allegory of Music*) or performances.

Notes to Pages 59–70 · 239

38. The standard work on the organization is Konrad Eisenbichler, *The Boys of the Archangel Raphael: A Youth Confraternity in Florence, 1411–1785* (Toronto: University of Toronto Press, 1998); see also John Walter Hill, "Oratory Music in Florence," pts. 1–3, *Acta Musicologica* 51 (1979): 108–36 and 246–67; 58 (1986): 129–79.

39. Why Bicilli's name was crossed out on f. 2 of the Vienna score is unclear.

40. Besides the reference to Sara's "ardor crudele," possibly Hagar's "riso" here is a reappropriation of Sarah's "laughter" (on the birth of Isaac) in Genesis 21:6.

41. Another possible argument for "È folle chi paventa" as the original is the way in which this aria's last words, referring to adversity finally overcome ("fioriscon le viole / dopo le brine e 'l gel" [the violets flower after frost and ice]), echo Ismaele's resignation to his Banishment in Part I ("Ecco m'invio. . . . dove fra il rigor d'eterne brine / in orrido confine / batto il freddo Aquilon vanni di gelo" [Look, I go . . . where the frigid North Wind blows amidst eternal frosts at the horrid icy end (of the earth)]).

42. This is I-Vnm Cod. 10658, containing many cantata/opera arias by Pasquini, Scarlatti, and others. My thanks to Margaret Murata for identifying the codex and confirming these details.

43. Oddly, Lino Bianchi's edition of the work omits "Ingrato Abramo" in its libretto but not its musical text (*Agar ed Ismaele esiliati* [Rome: Edizioni de Santis, 1965]); cfr. pp. xv and 120.

44. The Vienna manuscript of Bicilli's piece is a short score, missing violin parts for some arias, except for some cues in Ismaele's Part I aria "No, no, l'alma mia" and Agar's following "Sgombra pure i timori"; these are written out in the continuo part.

45. Just before Ismaele's entrance halfway through Part I, her concerns that Agar will dissuade the patriarch from the Banishment ("che un lusinghier sospiro . . . estingua nel tuo cor l'affetto mio" [that a sensuous sigh . . . might extinguish my love in your heart]) receive different kinds of underlining: Bicilli's hard *durezze*, or a turn to the Neapolitan in Scarlatti's section.

46. The libretto is in I-Bc (Lo. 1872); there is no record of a performance (nor a score). The piece seems to have escaped the Caldara literature.

47. Giacinto Tonti, *Secondo Avvento e Secondo Quaresimale . . . detto nell'augustissima Cesarea cappella* (Venice: Giuseppe Corona, 1730; Tonti had died in 1726 and the first editions of this and its companion collection are dedicated to Charles VI), 249–53, "Sermone nel Giovedì dopo la IV Domenica di Quaresima per l'Oratorio d'Ismaello Discacciato dal Padre." There survive about twenty-five copies of this edition south and north of the Alps; the printed form of the oratorio sermon comes in at about 3,000 words, suggesting an original oral version about half that length and perhaps of twenty minutes. This volume also includes the only written-out sermon for the Holy Week Tomb

services in the Hofburgkapelle, between the two parts of Pariati/Fux's *Cristo condennato*, as well as the sermons for *Sisara, Santa Ferma*, and *Il transito di San Giuseppe* (e.g., Thursday after the First Sunday in Lent), all performed that year.

48. Lawrence Bennett, "A Little-Known Collection of Early-Eighteenth-Century Vocal Music at Schloss Elisabethenburg, Meiningen," *Fontes Artis Musicae* 48 (2001): 250–302. On Perfetti, who also wrote a few other dramatic texts for Vienna in addition to other non-improvised works, see Françoise Waquet, *Rhétorique et poétique chrétiennes: Bernardino Perfetti et la poésie improvisée dans l'Italie du XVIIIe siècle* (Florence: Leo S. Olschki, 1992), and her entry on the poet in the *DBI* 82 (2015); her ideas in the former on Perfetti as a "Christian poet" are based on other works, not considering the oratorio's text.

49. Tonti also printed his sermons for the two oratorios and the Holy Week work.

50. Bernd Rill, *Karl VI. Habsburg als barocke Großmacht* (Graz: Styria-Verlag, 1992), 157–58, still the major treatment of the monarch's rule.

51. Phyllis Trible, "Ominous Beginnings for a Promise of Blessing," in Trible and L. M. Russell (eds.), *Hagar, Sarah, and Their Children*, 33–69.

52. Giovanni N. Rainieri Redi, *Ismaele in esilio, oratorio a cinque voci da cantarsi nella chiesa di S. Firenze il dì xxi. Dicembre* (Florence: n.p., 1747).

Chapter Four

1. The great Jesuit preacher Paolo Segneri viewed them as polar opposites in his explanation of why religious orders produced saints and also sinners: "Se miriamo la Casa d'Abramo, veggiamo che con ella con un Isacco ossequioso hebbe un Ismaele protervo," *Panegirici sacri* (Treviso: Pianta, 1704), pt. 1, 320.

2. Gregory of Nyssa, "De deitate Filii et Spiritus Sancti et in Abraham," in *Sermones*, pt. 3, ed. F. Mann (Leiden: Brill, 1996), at 130–40. For overall views of the story in our period, see *Isaaks Opferung (Gen 22) in den Konfessionen und Medien der Frühen Neuzeit*, ed. Johann A. Steiger and U. Heinen ("Arbeiten zur Kirchengeschichte," 101; Berlin, 2006), esp. B. Mahlmann on Gregory's *Oratio* at 314–19, and M. Reiser on the Jesuit commentary of Benito Perera, 453–81, while H. Jung considers Carissimi's oratorio at 700–703.

3. Metastasio's footnotes to *Isacco, figura del Redentore* mention Gregory's paraphrase.

4. These are discussed by Frits Noske, *Saints and Sinners: The Latin Musical Dialogue in the Seventeenth Century* (Oxford: Oxford University Press, 1992), 172–95.

Notes to Pages 76–81 · 241

5. Vittore Silvio Grandi, *Historia ecclesiastica* (Venice: Domenico Loviso, 1708), vol. 1, 16.

6. Bartoli considered that "the whole world, all humans, would be worthy to be the spectators and admirers of this action. . . . Was the father more ready to kill his only-born son [Ishmael tends to disappear in such accounts], or was the son more ready to receive death at the hand of his own father?" *Delle grandezze di Christo* (Rome: n.p., 1675), 383–84. On Bartoli, see Simon Ditchfield, "Baroque around the Clock: Daniello Bartoli SJ (1608–1685) and the Uses of Global History," *Transactions of the Royal Historical Society* 31 (2021): 49–73.

7. "Né il padre, / né l'uomo era più in me; la grazia avea / vinto già la natura," as he describes his own state while preparing to sacrifice his son (*Isacco, figura del Redentore*, ll. 452–54, with a possible reference to Thomas à Kempis's *De imitatione Christi*).

8. It will also be noted how some of these latter texts make explicit reference to the Isaac story in their characters' pleas for the Daughter's life to be spared.

9. Carlo Antonio Morone, *Annuale* (Parma: Rosati, 1706), 242–44.

10. On Scipione Agnelli's 1622 *Il sacrifizio d'Isac*, see most recently Simona Santacroce, "Dal Libro al libretto: Tre drammi musicali biblici del Seicento" (PhD diss., University of Turin, 2012), 14–63.

11. It should be noted that Carissimi's text omits the ancillary details of the ram found entrapped to be used as a substitute sacrifice, as well as remaining faithful to Genesis 22 by ignoring Sarah.

12. The 1637 *Isacco, azione sacra* done for the Seminario Romano has only its prologue in music. Its length and cast of characters are, however, in some ways the antithesis of Carissimi's economy.

13. The only partial exception was in Bologna; a 1732 *Sagrifizio d'Abramo* for three voices (no Sarah) was used for the vows of Cecilia Marescotti in the Benedictine house of SS. Gervasio e Protasio; it ends with a *licenza* for Sts. Benedict and Scholastica, who presented the new nun with her crown of thorns, having removed the one of flowers. This text begins with father and son preparing for the Binding on Mount Moriah, and God Himself—not an angel—intervenes to stop the sacrifice.

14. Some sixteen copies of *L'arpa celeste* survive in Italian libraries.

15. Even the nine-character 1674 Sienese *Sacrifizio d'Abramo* has no role for Sara. This absence from the whole (if sparse) Seicento repertory on the story is all the more striking in view of her role as one of the central voices in Gregory of Nyssa's envoicement.

16. The preface does mention the Ishmael story, perhaps a hint at the various versions of Genesis 21 that had been performed at the Oratorio in previous years. The piece is listed in Franchi, *Drammaturgia romana*, vol. 2, 57.

17. Not all the arias are da capo, as this one gives no repeat, and evidently Clemente preferred to end the part thusly.

18. On this piece, see Franchi, *Drammaturgia romana*, vol. 2, 56.

19. The emphasis on Nature's bounty is also found in some of the Viennese works but is strikingly absent from the homiletic and devotional literature; its relationship to the theme of sacrifice is still unclear.

20. The ever-inventive Palermo Jesuits seem to have put on the first production under this title as a Forty Hours' devotion with music in 1677.

21. Why the Crocifisso would have commissioned a work from the almost unknown de' Messi, active mainly in Milan (Ambrosian-rite church music in I-Ma), is unclear.

22. If Ottoboni was musically responsible for an aria, this one was probably not it; better candidates might be Sara's (or Abramo's; see above) "Quel rio mormorante," a pastoral item with omnipresent parallel thirds in the strings, or possibly her "Luce de gl'occhi miei," which has a competent but entirely crossed-out first page in the Manchester score, rather as if Bencini had suggested major changes to Ottoboni's insertion.

23. That the Viennese score gives "ignoto" for the librettist—the same fate that would befall Gian Francesco Bernini and his disappearance from the Habsburg score of Bicilli's *La vita humana*—might indicate that both poets were in some way *personae non gratae* in Vienna.

24. It is difficult to place the relatively short anonymous oratorio *Il sagrifizio d'Abramo* (A-Wn Mus. Hs. 18322), and I have omitted it here for its lack of context; the Viennese copy of an *Oratorio di Sant'Abramo* deals with a different (Christian) story.

25. There are a certain number of clarifications about more minor parts of her story, for example, rulers' desires for her.

26. Bernardoni could have roughly borrowed this idea from Segneri's *Il divoto di Maria Vergine* (Parma: Alberto Pazzoni, 1700), pt. 5, in which the Jesuit pointed out that the Binding was a sacrifice not only of the child but of all of Abraham's descendants (Ishmael again being conveniently omitted from this point), along with the idea that Mary's sorrow at the loss of her Son qualitatively exceeded any such sentiment on Sara's part.

27. The only other work in Italian during this period on St. Knud was a 1682 Jesuit tract in his honor; possibly the Viennese oratorio was a well-concealed tribute to Denmark's role on the anti-Swedish side in the Great Northern War (1700–1721), vaguely congruent with the War of the Spanish Succession. The Italian newspaper *Corriere ordinario* referred only generally to the Tuesday oratorios during Lent without naming pieces.

28. Rossi's oratorios are discussed, others besides *Il sacrificio* in greater detail, by Martina Natter, "Die vier Oratorien von Camilla de Rossi" (PhD diss., University of Innsbruck, 2003).

29. Problems with the part in tablature, in the Sinfonia to Part II, are that (a) it appears at all in an otherwise normally notated score and (b) the pitches indicated by the tablature numerals begin to diverge from the notated pitches in the strings which it is accompanying (e.g., on p. 100 of the A-Wn digital facsimile, bb. 2–7); this latter is possibly due to copyists' mistakes. My thanks to Franco Pavan for all this information.

30. "L'avere io introdotta Sara sul monte, egli è stato (nol niego) per abbozzare da lontano un immagine della Vergine appiè della Croce," Manzoni, "Argomento," *Il sagrifizio d'Abramo* (Vienna: van Ghelen, 1738), fol. A2. One late Roman oratorio before Metastasio's text was Nicolò Scalmani's *Il sagrifizio d'Abramo* (Rome, 1737), a trialogue with the Angel.

31. On Jommelli's version, see Herczog, *Il perfetto melodramma*, 224–32; the score is available at https://smcfava.regione.veneto.it/oratori/0005_jommelli_nicolo/isacco_figura_del_redentore/01_5_partitura/dsp.htm (accessed February 2. 2023).

32. On the text as a "hidden Passion," including Sara's paraphrases of Lamentations verses, see Stroppa, "*Fra notturni sereni*," 175–79.

33. Because of its relatively pedestrian nature, I omit detailed discussion of L. A. Predieri's original 1739 setting; for a detailed comparison of the overall structure and several arias in Predieri's and Jommelli's versions, see Gaetano Pitarresi, "*Isacco figura del Redentore* di Pietro Metastasio nelle intonazioni di Luca Antonio Predieri e di Niccolo Jommelli," in *Niccolò Jommelli: l'esperienza europea di un musicista "filosofo*," ed. Pitarresi (Reggio Calabria: Conservatorio di Musica F. Cilea, 2014; online at https://www.conservatoriocilea.it/index.php/produzione-e-ricerca-h/1111-pubblicazioni-on-line; accessed 21 January 2021).

34. It is striking that, although the poet thought of all his oratorios as being essentially Passion works, no matter what their nominal subject, there is very little use of Jeremiah's text in the other six others.

35. His decision to tell all was backed up with citations to Augustine, Gregory of Nyssa, Tirinius, and Calmet, among others.

36. What it meant in 1740 to go "off scene" in the *Hofburgkapelle* is not clear. There is a set design drawing by Ferdinando Galli Bibiena (Vienna, Albertina) for the anonymous replacement work of 1739, the little-known *azione sacra La Maria lebbrosa**, but no sketch that seems applicable to Metastasio's piece. The 1739 work shows the clear political meaning of the Viennese repertory, as it takes an otherwise untreated episode on Aaron's wife fomenting dissent against Moses (Numbers 12), clearly designed to warn any Imperial subject or relative from taking the anti-Austrian side in any upcoming conflict stemming from the succession to the Imperial throne; the libretto is anonymous (not Metastasio) and the music by G. Reutter Jr.

37. A point first made by Stroppa (ed.), *Metastasio: Oratori sacri*, 281.

38. In post-Predieri settings, this aria would be a central moment of demarcation, notably in Jommelli's and Mysliveček's versions.

39. The exceptions (i.e., performances of Metastasio's original 1739–40 text) include Palermo 1743, Florence 1747, and Dresden 1748/49, all three of these perhaps in deference to the original Viennese libretto, and Rome 1750. The 1749 Munich production had a different and obedient aria for Sara ("Signor, se il figlio chiedi"); as noted, it was also done in the court theater and has staging indications for the scenes into which the two parts are divided (D-Mbs).

40. The other story of attempted filicide was the far more obscure one from 1 Samuel 14:24–45, the inadvertent eating of honey by Saul's son Jonathan during battles against the Philistines, this happening on a day that Saul had forbidden food consumption to all Israelites on pain of death. The father's decision to kill him for violating the decree is the plot generator, and again a Scripturally absent mother turned out to be a central figure in many versions (this is also one of the few examples of mass action in the oratorio repertory, as 1 Samuel recounts how the men of Israel stopped Saul from carrying out the death sentence). The oratorio versions of this "Gionata" story normally added Saul's wife ("Achinoam" in Apostolo Zeno's 1728 Viennese libretto), and various high priests and captains. In a certain way, the Jonathan story came very close to the Isaac account, not least in its more or less happy ending. Space precludes a longer discussion of the musical settings of this tale.

Chapter Five

1. "*Et fecit ei sicut voverat*. La dificultad es gravissima. Ea, desatémosla, descubriendo nuevas luzes de la religiosa acción a que assistimos . . . ," J. A. Rosado y Haro, *Oración solemne en la profesión y velo que recibió . . . la Madre Soror Margarita Fernández de Córdova y Pimentel* (Seville: Widow of N. Rodríguez, 1673), 3, declaimed for a vesting ceremony in Córdoba.

2. For instance, the early study and catalogue of Wilbur O. Sypherd, *Jephthe and His Daughter: A Study in Comparative Literature* (Newark: University of Delaware Press, 1948), who, counting Protestant versions, came up with about 170 musical pieces on the story; a close reading of Sartori's catalogue, plus the Corago project (University of Bologna) and OpacSBN for Italy, leads to the numbers given here. The quantity is impressive.

3. The first case seems to be Francesco Acciarelli's 1695 Latin version for the Crocifisso, *Jefte infelix triumphans*, discussed below.

4. Such reduced pieces include a two-character 1726 version for the Seminario Romano, with music for Domenico Sarri (and a traditional Biblical end), repeated in the following two years (Macerata and Montefiascone), and

a three-character 1727 work by Antonino Reggio, probably for the Collegio Germanico (a mark that Carissimi's version, if it had been performed there originally, was out of the repertory by this point). This piece goes Carissimi one better by featuring a tragic end with the Sacrifice on stage. Pietro Avondano's 1771 Lisbon *Il voto di Jefte* has three characters plus a chorus of Hebrew virgins, also found in Perez's libretto.

5. Most of the literature on Handel's version has to do with the nonmartyrial ending and with the renunciation of marriage of the daughter Iphis, some of it inspired by the work of Mieke Bal; cf. Deborah W. Rooke, *Handel's Israelite Oratorio Libretti: Sacred Drama and Biblical Exegesis* (Oxford: Oxford University Press, 2012), 207–28. I leave the 1751 piece, and the Protestant tradition in general, out of consideration here, especially as George Buchanan's tragedy on the subject seems not to have influenced continental Catholicism except for the mother's name.

6. Pseudo-Philo, *The Biblical Antiquities of Philo*, trans. M. R. James (London: Macmillan, 1917), 191–94.

7. For late medieval and Reformed commentators, see Thompson, *Writing the Wrongs*, 100–178.

8. The Piedmontese Theatine Giovanni Battista Barralis even used the example of the unbidden Sacrifice (unlike Isaac's, as per Augustine) as a reproach of those parents who forced their daughters into monasteries only to save on dowries; *Quaresimale* (Turin: Gianfrancesco Mairesse, 1717), 129. For Arcangela Tarabotti's surprising excuses for Jephthe's behavior, and her praise of the Daughter's Sacrifice as a fulfillment of vows, see Joy A. Schroeder, "Envying Jephthah's Daughter: Judges 11 in the Thought of Arcangela Tarabotti (1604–1652)," in *Strangely Familiar: Protofeminist Interpretations of Patriarchal Biblical Texts*, ed. N. Calvert-Koyzis and H. E. Weir (Atlanta: Society of Biblical Literature, 2009), 75–91, and Ardissino, *Donne interpreti*, 248–49.

9. Saverio Vanalesti, *Prediche quaresimali* (Venice: G. B. Pasquali, 1743), 259–60.

10. On issues of past sacrifices in ancien régime opera, see Martha Feldman and Valerio Valeri, "L'opera e il sacrificio: passato e futuro mitologico nel teatro pre-rivoluzionario," in Valeri, *Uno spazio tra sé e sé* (Rome: Donzelli, 1999), 181–225.

11. The form "Jefet" is found in a number of Italian sources around midcentury, for example Benedict XIV's *Delle feste di Nostro Signore* (Venice, 1749 ed.), 1:258. Possibly it was brought to Dresden by the Italian Jesuits. "Sefa" is a variant of "Seila," first found in Galuppi's original 1749 libretto.

12. This is in Giovanni de Benedictis, *Azioni sacre* (Rome: S. G. Generoso, 1758), 165–84, with an explanation in the preface of the choice for a nonmartyrial ending. Ironically, in the same year, an anonymous reviewer of for-

eign literature criticized a supporter of the *lieto fine* (*Saggio critico della corrente letteratura straniera*, [Modena: n.p., 1758], vol. 3, no. 2, 248ff).

13. Possibly he was the same Arcadian figure "Penelao Molarchio" = abate Giuseppe Maria Calderara who wrote an encomiastic poem to the new Pope Pius VI in 1775 (found in *Triplice omaggio offerto dagli Arcadi al . . . Papa Pio VI* [Rome: Salomone, 1775]), with the libretto's form of his name being a mistake, deliberate or not. No other works by "Penelao" or "Peone" seem traceable.

14. Some of Alexandre's formulations include (*Historia ecclesiastica*, [Lucca: Leonardo Venturini, 1734]): "Sed de voto Jephthe suo loco differemus, expendemusque, an . . . virginis consecratione, ut quibusdam placuit, an mactatione cruenta? [vol. 1, 296]; "Verum figmenta ista [the Talmudic version in which the annual mourning of Hebrew women took place to console her for her living virginity] in dissertationibus referremus, et filiam Jephthe vere a patre mactatam probabimus" [1, 318]. The 1714 Paris edition of the *Dissertationes* has the same text in this passage. Similarly, Ignace Armat de Graveson's *Historia Ecclesiastica Veteris Testamenti* (Venice: G. B. Recurti, 1732) spent two pages (170–71) defending the traditional outcome of the story. Obviously, this recourse to tradition showed the strain under which the Sacrifice was beginning to labor.

15. "Oh quante belle / . . . verginelle, / . . . tue seguaci saranno; ed oltre ancor / le auree vie del Pattolo [the Pactolus River in Turkey] / e i confini del Gange . . ." (Molorchio, *Il Gefte*, 18).

16. At least two, possibly three, of Mattei's keyboard sonatas are scattered among GB-Lbl, F-Pn, US-LOu, and so on (opac.rism.info, accessed May 2022).

17. Possibly Maria Rosa was a daughter of the family that owned Palazzo Orlandini del Beccuto in via de' Pecori, sumptuously redone in the early Settecento.

18. Evidently there was no sermon, and the piece is in one part only. My deepest thanks to John Shepard at the Berkeley Music Library for making available this and the 1650 Palermo text discussed in the previous chapter.

19. Here again, the amount of work on proto-bourgeois father-daughter novels in England is not matched by the material on the Italian or Austrian family. I have attempted to use the Catholic family literature as a kind of background for the oratorios.

20. For example, the Jesuit Pietro Valle's *Prediche dette nel Palazzo Apostolico* (Venice: N. Pezzana, 1713, at 251), who used the story in a sermon for the feast of St. Thomas the Apostle to warn prelates against all extravagance, including that of making promises.

21. It is all the more frustrating that none of the scores by Jommelli, Perez, and Paisiello seem to survive. Domenico Cimarosa's setting of *Iefte* (?c. 1785) is transmitted only in fragmentary parts in I-Nc, X. 1712.

22. Just as the theme was beginning to receive more emphasis in the orato-

Notes to Pages 115–122 · 247

rio repertory, the Jesuit Menocchio devoted two pages to its canonical version in his *Stuore* (Rome, 1646; here Rome: Felice Cesaretti, 1689), vol. 1, 21–23. Here, the exegete refuted the happy-ending version of the tale, attributing it to "alcuni rabbini," but discussed the four possibilities of if, and at what point, Jephthe actually sinned with the vow. Perhaps surprisingly, he absolved the general of sin, both in taking and in executing the vow. The reprint testifies to the ongoing interest in the story.

23. I use Janet Beat's edition of this piece (London: Faber Music, 1974) for measure numbers.

24. It seems best to take the "source A" reading of "ut pugnaret contra vos" (Beat, m. 52) as better than "et pugnat contra vos," and probably closer to some putative Roman version.

25. Notably, except for its opening ("O hills . . . o mountains"), Carissimi's trope 3/lament is not related to the extended lament in pseudo-Philo for the Daughter's virginity.

26. Carlo Sigonio's *De republica Hebraeorum* (Bologna: Giovanni Rossi, 1582, at 92) considered the annual four-day lament for the Daughter to be a major commemoration in the Israelites' year.

27. The dual editions, both anonymous, are *Jephthé, tragédie en musique pour server d'intermedes a la piece latine que sera rappresentée au College de Louis-le-Grand* (Paris, 1686), and *Jephthes Tragoedia*, the latter of which noted the exact date (20 February) of performance.

28. Robert A. Low, *Marc-Antoine Charpentier et la musique au Collége des Jesuits* (Paris: Maisonneuve & Larose, 1966). Elizabeth Jacquet de la Guerre's 1711 cantata (from Book 2) on the subject ends with a slightly ambiguous Biblical denouement, while, with a completely non-sacrificial finish, Michel de Montéclair's *Jephthé* dates to 1732.

29. The text of his Jephthe piece, as well as that of Franchi discussed below, is Alaleona, *Studi su la storia dell'oratorio musicale in Italia*, 435–43 and 445–52, respectively.

30. Balbi would later do two oratorios for Christina of Sweden in 1679, giving some sense of his possibly heterodox sympathies; indeed, there is no imprimatur.

31. Margaret K. Murata, "Colpe mie venite a piangere: The Penitential Cantata in Baroque Rome," in *Listening to Early Modern Catholicism*, ed. M. Noone and D. Filippi (Leiden: Brill, 2017), at 215–16.

32. Abraham a Sancta Clara, *Mercks wol Soldat!* (Vienna: n.p., 1680), 49–50.

33. On the companion oratorio, also performed in Vienna in 1690, with text by San Carlo and music by Rubini, *Il finto Smeraldo, o la vera Eufrosina*—on the story of St. Euphrosyne of Alexandria, and the only Seicento oratorio to my knowledge for which the sermon between the parts, the libretto, and the music all survive—see my "Disguise, Difference, Deceit in a Sienese Oratorio-

Sermon," in *La crisi della modernità. Storie, riletture e revisioni per Gianvittorio Signorotto*, ed. M. Al-Katak, E. Fumagalli, and L. Ferrari (Rome: Viella Editrice, 2023).

34. The 1688 Siena libretto (I-Fc) is titled *Il riso e il pianto in contesa, ovvero La vittoria di Gefte*.

35. A brief line, not originally applicable to Vienna, on "una perla naufragata entro un mare di coralli/a pearl shipwrecked in a coral sea" might have raised Leopold's grief for his first wife Margarita ("a pearl"), who had been dead some seventeen years.

36. There is no cast list in the score.

37. The *Wienerisches Diarium* of 11 March, after reporting on events of 8 March, calls the next day "2," but this must be a misprint. The three roles were sung by Orsini, Carestini, and Praun (two castrati and a bass), who also take up a good part of Part I's opening with speculations as to Gefte's state of mind and (with various citations to Judges 11) how his traumatic youth might have caused his later instability.

38. The relatively minor singer (tenor) Gaetano Borghi was cast as Jefte; all of these figures had appeared, in roles larger and smaller, in Fux's *Costanza e Fortezza* of the previous year.

39. The 1716 payments for two new arias noted by Kirkendale seem to refer to recompositions of Jefte's aria and that of Andrìa's following "Di tua sorte le vicende," both in G minor and 3/8, possibly because of a change of singers for the 1716 reprise. Both these simpler versions, included in the D-MÜs score, are in the section in which the characters are coming to terms with the upcoming Sacrifice.

40. One can compare this part of the Iphigenia story with the Christian sacralizations of the Tauris section found in Edith Hall, *Adventures with Iphigenia in Tauris: A Cultural History of Euripides' Black Sea Tragedy* (Oxford: Oxford University Press, 2013), 158–82.

41. Since the later libretti for Perez's work refer to him as chapelmaster in Palermo, a job that he held in 1738–48, presumably the original setting was indeed the 1742 edition mentioned presently.

42. In spring 2022, there briefly appeared on the internet antiquarian market a copy of *Il sacrificio di Jefte oratorio a 4. Voci, e più Stromenti, da cantarsi nel Vener. ed Antico Monistero di S. Maria delle Vergini* (Palermo, 1742), with a manuscript note giving the poetry to Girolamo di Sant'Angelo and the music to Perez. This edition was first reported by Ilaria Grippaudo, "Attività musicale, patrocinio e condizione femminile nei monasteri palermitani (secc. XVII–XVIII)," in *Puta/puttana: donne musica teatro tra XVI e XVIII secolo*, ed. M. P. Altese and P. Cangemi (Palermo: Il Palindromo, 2016), at 53.

43. Scarpelli seems to have published nothing else, but the libretto made

Notes to Pages 132–143 · 249

its way to Bologna, Perugia, Mantua, Macerata, and Ferrara in the 1780s. Its dedicatee, Sisto Sforza-Cesarini (1730–1802), was count of Celano after his brother's death in 1764, which gives a rough dating of the piece. Luigi Caruso's 1789 Mantua setting of this text also survives (I-OS).

44. Piperno, *La Bibbia all'opera*, begins its discussion with Barthélemon's 1776 *Jefte in Masfa* before also considering the 1785–86 pasticcio *La figlia di Jefte*; 9–10 and 57–58.

45. Again, for the context of this piece, see Piperno, *La Bibbia in musica*, 9–10.

46. See Piperno, *La Bibbia*, for many of these pieces into the Ottocento: for example, 45–47, 57–58, 205–6, 210–11, 215–16, and 221–24.

47. On this piece, see Anja Morgenstern, *Die Oratorien von Johann Simon Mayr (1763–1845): Studien zu Biographik, Quellen, und Rezeption* (Munich: Katzbichler, 2007), 120–28 and 251–56.

48. Gillio, *L'attività musicale*.

49. Paisiello's first surviving oratorio on any topic was not until his Russian years, Metastasio's *Passione* done for the Catholic cathedral in St. Petersburg in 1782.

50. There is no second part and no indication of any break for a sermon.

Chapter Six

1. On the issues of marriage — including the traditional "leading the bride home" without a ceremony — after Trent, see Giuseppe Mazzanti, *Matrimoni post-tridentini: Un dibattito dottrinale fra continuità e cambiamento (secc. XVI–XVIII)* (Bologna: Bononia University Press, 2020).

2. Lapide, *Commentarius in Josue, Judicum, Ruth . . .* (Antwerp: M. Nutius, 1700), 198.

3. The breakdown is: Ruth three; Noemi, Tigea, and Boaz two, plus a duet for the spouses.

4. Herczog, *Il perfetto melodramma*, excludes the Latin-texted works from his considerations.

5. I have used the score of *Nuptiae Ruth* in I-Mc; the libretto is in I-Vgc.

6. Again, I have used "Tobit" to denominate the father and "Tobias" the son, in order to avoid confusion.

7. For Catholic Germany, the Benedictine monk Johann Baptist Hutschenreiter's *Azarias Fidelis Tobiae in via spiritualium Exercitiorum per octiduum* (Regensburg: J. B. Lang, 1741) provided an octave's worth of spiritual exercises dedicated to Raphael but focusing successively on these themes; it saw some four editions between Latin and German in the following fifteen years.

In a similar way, G. J. Werner at Eisenstadt wrote a 1759 German-language oratorio, *Tobias*; Haydn might have seen the score of this but not heard the premiere.

8. Carlo Tommaso Morone, *La vera politica economica cristiana insegnata dallo Spirito Santo nella casa di Tobbia* (Parma: Rosati, 1709).

9. Giuseppe Luigi Pellegrini, *Tobia: Ragionamenti* (Venice: Gaspare Storti, 1772), vol. 1, p. 2.

10. On these reprises of the work, and its rapidly aging appeal, see Marko Motnik, "Das Oratorium 'Il ritorno di Tobia' di Joseph Haydn: 'ein veraltetes Machwerk'?," *Eisenstädter Haydn-Berichte* 12 (2020): 175–96.

11. A 1751 Tobit piece on this occasion is noted in De Luca, *Musica e cultura urbana*, 56.

12. The Italian use of the theme for paintings seems, like the canvases on Hagar, to be aimed at domestic devotion/collection; two versions of the Healing by Bernardo Strozzi from his Venetian years in the 1630s (Hermitage and New York/Metropolitan Museum of Art), or the early copperplate image of the catching of the fish (?1616; Blanton Museum of Art, Austin, TX) by Guercino. By the 1670s, this last was in the collection of Maffeo Barberini (1631–85), the Prince of Palestrina, who had reopened the Teatro alle Quattro Fontane.

13. On this, see Julius Hirschberg, *Die Augenheilkunde in der Neuzeit*, vol. 3 (Berlin: Springer, 1899ff), 489–90, and https://www.geschichtewiki.wien .gv.at/Joseph_Barth (accessed March 4, 2022).

14. On Veneziano's piece, see Antonio Dell'Olio, "Il *Tobia sposo* (1690): scherzo drammatico di Gaetano Veneziano," in Dell'Olio (ed.), *L'oratorio musicale a Napoli nel tempo di Gaetano Veneziano* (Naples: I Figlioli di S. Maria di Loreto, 2016), 1–42.

15. Strikingly, these wedding works aimed at the urban patriciate totally omit references to priests or temple ceremonies.

16. The score is preserved in D-Hs, ND.VI.2478/1.

17. Jutta Sperling, *Convents and the Body Politic in Late Renaissance Venice* (Chicago: University of Chicago Press, 1999).

18. Its issues around the Healing would anticipate Part II of Haydn's *Il ritorno di Tobia*.

19. The score, in F-Pn, seems close to a holograph, due to the number of cross-outs and a few compositional corrections. No printed libretto seems to survive, and its incipit, "Quid restat misero michi? Quid amplius sperare possum?," is not a direct Biblical citation. The vocal scoring excludes the Venetian *ospedali* as a locus for the premiere.

20. On Bede, see Johann Gamberoni, *Die Auslegung des Buches Tobias in der griechisch-lateinischen Kirche der Antike und der Christenheit des Westens bis um 1600* (Munich, Kösel-Verlag, 1969), 107–23; and on Hugh, Gamberoni, *Die*

Auslegung des Buches Tobias, 138–41. Gamberoni's helpful history of exegesis stops with the early seventeenth-century Jesuit Nicolaus Serarius, noted also for his work on the meaning of litanies.

21. On Casali's work, see Herczog, *Il perfetto melodramma*, 472–78.

22. Here I refer only to Haydn's original 1775 version without the additions and cuts of the 1784 Vienna second performance, using the version of E. F. Schmid's work prepared by A. Oppenheimer (Munich: G. Henle Verlag, 2000/2009), with consideration of F. Mühle's excellent critical report (Munich: G. Henle Verlag, 2018).

23. The *Corriere ordinario* of 16 March noted Zeno's piece as performed on the 14th as a "bellissima Azzione Sacra." The longest discussion thus far is Herczog, *Il perfetto melodramma*, 142–46.

24. Augustine, *De dono providentiae*, chapter 15.

25. The reference to Tobias and his instinctual awareness might have been a highly veiled reference to the death of the Dowager Empress Eleonore Magdalene, which had just taken place on 19 January 1720. The references to loans are probably the closest approach in this libretto to Habsburg mercantilist policy.

26. Zeno must have revised his text after the premiere, as the 1735 edition of his works opens the piece with "Signor, al trono tuo" but Porsile's score with "Al tuo eccelso trono tuo."

27. Melani's poetry edition was dated 1722, and so this plus the two other texts (*Adamo* and *Ester*) must have been added in press as an appendix (and the original piece probably from that year). If this is the same Arcadian who published a few other oratorio libretti and a good deal of panegyric literature, he was active into the 1760s.

28. Currently there does not seem to be any contemporary image of Tobit and/or the Guardian Angel inside the Galliera's public area.

29. Metastasio's two longest texts are both around 680 lines (*Betulia liberata* and *Gioas*); Mozart's setting of the former as well as J. C. Bach's 1770 version of the latter both run more than two hours in recorded performances without onstage action (e.g., 2 hours 3 minutes [Challenge Classics, 2013] and 2 hours 15 minutes [CPO, 2002], respectively). As noted above, Boccherini's text for Haydn comes in at 650 lines, although the musical length of the arias renders the 1775 piece notably longer.

30. Tobit 6—the journey, capturing of the fish, and chaste wedding nights—represented the triumph over sin. The understanding of the Angel as Calasanz was explicit in the preface: "il soggetto del presente componimento, il quale tutto si aggira sopra l'Angelo . . . Egli [the Angel] non e' che un velo, di cui si copre la nostra divozione per rilevare il bel carattere di San Giuseppe Calasanzo . . . di Giuseppe pertanto si parla, quando si parla dell'Angelo, e perchè meglio in tutto risponda al figurato la figura," the last phrase another testimony to the problems of allegorical drama in this historical moment. For a thorough

discussion of this piece, see Ignacio Prats Arolas, "Music and Communication in Enlightenment Rome," (PhD diss., University of Illinois, 2015), 225–88.

31. The proximity of Benedict XIV to the Oratorians will become evident in the case of Giuseppe Barbieri in the next chapter.

32. Although he seems to have picked up no other dedications, the cardinal would keep his ties to the order; in 1803, his viewing was held at the Chiesa Nuova before interment in S. Maria Maggiore.

33. In the I-Rn copy these are all marked in pencil, rather as if someone were very aware of the changes to the arias.

34. By this point probably only parts of Casali's original recitative settings remained in the 1771 piece.

35. Whatever the audience might have been, one would assume a similar composition as for Mozart's *Betulia liberata* of two years later. There seems to be no direct information on the performance venue. Something close to the original of Mysliveček's score plus eight printed libretto copies are in I-Pca; other copies are scattered elsewhere around Europe.

36. "E non è diversamente del pio e tenero amor di famiglia, che qui pure spira per tutto: appunto simile a quello, che Voi ritenendo sovente nei comuni uffici di Madre, ci fece più meravigliar di Voi stessa negli studi difficili di Sovrana . . ."

37. "Un padre amoroso, ed una tenera madre non può a meno che non passare dolente i giorni . . ."

38. "Non può nessuno eccedere in giusta gratitudine verso i parenti, se non allora che preponessese a quella più giusta, che deve ciascuno a Dio. È Egli d'ogni paternità l'universale sorgente . . . del resto, ai parenti non si devono gli offici solo, che a loro ci prostestano grati; ma quelli ancora, che renderci possono a loro utili." With this last clause Pellegrini turns to the combination of Divine obedience and filial duty that undergirds the Healing of Tobit.

39. "[Anna] era femmina ed era madre— . . . or come è saggio quel solo, che serba in tutti i tempi alla ragione il suo luogo, cosi quel solo è devoto, che in tutti tempi da alla Religione il suo dritto."

40. "Il venire d'una sposa novella non è mai senza molto romore . . . ella però era leggiadra e graziosa. . . . È veramente raro, o Signori, che in una sola persona si uniscano insieme nascita e ricchezza e sanità e spirito e religione."

41. On the reception and reworking of Haydn's piece, see Emily M. Wuchner, "The Tonkünstler-Sozietät and the Oratorio in Vienna, 1771–1798" (PhD diss., University of Illinois–Urbana-Champaign, 2017), 173–97, especially for the changes in the 1784 version, including the new aria for Anna.

42. In defense of the libretto and score, see Smither, *History*, vol. 3, and Herczog, *Il perfetto melodramma*, 550–80.

43. What the actual economics behind Boccherini's text might be is unclear: nominally, the reason for the journey is to reclaim the owed money because

of Tobit's poverty, and different libretti pay different amounts of attention to this aspect. If Boccherini meant the audience to sympathize with Anna at this point, it would be a case of Imperial disdain for purely monetary relationships, especially among family.

44. Pellegrini's comment on the beginning was: "Ahi che la lontananza, o miei cari, è pure un lungo ed acerbo martirio del cuore umano" (*Ragionamenti*, vol. 2, 120), passing to his envoicing of Anna at p. 128 of his book.

45. There is no specific source for this moment in the Vulgate, and so Pallavicini's views on their joint suffering have to be inferred.

46. The 2 April 1775 playbill (A-Wgm) is reproduced in the 2009 study score of Schmid and Oppenheim; for cast lists, see Wuchner, "The Viennese Tonkünstler-Societät," 418.

47. He had been Nanni in Haydn's 1773 opera and would be "un calandro," a dervish, in the 1775 piece.

Chapter Seven

1. Gigli's work as linguistic reformer, librettist for works at Siena's Jesuit *Collegio Tolomei*, restorer of Catherine of Siena's cult, impresario, and many other facets has received new emphasis in the recent literature: Stefano Lorenzetti, "*Per ricreazione e diletto*: Accademie e opera in musica nel Collegio Tolomei di Siena," in *Il melodramma italiano in Italia e Germania nell'età barocca*, ed. A. Luppi et al. (Como: AMIS, 1995), 217–41; Jane Tylus, *Reclaiming Catherine of Siena: Literacy, Literature and the Signs of Others* (Chicago: University of Chicago Press, 2017); Colleen Reardon, *A Sociable Moment: Opera and Festive Culture in Baroque Siena* (New York: Oxford University Press, 2016), 165–76 and 208–19; and Chiara Frenquellucci, *Dalla Mancia a Siena al nuovo mondo: Don Chischiotte nel teatro di Girolamo Giglio* (Florence: L. S. Olschki, 2010). The oratorio libretti await further attention.

2. Similarly, Carlo Francesco Cesarini's *La sposa de' sacri cantici* (Rome, 1712, for the Collegio Clementino) is also an Assumption piece; my thanks to Luisa Nardini and Guido Olivieri for tracking this text down.

3. Girolamo Gigli, *La sposa de' cantici* (Siena: Bonetti, 1702), 3.

4. Colleen Reardon's standard work on Sienese nuns (*Holy Concord within Sacred Walls: Nuns and Music in Siena, 1575–1700* [New York: Oxford University Press, 2002]) came up with relatively little evidence for music at the house.

5. *La sposa de' cantici piamente considerata nella diletta consorte di Gesù appassionato Santa Catarina da Siena domenicana* (Padua, 1706, with a dedication to a patrician consororiry attached to the friars' church of Sant'Agostino in the city).

6. With a score in A-Wgm (III.17705/H. 28239), this piece is listed in

Johann Herczog, "Sulle trace della Cappella Cesarea: Gregor Joseph Werner e la tradizione oratoriale nell'Eisenstadt dei principi Esterházy," in *Symposium Musicae: Saggi e testimonianze in onore di Giancarlo Rostirolla per il suo 80° genetliaco*, ed. F. Nardacci and B. Cipriani (Faleria: Recercare, 2021), 197–232. The work was performed on 15 April ([re]copied 20 May); it features the Soul, Love, Penance, and two Angels, and begins with a macaronic recitative on "Fulcite me floribus," "Fulcite me mit Blumen." Its nine arias and varying instrumental obbligati (trombone, *violette*) render it a not insubstantial work.

7. Bernard McGinn, "Women Interpreting the Song of Songs, 1150–1700," in *A Companion to the Song of Songs in the History of Spirituality*, ed. T. H. Robinson (Leiden: Brill, 2021), 249–73.

8. Obviously, "Sposa" refers to Gigli's oratorio character, and "Sponsa" to the Biblical personage.

9. The Sposa's "Vengo nuda, e negletta / e mi basta venire adorna solo / del rossore . . ." is reminiscent of a phrase in a solo martyrial motet by Bonifazio Graziani: "sum puella, nuda, sola, / puellam doce, nudam arma . . ." ("Audi, clementissime Domine," in *Il quinto libro de mottetti a voce sola*, op. 16 [Rome, 1669]), 61.

10. For Ignazio Savini's Viennese court sermon of 1674 calling on his audience to imitate Mary by "burying" Christ in the "Tomb of the heart" and with a reference to Canticles 1:12, see Robert L. Kendrick, *Fruits of the Cross: Passiontide Theater in Habsburg Vienna* (Oakland: University of California Press, 2019), 100.

11. Although Furlanetto is often mentioned as the composer of the 1753 version, he was a barely trained fifteen-year-old at the time, and it seems unlikely that the Oratorians would have commissioned a large-scale piece for the opening of the Fava from him; in addition, one of the two libretto copies in I-Rn (call no. 35.D.04.11) includes a printed paste-in noting "Messo in musica l'anno 1767 dal Sig. D. Ventura Furlanetti." suggesting that his work was associated with the later date/performance.

12. Strikingly, the trajectory of the 1753 libretto does not include the fourteen Stations of the Cross, suggesting that these had not yet been put in at the Fava's new construction.

13. *La Sposa de' sacri cantici* (Francesco Vassalli/Domenico Conventati; published in Camerino and preserved in I-Fm).

14. The figure of the Mother has generated a certain amount of contemporary theological literature, while several essays in *Dying for the Faith, Killing for the Faith: Old-Testament Faith-Warriors (1 and 2 Maccabbes) in Historical Perspective*, ed. Gabriella Signori (Leiden: Brill, 2012), consider early modern interpretations of the books, without mention of her. Some of this has come from contemporary female self-martyrdom. For an overall discussion of the canonical book, I have used Robert Duran, *2 Maccabees: A Critical*

Notes to Page 179 · 255

Commentary (Minneapolis: Fortress Press, 2012). In general, there has been a large amount of recent exegetical literature on all the Maccabees books. Both a "literal" and a "spiritual" explanation were given by Le Maître de Sacy, *Sacra scrittura* 31 (Venice: Lorenzo Baseggio, 1780), 382–97. That the Mother remains "nameless" in the libretti suggests that the actual source was the early seventeenth-century French translation, or another version (unlike the Sephardic one) which does not name her.

15. On the issues of maternal agency and exegetical influence, respectively, see David A. deSilva, "Perfection of 'Love for Offspring': Representations of Maternal Affection and the Achievement of the Heroine of 4 Maccabees," *New Testament Studies* 52 (2006): 251–68, and deSilva, "An Example of How to Die Nobly for Faith: The Influence of 4 Maccabees on Origen's *Exhortatio ad Martyrium*," *Journal of Early Christian Studies* 17, no. 3 (2009): 337–55.

16. See variously Josephus, *Jewish Antiquities* (Cambridge, MA: Harvard University Press, 1997), book 12; Steven B. Bowman, *Sepher Yosippon: A Tenth-Century History of Ancient Israel* (Detroit: Wayne State University Press, 2023), chapter 15; and the *Passio Sanctorum Maccabaeorum*, trans. Luigi Franco Pizzolato, in *I sette fratelli Maccabei nella chiesa antica d'Occidente* (Milan: Vita e Pensiero, 2005), 130–69. The fifth-century *Passio* is notable for (1) its systematic excision of the concept of "law," which instead is quite present in the oratorio texts; (2) its granting a separate speech before death to each of the seven brothers (but not to the Mother); and (3) its reversal of the normative sequence of deaths in martyrological stories, in which the adult(s) should go first. In the roughly coetaneous *Carmen de Martyrio Maccabeorum*, the children are silenced and the Mother given the overwhelming part of the direct discourse in which the poem is largely composed (Clemens Weidmann, "Das Carmen de Martyrio Maccabaeorum," PhD diss., University of Vienna, 1995, at 49).

17. In the Roman breviary, the passages from 1 and 2 Maccabees, along with readings from Gregory Nazianzus's *Oratio 20 in Maccabeos*, were reserved for Matins of Monday–Tuesday in October's Week 5 (i.e., years with an October that had five Sundays), a time frame that often conflicted with the more important liturgies of All Saints/All Souls. The most recent such year had been 1684.

18. Ironically, the last echoes of the story were in prose theater of the Restoration for Paris and Vienna (L. Chandezon, 1817; I. F. Castelli, 1818; and Z. Werner [unperformed], 1820). One oratorio version in French, written for Max Emanuel of Bavaria's exiled court in Brussels around 1705, is Pietro Torre's *Le martir des Maccabées*; this was an attempt to use the story on the Bavarian (anti-Habsburg) side of the War of the Spanish Succession, 1700–1713. This battle of Mother stories in the middle of the war is striking.

19. Giovanni Paolo Oliva, *Sermoni domestici*, vol. 5 (Rome: Z. Conzatti, 1676), 34.

20. *La madre dei Maccabei, oratorio a tre voci fatto cantare in occasione delle feste di San Luigi Gonzaga e San Stanislao Kostka* . . . (Terni: n.p., 1727).

21. The standard modern work for both the text and the understanding of the apocryphal book is David A. deSilva, *4 Maccabees* (Septuagint Commentary Series; Leiden: Brill, 2006). For the details of this book's account of the martyrdom, see 157–242; for the text, translation, and comments on the brothers' interchanges with Antiochus, see 24–47 and 157–202; for the Mother, see 53–57, 61–63, and 217–42. Given this non-canonical text's influence on Patristic formulations, its "philosophical" tinge might well be traceable indirectly in the oratorio libretti, a task beyond the scope of this volume.

22. The wider parallels of the story include the derivative cult of St. Symphorosa and her sons in Rome, and it had resonances as late as the seven Cervi brothers, World War II partisans killed in a Nazi reprisal in 1943, along with this latter case's musical reflection in Italian popular music of the postwar period.

23. The emphasis on the boy's beauty seems to cut both ways: if he was a prefiguration of Christ, this relates to the cult of the Christ Child. Still, the ancient context, and Antioco's insistence, could have suggested an uglier sense of the tyrant's initiation of the boy via pagan pederasty.

24. This revival was for the feast of its patron St. Bartholomew, another figure linked via his martyrdom by knife; on the tradition of oratorios in Montefiascone, see Franchi, *Drammaturgia romana*, vol. 2, p. 3.

25. Angelo Paciuchelli, *Lezioni morali sopra il libro di Giona*, vol. 2 (Venice: P. Baglioni, 1677), 443 and 450.

26. Seventeenth-century examples of martyred Catholic women include the Englishwoman Anne Line (d. 1601) and the twenty-three Japanese laywomen executed between 1620 and 1628 as part of repression in the kingdom. On the group of twenty-six Japanese martyrs from 1597—none women—beatified by Urban VIII on 14 September 1627, see the sermon of Paolo Aresi, *Le rose giapponesi* (Tortona: P. G. Calenzano and Eliseo Viola, 1628), and for a modern consideration of the construction of the overall cult, see Rudy Roldán-Figueroa, *The Martyrs of Japan: Publication History and Catholic Missions in the Spanish World (Spain, New Spain, and the Philippines, 1597–1700)* (Leiden: Brill, 2021). The Japanese mother "Maddalena" and her son, from a persecution of 1604, figure in the prose tragedy of Giuseppe Berneri, *Li sacri eroi del Giappone* (Rome: Francesco Tizzoni, 1633). The link between the Mother and martyred Japanese parents/children ranged from Giacomo Lubrano's panegyric on the Japanese Jesuits ("Panegirico XX," in *Il solstizio della gloria divina* [Naples: D. A. Parrino and N. Muzio, 1692], 338), to a 1717 discourse on Dominican history by Teodosio Romano, "Orazione per il quinto secolo del sacro Ordine de' Predicatori," in *Nuova raccolta di varie e scelte orazioni*, vol. 4 (Venice: Giovanni Manfre, 1754), 241. A sermon by the great Portuguese homilist Antonio Vieira

on Francis Xavier's predictions of East Asian martyrdom referred to the Japanese mothers' strength, just like the example of 2 Maccabees (I use the Italian translation, Vieira, "Discorso XI," *Il Saverio addormentato e il Saverio vigilante* [Venice: Pietro Baglioni, 1712], 486).

27. For example, Agostino Alevazoli's Marian tract *La reina de' martiri compatita ne' suoi dolori*, pt. 1 (Milan: Agnelli, 1692), 135–37, compared Mary's multiple sufferings to that of the Mother as portrayed in the Old Testament.

28. Kathleen G. Elkins, *Mary, Mother of Martyrs: How Motherhood Became Self-Sacrifice in Early Christianity* (Eugene, OR: Wipf & Stock, 2018), 55–84, on 4 Maccabees. For the 1715 libretto, see Erika Kanduth's excellent introduction to the critical edition of Fux, *La donna forte*, xiv–xvii (*Sämtliche Werke*, III/ii [Graz: Akademische Druck- u. Verlagsanstalt, 1976]). Giovanna Gronda, *La carriera di un librettista: Pietro Pariati da Reggio di Emilia* (Bologna: Il Mulino, 1990), 224–25, lists but does not discuss the text. The catalogue entry of Thomas Hochradner, *Thematisches Verzeichnis der Werke von Johann Joseph Fux*, vol. 1 (Vienna: Hollitzer, 2016), 81–87, gives a complete list of sources and literature for the oratorio.

29. The idea of the Maccabees' constancy as a model for Habsburg children had come up already in a sermon for Nativity BVM by Eleonora Gonzaga's court preacher Francesco Maria Carracciolo, *Decade oratoria* (Padua: Pasquati, 1667), 61. Some of the devotional literature placed its emphasis on the sons, not the Mother (e.g., Antonio Lupis, *Il nuovo zodiaco* [Venice: Lorenzo Basegio, 1697], 241).

30. My thanks to Riccardo Pintus for checking on this.

31. The *sotto voce* nature of this aria is presumably a symbol for her Biblical address in Hebrew.

32. The short score put up for sale on the antiquarian market in 2023 is in the same hand as the full score in F-Pn.

33. *Wienerisches Diarium* of 22–26 March, p. 2; on a long Friday, the court "[hat] wieder in besagter Kayserl. Hof-Kapellen bey einem kleinen Welschen Oratorium, und Predigt sich eingefunden."

34. In terms of overall timing for Badia and Fux's pieces, the latter might come in at around eighty minutes, whereas a recording of Badia's 1702 *La fuga in Egitto* (nineteen concerted numbers as opposed to the thirteen of the 1709 work; ORF Edition Alte Musik CD 236 [Vienna, 1999]) takes an hour. The sectional numbers in my discussion of Fux refer to Kanduth/Wessely's edition and its numeration of arias and recitatives.

35. Looking at the *Corriere ordinario* (and not the *Wienerisches Diarium*), an "oratorio in musica" was listed for 8 April 1718 (exceptionally a Friday), the feast of the Seven Sorrows of Mary (it had been extended to the whole Empire in 1674). No oratorio took place on an earlier Thursday, 24 March, because other devotions for the Vigil of Annunciation BVM superseded any

dramatic work; another one was recorded on 17 March, so the precise date of Fux's reprise is uncertain. The *sepolcro* of Holy Week that year was Pariati/Fux's *Cristo nell'orto*.

36. I use the number system found in Kanduth/Wessely's critical edition. The two prophetic references have to do with the upcoming successful revolt of the Maccabees (#44; "Tempo verrrà, che il Maccabeo valore / renda le prede al tempio . . ."), and Antioco's own future fall from power (#48). Pariati's Maccabea is also Biblically aware, as she refers to Joshua and the stopping of the sun as an argument against sun worship (#46).

37. Josephus, *Jewish Antiquities*, book XII, chapter 5, passes over the story of the sons while alluding in general ways to Antiochus's torturing. The reception of 4 (and 5) Maccabees in early modern Italy is unclear. Pariati's original 1715 printed libretto, which would contain any such citations, seems lost (its only copy not currently traceable in I-Vnm), and there is no libretto source for the 1718 reprise.

38. The passepied as a figure of one character "following" another would be repeated, of course, in Bach's "Ich folge Dir gleichfalls" in the 1724 *St. John Passion*.

39. Presumably the following ritornello which introduces the Mother's recitative recognition of "Ei già morí" would have provided time for an onstage gesturing of Giacobbe's martyrdom.

40. Paolo Medici, *Dialogo sacro sopra i libri di Esdra, e de' Maccabei* (Florence: M. Nestenius, 1724), 596–611, at 604.

41. He is mentioned by Sebastiano Rumor, *Gli scrittori vicentini dei secoli dieciottavo e diecinono* (Venice: Tipografia Emiliana, 1900), vol. 1, 57–58. His brother Carlo, also an Oratorian, was a better-known writer and poet.

42. Possibly Barbieri's anti-Jesuit sentiments led him to bypass the explication of the story as found in Ferdinando Zucconi S.J., *Lezioni sagre sopra la Divina Scrittura* (Venice: P. Baglioni, 1741), vol. 2, 733–39, who elaborately envoiced the Sons in a way reminiscent of 4 Maccabees but gave the Mother only the paraphrase of her Biblical words.

43. Since it was presented by the Oratorians, presumably in their capacious (~600 square meters) and newly built oratory in the S. Firenze complex, perhaps this is another piece in honor of the order itself. Although they were little involved in missionary work and not subject to martyrdom, possibly this represents a feminization of St. Philip Neri (as "mother" of the order) and the Congregation's (his "sons'") fidelity, rather like the Jesuit piece noted above. The Jesuits had just been suppressed and the Oratorians had triumphed over their rivals.

44. Denis and Elsie Arnold, *The Oratorio in Venice* (London: Royal Musical Association, 1986); Wolfgang Osthoff's excellent study, "Antonio Sacchini als Oper- und Oratorienkomponist," in *Musik an den venezianischen Ospedali/*

Konservatorien vom 17. bis zum frühen 19. Jahrhundert (Rome: Edizioni di Storia e Letteratura, 2004), ed. H. Geyer and Osthoff, discusses this aspect well. On choral and ensemble treatment in *Machabaeorum Mater* and *Nuptiae Ruth*, see Geier, *Das venezianische Oratorium*, 97–107.

45. To annotate Burney's real version of his diary (*An Eighteenth-Century Musical Tour in France and Italy*, ed. P. A. Scholes [London: Oxford University Press, 1959], 130): Gabrieli was Antioco, starting in Part II with her accompanied recitative "Frustra adducis" and its bravura aria "Sinum mostra"; Conti's "Quasi per somnium" with her "infinite expression and taste"; and finally the closing duet between Mother and youngest Son, "Dulcis amor."

46. Although there is some evidence that the *ospedali's* libretti were printed in runs of 500, probably to handle both the titular day's performance as well as any repeats, possibly Burney did not have one.

47. Eleonora Bonincontro, *Il "festino straordinario" di Sant'Agata nel 1799: Politica e devozione nell'anno della Repubblica Partenopea* (Catania: G. Maimone, 2001); see also the listings of performances in De Luca, *Musica e cultura urbana*, 149 and 151.

48. By 1803, Lorenzo Barotti's *Lezioni sacre . . . sul libro de' Maccabei* (Venice: Adolfo Cesare, 1803, 5–6), would make the anti-Enlightenment use of the book quite clear: "Così a poco a poco per via di picciole scosse si sradicano da' cuori altrui quelle, come chiamanle, perverzioni messevi dall'allevamento, e nutritevi dal fanatismo [i.e., Christian faith] . . . or come . . . in tanta licenza . . . prenderà la vostra fede rinvigorimento, e saldezza? [Nei] Libri de' Maccaabei, ne' quali . . . troveremo degli esempi bellissimi di Religione e di Fede."

49. *Riflessioni sul nuovo calendario de' Francesi con una lettera di un curato di Parigi* (n.d., n.p.), "Lettera," pp. 30–32. In a similar vein, the Roman priest Gaetano Luigi del Giudice's adulatory tract of Catherine the Great, filled with anti-Republican invective, cited 2 Maccabees as examples of how to resist tyranny (i.e., the French); *La scoperta de' veri nemici della sovranità* (Rome: G. Zempel, 1794), 330.

Chapter Eight

1. For Leopold I there is no recent scholarly biography. For the general emphasis on family life in Charles's reign, and the importance of music, see Bernd Rill, *Karl VI: Habsburg als barocke Großmacht* (Graz: Styria-Verlag, 1992), especially 21–25 and 198–200. For the shifting politics leading to the proclamation of the Pragmatic Sanction as Imperial law in early February 1732, see Rill, *Karl VI*, 268–72. Metastasio gave detailed staging instructions for *Demetrio* and (to a lesser extent) *Issipile* in his letters of fall 1731 and winter 1732, but the task of writing *La morte d'Abel* evoked only ennui in him

(Metastasio, *Tutte le opere*, ed. B. Brunetti [Florence: Mondadori, 1943ff]), vol. 3, 60–64.

2. The entire season was put together in a hurry: Zeno wrote that he finished *Sedecia* in February, and Caldara's score for it is dated 7 March; see U. Kirkendale, *Antonio Caldara: Sein Leben und seine venezianisch-römischen Oratorien* (Graz: Böhlau, 1966), 138. The other major opera that year was for Karl's name day: Metastasio/Caldara, *Adriano in Siria*, done in November. This is more of a political work on loyalty, betrayal, and constancy; Farinelli did not stay to sing in it (the title role went to Gaetano Orsini).

3. His name is clearly given on the cast lists in Caldara's two scores in A-Wn.

4. The *Wienerisches Diarium* of 8 March opens with a rare report from Turin dated 22 February, giving a sense of travel/courier times as about two weeks that year; there were no articles on Farinelli's Carnival season performances for the Savoyards (Hasse's *Catone in Utica* and his own brother's *Merope*, familiar roles to him). These were staged in the pre-1740 theater, the "Teatro di Corte."

5. By comparison with the Abel piece of 1727 noted above, it will be noted how Reutter's compositional technique had made major progress in five years.

6. Although the citations to 2 Maccabees are duly marked, the other Scriptural references are implicit and there are no Patristic/exegetical marginalia; that is, this is not a text on the intellectual level of Zeno or Metastasio.

7. Hermione W. Williams, *Francesco Bartolomeo Conti: His Life and Music* (Aldershot: Ashgate, 1999), 143, noted the amount of accompanied recitative in both *Issipile* and *L'Osservanza*. One wonders if the enormous tasks of composing contributed to Conti's death later that year.

8. Praun's ability to imitate fury is also evident in Conti's writing for Antioco's Part II aria, with a wildly extravagant violin part, "Sciocchi, andate"; in general, the instrumental obbligati in this piece are extremely difficult (e.g., Son #7's Part II aria, "Già atroce il mio dolore," with hard bassoon and cello lines).

9. The play-like nature of the work is also shown in the numerous obbligati, largely for low and somber instruments: variously trombone, cello, pantaleon (i.e., hammered dulcimer, here unusually requiring a low C on the instrument and used for Dio's own aria, i.e., God's heavenly lyre), and bassoons for different numbers. This kind of instrumental variety links it to Renaissance *intermedi*. My thanks to Margit Übellacker for instrument-specific information on the aria with pantaleon, "Se l'incauto passager" (f. 117v of the score, toward the end of Part I).

10. Stroppa, *Fra notturni sereni*, 152–58, still the best treatment of the text. Several aspects of Metastasio's narration (notably Caino's anger) are derived from Augustin Calmet, *La storia dell'Antico e Nuovo Testamento* (It. trans., Venice: N. Pezzana, 1725), 11–13.

11. One of the two copies of the score in A-Wn can be seen at https://search.onb.ac.at/permalink/f/1n9tuav/ONB_alma21297309890003338 (accessed 28 September 2023). Oddly, although the two Viennese scores survive, there seems to be no copy of a separate 1732 printed libretto.

12. Again here, Leo's choice for the aria was different: a bucolic andante on F, largely stepwise and not florid, with thematic interconnections between the (shorter) A and B sections. There are more than twenty complete manuscript copies of Leo's setting in various parts of Europe.

BIBLIOGRAPHY

Abbate, Vincenzo, ed. *Serpotta e il suo tempo*. Milan: Silvana, 2017.

Abraham a Sancta Clara. *Mercks wol Soldat!* Vienna, 1680.

Alaleona, Domenico. *Studi su la storia dell'oratorio musicale in Italia*. Turin: Fratelli Bocca, 1908.

Alevazoli, Agostino. *La reina de' martiri compatita ne' suoi dolori*, pt. 1. Milan: Agnelli, 1692.

Alexandre, Natalis [= Noel]. *Historia ecclesiastica*, vol. 4. Lucca: Leonardo Venturini, 1734.

Ardissino, Erminia. *Donne interpreti della Bibbia nell'Italia della prima età moderna: comunità ermeneutiche e riscritture*. Turnhout: Brepols, 2020.

Aresi, Paolo. *Le rose giapponesi*. Tortona: P. G. Calenzano and Eliseo Viola, 1628.

Arnold, Denis, and E. Arnold. *The Oratorio in Venice*. London: Royal Musical Association, 1986.

Barotti, Lorenzo. *Lezioni sacre . . . sul libro de' Maccabei*. Venice: Adolfo Cesare, 1803.

Bartoli, Daniello. *Delle grandezze di Christo*. Rome: n.p., 1675.

Beat, Janet, ed. *Giacomo Carissimi: Jephthe*. London: Faber Music, 1974.

Benedictis, Giovanni de. *Azioni sacre*. Rome: S. G. Generoso, 1758.

Bennett, Lawrence. "A Little-Known Collection of Early-Eighteenth-Century Vocal Music at Schloss Elisabethenburg, Meiningen." *Fontes Artis Musicae* 48 (2001): 250–302.

Berneri, Giuseppe. *Li sacri eroi del Giappone*. Rome: Francesco Tizzoni, 1683.

Besutti, Paola, ed. *L'oratorio musicale italiano e i suoi contesti (secc. XVII–XVIII)*. Florence: Leo S. Olschki, 2002.

Bianchi, Lino, ed. *Alessandro Scarlatti, Agar ed Ismaele esiliati*. Rome: Edizioni de Sanctis, 1965.

―――. *Scarlatti, Il primo omicidio* (= *Cain*). Rome: Edizioni de Sanctis, 1968.

Bigarolo, Giovanni Battista. *Prediche quaresimali.* Milan: Francesco Vigone, 1686.

Boero, Stefano. "Gli Oratoriani all'Aquila tra Seicento e Settecento: cultura e spiritualità." *Annali di Storia moderna e contemporanea* 16 (2010): 485–516.

Bonincontro, Eleonora. *Il "festino straordinario" di Sant'Agata nel 1799: Politica e devozione nell'anno della Repubblica Partenopea.* Catania: G. Maimone, 2001.

Bono, Salvatore. *Schiavi musulmani nell'Italia moderna.* Naples: Edizioni scientifiche italiane, 1999.

―――. *Schiavi: una storia mediterranea (XVI–XIX secoli).* Bologna: Il Mulino, 2016.

Bowman, Steven B. *Sepher Yosippon: A Tenth-Century History of Ancient Israel.* Detroit: Wayne State University Press, 2023.

Budasz, Rogélio. *Opera in the Tropics: Music and Theater in Early Modern Brazil.* Oxford: Oxford University Press, 2019.

Burney, Charles. *An Eighteenth-Century Musical Tour in France and Italy*, ed. P. A. Scholes. London: Oxford University Press, 1959.

Calmet, Augustin. *La storia dell'Antico e Nuovo Testamento.* It. trans. Venice: N. Pezzana, 1725.

Carracciolo, Francesco Maria. *Decace oratoria.* Padua: Pasquati, 1667.

Cattelan, Vittorio. "'Se desideri Allah / egli è in ogni creatura': Metastasio a Costantinopoli nelle traduzioni di Giovanni Eremian." In *Orizzonti della musica italiana a Costantinopoli nel primo Ottocento*, 69–114. Lucca: LIM, 2021.

Celli, Andrea. "Figli di Agar e Ismaele: Riferimenti interreligiosi nei libretti per oratorio nel Seicento italiano?" In *Testi, tradizioni, attraversamenti: Prospettive comparatistiche sulla drammaturgia europea fra Sei e Settecento*, ed. A. Munari et al., 13–30. Padua: Padova University Press, 2019.

Chiappelli, Alberto. *Storia del teatro in Pistoia.* Pistoia: Officina tipografica cooperative, 1913.

Chirico, Teresa. "'Balconi dorati per i musici': la prassi rappresentativa dell'oratorio alla corte del cardinale Pietro Ottoboni fra il 1690 e il 1708." In *Spectacles et performances artistiques à Rome (1644–1740)*, ed. A.-M. Goulet, J. M. Dominguez, and É. Oriol, 151–65. Rome: École française de Rome, 2021.

Ciappelli, Giovanni. "Identità collettiva." In *Famiglia e religione in Europa*, ed. Ciappelli. Rome: Edizioni di Storia e Letteratura, 2011.

Clodinio, Girolamo [= Klodzinski, Hieronim]. *Discorsi per la novena e solennità . . .* Venice: G. G. Hertz, 1678.

Cordier, Jean. *La famiglia santa*, book 2. Macerata: G. F. Panelli, 1674.

Cox, Virginia. "Rethinking Counter-Reformation Literature." In *Innovation in the Italian Counter-Reformation*, ed. S. McHugh and A. Wainwright, 15–55. Newark: University of Delaware Press, 2020.

Crowther, Victor. *The Oratorio in Bologna (1650–1730)*. Oxford: Oxford University Press, 1999.

Da Molin, Giovanna. *Famiglia e matrimonia nell'Italia del Seicento*. Bari: Cucucci, 2000.

Deisinger, Marko. "Römische Oratorien am Hof der Habsburger in Wien in der zweiten Hälfte des 17. Jahrhunderts: Zur Einführung und Etablierung des Oratoriums in der kaiserlichen Residenz." *Musicologica austriaca* 29 (2010): 89–111.

Del Donna, Anthony R. *Opera, Theatrical Culture and Society in Late Eighteenth-Century Naples*. Farnham: Ashgate, 2012.

Del Giudice, Gaetano Luigi. *La scoperta de' veri nemici della sovranità*. Rome: G. Zempel, 1794.

Dell'Olio, Antonio. *Drammi sacri e oratori musicali in Puglia nei secoli XVII e XVIII*. Galatina: M. Congedo, 2013.

———. "Il *Tobia sposo* (1690): scherzo drammatico di Gaetano Veneziano." In *L'oratorio musicale a Napoli nel tempo di Gaetano Veneziano*, ed. Dell'Olio, 1–42. Naples: I Figlioli di S. Maria di Loreto, 2016.

De Lucca, Valeria. *The Politics of Princely Entertainment: Music and Spectacle in the Lives of Lorenzo Onofrio and Maria Mancini Colonna (1659–1689)*. New York: Oxford University Press, 2020.

deSilva, David A. "An Example of How to Die Nobly for Faith: The Influence of 4 Maccabees on Origen's *Exhortatio ad Martyrium*." *Journal of Early Christian Studies* 17, no. 3 (2009): 337–55.

———. *4 Maccabees*. Septuagint Commentary Series. Leiden: Brill, 2006.

———. "Perfection of 'Love for Offspring': Representations of Maternal Affection and the Achievement of the Heroine of 4 Maccabees." *New Testament Studies* 52 (2006): 251–68.

Ditchfield, Simon. "Baroque around the Clock: Daniello Bartoli SJ (1608–1685) and the Uses of Global History." *Transactions of the Royal Historical Society* 31 (2021): 49–73.

Dizionario biografico degli italiani (= DBI). Online at www.treccani.it.

Doerfler, Maria. *Jephthah's Daughter, Sarah's Son: The Death of Children in Late Antiquity*. Oakland: University of California Press, 2019.

Duran, Robert. *2 Maccabees: A Critical Commentary*. Minneapolis: Fortress Press, 2012.

Eisenbichler, Konrad. *The Boys of the Archangel Raphael: A Youth Confraternity in Florence, 1411–1785*. Toronto: University of Toronto Press, 1998.

Elkins, Kathleen G. *Mary, Mother of Martyrs: How Motherhood Became Self-Sacrifice in Early Christianity*. Eugene, OR: Wipf & Stock, 2020.

Emanuele di Gesù Maria. *Frutti del Carmelo, discorsi morali*. Rome: Filippo Maria Mancini, 1667.

Fedi, Maria. *"Tuo lumine": L'accademia dei Risvegliati e lo spettacolo a Pistoia tra Sei e Settecento*. Florence: Florence University Press, 2011.

Feldman, Martha, and V. Valeri. "L'opera e il sacrificio: passato e futuro mitologico nel teatro pre-rivoluzionario." In *Uno spazio tra sé e sé*, 181–225. Rome: Donzelli, 1999.

Fino, Clotilde. "Drammi e oratori nella corrispondenza di Francesco de Lemene con il cardinale Pietro Ottoboni." *Recercare* 30 (2018): 119–43.

Föcking, Marc. "Implicit Anti-Classicism: Imitating and Exhausting Old and New Classicisms in Spiritual Tragedy and Spiritual Petrarchism." In *A Companion to Anticlassicisms in the Cinquecento*, ed. Marc Föcking, Susanne Friede, Florian Mehltretter, and Angela Oster, 105–66. Berlin: de Gruyter, 2023.

Fosi, Irene. *Papal Justice: Subjects and Courts in the Papal State, 1500–1750*. Washington, DC: Catholic University Press, 2011.

Franchi, Saverio. *Drammaturgia romana*, vols. 1–2. Rome: IBIMUS, 1988–97.

———, ed. *Percorsi dell'oratorio romano da "Historia Sacra" a melodramma spirituale*. Rome: IBIMUS, 2002.

Frenquellucci, Chiara. *Dalla Mancia a Siena al Nuovo Mondo: Don Chisciotte nel teatro di Girolamo Giglio*. Florence: L. S. Olschki, 2010.

Frigo, Daniela. *Il padre di famiglia: governo della casa e governo civile nella tradizione della "economia" tra Cinque e Seicento*. Rome: Bulzoni, 1985.

Gamberoni, Johann. *Die Auslegung des Buches Tobias n der griechisch-lateinischen Kirche der Antike und der Christenheit des Westens bis um 1600*. Munich: Kösel-Verlag, 1969.

Geyer, Helen. *Das venezianische Oratorium*. Laaber: Laaber-Verlag, 2005.

Gigli, Girolamo. *La madre de' Maccabei*. Siena: n.p., 1688.

———. *La sposa de' cantici*. Siena: Bonetti, 1702.

Gillio, Pier Giuseppe. *L'attività musicale negli ospedali di Venezia*. Florence: L. S. Olschki, 2006.

Giuseppe da Como. *Annuale*, pt. 2. Venice: P. Baglioni, 1670.

Grandi, Vittore Silvio. *Historia ecclesiastica*. Venice: Domenico Loviso, 1708.

Graveson, Ignaz Armat de. *Historia Ecclesiastica Veteris Testamenti*. Venice: G. B. Recurti, 1732.

Gregory of Nyssa. "De deitate Filii et Spiritus Sancti et in Abraham." In *Sermones*, pt. 3, ed. Friedhelm Mann. Leiden: Brill, 1996.

Grippaudo, Ilaria. "Attività musicale, patrocinio e condizione femminile nei monasteri palermitani (secc. XVII–XVIII)." In *Puta/puttana: donne musica teatro tra XVI e XVIII secolo*, ed. M. P. Altese and P. Cangemi, 43–56. Palermo: Il Palindromo, 2016.

Gronda, Giovanna. *La carriera di un librettista: Pietro Pariati da Reggio di Emilia*. Bologna: Il Mulino, 1990.

Guercino: Master Painter of the Baroque. Washington, DC: National Gallery of Art, 1992.

Hall, Edith. *Adventures with Iphigenia in Tauris: A Cultural History of Euripides' Black Sea Tragedy*. Oxford: Oxford University Press, 2013.

Herczog, Johann. *Il perfetto melodramma spirituale: l'oratorio italiano nel suo period classico*. Rome: IBIMUS, 2013.

———. "Sulle trace della Cappella Cesarea: Gregor Joseph Werner e la tradizione oratoriale nell'Eisenstadt dei principi Esterházy." In *Symposium Musicae: Saggi e testimonianze in onore di Giancarlo Rostirolla per il suo 80° genetliaco*, ed. F. Nardacci/B. Cipriani, 197–232. Faleria: Recercare, 2021.

Hill, John W. "Oratory Music in Florence," pts. 1–3. *Acta Musicologica* 51 (1979): 108–36 and 246–67; 58 (1986): 129–79.

Hirschberg, Julius. *Die Augenheilkunde in der Neuzeit*, vol. 3. Berlin: Springer, 1899.

Hochradner, Thomas. *Thematisches Verzeichnis der Werke von Johann Joseph Fux*, vol. 1. Vienna: Hollitzer, 2016.

Hutschenreiter, Johann Baptist. *Azarias Fidelis Tobiae In Via spiritualium Exercitiorum per octiduum*. Regensburg: J. B. Lang, 1741.

Josephus, Flavius. *Jewish Antiquities*. Cambridge, MA: Harvard University Press, 1998.

Kanduth, Erika, and O. Wessely, eds. J. J. Fux, *La donna forte nella madre de' Maccabei, Sämtliche Werke*, series III, vol. ii. Graz: Akademische Druck-u. Verlagsanstalt, 1976.

Kendrick, Robert L. "Disguise, Difference, Deceit in a Sienese Oratorio-Sermon." In *La crisi della modernità. Storie, riletture e revisioni per Gianvittorio Signorotto*, ed. M. Al-Katak, E. Fumagalli, and L. Ferrari. Rome: Viella Editrice, 2023.

———. *Fruits of the Cross: Passiontide Theater in Habsburg Vienna*. Oakland: University of California Press, 2019.

Kertzer, David I., and M. Barbagli, eds. *Family Life in Early Modern Times 1500–1789*. New Haven, CT: Yale University Press, 2001.

Kirkendale, Ursula. *Antonio Caldara: Sein Leben und seine venezianisch-römischen Oratorien*. Graz: Böhlau, 1966.

Lapide, Cornelius a. *Commentaria in Josue, Judices . . .* 1st ed. Antwerp: J. Mersius, 1642.

———. *Commentarium in Pentateuchum*. 1st ed. Antwerp: Heirs of M. Nutius, 1616.

Lehner, Ulrich L. *The Catholic Enlightenment: The Global History of a Forgotten Movement*. New York: Oxford University Press, 2016.

Le Maître de Sacy. *Sacra scrittura*, vol. 31. Venice: Lorenzo Baseggio, 1780.

Lombardo, Carlo. *Sermoni domenicali*, pts. 1–2. Naples: Novello de Bonis, 1688.

Lorenzetti, Stefano. "*Per ricreazione e diletto*: Accademie e opera in musica nel Collegio Tolomei di Siena." In *Il melodramma italiano in Italia e Germania nell'età barocca*, ed. A. Luppi, Maurizio Padoan, and Alberto Colzani, 217–41. Como: AMIS, 1995.

Low, Robert A. *Marc-Antoine Charpentier et la musique au Collége des Jesuits*. Paris: Maisonneuve & Larose, 1966.

Lubrano, Giacomo. *Il solstizio della gloria divina*. Naples: D. A. Parrino and N. Muzio, 1692.

Lupis, Antonio. *Il nuovo zodiaco figurato*. Venice: Lorenzo Basegio, 1697.

Malanima, Paolo. "Italian Cities 1300–1800: A Quantitative Approach." *Rivista di Storia Economica* 14 (1998): 91–126.

Manni, Giovanni Battista. *Quaresimale prima*. Venice: Andrea Polletti, 1681.

Manzoni, Francesca. *Il sagrifizio d'Abramo*. Vienna: van Ghelen, 1738.

Masini, Antonio. *Bologna perlustrata*. Bologna: Vittorio Benacci, 1666.

Mattioda, Enrico. "Ifigenia e la figlia di Iefte: una polemica illuminista a teatro." In *Sacro e/o profano nel teatro fra Rinascimento ed Età dei Lumi*, ed. S. Castellaneta and F. Minervini, 213–29. Bari: Cacucci, 2009.

Mayno, Domenico. *Il decalogo descritto e spiegato*. Naples: M. L. Nuzi, 1697.

Mazzanti, Giuseppe. *Matrimoni post-tridentini: Un dibattito dottrinale fra continuità e cambiamento (secc. XVI–XVIII)*. Bologna: Bononia University Press, 2020.

McGinn, Bernard. "Women Interpreting the Song of Songs, 1150–1700." In *A Companion to the Song of Songs in the History of Spirituality*, ed. T. H. Robinson, 249–73. Leiden: Brill. 2021.

McLeod, Wallace. "The Range of the Ancient Bow." *Phoenix* 19 (1965): 1–14.

Medici, Paolo. *Dialogo sacro sopra I libri di Esdra, e de' Maccabei*. Florence: M. Nestenius, 1724.

Menochio, Giovanni Stefano. *Le Stuore*, vol. 2. Rome: Felice Cesaretti, 1689.

Metastasio, Pietro. *Oratori sacri*, ed. S. Stroppa. Venice: Marsilio, 1996.

Morelli, Arnaldo. *Il tempio armonico: Musica nell'oratorio dei Filippini in Roma (1575–1705)*. Laaber: Laaber-Verlag, 1991.

———. "La circolazione dell'oratorio italiano nel Seicento." *Studi musicali* 26 (1997): 105–86.

———. "La musica a Roma nella seconda metà del Seicento attraverso l'archivio Cartari-Febei." In *La musica a Roma attraverso le fonti d'archivio*, ed. B. M. Antolini, A. Morelli, and V. Vita Spagnuolo, 107–36. Lucca: LIM, 1994.

———. "'Un bell'oratorio all'uso di Roma': Patronage and secular context of the oratorio in Baroque Rome." In *Music Observed: Studies in Memory of William C. Holmes*, ed. C. Reardon and S. Parisi, 333–51. Warren, MI: Harmonie Park Press, 2005.

Morgenstern, Anja. *Die Oratorien von Johann Simon Mayr (1763–1845): Studien zu Biographik, Quellen, und Rezeption*. Munich: Katzbichler, 2007.

Mormando, Franco. "Gian Paolo Oliva: The Forgotten Celebrity of Baroque Rome." In *The Holy Name: Art of the Gesù, Bernini and His Age*, ed. Linda Wolk-Simon, 225–51. Philadelphia: St. Joseph's University Press, 2018).

Morone, Carlo Tommaso. *Annuale*. Parma: Rosati, 1706.

Motnik, Marko. "Das Oratorium 'Il ritorno di Tobia' di Joseph Haydn: 'ein veraltetes Machwerk'?" *Eisenstädter Haydn-Berichte* 12 (2020): 175–96.

———. "Oratorien am Wiener *Theater nächst der Burg* in der Ära Durazzos." *Studien zur Musikwissenschaft* 60 (2018): 45–125.

Mühle, Friederike. *J. Haydn, Il ritorno di Tobia, Kritischer Bericht*. Munich: G. Henle Verlag, 2018.

Murata, Margaret K. "Colpe mie venite a piangere: The Penitential Cantata in Baroque Rome." In *Listening to Early Modern Catholicism*, ed. M. Noone and D. Filippi, 204–32. Leiden: Brill, 2017.

Muurling, Sanne. *Everyday Crime, Criminal Justice, and Gender in Early Modern Bologna*. Leiden: Brill, 2021.

Nannini, Remigio. *Epistole e evangelii, che si leggano tutto l'anno alla Messa*. Venice: G. B. Gagliani, 1599.

Natter, Martina. "Die vier Oratorien von Camilla de Rossi." PhD diss., University of Innsbruck, 2003.

Noske, Frits. *Saints and Sinners: The Latin Musical Dialogue in the Seventeenth Century*. Oxford: Oxford University Press, 1992.

Oliva, Giovanni Paolo. *In selecta Scripturae loca ethicae commentationes . . . in Genesim*. Lyons: Annison & Posuel, 1677.

———. *Sermoni domestici*, pts. 1–10. Rome: Z. Conzatti, 1671–82.

Olszewski, Edward J. *The Inventory of Paintings of Cardinal Pietro Ottoboni (1667–1740)*. New York: Peter Lang, 2004.

Orlandi, Pellegrino Antonio. *Notizie degli scrittori bolognesi e dell'opere loro stampate*. Bologna: C. Pissari, 1714.

Osthoff, Wolfgang, "Antonio Sacchini als Oper- und Oratorienkomponist." In *Musik an den venezianischen Ospedali/Konservatorien vom 17. bis zum frühen 19. Jahrhundert*, ed. H. Geyer and Wolfgang Osthoff. Rome: Edizioni di Storia e Letteratura, 2004.

Over, Berthold. *"Per la gloria di Dio": soloistische Kirchenmusik an den venezianischen Ospedali.* Bonn: Orpheus-Verlag, 1998.

Paciuchelli, Angelo. *Lezioni morali sop-a Giona profeta,* vol. 3. Venice: P. Baglioni, 1677.

Palermo, Guido. *Guida istruttiva per Falermo.* Palermo: Reale Stamperia, 1816.

Pellegrini, Almachilde. "Spettacoli lucchesi: 1697–1700." *Memorie e documenti per servire alla storia di Lucca* 14, no. 1 (1914): 193–95.

Pellegrini, Giuseppe Luigi. *Tobia: Ragionamenti.* Venice: Gaspare Storti, 1772.

Piperno, Franco. *La Bibbia all'opera: drammi sacri in Italia dal tardo Settecento al Nabucco.* Rome: NeoClassica, 2018.

Pitarresi, Gaetano. "*Isacco figura del Redentore* di Pietro Metastasio nelle intonazioni di Luca Antonio Predieri e di Niccolo Jommelli." In *Niccolò Jommelli: l'esperienza europea di un musicista "filosofo."* Reggio Calabria: Conservatorio F. Cilea, 2014.

Pizzolato, Luigi Franco. *I sette fratelli Maccabei nella chiesa antica d'Occidente.* Milan: Vita & Pensiero, 2005.

Prats Arolas, Ignacio. "Music and Communication in Enlightenment Rome." PhD diss., University of Illinois, 2015.

Prevot, Andrew. *Theology and Race: Black and Womenist Traditions in the United States.* Leiden: Brill, 2020.

Rainieri Redi, Giovanni Nicola. *Ismaele in esilio, oratorio a cinque voci da cantarsi nella chiesa di S. Firenze il dì xxi. Dicembre.* Florence, 1747.

Ranaldi, Antonella. "La chiesa di S. Maria del Soccorso e le chiese sulle mura. Domenico Tibaldi e il cardinale Gabriele Paleotti." In *Domenico e Pellegrino Tibaldi. Architettura e Arte a Bologna nel secondo Cinquecento,* ed. F. Ceccarelli and D. Lenzi, 221–22. Venice: Marsilio, 2011.

Reardon, Colleen. *Holy Concord within Sacred Walls: Nuns and Music in Siena, 1575–1700.* New York: Oxford University Press, 2002.

———. *A Sociable Moment: Opera and Festive Culture in Baroque Siena.* New York: Oxford University Press, 2016.

Rho, Giovanni. *Orazioni sagre sopra la Divina Scrittura,* pt. 2. Milan: F. Ghisolfi, 1671.

Riepe, Juliane. *Die Arciconfraternita di S. Maria della Morte in Bologna.* Paderborn: F. Schöningh, 1998.

Riflessioni sul nuovo calendario de' Francesi con una lettera di un curato di Parigi. N.d., n.p..

Rill, Bernd. *Karl VI. Habsburg als barocke Großmacht.* Graz: Verlag Styria, 1992.

Roldán-Figueroa, Rady. *The Martyrs of Japan: Publication History and Catho-*

lic Missions in the Spanish World (Spain, New Spain, and the Philippines, 1597–1700). Leiden: Brill, 2021.

Romano, Teodosio. "Orazione per il quinto secolo del sacro Ordine de' Predicatori." In *Nuova raccolta di varie e scelte orazioni*, vol. 4. Venice: Giovanni Manfre, 1754.

Rooke, Deborah W. *Handel's Israelite Oratorio Libretti: Sacred Drama and Biblical Exegesis*. Oxford: Oxford University Press, 2012.

Rosado y Haro, J. A. *Oración solemne en la profesión y velo que recibió . . . la Madre Soror Margarita Fernández de Córdova y Pimentel*. Seville: Widow of N. Rodríguez, 1673.

Rose, Colin. *A Renaissance of Violence: Homicide in Early Modern Italy*. Cambridge: Cambridge University Press, 2019.

Rumor, Sebastiano. *Gli scrittori vicentini dei secoli dieciottavo e diecinono*. Venice: Tipografia Emiliana, 1900.

Santacroce, Simona. "Dal Libro al libretto: Tre drammi musicali biblici del Seicento." PhD diss., University of Turin, 2012.

Sarti, Raffaella. "Bolognesi schiavi dei 'Turchi' e schiavi 'turchi' a Bologna tra Cinque e Settecento: alterità etnico-religiosa e riduzione in schiavitù." *Quaderni storici* 2 (2001): 437–74.

Sartori, Claudio. *I libretti italiani a stampa dalle origini al 1800*. Cuneo: Bertola & Locatelli, 1990–93.

Schmid, Ernst Franz, and A. Oppermann, eds. *Haydn, Il ritorno di Tobia*. Munich: G. Henle Verlag, 2009.

Schroeder, Joy A. "Envying Jephthah's Daughter: Judges 11 in the Thought of Arcangela Tarabotti (1604–1652)." In *Strangely Familiar: Proto-feminist Interpretations of Patriarchal Biblical Texts*, ed. N. Calvert-Koyzis and H. E. Weir, 75–91. Atlanta: Society of Biblical Literature, 2009.

Segneri, Paolo. *Il divoto di Maria Vergine*. Parma: Alberto Pazzoni, 1700.

———. *Panegirici sacri*. Treviso: Pianta, 1704.

Sellin, Christina P. *Fractured Families and Rebel Maidservants: The Biblical Hagar in Seventeenth-Century Dutch Art and Literature*. New York: Continuum, 2006.

Selmi, Elisabetta. "Riscritture bibliche nel dramma sacro fra Seicento e Settecento." In *Gli italiani e la Bibbia nella prima età moderna: Leggere, riscrivere, interpretare*, ed. E. Ardissino and E. Boillet. Turnhout: Brepols, 2018.

Setaioli, Filippo. *Orationi e discorsi*, pt. 2. Venice: Baglioni, 1678.

Siebenhüner, Kim. *Bigamie und Inquisition in Italien 1600–1750*. Paderborn: F. Schöningh, 2006.

Signori, Gabriella, ed. *Dying for the Faith, Killing for the Faith: Old-Testament*

Faith-Warriors (1 and 2 Maccabees) in Historical Perspective. Leiden: Brill, 2012.

Sigonio, Carlo. *De republica Hebraeorum*. Bologna: Giovanni Rossi, 1582.

Smither, Howard E. *A History of the Oratorio*, vols. 1–4. Chapel Hill: University of North Carolina Press, 1977–2000.

———, ed. *Alessandro Melani, Il sacrificio di Abel*. Italian Oratorio 1650–1800, vol. 3. New York: Garland Publishing, 1986.

Speck, Christian. *Das italienische Oratorium 1625–1665: Musik und Dichtung*. Turnhout: Brepols, 2003.

Sperling, Jutta. *Convents and the Body Politic in Late Renaissance Venice*. Chicago: University of Chicago Press, 1999.

Steiger, Johann A., and Ulrich Heinen, eds. *Isaaks Opferung (Gen 22) in den Konfessionen und Medien der Frühen Neuzeit*. Arbeiten zur Kirchengeschichte, vol. 101. Berlin: de Gruyter, 2006.

Stroppa, Sabrina, ed. P. Metastasio, *Oratori sacri*. Venice, Marsilio, 1993.

Sypherd, Wilbur O. *Jephthah and His Daughter: A Study in Comparative Literature*. Newark: University of Delaware Press, 1948.

Thompson, John L. *Writing the Wrongs: Women of the Old Testament Among Biblical Commentators from Philo through the Reformation*. New York: Oxford University Press, 2001.

Thum, Agnes. *Schutzengel: 1200 Jahre Bildgeschichte zwischen Devotion und Dikaktik*. Regensburg: Schnell & Steiner, 2014.

Tirinus (Tiran), Jacobus. *Commentarius in Vetus et Novum Testamentum*. Antwerp: M. Nutius, 1632.

Tonelli, Vanessa. "*Le Figlie Di Coro*: Women's Musical Education and Performance at the Venetian Ospedali Maggiori, 1660–1740." PhD diss., Northwestern University, 2022.

Tonti, Giacinto. *Secondo Avvento e Secondo Quaresimale . . . detto nell'augustissima Cesarea cappella*. Venice: Giuseppe Corona, 1730.

Trible, Phyllis. "Ominous Beginnings for a Promise of Blessing." In *Hagar, Sarah, and Their Children: Jewish, Christian, and Muslim Perspectives*, ed. Trible and L. M. Russell, 33–69. Louisville: Westminster John Knox Press, 2006.

Tylus, Jane. *Reclaiming Catherine of Siena: Literacy, Literature and the Signs of Others*. Chicago: University of Chicago Press, 2017.

Valle, Pietro. *Prediche dette nel Palazzo Apostolico*. Venice: N. Pezzana, 1713.

Vanalesti, Saverio. *Prediche quaresimali*. Venice: G. B. Pasquali, 1743.

van der Linden, Huub. "Eighteenth-Century Oratorio Reform in Practice: Apostolo Zeno Revises a Florentine Libretto." *Eighteenth-Century Music* 26 (2019): 31–52.

———. "A Family at the Opera: The Bolognetti as an Audience at the Theatres of Rome, (1694–1736)." *Recercare* 30 (2018): 145–200.

———. "The Unexplored Giant: Use Histories of Italian Oratorio around 1700." PhD diss., European History Institute Florence, 2012.

Vieira, Antonio. "Discorso XI." In *Il Saverio addormentato e il Saverio vigilante*. Venice: Pietro Baglioni, 1712.

Waquet, Françoise. *Rhétorique et poétique chrétiennes: Bernardino Perfetti et la poésie improvisée dans l'Italie du XVIIIe siècle*. Florence: Leo S. Olschki, 1992.

Weidmann, Clemens. "Das Carmen de Martyrio Maccabaeorum." PhD diss., University of Vienna, 1995.

Weilen, Alexander von. *Zur Wiener Theatergeschichte. Die vom Jahre 1629 bis zum Jahre 1740 am Wiener Hofe zur Aufführung gelangten Werke theatralischen Charakters und Oratorien*. Vienna: Alfred Hölder, 1901.

Williams, Delores S. "Hagar in African American Biblical Appropriation." In *Hagar, Sarah, and Their Children: Jewish, Christian, and Muslim Perspectives*, ed. P. Trible and L. M. Russell, 171–84. Louisville: Westminster John Knox Press, 2006.

Williams, Hermione W. *Francesco Bartolomeo Conti: His Life and Music*. Aldershot: Ashgate, 1999.

Wuchner, Emily M. "The Tonkünstler-Sozietät and the Oratorio in Vienna, 1771–1798." PhD diss., University of Illinois/Urbana-Champaign, 2017.

Zucconi, Ferdinando. *Lezioni sagre sopra la Sacra Scrittura*, vol. 1. Venice: P. Baglioni, 1741.

———. *Lezioni scritturali*, vols. 14–15. Venice: P. Baglioni, 1714.

INDEX

Page numbers in italics refer to musical examples.

Abel. *See* Cain and Abel
Abraham, 1, 3, 120, 132, 149, 191; as
   father of Isaac, 75–104; as father
   of Ishmael, 39–74; as husband of
   Sarah, 39–74, 75–104
Abraham a Sancta Clara, 121
Acciarelli, Francesco, 119, 139
Adam and Eve, 15–38, 213–14
Albrici, Vincenzo, 117
Aldrovandini, Giuseppe Antonio,
   175
Alexandre, Noel, 112–13
Ambrose, Saint, 8, 148
Anfossi, Pasquale, 195–99, *198*
Angelelli, Antonio Maria, 90
anonymous oratorios, 15–17, 23, 130
Ardissino, Erminia, 227n, 234n
Ariosti, Attilio, 10, 184–91, *186*
Augustine, Saint, 8, 80–81, 98, 148,
   183, 251n

Badia, Carlo Antonio, 70, 257n
Balbi, Benedetto, 120–21
Barbieri, Giuseppe, 193–95, 199
Barth, Joseph, 145

Barthelémon, François-Henri, 132–33
Bartoli, Daniele, 76
Bencini, Pietro Paolo, 80, 83–85, *87*
Benedict XIII, Pope, 16
Benedict XIV, Pope (Prospero Lam-
   bertini), 15
Bernardoni, Pietro Antonio, 91, 94
Bicilli, Giovanni, 54, 59–66, 183
Boccherini, Giovanni Gastone, 147,
   159–67
Bologna, 2, 8, 11, 13, 21, 43, 47–49,
   139; Palazzo Orsi, 47; SS. Sebas-
   tiano e Rocco, Oratory of, 89
Bono, Salvatore, 236n
Borghese, Maria Virginia, 180
Borrini, Rainaldo, 92, 185
Bridget of Sweden, 184
Buonaccorsi, Giacomo, 80, 83–86, 98
Burney, Charles, 200–204

Caffarelli, Giovan Paolo, 55–56
Cain and Abel, 1, 7, 12, 14, 16, 18–38,
   180, 206–18
Caldana, Nicolo, 88
Caldara, Antonio, 68–70, 109, 129,

Caldara, Antonio (*continued*) 214, 215–18; *Abramo*, 68–70; *La morte d'Abel*, 215–18; 217
Calmet, Augustin, 8, 116, 148, 260n
Carissimi, Giacomo, 78, 108; *Jephthe*, 108, 114–18
Carmelites, Discalced, 11, 16
Castel San Pietro (Terme), 14, 16–21, 104
Catania, 145, 198, 204
Cazzati, Maurizio: 14, 59; *Il Caino condennato*, 21–22
Celani, Giovanni, 60–61
Charles VI, Emperor, 70, 86, 91, 99–102, 129, 189, 206–10
Charpentier, Marc-Antoine, 76, 115–17
Chiari, Pietro, 5, 134, 142–43, 199
Chigi, Agostino, 180
child mortality, 2
Cimarosa, Domenico, 103
Clementi, Francesco, 81–82
Conti, Francesco Bartolomeo, 97, 149, 185, 187, 207, 260n; *L'osservanza della divina legge nella madre de' Macabei*, 206, 209–13, 213
Conticini, Giovanni, 79
Cordier, Jean, 6–7
Cupeda, Donato, 58, 172, 176

dancing, 17
Dario, Francesco Maria, 94, 97–98
D'Este, Rinaldo I, 52
De Lummene, Jacques, 107
De' Messi, Francesco, 80
De Totis, Giovanni Domenico, 57
Discalced Carmelites, 11, 16
Duviel, Jacques, 145

Eleonore Magdalene of Neuburg, Dowager Empress, 91, 188
Elizabeth Christiane, Empress, 102, 189

Emanuele di Gesù Maria, 21, 233n
Esau, and Jacob, 19
Esterházy family, 173
Eve, and Adam, 15–38, 213–14

Fabbrini, Giuseppe, 173
family size, 2
Farinelli (Carlo Broschi), 206, 215–17
female infanticide, 2, 108
Feo, Francesco, 141, 147
Florence, oratorios in, 10, 58–59, 102, 145–46, 197; Compagnia dell'Arcangelo Raffaello, oratorios for, 59, 145–46
Fosi, Irene, 3
Franchi, Saverio, 9–10
fratricide, 19–21, 79, 207
Frigimelica Roberti, Girolamo, 121, 123–24
Fritelli, Giacomo, 56
Furlanetto, Bonaventura, 175, 177–78, 254n
Fux, Johann Joseph, 3, 124, 149, 212, 257n; *La donna forte nella madre de' sette Macabei*, 187–93, 192

Gabrieli, Francesca, 142
Galuppi, Baldassare, 104, 113, 146, 178
García Fajer, Francisco Javier, 148, 154
Gatti, Luigi, 195, 197
Genesis, Book of, 1–4, 16, 18–38, 39–74, 75–104
Giacobbi, Antonio, 46
Gigli, Girolamo, 123, 170–75, 179–84, 210
Gini, Paolo, 67–68
Girolamo di San Carlo O.C.D., 121–23
Giubilei, Pietro, 118–19

Index • 277

Glielmo, Antonio, 42
Gonzaga, Empress Eleonora (II), 57, 183–84
Gonzaga, Luigi (Saint), 153
Gregory of Nazianzus, Saint, 183, 255n
Gregory of Nyssa, Saint, 76–77
Grippaudo, Ilaria, 248n
Guercino (G. F. Barbierini), 43
Guglielmi, Pietro, 193
Guidotti, Curzio Maria, 22

Habsburg dynasty, 3, 8, 70–73, 102, 129, 132, 149–51, 206, 212; ideology of 10, 57, 182–91, 197; problems with male succession in, 85–90
Hagar, 1–3, 7, 12, 16, 39–74, 81, 139, 207–10
Haydn, Joseph, *Il ritorno di Tobia*, 9, 13, 144, 159–68, *163*, 221
Herczog, Johann, 243n, 253n
Hypostatic Union, 6, 230n

Incontri, Francesco, 73
infanticide, female, 2, 108
Iphigenia, 4, 10, 107–13, 129–30
Isaac, 1–4, 10, 15, 40–45, 53–57, 68–74, 75–104, 109, 112–13, 139–44, 154, 191, 208–9
Ishmael, 1, 7, 16, 39–74, 81, 89, 207–9

Jacob and Esau, 19
Jacquet de la Guerre, Elizabeth, 247n
Jephthe, 2–4, 11, 79, 105–37, 140, 220
Jephthe's daughter (various names), 1–4, 105–37
Jesuits, 78, 117, 141, 179
John Chrysostom, 99
John of the Cross, Saint, 16, 179, 209

Jommelli, Nicolo, 77, 99, 102–3, 114, 130, 200
Jonathan (Saul's son), 244n
Joseph I, Emperor, 85, 94, 107, 124–25, 188
Josephus, Flavius, 99, 179, 193, 255n, 258n
Judges, Book of, 105–37

Kanduth, Erika, 257n

Lamberg, Joseph von, 72
Landin-Conti, Maria, 151
Lang, Katherine, 197
Lapide, Cornelius a, 8, 40, 98, 116
Leo, Leonardo, 216–18, *217*
Leonardi, Giovanni, 6
Leopold I, Emperor, 66, 88–90, 121, 143, 181–85
Lora, Francesco, 235n, 237–38n
Lorrain, Claude, 43
Lotti, Antonio, 124–26, *126*, 151–53
Lucca, 17, 145
Luchini, Antonio Maria, 206–11

Maccabees, Second Book of, 57, 170–205, 209–12
Maccabees, Fourth Book of, 179–80, 190, 194
Maccabees, Mother of Seven Sons (various names), 1–10, 29, 132, 170–205, 209–20
Magnani, Giovanni Antonio, 119
Manni, Giovanni Battista, 41, 71
Manzoni-Giusti, Francesca, 76, 89, 99, 189
Mariana, Juan de, 108
Maria Theresia, Empress, 158, 189, 207, 212
martyrdom, intercontinental, 182
Massarotti, Angelo, 181
Mattei, Beatrice, 113

Maurizio, Giovanni Battista, 47
Mayno, Domenico, 42
Medici, Paolo, 153, 193, 195
Melani, Alessandro, 24–27, 27
Melani, Girolamo, 151–52
Mendoza, Francisco de, 182
Mesquita, Salvador de, 45, 56, 117
Metastasio, Pietro, 3–4, 8, 10, 16, 20,
    76–77, 80, 86, 98–104, 207, 212–
    21, 251n, 259n; *Isacco, figura del
    Redentore* (1739/40), 100–104;
    La morte d'Abel (1732), 218–21
"Molorchio, Peore," 112
Monari, Bartolomeo, 52–53
Monteclair, Michel de, 247n
Morean War, First, 36
Morelli, Arnaldo, 28, 54, 229n, 233n,
    238n
Morone, Carlo Tommaso, 77, 144
Morosini, Giovanni Francesco, 29
Motnik, Marko, 250n
Murata, Margaret K., 239n, 247n
Muratori, Ludovico Antonio, 7, 51, 193
Mysliveček, Josef, 153, 155–58, 157

Nencini, Bartolomeo, 53–54, 73
Nicholas of Lyra, 108
nuns and their professions, 4, 8, 106,
    113, 139, 148

Odescalchi, Livio, 9, 67
Oliva, Gian Paolo, 8, 41, 179, 235n,
    255n
ophthalmology, 145–46
Oratorian order, 11, 53, 68, 70, 114,
    131–32, 153, 177–78
oratorio, nature and genre of, 1–17
Orazio di Parma, 153, 195
Orlandini, Maria Rosa, 110
orphans, 5, 146
Orsi, Astorre, 2, 44, 47

Orsi Montecuccioli, Chiara, 47
Orsini, Gaetano, 94, 185, 188, 207,
    209, 214, 218–19
ospedali (female orphanages) in
    Venice, 5; Ospedale dei Derelitti,
    12–14, 141, 199–201
Ottoboni, Pietro, 31, 79, 83, 85, 230n,
    242n

Paciuchelli, Angelo, 182
Paisiello, Giovanni, 133–34
Palermo, 9, 13, 32, 54, 58, 61, 78–79,
    131, 141, 147
Palumbo, Lelio, 78
Pamphili, Benedetto, 24, 57
Paolacci, Agostino, 54
Pariati, Pietro, 3, 70, 124, 189–93,
    210
Pasquini, Bernardo, 28, 53–55
Pasquini, Giovanni Claudio, 206,
    214, 219–20
Passerini, Francesco, 86–90
Passignani, Maria Luisa, 112
Passion meditation, 172–78, 197
Paul, Saint, 40, 73
Pellegrini, Giuseppe Luigi, 144,
    158–59
Perez, David, 9, 130, 147
Perfetti, Bernardino, 7, 70–72
Perti, Giacomo Antonio, 40, 49–52,
    50, 72
Petrucci, Pier Maria, 11, 176
Pichi, Giovanni Battista, 79–80
Pignatta, Pietro, 146
Porsile, Giuseppe, 121, 125, 148, 189,
    212
Praun, Christoph, 207, 210, 212, 214,
    219, 260n
Predieri, Luca Antonio, 86, 98–100,
    243n
Pusterla, Francesco, 29–30

quaresimale, 7, 11, 209

Ranieri Redi, Giovanni Nicola, 73
Reggio, Antonino, 245n
Reutter, Theresia, 207, 218
Reutter, Georg, Jr., 42, 206, 214–15, 220–21
Rhò, Giovanni, 28
Rome, Oratorian order in (Chiesa Nuova and S. Girolamo della Carità), 11, 53, 131, 148, 153, 175, 178; Oratorio del Crocifisso, oratorios in, 4, 13–14, 28, 55, 67, 115–21, 139–40, 235n, 242n, 244n; other oratorios in, 9–11, 13, 29–32, 36, 44–47, 53–58, 65–67, 81–84, 107–9, 122, 130–33, 153–55, 168, 193
Roncaglia, Costantino, 6
Rossi, Camilla de', *Il sacrifizio di Abramo*, 96, 104–8
Rubini, Gaetano, 121–22
Ruth, Book of, 1, 5, 14, 140–43, 168

Sacchini, Antonio, 5; *Jephthes sacrificium*, 134–37, 136; *Mater machabaeorum*, 199–203, 202; *Nuptiae Ruth*, 140–43
Sacra rappresentazione, 13, 20–23, 28, 45, 56, 81, 88, 117, 120–22, 143
Salio, Giuseppe, 121, 125–27, 212–13
Sammartini, Giovanni Battista, 20
Sancta Clara, Abraham a. *See* Abraham a Sancta Clara
Santi, Ippolita, 134–35, 143, 199
Sarti, Raffaella, 237n
Savaro, Giovanni Francesco, 21–22
Sbarra, Francesco, 183–84
Scarlatti, Alessandro, 15, 24, 74, 89, 171; *Agar ed Ismaele esiliati*, 57–67, 62, 64; *Cain, ovvero Il primo omicidio*, 28–38, 35, 37

Scarpelli, Angelo, 131–32
Schoonjans, Regina, 125–26, 151
Segneri, Paolo, 8, 11
Serpotta, Giacomo, 58
Serrarrio, Stefano, 172
Siebenhühner, Kim, 43, 236n
Siena, 43, 121, 171–78; Collegio Tolomei, 180, S. Caterina del Paradiso, 172–73
slavery and families, 40–48, 56, 66–69
Smither, Howard E., 229n
Song of Songs, 1, 12, 17, 131, 148, 170–78; tropological interpretation of, 171–72
Sozzafanti, Aurelio, 172
Spanish Succession, War of, 57, 85, 95, 125, 187–88
Spengler, Margarete, 168
Spengler-Friberth, Magdalene, 168
Stampiglia, Silvio, 187–89
Stanzani, Tommaso, 89–90
Stroppa, Sabrina, 215, 218, 229n

Tanara, Sebastiano, 175
Tarabotti, Archangela, 234n
Thompson, John, 235n
Tirin, Jacob, 116
Tobit, Book of, 1–14, 59, 138–69, 206, 219–21
Tollini, Domenico, 188
Tomasini, Luigi, 161
Tonti, Giacinto, 70–71, 239n
Traetta, Tommaso, 10, 130

Urbino, 175

Vacondio, Giovanni Battista, 139–40
Vanalesti, Saverio, 245n
van der Linden, Huub, 9, 230–31n

Vannuchi, Antonio Maria, 110–11
Veneziano, Gaetano, 146
Venice, oratorios in: 11, 31, 36, 103, 133; Ospedale dei Derelitti, 5, 134–37, 142–44, 199–202; Santa Maria della Consolazione ("La Fava"), 175–79
Verazi, Matteo, 109
Vieira, Antonio, 257n
Vienna, oratorios in: 4–8, 10–11, 13, 36, 42, 52–53, 57, 68, 70, 80, 86–97, 120–27, 132, 145–46, 158–68, 172, 185, 206–20; situation in after 1740, 157

Visconti, Giambattista Antonio, 148, 154
Vitali, Giovanni Battista, 47–48, 120–21
Volto Santo (Lucca), 17

Werner, Gregor Joseph, 173
wifehood, Christian, 39–58
Wilhelmine Amalia, Empress, 187, 188, 210

Zeno, Apostolo, 3, 13, 149–50, 206, 220
Ziani, Marc'Antonio, 91–94, 93